THE SAT ADVANTAGE
Beat Your Best Score!

XAMonline, Inc., Melrose, MA 02176
© 2015 by Sharon A. Wynne (text and illustrations)

Published 2015
Printed in the United States
1 2 3 4 5 6 7 13 12 11 10 09 08

All rights reserved. No part of the material protected by this copyright may be reproduced or utilized in any form or by any means, electronic or mechanical, including photocopying, recording or by any information storage and retrieval system, without written permission from the copyright holder.

To obtain permission(s) to use the material from this work for any purpose, including workshops or seminars, please submit a written request to:

XAMonline, Inc.
21 Orient Avenue
Melrose, MA 02176
Toll Free 1-800-301-4647
Fax: 1-617-583-5552
Email: info@xamonline.com
Web: www.xamonline.com

Test and illustrations: Sharon A. Wynne

Contributing authors:
Sreela Datta
Steve Reiss, The Math Magician, Reiss SAT Seminars (www.reisssat.com)
June Saunders
Jana Sweeney
Vicki Wilt, Tucker Seven Editorial Associates, Inc.

Contributing illustrator: Paige Larkin.
Cover Photos © Stephen Coburn I Dreamstime.com; © Can Stock Photo Inc. / gajdamak; © Can Stock Photo Inc. / darrin

Library of Congress Catalog Card Number: (pending)

Wynne, Sharon A.
 The SAT advantage: beat your best score!

 428., ill.
 1. Title 2. SAT (educational test) – Study guides 4. Scholastic aptitude test (educational test) Study guides 5. Achievement tests – Study guides 6. Study guides 7. National merit scholarship qualifying test – Study guides

 LB2353.57 W966 2012 378.1662 W99 2012

 ISBN: 978-1-60787-489-8

TABLE OF CONTENTS

INTRODUCTION TO THE SAT	1
CRITICAL READING STRATEGIES	7
MATHEMATICS STRATEGIES	30
WRITING STRATEGIES	47

PRACTICE TEST 1
Section 1 Writing	66
Section 2 Critical Reading	69
Section 3 Mathematics	78
Section 4 Critical Reading	84
Section 5 Mathematics	92
Section 6 Writing	98
Section 7 Critical Reading	108
Section 8 Mathematics	116
Section 9 Writing	121
Practice Test 1 Answer Key	127
Practice Test 1 Answer Rationales	131

PRACTICE TEST 2
Section 1 Writing	172
Section 2 Critical Reading	175
Section 3 Mathematics	186
Section 4 Critical Reading	192
Section 5 Mathematics	204
Section 6 Writing	211
Section 7 Critical Reading	222
Section 8 Mathematics	229
Section 9 Writing	234
Practice Test 2 Answer Key	239
Practice Test 2 Answer Rationales	243

PRACTICE TEST 3
Section 1 Writing	292
Section 2 Critical Reading	295
Section 3 Mathematics	303
Section 4 Critical Reading	309
Section 5 Mathematics	318
Section 6 Writing	324
Section 7 Critical Reading	337
Section 8 Mathematics	344
Section 9 Writing	349
Practice Test 3 Answer Key	355
Practice Test 3 Answer Rationales	359

Answer Sheet Templates	405

THE SAT ADVANTAGE
Beat Your Best Score!

INTRODUCTION TO THE SAT

WHAT IS THE SAT?

The SAT is a standardized test for college admissions. It is administered by the College Board. The SAT tests a student's knowledge of critical reading, mathematics, and writing. Most colleges require the SAT; some require either the SAT or the ACT. Be sure to check the admissions requirements for each school that you are interested in.

A student's score on the SAT is one of many factors that college admissions officers use to determine a student's ability to do college-level work. Other factors may include grade point average, extracurricular activities, teacher recommendations, and college admission essays.

WHAT ARE THE SAT SUBJECT TESTS?

The SAT is a general knowledge and skills test in reading, mathematics, and writing. There are also 20 different SAT Subject Tests, which test subject-specific knowledge. Each hour-long SAT Subject Test covers a topic in English, history, languages, mathematics, or science.

Some colleges require or recommend SAT Subject Tests and some do not. Check the college's admissions requirements to determine whether SAT Subject Tests are required. Even if they are not required for admission, taking SAT Subject Tests can improve your chances of being accepted into college by allowing you to highlight subjects in which you excel. Taking SAT Subject Tests can also potentially place you out of introductory college courses.

WHEN SHOULD I TAKE THE SAT?

The SAT is usually taken during a student's junior or senior year in high school, and many students take the test more than once. Most often, students take the SAT for the first time during the spring of their junior year and then again during the fall of their senior year but you are not required to take it more than once.

Taking the PSAT/NMSQT (Preliminary SAT/National Merit Scholarship Qualifying Test) will prepare students for the SAT and enter them in the competition for a National Merit Scholarship, but taking the preliminary test not a requirement for taking the SAT.

HOW CAN I REGISTER FOR THE SAT?

Students can register for the SAT online or by mail. To register online, visit the official College Board website, www.collegeboard.org, click on *SAT*, and then click on *Register Now*. Once you sign up on the website, you can register, print your admission ticket, receive and send SAT scores, apply for colleges online, and more.

In some situations, students need to register by mail. See the registration information on the College Board website to see if you qualify to register online. To register by mail, get an SAT Paper Registration Guide from your high school counselor and follow the instructions.

HOW MUCH DOES THE SAT COST?

The fee to register for the SAT is $52.50. The $52.50 fee covers the test fee and scoring reports for you, your high school, and up to four colleges and scholarship programs. There are additional fees for late registration, standby testing, international processing, changing test centers or test dates, rush reporting, and other additional services and products.

Families who cannot afford the fee can request a waiver from their school counselor. Fee waivers are not available through the College Board website. Each fee waiver covers the registration fees for one test date.

The registration fee for SAT Subject Tests is $23 for the first test and $12 for each additional subject test. The fee for each language with a listening test is $23.

WHEN IS THE TEST OFFERED?

The SAT is administered seven times a year in October, November, December, January, March, May, and June. It is offered on select Saturdays during the school year. It is usually offered on the first Saturday of the month for November, December, May, and June. Sunday testing is available for those who cannot take the test on Saturday because of religious observances.

Go to www.collegeboard.org to see upcoming test dates. A student may take either the SAT or up to three SAT Subject Tests on the same test date.

WHAT SHOULD I BRING ON TEST DAY?

Your Admission Ticket
You can print your admission ticket by signing into your account on www.collegeboard.org.

Proper Identification
Acceptable forms of identification include photo IDs such as a driver's license, a school identification card, or a valid passport. Social security cards, birth certificates, and credit cards will not be accepted, even if the credit card has a photograph. For more information about the identification policies for the SAT, go to www.collegeboard.org and click on *Register*.

Two Number 2 Pencils and a Soft Eraser
Number 2 pencils are the only acceptable writing instruments to use on the test so be sure to bring your own and have them already sharpened and ready to use.

A Calculator
Graphing calculators and scientific calculators are permitted during the test. Four-function calculators are also permitted, but they are not recommended. Among the calculators that are not permitted are calculators on laptops or a handheld computer, cell phone calculators, and calculators that use an electrical outlet, make noise, or have a paper tape. To see the SAT Calculator Policy go to www.collegeboard.org.

Recommended but Not Required:
- A watch with no alarm
- Extra batteries for a watch or calculator
- A bag or backpack
- A drink or snack for the break

Note: Cell phones, smartphones, laptops, notebooks, iPods, iPads, MP3 players, timers, recording devices, and cameras are just some of the devices not permitted in SAT test centers. For more information, go to www.collegeboard.org.

WHAT IS ON THE TEST?

The SAT has a total of 170 questions. The total actual test time is 3 hours and 45 minutes. There are also two 10-minute breaks.

The SAT has three sections: Critical Reading, Mathematics, and Writing. Each section is divided into three subsections. In addition to the nine subsections, there is an additional 25-minute *experimental* subsection that may be in critical reading, mathematics, or writing. The experimental subsection does not count toward the final score.

The unscored experimental subsection is used by test developers to try out new questions before including them on actual tests as scored questions. It may appear anywhere on the test, and it will look just like any other subsection. Do not try to guess which subsection is the experimental subsection. You will not be able to distinguish it from the others. Complete all ten subsections as if they all counted toward the final score.

NOTE: Since the practice tests in this book do not include an experimental section, you should only allot 3 hours and 20 minutes to complete the practice tests.

WHAT SHOULD I EXPECT WHEN I TAKE THE TEST?

The first subsection on the test is always the Writing subsection 1, so you will always begin by writing a short essay. The eighth and ninth subsections are either Critical Reading or Mathematics, and the last subsection is always Writing. The other six subsections can appear in any order.

NOTE: Since the practice tests in this book do not include an experimental section, some of the section numbers in this book will be different than explained above.

Test questions are generally tricky. They are written to test the things that people *most often get wrong or misunderstand* in each subject area. Answer choices often contain choices that would seem right if you made a common mistake or held a common misunderstanding—so be careful in selecting your answers!

When taking the test, you cannot switch back and forth between sections or return to earlier sections to change your answers. You can only spend the allotted amount of time for each section and then move on to the next section. You can, though, move around within each section.

HOW IS THE ESSAY SCORED?

The essay can receive a maximum score of 12. Two trained readers assign each essay a score between 0 and 6, where 0 is for essays that are blank, off-topic, non-English, not written with number 2 pencil, or illegible. Scores are summed to produce a final score from 2-12 (or 0). If the two readers' scores differ by more than 1 point, a third reader decides the score. Each reader spends approximately 3 minutes on each essay.

HOW IS THE TOTAL SCORE DETERMINED?

The highest possible score on the SAT is 800 per section, for a total possible score of 2400. All questions are weighted equally. For each correct answer, 1 raw point is added. For each incorrect answer one-quarter of one point is deducted. No points are deducted for incorrect math grid-in questions or skipped questions.

The totals for the subsections are added together to produce three raw scores, one for each section. These raw scores equal the number of questions you got right *minus* a fraction of the number you got wrong. These scores are then converted into scaled scores, with 200 as the lowest and 800 as the highest per section. Each raw point is worth approximately 10 scaled points.

Final total scores range from 600 to 2400. The final score combines results from the three 200–800 point sections (Critical Reading, Mathematics, and Writing).

SERVICES PROVIDED BY THE COLLEGE BOARD

The College Board provides its test takers the following services:

Score Choice
Score Choice gives you the option of sending some or all of your test scores to colleges. Although you cannot selectively send a reading, writing, or math score, you can choose to send or not send entire test scores you have earned in the past.

Question-and-Answer Service (QAS)
The Question-and-Answer Service (QAS) provides test takers with a report that details the following:
- the correct answer
- your answer
- the type of question
- the difficulty level of the question

In addition, you will also receive the actual questions from the test you took. This service is usually offered for the October, January and May administrations.

Student Answer Service (SAS)
The Student Answer Service (SAS) is similar to the Question-and-Answer Service, but the actual questions are not provided. The Student Answer Service (SAS) is offered for all test administrations that do not provide the Question-and-Answer Service (QAS)

THE THREE SECTIONS OF THE SAT

CRITICAL READING SECTION

The total time for the Critical Reading section is 70 minutes. There are 67 questions total. This section includes sentence completion questions and questions based on reading passages.

In the sentence completion questions, the test taker chooses a word or words to complete a sentence. The sentence completion questions test vocabulary knowledge and understanding of sentence structure. Sentence completion questions get progressively harder; easy ones come first, followed by increasingly difficult questions.

The reading comprehension questions are based on long passages, short passages, and double passages. The questions test your understanding of what is stated explicitly and implied in the passages. After reading a double passage, the student compares and contrasts the passages or uses information in both passages to answer the questions. The reading questions are arranged chronologically rather than level of difficulty.

See the Critical Reading Strategies chapter for detailed information about and specific strategies for the types of questions in this section.

The Critical Reading section has three subsections.

	SUBSECTION 1	SUBSECTION 2	SUBSECTION 3
Time	25 minutes	25 minutes	20 minutes
Description	24 multiple-choice questions (8 sentence completion questions followed by 16 passage-based questions)	24 multiple-choice questions (5 sentence completion questions followed by 19 passage-based questions)	19 multiple-choice questions (6 sentence completion questions followed by 13 passage-based questions)

MATHEMATICS SECTION

The total time for the Mathematics section is 70 minutes. There are 54 questions total. In this section, the student answers multiple-choice and grid-in questions. For grid-in questions, the student is not given answers to choose from. Instead, he or she needs to solve the problem and then enter the answer in a grid. The mathematics questions get progressively harder; easy ones come first, followed by increasingly difficult questions. Topics include numerical operations, algebra, geometry, statistics, and probability.

During the test, students are provided with a math reference sheet. The reference sheet includes basic geometric formulas such as the area of a triangle, circumference of a circle, and volume of cylinder. It also includes information on special right triangles.

See the Mathematics Strategies chapter for detailed information about and specific strategies for the types of questions in this section.

The SAT Advantage

The Mathematics section has three subsections.

	SUBSECTION 1	SUBSECTION 2	SUBSECTION 3
Time	25 minutes	25 minutes	20 minutes
Description	20 multiple-choice questions	8 multiple-choice questions followed by 10 grid-in questions	16 multiple-choice questions

WRITING SECTION

The total time for the Writing section is 60 minutes. There are 49 questions total plus one essay. In this section, the test taker writes a short essay in response to a prompt and answers multiple-choice questions on improving sentences, identifying errors in sentences, and improving paragraphs. Topics include grammar, punctuation, usage, word choice, sentence structure, and paragraph organization and development.

See the Writing Strategies chapter for detailed information about and specific strategies for the types of questions in this section.

The Writing section has three subsections.

	SUBSECTION 1	SUBSECTION 2	SUBSECTION 3
Time	25 minutes	25 minutes	10 minutes
Description	Write one short essay in response to a prompt. In the essay, you will present and support a point of view	35 multiple-choice questions (11 improving sentence questions, 18 identifying sentence error questions, and 6 improving paragraph questions)	14 multiple-choice questions on improving sentences

The SAT Advantage

CRITICAL READING STRATEGIES

The Critical Reading section of the SAT tests your vocabulary knowledge and ability to understand sentences and passages. The Critical Reading section is divided into three subsections. Each subsection includes both sentence completion questions and passage-based reading questions.

There are two types of sentence completion questions:
- Vocabulary-in-context questions
- Logic-based questions

There are three types of passage-based reading questions:
- Extended reading questions
- Vocabulary-in-context questions
- Literal comprehension questions

Here are strategies for approaching each question type. The strategies are followed by sample questions, each with a detailed explanation, walking you through the steps to find the correct answer.

VOCABULARY-IN-CONTEXT SENTENCE COMPLETION QUESTIONS

Vocabulary-in-context questions test your knowledge of vocabulary. In the vocabulary-in-context questions, you will choose a word that best completes a sentence by looking at the context, or meaning, of the sentence.

There are both one-blank and two-blank vocabulary-in-context questions. Here is an example of a one-blank vocabulary-in-context question. We'll answer this question later in the chapter.

> Because none of the students had any questions, the teacher made the -------- that everyone was ready to move on to more difficult material.
>
> (A) hypothesis
> (B) assumption
> (C) integration
> (D) requirement
> (E) compilation

STRATEGIES FOR SUCCESS

Here are some strategies for preparing for and approaching for vocabulary-in-context questions. **Important Note!** Many of these strategies will help you prepare for the *entire* Critical Reading section because building a strong vocabulary is vital for earning a high score on both sentence completion questions and passage-based reading questions.

The SAT Advantage

1. **Create Your Own SAT Vocabulary Notebook**
   Buy a large notebook *today* and begin your own SAT vocabulary list. Every day, write down words that are new to you—interesting words you hear in a news program, a word you don't know the meaning of in an online technology article, every vocabulary word you don't know in this book, and on and on.

   Next to each word, write the meaning. Also, because the SAT tests vocabulary by having you choose a word or words that complete a sentence, write down two different sentences that use the word. Be creative—don't copy sample sentences from a dictionary; create your own. You will be more likely to remember the meaning.

2. **Make an Online Dictionary Your Best Friend**
   Every time you hear or read a word you don't know, look it up in an online dictionary. Online dictionaries are an invaluable resource, not only because you can look up the meaning of words, but also because when you look up a word, there are often links to related words. Click on the related words, and the definition of the related words will appear.

3. **Expand Your Vocabulary Using an Online Thesaurus**
   Using a thesaurus, you can look up synonyms, words with the same or similar meanings. You can search the Internet for a thesaurus program—or just look in your online dictionary. Most online dictionaries have a thesaurus feature. You can even use the dictionary to find the meaning of a word, and then switch to the thesaurus to see a list of synonyms.

   Using an online thesaurus is one of the fastest ways to expand your vocabulary. Just go to an online thesaurus and look up a word, almost any word. Try typing "magic," "clever," "entertainment," or "innovative." Almost any word will bring up an interesting list of new words, and you will associate them in your mind because they have similar meanings.

   The powerful part of using an online thesaurus is that after you look up synonyms for a word, you can then click on one of the synonyms and get a new list of words. This can get addictive! You might begin with the word "thunder" and, after a half of an hour end with the word "eccentric." When you find words that are new to you, add them to your SAT vocabulary notebook.

4. **Brainstorm to Find New Vocabulary Words**
   To expand your list of new words, try brainstorming. Begin with an interesting word that you don't quite know the meaning of. Maybe you can think of one. If not, use a word from this chapter or a practice test. Then brainstorm! From that word, write down a word that rhymes with it, sounds like it, has the same meaning, or reminds you of it.

   Here's a sample brainstorming list:

   - detest
   - deflect
   - detect
   - inspect
   - inject
   - injection

- injunction
- inflection
- interference
- inference
- infer
- defer
- confer
- conspire
- aspire

There are some great SAT words on this list—deflect, injunction, infer, aspire, and more.

This can be a lot of fun, and it's an effective way to expand your vocabulary. You can think of many new words this way that you've heard but don't quite know the meaning of. Write down the words in your notebook, look up the meaning of the words in the dictionary, and use each word in two sentences.

5. **Use Prefixes, Suffixes, and Roots to Determine the Meaning of Words**

   Prefixes, suffixes, and roots are word parts that make up words. A prefix is added to the beginning of another word or word part. A suffix is added to the end of another word or word part. For example, the prefix sub- means "under or below." When the prefix sub- is added to the word "zero" the definition changes. "Subzero" means "below zero."

   By learning the meaning of prefixes, suffixes, and roots, you can often get a clue to the meaning of a word. For example, the prefix mal- means "bad." Knowing the meaning of the prefix mal- could help you deduce that "malnourished" means "poorly nourished." Here are more examples of how knowing the meaning of word parts can help you guess the meaning of a word.

   Prefixes
   The prefix bi- means "two." Knowing the meaning of the prefix can help you deduce that "bilateral" means "having two sides."

   "Circumfluent" contains the prefix circum-, meaning "around." The prefix gives you a clue to the meaning of the word, "flowing around; encompassing."

   Suffixes
   The suffix -ify means "to make or form into." Knowing the meaning of the suffix, you can figure out that "personify" means "to represent something as having human qualities."

   The suffix -ive means "that which" or "having the quality of." Putting that together with what you know about the word "punish," you could figure out that "punitive" means "corrective or penalizing."

   Roots
   "Voracious" contains the root "vor," meaning "eat," so you know that the word is related to eating. That gives you a clue to the meaning of the word, "craving or consuming large amounts of food."

"Dysfunctional" contains the root "dys," meaning "abnormal or bad." The definition of "dysfunctional" is "not working normally or properly."

Learning Prefixes, Suffixes, and Roots

To learn new words using prefixes, suffixes, and roots, begin by searching the Internet for these three terms. Then create tables of prefixes, suffixes, and roots. Include their meanings and examples of each. Here is a table of some prefixes to get you started:

Prefix	Meaning	Example
ante-	Before	anterior, anteroom
anti-	Against	antibiotic, antioxidant
bene-	Good	benefit, benefactor, benevolent
circum-	Around	circumvent, circumnavigate, circumference
de-	Away from, reverse action of	derail, decline, defrost, dejected
il-	Not	illogical, illegible
im-	Not	immature, immaterial
in-	Not	insatiable, incorrigible
inter-	Between, among	international, interact, interject
intra-	Between or within	intramural, intravenous
ir-	Not	irregular, irreducible
mal-	Bad	maltreat, malcontent, malevolent
pan-	All or whole	panacea, panorama
pre-	Before	precede, precedent, prelude
post-	After in time, space	postpone, postwar
pro-	Before, in front of	prologue, proactive
re-	Again	reiterate, revert, rejuvenate
sub-	Below	submarine, subversive
super-	Over and above, very large	superlative, superfluous
un-	Not, reverse of	unleashed, unrelenting

6. **Don't Get Bogged Down on Difficult Questions**
   Every question on the SAT is worth the same number of points. Whether you spend a few seconds or several minutes answering a question, you will get the same number of points for a correct answer, so be sure not to spend too much time on any one question.

   The vocabulary-in-context questions get progressively harder throughout each subsection. The easiest questions come first, and the most difficult are last. Because each question is worth the same number of points, be careful not to spend too much time on the harder questions. You are more likely to get the earlier questions correct, so don't get bogged down on the last few.

7. **Note the Half-Way Point of Each Subsection**
   Each subsection of the SAT has an allotted amount of time. Each subsection of Critical Reading is 20 or 25 minutes long. Note the time that each subsection begins. Half way through the allotted time, stop and see how much of the subsection you've completed. If you've completed less than half of the questions, try spending less time on the more challenging questions. Managing your time like this will assure that you have time to try to answer each question.

8. **Read the Sentence to Yourself**
    Begin each sentence completion question by reading the sentence, either aloud while you're studying, or silently while you're taking the test. Pause where each blank is. Reading the entire sentence will give you a good idea what the sentence is about and what word or words complete the sentence.

9. **Rephrase Each Sentence**
    If you have trouble understanding the meaning of a sentence, simplify it by rewording it to yourself. Take this sentence as an example:

    Because Lucy hasn't returned three overdue books and two DVDs, her library privileges might be --------.

    After reading the sentence, simplify it by rewording it to yourself. You might say, "Because Lucy hasn't returned some items, something might happen to her library privileges." Rewording it this way can help you find the correct answer. For this sentence, the correct answer might be "revoked."

10. **Look for Key Words and Phrases**
    Look for specific, descriptive words and phrases that can be keys to understanding the meaning of a sentence. Read this sentence:

    Rudy held his head up high and marched -------- into the boardroom.

    What words or phrases might help you understand the meaning of the sentence? The phrase "held his head up high" suggests being proud and the word "marched" suggests confidence. To help find the correct answer, you can underline the key words and phrases:

    Rudy <u>held his head up high</u> and <u>marched</u> -------- into the boardroom.

    The key words and phrases suggest being proud and confident. The key words and phrases can help you find the correct answer. One word that fits well in this sentence is "boldly."

11. **Guess What the Word Might Be**
    A great approach to vocabulary-in-context questions is to read the sentence, and then guess what the missing word or words might be. You can often take a good guess by looking at the meaning of the sentence. The correct answer will often be a synonym of the word that you guessed. Here's an example:

    The signed agreement -------- that all team members must attend training.

    After reading the sentence, you might guess that the missing word is "states" or "specifies." The correct answer probably has a similar meaning to both words. The correct answer could be "stipulates."

12. **Eliminate Answer Choices**
    Once you have an idea what word or words you might be looking for, begin eliminating answer choices. Eliminate any answer choice that is not the type of word that you're

looking for. Be sure to eliminate any answer choice in which the word has the *opposite* meaning of the word you're looking for.

For example, read this sentence:

Our early ancestors used -------- stone tools to dig, hunt, and defend themselves.

You're looking for a word that would describe stone tools that our early ancestors used to dig, hunt, and defend themselves. Now look at the answer choices:

(A) refined
(B) simplistic
(C) primitive
(D) sophisticated
(E) obsolete

You can eliminate words that would not describe these stone tools. Two words clearly seem to not work. "Refined" suggests that the tools have been improved, which doesn't work in this sentence. The word "sophisticated" also doesn't work. Go ahead and cross out the answer choices that do not work.

(A) refined
(B) simplistic
(C) primitive
(D) sophisticated
(E) obsolete

For sentences that have two blanks, first check to see if either word does not work in the sentence. If *either* word doesn't work, eliminate the answer choice.

13. **Choose the *Best* Answer**
It is not enough to find an answer choice that works; you need to select the *best* answer. To make sure you find the *best* answer, be sure to look at all of the answer choices. Do not go on to the next question as soon as you find an answer choice that seems to work. The best answer choice is the answer choice in which the word or words match the meaning of the sentence most specifically.

14. **Notice the Subtle Differences Between Words**
Many questions will come down to subtle differences in the meaning of words. After you've eliminated answer choices that are not possibilities, the remaining answers may have similar meanings. You might end up with two or three words with similar meanings such as "certification" and "qualification."

To find the correct answer read the sentence again, inserting each possible answer choice. Some words might not work in the context of the sentence. Other words might work but might not be the best choice. Read the sentence once, inserting each answer choice to see which word is the correct answer.

Take this sentence as an example:

> At the graduation party this evening, he plans to stand in front of his many friends and family members and proudly -------- his plans to start his own business.

After eliminating answer choices, you might need to choose between the words "articulate," "announce," and "predict." Read the sentence, inserting each possible answer choice:

> At the graduation party this evening, he plans to stand in front of his many friends and family members and proudly *articulate* his plans to start his own business.

> At the graduation party this evening, he plans to stand in front of his many friends and family members and proudly *announce* his plans to start his own business.

> At the graduation party this evening, he plans to stand in front of his many friends and family members and proudly *predict* his plans to start his own business.

"Predict" isn't quite right because he isn't forecasting what is to come. "Articulate" is close because it means "to voice or put into words." The key word "proudly," though, lets you know that he plans to state his plans with confidence, so the word "announce" is the best fit.

15. **Relate Words to Words You Already Know**
Use words that you know to help you decode words that are new to you. For example, let's say that you've eliminated three answer choices, and one of the remaining possibilities is the word "redemption." You might not know the word "redemption," but you might know what it means to "redeem" yourself. Knowing the meaning of "redeem," you might be able to figure out that "redemption" means "the act of saving or being saved."

Or you might be trying to figure out the meaning of the word "aerobe." Let's say that you can tell from the sentence that it is a thing, but you don't know the meaning. Is there a word that you know that is similar to "aerobe"? How about "aerobics"? Knowing the meaning of "aerobics" can help you figure out that "aerobe" means "a living thing that breathes or needs oxygen to live."

16. **Read the Sentence Again**
After choosing the correct answer, read the sentence one last time with the word or words inserted in the sentence. You might have selected words that seem to fit, but you might not notice that one or both words are not a fit until you read the sentence again.

EXAMPLE QUESTIONS

Example 1
Because none of the students had any questions, the teacher made the -------- that everyone was ready to move on to more difficult material.

(A) hypothesis
(B) assumption
(C) integration
(D) requirement
(E) compilation

Explanation
Begin by reading the sentence, pausing where the blank is. Because the students didn't have any questions, the teacher made the *something* that everyone was ready to move on. She came to the conclusion that everyone was ready to move on. Read the answer choices to see which have a meaning related to coming to a conclusion.

Eliminate any answer choices that do not fit. For example, the word "compilation" is not related to coming to a conclusion. Cross out the words that do not work:

(A) hypothesis
(B) assumption
~~(C) integration~~
~~(D) requirement~~
~~(E) compilation~~

Three answer choices are now eliminated. The answer choices that remain are related to coming to a conclusion. Now read the sentence again, inserting each answer choice:

> Because none of the students had any questions, the teacher made the *hypothesis* that everyone was ready to move on to more difficult material.

> Because none of the students had any questions, the teacher made the *assumption* that everyone was ready to move on to more difficult material.

The words "hypothesis" and "assumption" have similar meanings. The word "hypothesis" is close, but a hypothesis is a tentative assumption that will be tested, like a hypothesis that is tested in a scientific experiment. The correct answer to this question is answer choice B: assumption.

Take a moment to read the sentence again with the correct word inserted in the blank:

> Because none of the students had any questions, the teacher made the assumption that everyone was ready to move on to more difficult material.

The SAT Advantage

Example 2
Petra's dad was chatting with her casually about school, but she knew that the -------- of the conversation was more serious.

(A) segue
(B) condemnation
(C) subtext
(D) conjecture
(E) antidote

Explanation
Begin by reading the sentence, pausing where the blank is. Her dad was chatting with her casually, but something about the conversation was more serious. By looking at the meaning of the sentence, try to guess what the missing word might be. Petra knew that the "hidden meaning" or "undercurrent" of the conversation was more serious.

Eliminate any answer choice that you know does not mean something like "hidden meaning" or "undercurrent." Cross out the words that do not work:

(A) segue
(B) condemnation
(C) subtext
(D) conjecture
(E) antidote

Two answer choices are now eliminated. Let's say that you don't know the meaning of the remaining three answer choices. Notice that you might be able to figure out the meaning of one of the answer choices if you know some common prefixes. The word "subtext" contains the prefix sub-, which means "under." "Subtext" is the text under other text, or underlying meaning. Try substituting the word into the sentence:

> Petra's dad was chatting with her casually about school, but she knew that the *subtext* of the conversation was more serious.

"Subtext" is the best word to complete this sentence, so the correct answer is answer choice C.

Example 3
Lisa's --------, -------- work experience made her an excellent candidate for the job.

(A) extensive ... diverse
(B) sketchy ... successful
(C) insightful ... varied
(D) jubilant ... vast
(E) outstanding ... tepid

Explanation
Begin by reading the sentence, pausing where the blanks are. You'll see that some type of work experience made Lisa an excellent job candidate. Ask yourself, "What type of experience would make her an excellent candidate?" You don't know specifically, but the two adjectives must be positive.

The SAT Advantage

Eliminate any answer choice in which either word is not positive. Cross out the words that do not work:

(A) extensive ... diverse
(B) ~~sketchy~~ ... successful
(C) insightful ... varied
(D) jubilant ... vast
(E) outstanding ... ~~tepid~~

Two answer choices are now eliminated. The answer choices that remain are pairs of positive adjectives. The adjectives need to not only be positive, though; they need to be words that can describe work experience. Look through the answer choices again and cross out any words that clearly cannot describe work experience:

(A) extensive ... diverse
(C) insightful ... varied
(D) ~~jubilant~~ ... vast

The word "jubilant" means "filled with joy," so the phrase "jubilant work experience" doesn't make sense. You are left with two possible answer choices: extensive ... diverse and insightful ... varied. Now read the sentence again, inserting the words for each answer choice:

> Lisa's *extensive, diverse* work experience made her an excellent candidate for the job.

> Lisa's *insightful, varied* work experience made her an excellent candidate for the job.

The word "insightful" means "full of insight," in other words, showing a deep understanding of something. Answers to interview questions can be insightful, but job experience can't really be "full of insight." Therefore, the correct answer is answer choice A: extensive ... diverse.

Take a moment to read the sentence again with the correct words inserted in the blanks:

> Lisa's extensive, diverse work experience made her an excellent candidate for the job.

The SAT Advantage

LOGIC-BASED SENTENCE COMPLETION QUESTIONS

Logic-based questions test your knowledge of vocabulary and your ability to understand complex sentences. In the logic-based sentence completion questions, you will choose one or two words to best complete a sentence by looking at the logic and overall structure of the sentence.

There are both one-blank and two-blank logic-based questions. Here is an example of a one-blank logic-based question. We'll answer this question later in the chapter.

> Despite early-morning laps five days a week, swimming lessons since he was five years old, and two years with a private coach, Raaj felt somewhat -------- before his first college swim meet.
>
> (A) tranquil
> (B) terrified
> (C) anxious
> (D) confident
> (E) foolish

STRATEGIES FOR SUCCESS

1. **Don't Get Bogged Down on Difficult Questions**
   Remember that every question on the SAT is worth the same number of points. Like the vocabulary-in-context questions, the logic-based questions get progressively harder throughout each subsection. You are more likely to get the earlier questions correct. Skip difficult questions and come back to them if you have time.

2. **Look for Introductory and Transition Words and Phrases**
   Introductory and transition words and phrases are critical to understanding the sentences in logic-based questions. These words show how the first and second parts of a sentence relate to each other. They indicate whether two parts of a sentence contradict each other, compare and contrast with each other, or simply add additional, complementary information.

   For example, the transition word "however" lets you know that *even though* one thing is true, something you might not expect is also true. "Rain is predicted in the forecast tomorrow; however, we still plan to go to the concert in the park." *Even though* rain is predicted, we will still go to the concert.

   Notice the introductory word in this sentence:

   > Despite the -------- of volunteers, no one is available to help clean up.

   In this sentence, the word "despite" lets you know that it is surprising that no one is available to help clean up. Let's say the two possible answer choices for this sentence are "plethora" and "dearth." Would it be surprising that no one is available to help clean up if there were a *plethora* or a *dearth* of volunteers? "Plethora" means "abundance," and "dearth" means "scarcity." It would be surprising if there were an abundance of volunteers and still no volunteers were available to help clean up, so the correct answer is "plethora."

Here are some examples of introductory and transition words and phrases that demonstrate contradiction:

- although
- before
- but
- despite
- even though
- however
- in spite of
- instead of
- in the end
- nevertheless
- nonetheless
- notwithstanding
- rather than
- while
- yet

Here are some introductory and transition words that demonstrate agreement:

- also
- because
- finally
- in addition to
- plus
- since
- therefore
- too

3. **Look for Key Words and Phrases**
In addition to introductory and transition words and phrases, look for specific, descriptive words and phrases that can be keys to understanding the meaning of a sentence. Here are some examples:

- admired
- brilliant
- contrary
- courage
- dreaded
- hazy
- heartbreaking
- hopeful
- ironically
- suddenly
- willingly

For example, the key words "hesitate" and "stumble" suggest a lack of experience or confidence.

4. **Get a Sense for the Logic of the Sentence**
   As with the vocabulary-in-context questions, begin by reading each sentence to yourself, pausing at the blank or blanks. For the logic-based questions, though, follow the logic of the sentence as you read. Make sense of the sentence *without* the answers filled in. Does the first part of the sentence describe something that happened earlier and the second part something that happened after? Does the second part of the sentence follow the first part of the sentence, or does it take an unexpected turn? Do the two parts of the sentence compare and contrast something?

   For example, if you read the sentence, "Joy and her colleagues expected the seminar to be --------, but they were astonished to see a renowned inventor and author at the podium." Even without filling in the blank, you can get a sense for the *logic* of the sentence—the word "but" lets you know that the sentence starts one way, but takes an unexpected turn.

5. **Guess What the Word Might Be**
   Just like with the vocabulary-in-context questions, an excellent approach to logic-based questions is to read the sentence and then guess what the missing word or words might be. Take the sentence above as an example.

   > Joy and her colleagues expected the seminar to be --------, but they were astonished to see a renowned inventor and author at the podium.

   They expected the seminar to be a certain way, but they were astonished, or surprised, to see a renowned, or famous, person at the podium. How do you think they expected the seminar to be? If they expected the seminar to be fascinating, they wouldn't be surprised to see a famous person at the podium. You might guess that the missing word is "dull" or "uninspiring." There is a good chance that the word you guess will be similar to the correct answer.

6. **Be Careful When You See Negative Words**
   Sentences with negative words in them—not, never, no, cannot, didn't, won't, and so on—can be tricky. Take an extra moment or two with these questions to make sure you understand the meaning. For example, read the following sentence:

   > It was never Ami's intention to take three laboratory courses in one semester, but she couldn't -------- the opportunity to do field work in biology.

   This sentence has two negatives in it—"never" and "couldn't." It helps to simplify a sentence containing negatives by rewording it. You might reword it like this:

   > She didn't plan to take three laboratory courses, but she couldn't -------- the chance to do field work.

   By reading this simpler sentence, you might be able to guess that the missing word is "miss" or "squander."

The SAT Advantage

7.   Read the Sentence Again
After choosing the correct answer, read the sentence one last time with the word or words inserted in the sentence. Reading the complete sentence confirms that you have chosen the correct answer.

EXAMPLE QUESTIONS

Example 1
Despite early-morning laps five days a week, swimming lessons since he was five years old, and two years with a private coach, Raaj felt somewhat -------- before his first college swim meet.

(A) tranquil
(B) terrified
(C) anxious
(D) confident
(E) foolish

Explanation
Begin by reading the sentence, pausing where the blank is. You'll see that there are two parts to this sentence. The first part tells you about Raaj's swim training and practice, and the second part states that he feels a certain way before his first college swim meet.

There are several phrases that are important clues. "Early-morning laps," "swimming lessons since he was five years old," and "two years with a private coach" suggest that Raaj is well prepared. However, the sentence begins with the introductory word "despite." This tells you that the second part of the sentence will state something contrary to what you would expect from the first part of the sentence.

Despite laps five days a week, swimming lessons, and two years with a private coach, Raaj felt a certain way before the swim meet. A lot of practice and training would suggest that someone would feel confident before a swim meet, but the word *despite* lets you know that he felt another way.

Eliminate any answer choice that you would associate with feeling well prepared and confident. Cross out the words that do not work:

(A) tranquil
(B) terrified
(C) anxious
(D) confident
(E) foolish

You are left with three possible answer choices: terrified, anxious, and foolish. Now read the sentence again, inserting each possible answer choice:

> Despite early-morning laps five days a week, swimming lessons since he was five years old, and two years with a private coach, Raaj felt somewhat *terrified* before his first college swim meet.

The SAT Advantage

> Despite early-morning laps five days a week, swimming lessons since he was five years old, and two years with a private coach, Raaj felt somewhat *anxious* before his first college swim meet.
>
> Despite early-morning laps five days a week, swimming lessons since he was five years old, and two years with a private coach, Raaj felt somewhat *foolish* before his first college swim meet.

"Terrified" is an intense feeling, so the phrase "somewhat terrified" doesn't quite make sense, and you can eliminate that answer choice. There's nothing in the sentence to suggest that Raaj feels "foolish," so you can eliminate that answer choice. The correct answer, therefore, is answer choice C: anxious.

Another approach to this question would be to guess what the word that goes in the blank might be. You might guess that Raaj was a bit "nervous" before his first swim meet. Then, find the word that is closest in meaning to "nervous." That word is "anxious."

Take a moment to read the sentence again with the correct word inserted in the blank:

> Despite early-morning laps five days a week, swimming lessons since he was five years old, and two years with a private coach, Raaj felt somewhat anxious before his first college swim meet.

Example 2
Because of cats' -------- instinct to hunt, they do not need to be trained to chase a toy mouse.

(A) apathetic
(B) innate
(C) subliminal
(D) unabashed
(E) callous

Explanation
Begin by reading the sentence, pausing where the blank is. Because of some type of instinct to hunt, cats do not need to be trained to chase a toy mouse. Try to guess what the missing word might be. What type of instinct is a cat's instinct to hunt? You might guess the word "natural" or "automatic."

Eliminate any answer choice that you know does not have a meaning similar to "natural" or "automatic." Cross out the words that do not work:

(A) ~~apathetic~~
(B) innate
(C) subliminal
(D) ~~unabashed~~
(E) ~~callous~~

Three answer choices are eliminated. Now read the sentence again, inserting each possible answer choice:

The SAT Advantage

> Because of cats' *innate* instinct to hunt, they do not need to be trained to chase a toy mouse.
>
> Because of cats' *subliminal* instinct to hunt, they do not need to be trained to chase a toy mouse.

"Innate" means "inborn," and "subliminal" means "subconscious." Because you're describing a cat's inborn instinct to hunt, the correct answer is answer choice B: innate.

Example 3
The town of Milton had suffered one of the most -------- droughts in the past 50 years, with less than two inches of rainfall all summer, so Elizabeth was surprised to see a -------- garden in front of the courthouse.

(A) moderate ... flourishing
(B) uncomfortable ... colorful
(C) humid ... vivacious
(D) ruthless ... pale
(E) brutal ... vibrant

Explanation
Begin by reading the sentence, pausing where the two blanks are. You'll see that there are two parts to the sentence. The first part states that Milton had suffered a drought. The second part said that Elizabeth was surprised to see some type of garden in front of the courthouse.

There are several clues in this sentence. In the first part of the sentence, the words and phrases "suffered," "in the past 50 years," and "with less than two inches of rainfall" suggest that the drought was severe. In the second part of the sentence, the word "surprised" lets you know that the garden is not what she would have expected. In a severe drought, you would not expect a garden to be healthy and thriving.

You know that the first word needs to be an adjective that would describe a severe drought, and the second word needs to be an adjective that would describe a healthy and thriving garden. Eliminate any answer choices in which the first word would not describe a severe drought or the second word would not describe a healthy and thriving garden. Cross out the words that do not work:

(A) ~~moderate~~ ... flourishing
(B) uncomfortable ... colorful
(C) ~~humid~~ ... vivacious
(D) ruthless ... ~~pale~~
(E) brutal ... vibrant

You are left with two possible answer choices: uncomfortable ... colorful and brutal ... vibrant. Now read the sentence again, inserting the words for each answer choice:

> The town of Milton had suffered one of the most *uncomfortable* droughts in the past 50 years, with less than two inches of rainfall all summer, so Elizabeth was surprised to see a *colorful* garden in front of the courthouse.

> The town of Milton had suffered one of the most *brutal* droughts in the past 50 years, with less than two inches of rainfall all summer, so Elizabeth was surprised to see a *vibrant* garden in front of the courthouse.

Both sentences now make sense, but you were asked to choose the *best* answer choice, not just an answer choice that makes sense. Which pair of words works better? The phrases "colorful garden" and "vibrant garden" both describe a garden that is healthy and thriving, but look at the first word in each answer choice. Milton had suffered one of the worst droughts in the past 50 years. Although a terrible drought would be "uncomfortable," the word "brutal" means "harsh or severe" which is a better fit for this sentence.

Therefore the correct answer to this question is answer choice E: brutal ... vibrant. Take a moment to read the sentence again with the correct words inserted in the blanks:

> The town of Milton had suffered one of the most brutal droughts in the past 50 years, with less than two inches of rainfall all summer, so Elizabeth was surprised to see a vibrant garden in front of the courthouse.

EXTENDED READING QUESTIONS

Reading questions are based on short passages, long passages, and paired passages. Short passages are often 100-150 words, and long passages are often 400-850 words. Paired passages are two passages with a common theme or topic. After reading paired passages, you will use information in both passages to answer the questions. You might be asked to compare information in the two passages or to combine information in both passages to answer a question.

Passage-based reading questions test your understanding of what is both stated and implied in the passages. The lines of each passage are numbered, and some questions refer to specific line numbers to help you find the information that you need to answer the question.

There are three types of passage-based reading passages. The first type we will cover is extended reading questions. In extended reading questions, you will need to evaluate information in a passage. Answers to these questions are often *implied* and not stated directly.

In an extended reading question, you might be asked to draw conclusions, find the main idea, or identify a similar idea to an idea presented in the passage. You might also be asked about the author's tone, attitude, or purpose for the writing passage. You might be asked why the author included a particular quotation or example in the passage or how the author would be likely to react to certain ideas.

For extended reading questions, you will need to understand the passage as a whole. Use these strategies to help understand the entire passage as you're reading it and to refer back to the passage to answer the questions.

The SAT Advantage

STRATEGIES FOR SUCCESS

1. **Be Engaged with the Passage**
   Don't simply read each passage: be engaged with it. Pretend it is a news program or movie that interests you. As you're reading the passage, think about how you might explain it to someone else, how it relates to something else you've learned about, or whether or not you agree with what is being said.

   Ask yourself questions while you read. What type of passage is this, factual or an opinion? Why did the author write this passage? Before you reach the end, predict how the passage will conclude. The more involved you are with the passage, the better you will understand it and the more you will remember it.

2. **Summarize Each Paragraph or Section**
   While you are reading the passage, make a short note in the margin next to each paragraph or section of two or three paragraphs. In the note, summarize what you have read in a few words. These notes will help you understand what you have read, and they will help you find the parts of the passage you need in order to answer questions.

   When you have finished reading the passage, take a moment to summarize the passage in a sentence or two in your mind or on paper. Then continue on to the questions.

3. **Keep in Mind that the Answer May Be Implied**
   Answers to extended reading questions are not usually given directly. You will often need to make inferences, or conclusions, based on what you have read. For example, read this sentence:

   > Henry dropped his bags on the table, collapsed on the couch, and fell into a blissful sleep.

   The sentence doesn't explicitly *state* that Henry was exhausted and had a long day, but it does *imply* it.

4. **Approach Paired Passages One at a Time**
   When answering questions on paired passages, look back at one passage, and then look back at the other. For example, if the question asks if the authors of two passages have the same opinion on a certain topic, review one of the passages, and then review the other.

5. **Don't Spend Too Much Time on One Question**
   The reading questions are ordered chronologically not based on difficulty. Don't spend too much time on any one question. Each question is worth the same number of points, so make sure you have time to try to answer each question. If you get stuck on a question, skip it and come back to it if you have time.

6. **Notice the Tone of the Passage**
   The tone, or feel, of the passage tells you a lot about the author's purpose, attitude, and opinions. Notice the tone. Is it upbeat and positive? Is it somber, argumentative, or angry? Establishing the tone can help you determine if the author is trying to entertain, persuade, or simply inform the reader.

7. **Choose the *Best* Answer**
   Remember that you are not just asked to choose an answer that works; you are asked to choose the *best* answer. After you have chosen the correct answer, always look at the other answer choices to see if there's a better answer.

VOCABULARY-IN-CONTEXT QUESTIONS

Vocabulary-in-context questions ask about the meaning of a word or phrase in the context of a passage.

STRATEGIES FOR SUCCESS

1. **Read the Word in Context**
   You will be asked not only to determine the meaning, but to determine the meaning in the context of the passage. Reread the sentence containing the word or phrase. If you cannot determine the meaning from the sentence, reread the surrounding sentences to gain a more complete understanding of the text.

2. **Determine the Meaning**
   If you don't know the meaning of the word, try using the strategies introduced earlier in this chapter: using prefixes, suffixes, and roots, reading the sentence to yourself, looking for key words and phrases in the sentence and surrounding sentences, eliminating answer choices, noticing the subtle differences between words, and relating the words to words you already know. Reread these strategies to help you answer the passage-based vocabulary-in-context questions.

3. **Distinguish Between Meanings**
   One word can have more than one meaning. You will be asked for the meaning of the word *in the context* of the passage. For example, the word "dark" can mean "devoid of light," "evil," or "gloomy." Read the sentence to determine the meaning as the word is used in the passage.

LITERAL COMPREHENSION QUESTIONS

Literal comprehension questions test your understanding of what is directly stated in a passage.

STRATEGIES FOR SUCCESS

1. **Understand the Question**
   Be aware that the wording of the question might be different from the wording in the passage. It can help to reword the question before looking for the answer, for example, "I'm being asked for the location of the dairy farm." Be sure you understand the question; then refer back to the passage to find the answer.

2. **Skim**
   If you don't remember the answer to a question from reading the passage, skim the passage to see where the answer might be and reread that section. Remember to use

the notes that you made in the margins to help find the paragraph or paragraphs that you need quickly.

3. **Eliminate Answer Choices**
   Before you even refer back to the passage, cross out answer choices that you know are not correct. Then read the remaining answer choices. Eliminating answer choices makes it easier to identify the correct answer.

4. **Only Use Information that is in the Passage**
   Be careful not to guess or assume that you know the answer based on information that you already know. The answer to the question will be stated in the passage itself.

EXAMPLE QUESTIONS

The following long passage is followed by examples of all three types of passage-based reading questions: extended reading questions, vocabulary-in-context questions, and literal comprehension questions.

Read the passage and answer the questions that follow. Answer the questions based on what is stated or implied in the passage.

The famous Lincoln-Douglas Debates changed the course of the nation's history. The seven debates took place during Abraham Lincoln's unsuccessful run for a Senate seat. This was in 1858, two years before the presidential election of 1860, when Lincoln was elected President of the United States. The Lincoln-Douglas Debates propelled Lincoln into
5 the national limelight. Transcripts from the debates were published and distributed all over the country. The Debates gave Lincoln a reputation for wit, eloquence, courage, and the moral high ground of having spoken out against slavery.
   The Lincoln-Douglas Debates revolved around the subject of slavery. Lincoln's position on slavery was not a simple one. On a personal level, he said that slavery made him
10 miserable and that he considered it a "monstrous injustice," "a vast moral evil," and that it disturbed him to see escaped slaves returned to their "unrequited stripes and toil." On a political level, however, he could not find in the Constitution any prohibition against slavery. He did not think the government had the legal power to take slavery away from states that had joined the country with slavery in place when they did so. His hope was that slavery
15 would die a natural death if it was quarantined to the slave states where it already existed and not allowed to spread. He strongly opposed any expansion of slavery.
   Lincoln's opponent in the debates, Stephen A. Douglas, was the author of legislation that allowed territories entering the Union as new states to vote as to whether they would be slave states or free. Indeed, slavery supporters and anti-slavery supporters moved into new
20 states like Kansas and Nebraska in droves to try to sway the votes on slavery or freedom in those states.
   The Supreme Court also had handed down the Dred Scott Decision, declaring that slaves in free states were still slaves. Dred Scott was a slave whose master had moved to a free state. After a time, Dred Scott sued for his freedom, but the Dred Scott decision said he
25 must remain a slave whether he lived in a slave state or a free state.
   To Lincoln, both of these pieces of legislation meant that slavery was going to expand. New states could become slave states. Slave owners could bring their slaves into free states and fill those states with slavery if enough of them moved in. Slavery was not dying a

slow death by quarantine. It was spreading, and it now had the potential to expand into new territories and to change free states into slave-holding states.

This was the reason Lincoln challenged the incumbent senator from Illinois and tried to unseat him from the Senate through the debates. The candidates held seven debates in seven different cities in Illinois.

In that pre-television era, great crowds turned out to see the debaters. The issues were also compelling. Lincoln and Douglas wrestled publicly with such profound moral questions as what is ultimately right and wrong, what is the nature of a man (and a woman, as Lincoln was a supporter of women's rights), what did it mean to be a human being, and did the Declaration of Independence apply to all people or only to a select few?

Douglas stated that he believed that the government was "made by the white man, for the benefit of the white man, to be administered by white men." Douglas did not believe that the Declaration of Independence applied to black men or women.

Lincoln said that the Declaration was a universal document, a "standard maxim for a free society." It should be looked to, labored for, and approximated, even if people could not attain to it perfectly. It should be "constantly spreading and deepening its influence, and augmenting the happiness and value of life to all people of all colors everywhere."

When he was chosen by the Republicans as their candidate to run against Douglas for the Senate seat, Lincoln made his immortal "House Divided" speech: "A house divided against itself cannot stand. I believe this Government cannot endure permanently half slave and half free."

Although Mr. Lincoln lost the election to the Senate, he made an indelible impression on his audiences. As a speaker, Lincoln had many physical shortcomings. He was homely and ungainly with a high, thin speaking voice. He tended to make graceless gestures, such as lifting both of his long arms up high for emphasis. Yet his words and spirit were so compelling, reporters sometimes forgot to record his speeches, they were so entranced by listening to him. At an early state convention of the Republican Party, Mr. Lincoln gave what may have been his greatest speech, yet no one knows what he said. All the reporters put down their pens to listen to him. When the speech was finished, one reporter said, "The audience rose from their chairs and with pale faces and quivering lips pressed unconsciously toward him [Lincoln]." The editor of a newspaper said, "Beyond and above all skill was the overwhelming conviction imposed upon the audience that the speaker himself was charged with an irresistible and inspiring duty to his fellow men."

Although one may say Lincoln "lost" the Lincoln-Douglas Debates because he lost the election to the Senate, Lincoln won many things through the Debates. He won the Presidency two years later on the strength of his debate performances. He won a unified nation through his tireless leadership through the Civil War. He abolished slavery through his war powers as President, winning the freedom of millions of human beings. He also won himself a place in history as perhaps the greatest of all American Presidents.

Example 1
Lines 8 – 16 distinguish between:

(A) The positions of Douglas and Lincoln on slavery
(B) The positions of North and South on slavery
(C) Douglas's history of pro-slavery legislation
(D) Constitutional as opposed to state legislation on slavery
(E) Lincoln's personal and political positions on slavery

The SAT Advantage

Explanation
The correct answer is (E): Lincoln's personal and political positions on slavery
This is an example of an extended reading question. After introducing the idea that slavery was the subject of the debates, the paragraph goes on to explain Lincoln's position on slavery. The words "On a personal level" introduce Lincoln's personal reactions to slavery with direct quotations from Lincoln himself. Later lines introduce Lincoln's political position with the words "On a political level" and discuss political considerations such as "the Constitution," governmental "legal power," legal quarantining of slavery, and Lincoln's strong opposition to "any expansion of slavery." Douglas's position on slavery, the positions of the North and South on slavery, and the Constitution as opposed to state legislation are not discussed in the passage, so you can eliminate all of the other answer choices.

Example 2
What were the implications of the Supreme Court decision described in lines 22 – 25?

(A) the Supreme Court wanted the abolition of slavery
(B) free states were different from free territories
(C) slavery could be brought into free states
(D) slavery would be quarantined to where it already existed
(E) Dred Scott was a free man

Explanation
The correct answer is (C): slavery could be brought into free states
This is also an example of an extended reading question. Describing the Dred Scott Decision, these lines state, "slaves in free states were still slaves," and describe the decision as meaning that Dred Scott "must remain a slave whether he lived in a slave state or a free state." The implications of this decision was that if enough slave owners brought their slaves into free states, the states might end up being free in name only, while slavery grew and flourished within them.

Example 3
In line 31, the word "incumbent" means:

(A) incipient senator
(B) incubating senator
(C) recently retired senator
(D) sitting senator
(E) current congresswoman

Explanation
The correct answer is (D): sitting senator
This is an example of a vocabulary-in-context question. The passage states that Lincoln challenged Douglas "and tried to unseat him from the Senate." This wording implies that Douglas was a "sitting senator" or a present senator. In answer (A) "incipient" means beginning. In answer (B) "incubating" means a time when an embryo or infant is exposed to special supporting conditions for growth. If the senator were "recently retired" as in answer (C), he would not be running for the Senate. We know that Senator Stephen A. Douglas was a man, so answer (E) referring to a congresswoman is not correct.

The SAT Advantage

Example 4
In line 42, "universal" is closest in meaning to:

(A) terrestrialism
(B) utilitarianism
(C) applying to all of humankind
(D) applying to universities and sectors
(E) applying to verisimilitudes

Explanation
The correct answer is (C): applying to all humankind
This is also an example of a vocabulary-in-context question. The key to the answer to this question lies in the context of the rest of the paragraph and especially the line wherein Lincoln used the phrase "all people of all colors everywhere." The word "universal" means all people of all times, places, nationalities, colors, etc. It means something that applies to all of humankind, which is the wording of answer (C).

Example 5
The last paragraph states that Lincoln lost many things. What is one thing that he won?

(A) a unified nation
(B) election to the Senate
(C) the Presidential election of 1856
(D) the support of all American women
(E) the Lincoln-Douglas Debates

Explanation
The correct answer is (A): A unified nation
This is an example of a literal comprehension question, because the answer is stated directly in the passage. Because the question references the last paragraph, begin by looking there for the answer. The paragraph states that he lost the election to the Senate, so you can eliminate answer (B). Answer (C) is not correct because, even though he did win the Presidential election, he did not win the Presidential election of 1856. Although the passage states that Lincoln was a supporter of women's rights, it does not state that he won the support of all American women, so you can eliminate answer (D). Answer (E) is not correct because the paragraph states, "Although one may say Lincoln "lost" the Lincoln-Douglas Debates because he lost the election to the Senate, Lincoln won many things through the Debates." The correct answer is stated directly: "He won a unified nation through his tireless leadership through the Civil War." Therefore, the correct answer is (A).

The SAT Advantage

MATHEMATICS STRATEGIES

The Mathematics section of the SAT tests your ability to solve math problems. Areas covered include numerical operations, algebra, geometry, statistics, and probability. The Mathematics section is divided into three subsections. Each subsection includes multiple choice questions, and one section also includes student-produced response questions, in which you enter your answer in a special grid.

During the test, you will be given the following reference information. It includes basic geometric formulas such as the area of a triangle, circumference of a circle, and volume of cylinder. It also includes information on special right triangles.

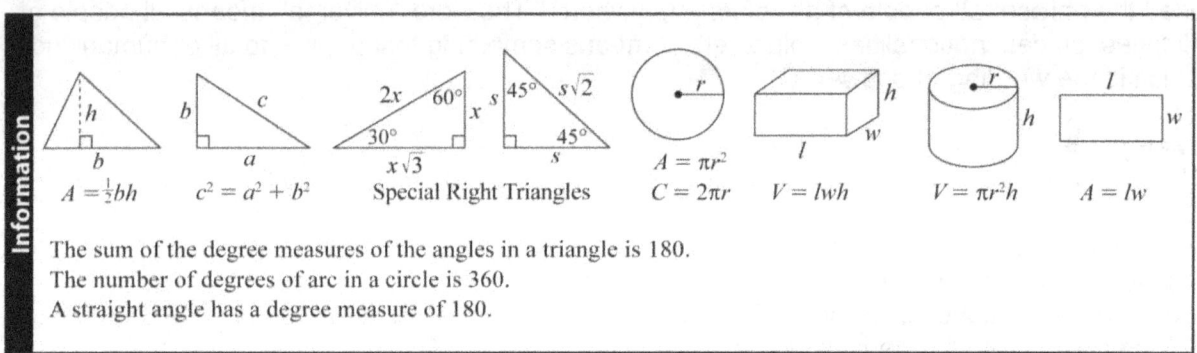

There are also three formulas that do not appear in the reference section that need to be committed to memory:

- The slope formula: $\dfrac{y_2 - y_1}{x_2 - x_1}$

- The midpoint formula: $\dfrac{x_1 + x_2}{2}, \dfrac{y_1 + y_2}{2}$

- The distance formula: $\sqrt{(x_1 - x_2)^2 + (y_1 - y_2)^2}$

There are two types of math questions on the SAT:
- Multiple choice questions
- Student-produced response questions

Here are strategies for approaching each question type. The strategies are followed by sample questions, each with a detailed explanation that walks you through finding the correct answer.

The SAT Advantage

MULTIPLE-CHOICE QUESTIONS

For multiple-choice questions, you solve a problem and then choose the correct answer from five possible answer choices. Here is an example of a multiple-choice question. We will solve this problem later in the chapter.

> The area of Lisa's vegetable garden is 84 square ft. What could the dimensions of her vegetable garden be?
>
> (A) 9 ft by 9 ft
> (B) 6 ft by 14 ft
> (C) 5 ft by 13 ft
> (D) 8 ft by 12 ft
> (E) 10 ft by 12 ft

STRATEGIES FOR SUCCESS

1. **Prepare**
   Search the Internet for topics that you want to review before the test. As you answer practice questions, make a note of topics that you need to review. Then search for them on the Internet using keywords. For example, you might search for "central angle," "probability," "factoring polynomials," or "cube root."

2. **Don't Get Bogged Down on Difficult Questions**
   Every question on the SAT is worth the same number of points. Whether you spend a few seconds or several minutes answering a question, you will get the same number of points for a correct answer, so be sure not to spend too much time on any one question.

   Math questions get progressively harder throughout each subsection. The easiest questions come first, and the most difficult are last. Because each question is worth the same number of points, be careful not to spend too much time on the harder questions. You are more likely to get the earlier questions correct, so don't get bogged down on the last few.

3. **Note the Half-Way Point of Each Subsection**
   Each subsection of the SAT has an allotted amount of time. Each subsection of Mathematics is 20 or 25 minutes long. Note the time that each subsection begins. Half way through the allotted time, stop and see how much of the subsection you've completed. If you've completed fewer than half of the questions, try spending less time on each question. Managing your time like this will assure that you have time to try to answer all of the questions.

4. **Do Not Fill in Answers Randomly**
   For the multiple-choice questions, one-quarter of a point is deducted for each incorrect answer, so do <u>not</u> fill in answers randomly if you run out of time. If you can make an educated guess, then fill in the answer. If not, skip the question.

5. **Read Each Question Carefully**
Read the entire question before you begin working. It can be tempting to begin doing calculations as soon as you read the first few words of a question, but be sure to read the *entire* question. Reading the entire question assures that you know exactly what you're being asked to find.

Also, read carefully. Are you being asked to find the tip or the total cost of the meal? The distance traveled or the distance remaining? Be careful because the answer to each one of these will probably be one of the answer choices. It would be a shame to get the wrong answer because you missed a key word or phrase in the question.

6. **Ask Yourself These Questions**
When you begin each problem, ask yourself these questions: "What information do I have?" and "What do I need to find?" Answering these two questions will help you solve the problem. For example, you might say to yourself, "I have been given the cost of a shirt and the total amount spent, and I need to find the tax rate."

7. **Eliminate Answer Choices**
After you read a question, try to eliminate one or more answer choices. Eliminate any answer choice that is not realistic. For example, the square footage of a house cannot be 120 square feet. Also eliminate any answer choices that are the wrong number type. For example, it doesn't make sense for the number of employees in a company to be negative. Eliminating one or more answer choices makes it easier to find the correct answer.

8. **Study the Diagrams Given**
Look carefully at any diagrams or figures given in a question. Some information will only be found in the diagram and will not be given in the question. Pay special attention to labels and units. For example, is a pie chart showing the number of students or the percent of students? Is a length given in centimeters or meters? By looking carefully at the diagram, you might discover that you need to do a unit conversion.

Also feel free to mark up the diagrams with additional information to help you solve the problem. It can be helpful to draw a line through a scatter plot, label the sides of a trapezoid, or draw a transformed figure on a coordinate grid.

The figures in the test are drawn to scale unless otherwise noted. For example, if one rectangle looks about three times longer than another, then you can use that information to help you find the correct answer.

9. **Make a Sketch**
If a question does not include a diagram, making a quick sketch will often help you find the answer. You might draw a sketch of a ladder leaning against a house, an L-shaped swimming pool, or a football field. Or you might make a tree diagram to count possibilities in a counting problem. Even if you think you can find the answer by picturing something in your head, make a quick sketch to make sure that you've included all of the information and calculated correctly.

The SAT Advantage

10. **Work out the Answer on Paper**
    Work out the problems in blank spaces of your test booklet. You are less likely to make mistakes if you write out the answer instead of doing calculations in your head. And be sure to write out every step. Writing out every step helps avoid common mistakes.

    You will only be scored on the answers marked on your answer sheet, but working out the problems in your test booklet will improve your chances of finding the correct answer.

11. **Use the Reference Information**
    Even if you think you know a formula, it doesn't hurt to double check the reference information. For example, it's easy to mix up the formulas for area of a circle and circumference of a circle. Study the reference information ahead of time and make sure you know how to use all of the formulas and other information given.

12. **Use a Calculator**
    You are permitted (and encouraged!) to bring a graphing calculator or scientific calculator to the test. Be sure to use it. You are more likely to make mistakes if you do calculations in your head, so use a calculator to perform calculations—and to double check your work.

13. **Check to See if Your Answer is Reasonable**
    After finding the correct answer, check to see if it is reasonable. Is it realistic? If you solve a problem and find that a family drove 225 miles per hour from Maine to Florida, you need to recheck your work. Similarly, it doesn't make sense to say that there are 12.5 girls in a club or that a car weighs 82 pounds. The outdoor temperature in winter or the balance of a checking account could be a negative number, but the number of apples in a barrel could not.

14. **Double Check Your Work Using Estimation**
    After solving a problem, use estimation to double check your work. You can round the original numbers you were given and then quickly perform a calculation in your head to see if your answer is on target.

    For example, let's say you were asked to find the area of a triangle with a base of 5.84 and a height of 7.2, and your answer is 42.048. You can quickly double check your answer using estimation.

    As you see in the reference information, the area of a triangle is one half the base times the height. Round 5.84 to 6 and round 7.2 to 7. You can quickly find half of 6 times 7 in your head; it's 21, so you know that the answer should be approximately 21. Your answer was 42.048, so you know that you need to recheck your calculation. The correct answer is 21.024.

15. **Plug-and -Check Strategy**
    If you do not know the answer to a problem, try a plug-and-check strategy. Since all numerical answers are arranged from least to greatest, always begin your plug-and-check strategy with selection C. If the value is too large, proceed to A and B. If the value is too small, proceed to D and E. You will find at least one problem on the SAT that is unsolveable; you *must* choose a plug-and-check strategy.

The SAT Advantage

EXAMPLE QUESTIONS

Example 1
The area of Lisa's rectangular vegetable garden is 84 square ft. What could be the dimensions of her vegetable garden?

(A) 9 ft by 9 ft
(B) 6 ft by 14 ft
(C) 5 ft by 13 ft
(D) 8 ft by 12 ft
(E) 10 ft by 12 ft

Explanation
Ask yourself two questions: What information do I have? What do I need to find? You were given the area of a rectangular garden and need to find the possible dimensions. Remember that you don't have to memorize formulas. They are given to you in the reference information. You'll see that the formula for the area of a rectangle is $A = lw$ or $A = l \times w$.

See if you can eliminate any answer choices. Let's say that you know that 9×9 is 81, and you know that 10×12 is 120. You can therefore eliminate answer choices A and E. Cross out the answers that you know are not correct:

(A) 9 ft by 9 ft
(B) 6 ft by 14 ft
(C) 5 ft by 13 ft
(D) 8 ft by 12 ft
(E) 10 ft by 12 ft

Remember that the area of a rectangle is length times width. From the remaining three answer choices, find the answer choice with a product of 84. Since $6 \times 14 = 84$, the correct answer is answer choice B.

Example 2
A bag contains 6 red marbles, 8 blue marbles, and 3 yellow marbles. If Juan reaches into the bag and pulls out one marble, what is the probability that it will be blue?

(A) 1/2
(B) 8/14
(C) 8/11
(D) 8/17
(E) 6/17

Explanation
This is a probability question. To find the probability that Juan will choose a blue marble, you need to find the number of favorable outcomes (the number of blue marbles) and the number of total possible outcomes (the total number of marbles). The total number of marbles is 17. Out of the 17 marbles, 8 are blue, so the probability of choosing a blue marble is 8 out of 17, also written 8/17. Therefore the correct answer is answer choice D.

The SAT Advantage

Example 3
A football team has played 5 games this year. The final score of each game is shown below:

25, 7, 20, 21, 7

What is the median of their scores?

(A) 7
(B) 16
(C) 18
(D) 20
(E) 21

Explanation
This is a statistics question. You are given data and need to find the median. Statistics terms can be confusing. Answer choices A, B, and C are other measures of center and range for this data. The mode, or value that occurs most often, is 7. The mean, or average of the data, is 16. The range of the data is 18.

The median is the middle number in a set of numbers. In order to find the median, you first need to arrange the numbers in ascending order.

7, 7, 20, 21, 25

The middle number is 20, so the median of this set of data is 20. Therefore the correct answer is answer choice D.

Example 4
Evaluate the following expression when $b = 5$.

$b^3 \times 16b + b^4$

(A) 1220
(B) 10,125
(C) 10,625
(D) 1,250,125
(E) 1,250,625

Explanation
For this question, be sure to write out each step of your work. To evaluate an expression, substitute the value given for the variable. In this case, substitute 5 for b.

$5^3 \times 16 \times 5 + 5^4$

When a number is raised to a power, multiply that number by itself the number of times indicated by the exponent.

$5 \times 5 \times 5 \times 16 \times 5 + 5 \times 5 \times 5 \times 5$

Now remember the correct order of operations: multiply before you add.

Mathematics Strategies

The SAT Advantage

$5 \times 5 \times 5 \times 16 \times 5 + 5 \times 5 \times 5 \times 5$

$10{,}000 + 625$

Therefore, the correct answer is answer choice C, 10,625.

Note: Much of this work can be done on a calculator. You can put this information into a scientific or graphing calculator as follows:

5^3 x 16+5^4= 10,625

The calculator will automatically follow the order of operations and arrive at the correct solution.

Example 5
If a line has a y-intercept at (0, 2) and an x-intercept at (3, 0), what is the slope of the line?

(A) $-\dfrac{3}{2}$

(B) $-\dfrac{2}{3}$

(C) $-\dfrac{1}{2}$

(D) $\dfrac{2}{3}$

(E) $\dfrac{3}{2}$

Explanation
For a question about slope, it helps to draw a sketch. Make a quick sketch of the x- and y-axes and mark the x- and y-intercepts.

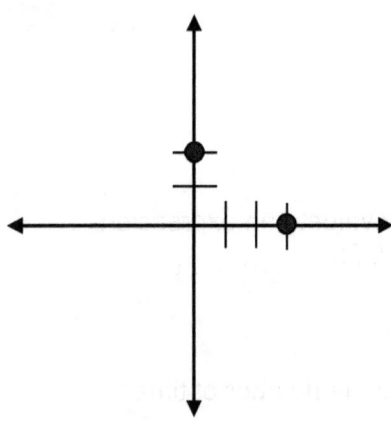

Mathematics Strategies

Then draw a line through the two points.

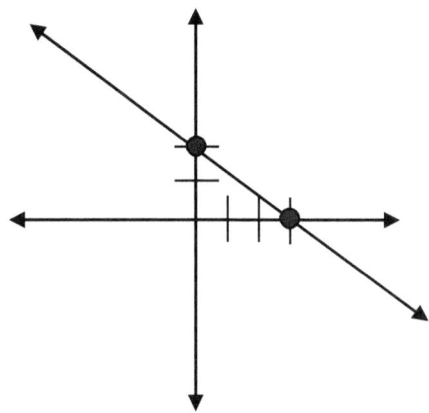

Remember that slope is "rise over run," or the change in y over the change in x ($\frac{y_2 - y_1}{x_2 - x_1}$). To find the slope of this line, subtract the y values and subtract the x values. The slope, therefore, is: $\frac{2-0}{0-3}$

2 over –3 is equal to $-\frac{2}{3}$, so the slope is $-\frac{2}{3}$. Drawing a sketch helps you with this question, because you can confirm that the slope should be negative. Lines that go "downhill" have a negative slope, and lines that go "uphill" have a positive slope.

The correct answer is answer choice B: $-\frac{2}{3}$

Example 6
What is the value of n in the following equation?
$$2^n = \frac{n}{.25}$$

(A) 2
(B) 3
(C) 4
(D) 5
(E) 6

Explanation
This problem is not solveable; you must use a plug-and-check strategy. Since the answers are arrayed from least to greatest, begin with selection C and assess the result.

$$2^4 = \frac{4}{.25}$$
$$16 = 16$$

The SAT Advantage

Using a plug-and-check strategy quickly helped us solve what could have been a time-consuming problem.

STUDENT-PRODUCED RESPONSE QUESTIONS

For student-produced response questions, you must solve the problem and enter the answer in a grid. You are not given answer choices to choose from, so you need to work carefully to make sure that you've found the correct answer. Write your answer in the boxes, and then fill in the circles in the special four-column grid. In each column, you can fill in a circle for a number, a decimal point, or a slash.

Fill in no more than one circle in any column. For example, to indicate the answer 2.67, you would fill in the circle for the 2 in the first column, the decimal point in the second column, the 6 in the third column, and the 7 in the fourth column.

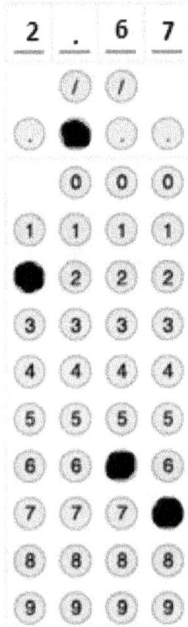

You don't get credit for writing your answer in the boxes at the top of the grid, but it helps assure that you fill in the circles correctly. The answer sheet will be scored by a machine, so be sure to fill in each circle completely.

If the answer requires that you fill in fewer than four columns, you begin in any column as long as the answer fits. For example, to indicate the answer 23, you can begin in the first, second, or third column.

For fractions, use the slash. For example, for the fraction 7/8, you would fill in the circle for the 7, then the slash, and then the 8.

The SAT Advantage

```
 7  /  8  _
    ●  ⊘
 ⊙  ⊙  ⊙  ⊙
    ⓪  ⓪  ⓪
 ①  ①  ①  ①
 ②  ②  ②  ②
 ③  ③  ③  ③
 ④  ④  ④  ④
 ⑤  ⑤  ⑤  ⑤
 ⑥  ⑥  ⑥  ⑥
 ●  ⑦  ⑦  ⑦
 ⑧  ⑧  ●  ⑧
 ⑨  ⑨  ⑨  ⑨
```

If the answer is a decimal that is less than 1, you do not need to mark a zero before the decimal point. For example, if the answer is 0.25, you would fill in the circle for the decimal point, then the 2, and then the 5.

Note: Don't be alarmed if you notice that a question has more than one correct answer. Simply select one of the correct answers and you will receive full credit.

STRATEGIES FOR SUCCESS

1. **Don't Get Bogged Down on Difficult Questions**
   Remember that every question is worth the same number of points, so be sure not to spend too much time on any one question. Just like the multiple-choice questions, the student-produced response questions get progressively harder throughout the subsection. You are more likely to get the earlier questions correct, so don't spend too much time on the last few.

2. **Convert Mixed Numbers**
   Mixed numbers cannot be entered into the grid. For example, if you tried to indicate the mixed number $4\frac{1}{2}$ by filling in the circle for the 4, then the 1, then the slash, and then the 2, the answer would be interpreted as 41 over 2, not $4\frac{1}{2}$.

   If the answer to a question is a mixed number, you need to convert it to either a decimal or an improper fraction. For example, if the answer is $4\frac{1}{2}$, convert it to either 4.5 or 9/2 and enter it on the grid.

Mathematics Strategies

The SAT Advantage

Tip! Don't remember how to convert mixed numbers to decimals or improper fractions? This is a great example of a skill to brush up on by searching for the phrase "convert mixed numbers to decimals and improper fractions" on the Internet.

3. **Be Careful with Long Decimals**
You will mark your answer in a four column grid. If your answer has a decimal point, you will use one of the columns to indicate the decimal point. If the answer is a decimal with too many digits to fit in the grid, round the decimal.

For example, let's say this is the question:

What is $\frac{1}{3}$ expressed as a decimal?

The correct answer is 0.33333.... There are only four columns in the grid, though, so to mark this answer, round the number to 0.333. In the grid, mark the following answer: .333

If the decimal is too long to fit in the grid, you must use every column. For example, for the answer 0.33333..., it would be incorrect to mark the following answer: .33

4. **Know that the Answer Will Always Be Positive**
No question in the student-produced responses has a negative answer—or an answer greater than 9,999. Knowing that the answer must be positive and cannot be greater than 9,999 might help you find the correct question. If you solve a problem and get an answer that is negative or greater than 9,999, you will know that you took a wrong turn at some point and need to recheck your work.

5. **Write the Correct Answer on Scratch Paper First**
Write your answer on scratch paper so you will know how it will be entered into the grid. For example, $4\frac{2}{3}$ needs to be entered as 4.67 or 14/3, as explained above. And the decimal 0.24732 needs to be entered as .247. Writing the answer on scratch paper will help assure that you enter it correctly in the grid.

6. **Take a Guess**
You are not penalized for incorrect answers on student-produced response questions, so don't leave an answer blank. If possible, make an educated guess. If you cannot make an educated guess, try filling in one of the following answers:
 - the product of two of the numbers in the question
 - the mean of two of the numbers in the question
 - 1
 - 0

7. **Perform Each Calculation Twice**
Because you are not choosing from answer choices given, perform each calculation twice. That will confirm that you have found the correct answer.

EXAMPLE QUESTIONS

Example 1
Solve the equation for the positive value of y when $x = 7$.

$y^2 = x^3 - 6x - 45$

Explanation
Begin by substituting 7 for x. Remember to write out every step.

$y^2 = 7^3 - 6 \times 7 - 45$

Now simplify the right side of the equation. Remember the order of operations: exponents, then multiplication, and then subtraction.

$y^2 = 343 - 42 - 45$

$y^2 = 256$

To solve for y, take the square root of both sides.

$y = 16$

Example 2
The pie chart below shows the number of students who attend Milford High School.

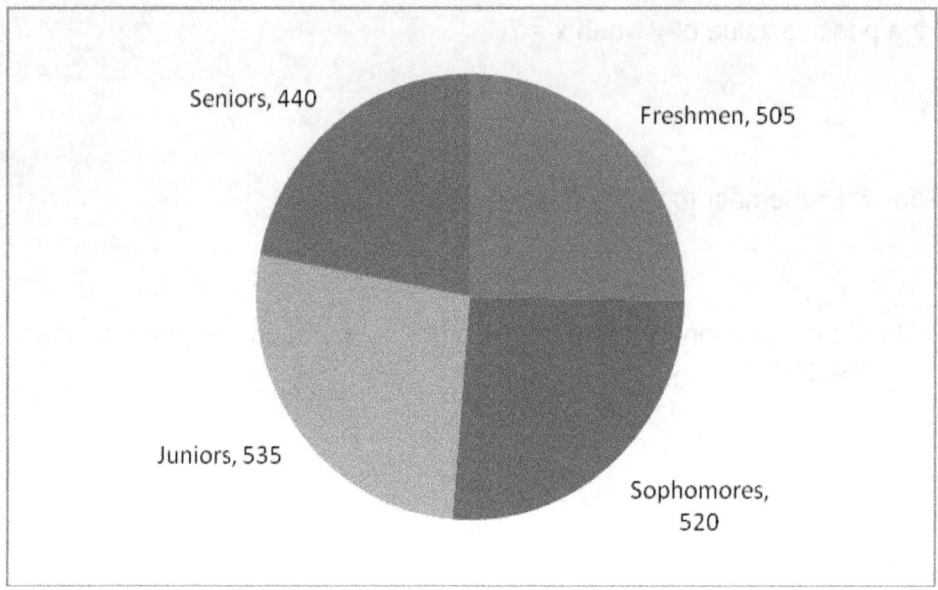

What percent of the students are sophomores?

Explanation
You are given the number of students in each grade, and you are asked to find the percent that are sophomores. To find the percent of students who are sophomores, divide the number of sophomores by the total number of students in the high school.

520 ÷ (505 + 520 + 535 + 440)

520 ÷ 2,000

0.26

0.26 is equal to 26%, so 26% of students in the high school are sophomores. Record your answer on the grid.

The SAT Advantage

```
  2   6   _   _
     (/) (/)
 (.) (.) (.) (.)
     (0) (0) (0)
 (1) (1) (1) (1)
  ●  (2) (2) (2)
 (3) (3) (3) (3)
 (4) (4) (4) (4)
 (5) (5) (5) (5)
 (6)  ●  (6) (6)
 (7) (7) (7) (7)
 (8) (8) (8) (8)
 (9) (9) (9) (9)
```

Example 3
A rectangular prism has a volume of 272.25 cm³. The length of the prism is 11 cm, and the height is 4.5 cm. What is the width?

Explanation
For this question, it can help to draw a quick sketch. A rectangular prism is a box. You know two of the dimensions, so draw a box and label two of the sides. You don't know the other dimension, so you don't need to worry about drawing the prism to scale. Mark the side you don't know with a question mark or a variable, whichever makes more sense to you.

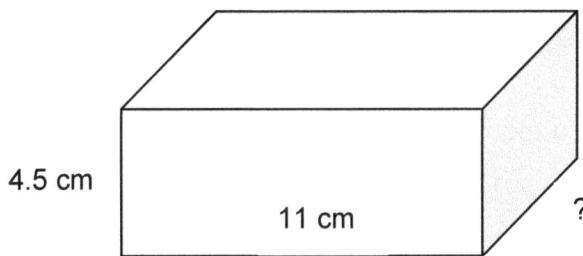

Remember that you don't have to memorize formulas. They are given to you in the reference information. You'll see in the reference information that the formula for the volume of a rectangular prism is $V = lwh$, or $V = l \times w \times h$.

Ask yourself these questions: What information do I have? What do I need to find? You were given the length, height, and volume. You need to find the width. Begin by writing the formula.

$V = l \times w \times h$

Then substitute the values that you were given.

$272.25 = 11 \times w \times 4.5$

Simplify the equation.

272.25 = 49.5 × w

To find the answer, divide both sides by 49.5. Remember that you're allowed to use your calculator.

W =5.5

Therefore, the width is 5.5 cm. Write your answer in the boxes, and mark the grid by filling in the circle for a 5, then the decimal point, and then the 5.

Example 4
What is the sum of the measures of the angles in a regular hexagon?

Explanation
To find the sum of the measures of the angles in any regular polygon, use the formula (n-2)(180), where n represents the number of sides. Since a hexagon has 6 sides, replace n with 6 in the formula:

(6 - 2)(180) = 4 x 180 = 720

Enter the correct answer, 720, in the grid.

The SAT Advantage

```
 7   2   0
    (/) (/)
(.) (.) (.) (.)
    (0) ●  (0)
(1) (1) (1) (1)
(2) ●  (2) (2)
(3) (3) (3) (3)
(4) (4) (4) (4)
(5) (5) (5) (5)
(6) (6) (6) (6)
 ●  (7) (7) (7)
(8) (8) (8) (8)
(9) (9) (9) (9)
```

Example 5
A carpenter has a piece of wood that is 7 feet long. He is going to cut the board into 4-inch pieces. How many pieces will he be able to make?

Explanation
Ask yourself the two questions: What information do I have? What do I need to find? You are given the length of the board and the length of the small pieces that he wants to make. You are asked to find the number of pieces that he will be able to make.

Read carefully: you are given measurements in both feet and inches, so you need to convert units. You need both measurements to be in either inches or feet. 4 inches would be a fraction of a foot, which would be more difficult to work with, so it would be easier to convert 7 feet to inches. Remember, there are 12 inches in every foot (12 inches = 1 foot).

7 ft × 12 in = 84 in

Therefore, the board is 84 inches long. How many 4-inch pieces can he make from an 84-inch-long board? To find the answer, divide.

84 ÷ 4 = 21

Therefore he will be able to cut 21 four-inch pieces of wood from the seven-foot board. Enter the correct answer in the grid.

The SAT Advantage

2	1		
	/	/	
.	.	.	.
	0	0	0
1	●	1	1
●	2	2	2
3	3	3	3
4	4	4	4
5	5	5	5
6	6	6	6
7	7	7	7
8	8	8	8
9	9	9	9

The SAT Advantage

WRITING STRATEGIES

The Writing section of the SAT tests your ability to write an essay and identify errors in sentences and paragraphs. The Writing section is divided into three subsections. In the first subsection, you will write a short essay in response to a prompt. In the other two subsections, you will answer multiple-choice questions on identifying errors in sentences and improving sentences and paragraphs. Topics include grammar, punctuation, usage, word choice, sentence structure, and paragraph organization and development.

In the Writing section, there are three types of questions, plus one essay:
- Improving sentences questions
- Identifying sentence error questions
- Improving paragraphs questions
- Essay

Here are strategies for approaching each question type and the essay. The strategies are followed by sample questions, each with a sample response or a detailed explanation that walks you through finding the correct answer.

IMPROVING SENTENCES QUESTIONS

The improving sentences questions test your knowledge of grammar, usage, and sentence structure and your ability to recognize effective sentences and identify and correct mistakes. The questions cover topics such as punctuation, verb usage, subject-verb agreement, pronoun usage, active versus passive voice, parallel structure, wordiness, run-on sentences, and fragments.

You will be shown a sentence with a portion of the sentence underlined. You will then be given five answer choices. Each answer choice is a replacement for the underlined portion of the sentence. The first answer choice will always be the same as the underlined portion of the original sentence, so to indicate that there should be no change, you will choose answer choice A.

Here is an example of an improving sentences question. We will answer this question later in the chapter.

> June was so excited about her vacation that she couldn't sleep; she just laid in bed, staring at the ceiling, thinking about all of the places she would visit.
>
> (A) sleep; she just laid in bed
> (B) sleep, she just laid in bed
> (C) sleep, she just lay in bed
> (D) sleep; she just lied in bed
> (E) sleep; she just lay in bed

Writing Strategies

The SAT Advantage

STRATEGIES FOR SUCCESS

1. **Prepare**
   Improving sentences questions test your knowledge of standard written English, including grammar, usage, and punctuation. To help prepare for the test, search the Internet for topics that you need to learn more about. As you answer practice test questions, make a note of topics that you need to review more. Then search for the topics on the Internet using keywords. For example, you might search for "pronoun antecedents," "dangling modifiers," "semicolons," or "active and passive voice."

2. **Don't Get Bogged Down on Difficult Questions**
   Every question on the SAT is worth the same number of points, so don't spend too much time on any one question. Be sure to allow enough time to try to answer each question. The questions are arranged in order of difficulty, so the easiest questions will be the first few.

3. **Note the Half-Way Point of Each Subsection**
   Each subsection of the SAT has an allotted amount of time. Each subsection of Writing is 10 or 25 minutes long. Note the time that each subsection begins. Half way through the allotted time, stop and see how much of the subsection you've completed. If you've completed fewer than half of the questions or written less than half of the essay, adjust your timing accordingly.

4. **Do Not Fill in Answers Randomly**
   For the multiple-choice questions, one-quarter of a point is deducted for each incorrect answer, so do <u>not</u> fill in answers randomly if you run out of time. If you can make an educated guess, then fill in the answer. If not, skip the question.

5. **Read the Sentence Quickly and Naturally**
   Begin by reading the sentence quickly to see if it sounds correct as written. Read it naturally, as if you're speaking the sentence, not slowly as if you're trying to find a mistake. Reading the sentence naturally can help you find mistakes.

   When you see a comma in a sentence, pause. Pausing at each comma will help determine whether the comma is needed.

   Choose the answer choice that creates a sentence with correct grammar, usage, and punctuation. The sentence must be clear and precise and must follow the conventions of standard written English.

6. **Look for Both Corrections and Improvements**
   The problem with a sentence might not be an actual error; the sentence might just need to be improved. For example, read this sentence:

   > I keep an umbrella in the trunk of my car, and I never know when it might rain.

   This sentence is technically correct. There are no grammatical errors. However, the sentence doesn't show the cause-and-effect relationship between the two parts of the sentence. Try replacing the word "and" with "because" and read the sentence again:

   > I keep an umbrella in the trunk of my car, because I never know when it might rain.

This is sentence is a better choice because it gives the reader more information. It shows the relationship between the first part of the sentence and the second part of the sentence.

7. **Read All Five Answer Choices**
   After reading the sentence, always read all five answer choices, even if the original sentence sounds correct as written. As you read each answer choice, you might see that one of the phrases fixes a mistake that you hadn't noticed.

   For example, one of the answer choices might insert a comma in the underlined portion of the sentence. You might not have noticed that a comma was needed, but after looking at the answer choice, you might see that a comma was needed to set off an introductory or parenthetical phrase.

8. **Eliminate Answer Choices**
   After you read a question, try to eliminate one or more answer choices. Eliminate any answer choice that you know is incorrect or sounds awkward. If an answer choice creates a sentence that is wordy and confusing or contains a punctuation or grammatical error, go ahead and cross it out. Eliminating one or more answer choices makes it easier to find the correct answer.

9. **Read the Sentence Using Each Answer Choice**
   If you're having problems finding the correct answer, read the sentence once for each answer choice. Read the entire sentence, replacing the underlined portion of the sentence with the answer choice. Reading the sentence, aloud if you're practicing, or silently to yourself during the test, can help you decide which answer choice is correct.

   For example, look at the following question:

   Elizabeth's mother told her, "After you finish your chores, you can go to the <u>movies with your brother and I</u>."

   (A) movies with your brother and I
   (B) movies, with your brother and I
   (C) movies, with your brother and me
   (D) movies with your brother and me
   (E) movies with your brother and myself

   Let's say that you've read the original sentence and you've looked at all five answer choices, but you're still having trouble finding the correct answer. Try reading the sentence five times, once for each answer choice. By reading the sentence using answer choices B and C, you might notice that pausing after the word "movies" doesn't sound quite right, so the comma does not seem to be needed. You can eliminate answer choices B and C.

   Try reading the sentence using answer choice D:

   Elizabeth's mother told her, "After you finish your chores, you can go to the <u>movies with your brother and me</u>."

Reading that sentence might remind you of something you learned—that you wouldn't say, "go to the movies with I," so you shouldn't say, "go to the movies with your brother and I." You *would*, though, say, "go to the movies with me," so you should say, "go to the movies with your brother and me." The correct answer to this question is answer choice D.

10. **Look for the Clearest Sentence**
    The correct answer is often the one that simply sounds the clearest. If an answer choice makes the sentence easier to understand, there's a good chance that it's the correct answer. The correct answer choice will make the sentence unambiguous and precise. For example, read these two sentences. Which one is clearer?

    Many events that are sponsored by the library during the year, and the book swap is my favorite.

    There are many events sponsored by the library during the year, and the book swap is my favorite.

    The second sentence is clearer, and it's the correct answer. The first choice is not a complete sentence, and it shows—it sounds awkward.

    The correct answer is sometimes one of the shortest answer choices because the correct answer often reduces wordiness. Improving the sentence by choosing the correct answer will often involve eliminating repeated words. For example, read these two sentences:

    My favorite professor is Ms. Powers, and Ms. Powers was featured in a documentary.

    My favorite professor, Ms. Powers, was featured in a documentary.

    You'll see that the second sentence reduces wordiness by eliminating the repeated words "Ms. Powers." The second sentence is shorter and easy to understand.

11. **Choose the *Best* Answer**
    Remember that you're not simply looking for an answer that is technically correct; you're looking for the *best* answer. Even if you find an answer choice that seems to be the correct answer, be sure to read *all* of the answer choices. The correct answer is the answer choice that creates a sentence that follows the conventions of standard written English and is the most precise and clear.

12. **Read the Sentence Again**
    After choosing the correct answer, read the sentence one last time with the underlined portion of the sentence replaced with the correct answer. You might have a phrase that seems to fit, but you might not notice a problem with the answer choice until you read the sentence again.

EXAMPLE QUESTIONS

Example 1
June was so excited about her vacation that she couldn't <u>sleep; she just laid in bed</u>, staring at the ceiling, thinking about all of the places she would visit.

(A) sleep; she just laid in bed
(B) sleep, she just laid in bed
(C) sleep, she just lay in bed
(D) sleep; she just lied in bed
(E) sleep; she just lay in bed

Explanation
Read the sentence as written. Remember to read it quickly and naturally. Then read the answer choices. See if you can eliminate any answer choices that you know are incorrect or sound awkward.

Notice that if you divided the sentence into two parts before and after the semicolon, each part would be a complete sentence:

> June was so excited about her vacation that she couldn't sleep.

> She just laid in bed, staring at the ceiling, thinking about all of the places she would visit.

Two phrases that could be complete sentences on their own (also called independent clauses) cannot be joined using a comma, so you can eliminate answer choices B and C. Let's say that you also know that "she just lied in bed" is not correct. The past tense of "lie" is not "lied." Go ahead and cross out the answer choices that you know are not correct:

(A) sleep; she just laid in bed
~~(B) sleep, she just laid in bed~~
~~(C) sleep, she just lay in bed~~
~~(D) sleep; she just lied in bed~~
(E) sleep; she just lay in bed

You now have two answer choices to choose from. You need to decide which is correct: "she just laid in bed" or "she just lay in bed." You are looking for the past tense of the verb "lie," not "lay." Someone does not *lay* in bed; someone *lies* in bed. The past tense of "lie" is "lay," so the correct answer is answer choice E: sleep; she just lay in bed.

To check to make sure that you've found the right answer, take a moment to read the sentence again with the underlined portion of the sentence replaced with answer choice E:

> June was so excited about her vacation that she couldn't sleep; she just lay in bed, staring at the ceiling, thinking about all of the places she would visit.

The SAT Advantage

Example 2
Every member of the women's volleyball team is responsible <u>for buying their own bus ticket</u> to New York.

(A) for buying their own bus ticket
(B) for buying her own bus ticket
(C) for buying there own bus ticket
(D) to buy their own bus ticket
(E) to buy her own bus ticket

Explanation
Read the sentence as written. Remember to read it quickly and naturally. Then read the answer choices. Begin by eliminating any answer choices that you know are incorrect or sound awkward. Notice that answer choices D and E make sentences that sound awkward. For example, read the sentence using answer choice D:

> Every member of the women's volleyball team is responsible <u>to buy their own bus ticket</u> to New York.

That sentence sounds awkward because it's not idiomatic in standard written English to say, "responsible to buy;" we say, "responsible for buying." Therefore, you can eliminate answer choices D and E.

Let's say that you also know that "for buying there own bus ticket" is incorrect because the pronoun is not spelled "there;" it's spelled "their." Therefore, you can eliminate answer choice C. Remember that it helps to actually cross out the answer choices that you know are not correct:

(A) for buying their own bus ticket
(B) for buying her own bus ticket
~~(C) for buying there own bus ticket~~
~~(D) to buy their own bus ticket~~
~~(E) to buy her own bus ticket~~

You now have two answer choices to choose from: "for buying their own bus ticket" and "for buying her own bus ticket." You need to choose between the pronouns "their" and "her." The pronoun needs to agree in number with "every member of the women's volleyball team." In general, disregard prepositional phrases that begin with the word "of." The pronoun needs to agree in number with "every member." "Every member," like "each member" or "any member," is singular, so the pronoun must be singular. It is correct to say, "Every member is responsible for buying her own ticket," not "Every member is responsible for buying their own ticket." Therefore, the correct answer is answer choice B: for buying her own bus ticket.

To check to make sure that you've found the right answer, take a moment read the sentence again with the underlined portion of the sentence replaced with answer choice B:

> Every member of the women's volleyball team is responsible for buying her own bus ticket to New York.

Writing Strategies

The SAT Advantage

Example 3
The cats in the neighborhood hide and every <u>dog howls, the fireworks</u> explode in the distance each Fourth of July.

(A) dog howls, the fireworks
(B) dog howls; when the fireworks
(C) dog howls, and the fireworks
(D) dog howls, when the fireworks
(E) dog howls; the fireworks

Explanation
Begin by reading the sentence, pausing at the comma. You'll see that, as written, the sentence is awkward and sounds like it's missing something. Also, if you split the sentence into two before and after the comma, you would create two complete sentences:

> Cats in the neighborhood hide and every dog howls.
>
> The fireworks explode in the distance each Fourth of July.

Because two independent clauses are joined by a comma, the original sentence is an example of a comma splice and needs to be corrected. To correct the comma splice, replace the comma with a semicolon.

Read the answer choices, and eliminate any answer choices that you know are incorrect or sound awkward. We've eliminated the sentence as it is written, so we've eliminated answer choice A. Replacing the comma with a semicolon fixes the comma splice, but it still sounds like something is missing, so you can eliminate answer choice E. Cross out the answer choices that you know are not correct:

(A) ~~dog howls, the fireworks~~
(B) dog howls; when the fireworks
(C) dog howls, and the fireworks
(D) dog howls, when the fireworks
(E) ~~dog howls; the fireworks~~

There are three remaining answer choices. Now read the sentence replacing the underlined portion with each answer choice. The answer choices add the word "when" or "and" to the sentence. Look at the sentence using answer choice C:

> Cats in the neighborhood hide and every <u>dog howls, and the fireworks</u> explode in the distance each Fourth of July.

This sentence is grammatically correct, but it does not show the relationship between the first and second parts of the sentence. The conjunction "and" makes both parts of the sentence equally true; it doesn't show the correct relationship between them. Now read the sentence using answer choice D:

> Cats in the neighborhood hide and every <u>dog howls, when the fireworks</u> explode in the distance each Fourth of July.

Writing Strategies

This sentence is clear and precise. The word "when" shows the relationship between "Cats in the neighborhood hide and every dog howls" and "the fireworks explode in the distance each Fourth of July."

Answer choice B is not correct: the comma cannot be replaced with a semicolon because "when the fireworks explode in the distance each Fourth of July" is not an independent clause.

Therefore, the correct answer is answer choice D: dog howls, when the fireworks.

IDENTIFYING SENTENCE ERROR QUESTIONS

Identifying sentence error questions test your knowledge of grammar, usage, and sentence structure by having you *identify* errors in sentences. The questions cover topics such as punctuation, parallel structure, active versus passive voice, and common grammatical errors involving pronouns, verbs, comma splices, and fragments.

You will be shown a sentence with four words or phrases underlined and marked (A) through (D). Each sentence is followed by the underlined words "No error" marked (E). To indicate that there is no error in the sentence, you will choose answer choice E.

Here is an example of an identifying sentence error question. We will answer this question later in the chapter.

<u>Always the first to volunteer,</u> Melissa offered to find a location for the <u>drama club's</u> car
              A   B

wash, make posters <u>to hang in shops around town</u>, buy supplies, and <u>to bring</u> drinks for
                                        C   D

the workers. <u>No error</u>
                      E

STRATEGIES FOR SUCCESS

1. **Don't Get Bogged Down on Difficult Questions**
   Remember that every question on the SAT is worth the same number of points, so don't spend too much time on any one question. Like the improving sentence questions, the identifying sentence error questions are arranged in order of difficulty, so the easiest questions will be in the beginning. Keep an eye on the time, and be sure to allow enough time to try to answer each question.

2. **Read the Sentence Quickly and Naturally**
   Begin by reading the sentence quickly. Read it naturally, as if you're speaking the sentence, not slowly as if you're trying to find a mistake. Then read it a second time, paying close attention to each underlined word or phrase. When you see a comma in a sentence, pause. Pausing at each comma will help determine whether the comma is needed.

3. **Eliminate Answer Choices**
   After you read a question, try to eliminate one or more answer choices. Because you are looking for errors in the sentence, eliminate any underlined word or phrase that you know is not an error. It can help to put a small checkmark next to the word or phrase that

you know is written correctly. If it helps you, circle the remaining answer choices. Eliminating one or more answer choices makes it easier to find the error.

4. **Read a Portion of the Sentence**
   To help determine if an underlined word or phrase contains and error, read a larger portion of the sentence. Take this sentence as an example:

   In the new high <u>school, each</u> locker room <u>is equipped</u> with an office for a <u>coach, and</u>
                    A   B   C
   each math classroom has <u>it's own</u> computer lab. <u>No error</u>
                             D   E

   Let's say that you're trying to figure out if answer choice B is written correctly. Try reading a larger portion of the sentence that includes the underlined phrase:

      each locker room <u>is equipped</u> with an office for a coach

   Reading that part of the sentence helps you see that the underlined phrase is written correctly.

5. **You Might Need to Read the Entire Sentence to See the Error**
   Even though the error will be a word or phrase in the sentence, you might need to look at the sentence as a whole to see the mistake. For example, an underlined phrase might be causing the sentence to be a fragment instead of a complete sentence, or one word might be creating problems with parallel structure in the sentence.

6. **Read the Sentence Again**
   After finding the error in the sentence, read the sentence again and replace the mistake with a correct word or phrase. Reading the sentence with the error corrected can help you check to make sure you've found the correct answer.

EXAMPLE QUESTIONS

Example 1
<u>Always the first to volunteer,</u> Melissa offered to find a location for the <u>drama club's</u> car wash,
             A   B
make posters <u>to hang in shops around town</u>, buy supplies, and <u>to bring</u> drinks for the workers.
                         C   D
<u>No error</u>
   E

Explanation
First read the sentence quickly, and then read it again, noticing each underlined phrase. You are looking for the mistake in the sentence, if any.

Begin by eliminating any underlined phrases that you know are correct. The phrase "Always the first to volunteer" describes the word that it is closest to, "Melissa," so it is correct and you can eliminate answer choice A. The phrase "drama club's" is a possessive, describing the car wash, so it is spelled correctly. Therefore, you can eliminate answer choice B. It can be helpful to put a small checkmark next to those two options to remind yourself that they are correct.

To see if answer choice C is written correctly, try reading a larger portion of the sentence including that phrase:

> make posters <u>to hang in shops around town</u>

The phrase "make posters to hang in shops around town" is written correctly, so you can eliminate answer choice C.

In order to see if answer choice D is written correctly, you need to read the entire sentence:

> Always the first to volunteer, Melissa offered to find a location for the drama club's car wash, make posters to hang in shops around town, buy supplies, and <u>to bring</u> drinks for the workers.

There is a problem with parallel structure in the sentence. Melissa offered to do three things: *find* a location, *make* posters, and *bring* drinks. These verbs need to be written in the same way, so the word "to" should be removed from the phrase "to bring." Therefore, the correct answer is answer choice D.

To make sure you've found the correct answer, take a moment to read the sentence with the mistake corrected:

> Always the first to volunteer, Melissa offered to find a location for the drama club's car wash, make posters to hang in shops around town, buy supplies, and bring drinks for the workers.

Example 2
In our new house, the temperature in the <u>bedrooms were</u> always lower than in the living <u>room,</u>
                                                    A   B
<u>so</u> my <u>mom set up</u> a fan to circulate the <u>air and make</u> the whole house comfortable. <u>No error</u>
 C   D   E

Explanation
First read the sentence quickly, pausing at each comma, and then read it again, noticing each underlined phrase. You are looking for the mistake in the sentence, if any.

Begin by eliminating any underlined phrases that you know are correct. The comma after "living room" precedes the conjunction "so," which is correct. Therefore, you can eliminate answer choice B. To see if answer choice C is written correctly, read a larger portion of the sentence:

> my <u>mom set up</u> a fan to circulate the air

The word "mom" is not used as a name because it follows the word "my;" therefore it does not need to capitalized and you can eliminate answer choice C. Reading the sentence, you may be able to tell that a comma is not needed before the word "and" in answer choice D, so you can eliminate that answer choice also.

To see if answer choice A is written correctly, read a larger portion of the sentence including that phrase:

> the temperature in the <u>bedrooms were</u> always lower than in the living room

The verb needs to agree in number with the word "temperature," not "bedrooms." The *temperature* was always lower; the *bedrooms* weren't lower. Therefore, the verb "were" needs to be changed to "was," and answer choice A is the correct answer.

To make sure you've found the right answer, take a moment to read the sentence with the mistake corrected:

> In our new house, the temperature in the bedrooms was always lower than in the living room, so my mom set up a fan to circulate the air and make the whole house comfortable.

Example 3
In the new high <u>school, each</u> locker room <u>is equipped</u> with an office for a <u>coach, and</u> each math
                          A   B   C
classroom has <u>it's own</u> computer lab. <u>No error</u>
                  D   E

Explanation
First read the sentence quickly, pausing at each comma, and then read it again, noticing each underlined phrase. You are looking for the mistake in the sentence, if any.

Begin by eliminating any underlined phrases that you know are correct. The comma after "high school" sets off the introductory phrase "In the new high school," so that is correct, and the verb "is" in answer choice B agrees in number with "each locker room." Therefore, you can eliminate answer choices A and B. In answer choice C, the comma precedes the conjunction "and," so it is also correct.

To see if answer choice D is correct, read a larger portion of the sentence:

> each math classroom has <u>it's own</u> computer lab

The word "it's" is a contraction of "it is," and "each math classroom has it is own computer lab" does not make sense. The correct spelling the word is "its." Therefore, the correct answer is answer choice D.

To make sure you've found the right answer, take a moment to read the sentence with the mistake corrected:

> In the new high school, each locker room is equipped with an office for a coach, and each math classroom has its own computer lab.

The SAT Advantage

IMPROVING PARAGRAPHS QUESTIONS

Improving paragraph questions test your ability to improve paragraphs and sentences within the context of a paragraph by identifying changes that need to be made. The errors in the paragraph might be related to the organization and coherence of the paragraph or conventions of standard written English. Topics include subordination of ideas, coordination of ideas, transitions, and coherence and unity of paragraphs.

You will be shown a passage made up of one or more paragraphs. The passages are meant to be drafts, so you will notice errors. You will be asked about one or more of the errors in the passages.

Here is an example of an improving paragraphs question. We will answer this question later in the chapter.

Read the passage provided and select the best answer choice for the question that follows.

> (1) Square dancing is popular across the United States. (2) Square dancing is done in "squares" of eight people. (3) It is made up of four couples, each couple standing next to each other facing one wall of the room. (4) I have been square dancing for five years.
>
> (5) In square dancing, the dancers do a series of dance moves called "calls." (6) The square dance caller is the person who tells the dancers which call to do next. (7) You might have seen movies where a square dance caller says, "Swing your partner and promenade home." (8) "Swing" and "promenade" are both square dance calls.
>
> (9) One type of square dancing is called modern western square dancing. (10) Classes are taken by modern western square dancers in order to learn specific lists of calls. (11) Some calls just take a few seconds to complete, others are quite long and complex. (12) In modern western squares, the dances aren't scripted, planned, or memorized. (13) The dancers don't know which call is going to come next.
>
> To improve this paragraph, which sentence should be deleted?
>
> (A) Sentence 1
> (B) Sentence 4
> (C) Sentence 6
> (D) Sentence 12
> (E) Sentence 13

STRATEGIES FOR SUCCESS

1. **Read the Passage First**
   Before you read any of the questions, read the entire passage to understand the meaning of the passage as a whole. Some questions involve an entire passage or more than one paragraph, so you cannot look at one sentence at a time.

   For example, if you are asked whether a sentence should be moved to another part of the passage, you need to be familiar with the entire passage. The sentence you are moving might introduce a paragraph, so it might need to be moved to the beginning of that paragraph.

Or you may be asked which sentence should be deleted from a passage. A sentence should be deleted if it is unrelated or not closely related to the rest of the passage. If you've read the entire passage, you will know which sentences are the most closely related to the rest of the passage.

2. **Read Each Sentence in Context**
   If there is a question about one sentence in the passage, look at the sentence in the context of the passage. Many questions will deal with problems that involve transitions within the passage or relationships between sentences. Read the entire sentence again, and then read it in context, including the sentence before and after it.

   For example, if you look at only one sentence, you might not realize that the pronoun "her" is ambiguous because it could refer to one of two women mentioned in the previous sentence. Or you might not realize that in order for a sentence to follow logically from the previous sentence, it needs to begin with the word "therefore."

3. **Look for Both Corrections and Improvements**
   The change that needs to be made to the passage might not be an actual error; it might just be an improvement. Don't look only for errors in grammar, punctuation, etc.; also look for changes that would improve the coherence and flow of the passage.

EXAMPLE QUESTIONS

Read the passage provided and select the best answer choice for each question. Some questions are about individual sentences or parts of individual sentences and ask you to improve the sentence structure or word choice. Some questions are about multiple sentences ask you to consider the overall organization of the passage as a whole. In making your selection, follow the requirements of standard written English.

(1) Square dancing is popular across the United States. (2) Square dancing is done in "squares" of eight people. (3) It is made up of four couples, each couple standing next to each other facing one wall of the room. (4) I have been square dancing for five years.

(5) In square dancing, the dancers do a series of dance moves called "calls." (6) The square dance caller is the person who tells the dancers which call to do next. (7) You might have seen movies where a square dance caller says, "Swing your partner and promenade home." (8) "Swing" and "promenade" are both square dance calls.

(9) One type of square dancing is called modern western square dancing. (10) Classes are taken by modern western square dancers in order to learn specific lists of calls. (11) Some calls just take a few seconds to complete, others are quite long and complex. (12) In modern western squares, the dances aren't scripted, planned, or memorized. (13) The dancers don't know which call is going to come next.

The SAT Advantage

Example 1
To improve this paragraph, which sentence should be deleted?

(A) Sentence 1
(B) Sentence 4
(C) Sentence 6
(D) Sentence 12
(E) Sentence 13

Explanation
You have been asked which sentence should be deleted, so look for the sentence that is the least closely related to the passage. The sentence might still be on the same topic, but may not be related closely enough to be included in the passage. Removing sentences that are not closely related to the rest of a passage makes the passage stronger.

Look at each answer choice and see if that sentence relates closely to the passage. Ask yourself if the passage would be improved by removing the sentence. For example, sentence 1 is the introductory sentence and should not be deleted. Sentence 6 explains who a square dance caller is, and sentence 7 then refers to a square dancer caller, so sentence 6 is necessary in order to introduce the topic of square dance callers.

Look at sentence 4, "I have been square dancing for five years." The sentence is related to square dancing, the topic of the passage. However, the passage is informational, not personal. The sentence "I have been square dancing for five years" is told from the first person point of view. It does not fit in the passage and should be deleted. Therefore, the correct answer is answer choice B.

Example 2
Which change would best improve sentence 3, reproduced below?

It is made up of four couples, each couple standing next to each other facing one wall of the room.

(A) Change "It" to "A square".
(B) Change the comma to a semicolon.
(C) Move it before sentence 2.
(D) Insert "and is" before "facing".
(E) Delete "facing one wall of the room".

Explanation
Begin by reading the sentence how it is written. Then read it in the context of the paragraph to see if there is an error related to how the sentence relates to the surrounding sentences. Ask yourself: Is there anything ambiguous about the sentence? The sentence begins, "It is made up of four couples." What is made up of four couples? Answer choice A is to change "It" to "A square". "A square is made up of four couples" is clear and not ambiguous, so that is the change that needs to be made.

Remember: even if you think you've found the correct answer, be sure to check the other answer choices. The comma is correct in the sentence, so it does not need to be changed. The sentence would not make sense if it were moved before sentence 2, so that answer choice is incorrect. The sentence would be wordy if "and is" were inserted before "facing," so that's not the correct answer. And the sentence would not provide enough information if "facing one wall of the room" were deleted.

To make sure you've found the correct answer, read the sentence again, making the change indicated in answer choice A:

> A square is made up of four couples, each couple standing next to each other facing one wall of the room.

Example 3
Which sentence should be changed from the passive voice to the active voice?

(A) Sentence 5
(B) Sentence 7
(C) Sentence 8
(D) Sentence 10
(E) Sentence 12

Explanation
Changing a sentence from the passive voice to the active voice makes it stronger. For example, this sentence is written in the passive voice:

> The crafts were made by the children.

To change it to the active voice, begin with the noun that performed the action:

> The children made the crafts.

Switching to the active voice makes sentences stronger, and often makes them shorter, eliminating wordiness.

Look at all five answer choices. Which of these sentences is written in the passive voice and would be improved by switching to the active voice? Look at answer choice D, sentence 10:

> Classes are taken by modern western square dancers in order to learn specific lists of calls.

That sentence is written in the passive voice. Switching the sentence around and writing it in the active voice makes in stronger:

> Modern western square dancers take classes in order to learn specific lists of calls.

This sentence tells who is taking the classes. Therefore, the correct answer is answer choice D.

ESSAY

The essay is always the first subsection of the SAT. You will be given a prompt and will be asked to write a short essay presenting and supporting a point of view. You will have 25 minutes to write the essay, so it is not expected to be free from errors. The essay tests your ability to support your point of view with examples and reasoning based on your studies, experience, or observations.

There isn't a length requirement for the essay, but it should be approximately one page long. To make sure you have enough room for your essay, use every line provided and don't leave wide margins on the page.

Extra points are not awarded for longer essays. It's more important to develop your ideas thoroughly and provide examples that support your point of view.

Here is an example of an essay prompt. There will be a sample essay responding to this prompt later in the chapter.

Think carefully about the issue presented in the following excerpt and the assignment below.

> **Topic:** Modern technology is often credited for connecting people. Technological advances such as computers, the Internet, and smart phones allow people to communicate in ways that they never have before. However, the rise of technology has also meant a decrease in the time people spend together face to face. Overall, technology has encouraged people to spend more time alone and less time building communities.
>
> **Assignment:** Do technological advances bring people together or make people more isolated? Plan and write an essay in which you develop your point of view on this issue. Support your position with reasoning and examples taken from your reading, studies, experience, or observations.

STRATEGIES FOR SUCCESS

1. **Take a Stand**

   Express your viewpoint clearly in the first or second sentence. Don't allude to it; actually state it outright. Then state your viewpoint again in the last sentence.

   Your essay will be more effective if you take a strong stand one way or the other. Do not give some reasons to support one point of view and other reasons to support another. Don't even write part of a sentence addressing the other viewpoint. For example, avoid sentences like this:

   > Even though a lot of my friends think it's important to have a part-time job, I think there are more effective ways that teenagers can spend their time.

   Instead, take a strong stand and state it:

   > I don't think that teenagers should have part-time jobs. There are more effective ways that teenagers can spend their time.

Even if you're actually on the fence about the topic, choose a point of view and support it.

2. **Provide Strong Examples**
   Provide examples to support your point of view, and develop them. Don't just list four part-time jobs that you've had that were helpful. Instead, give examples of two of them, and provide interesting stories and details about each job.

3. **Practice Writing Both Sides**
   A great way to practice for the SAT essay is to write two responses to each practice essay—one taking each side. If you can fully support two different viewpoints, you will develop the skills needed to write a strong essay, no matter the topic.

4. **Use Effective Language**
   Choose effective language and strong words for your essay. Use active verbs—progressed, created, assured, initiated. Use descriptive, vivid adjectives—educated, elusive, self-assured, compassionate, etc.

   Vary your language. Avoid saying, "One advantage of having a part-time job is…" and "Another advantage of having a part-time job is…" Instead, you might say, "Working after school also gives you the opportunity to…"

EXAMPLE QUESTIONS

Think carefully about the issue presented in the following excerpt and the assignment below.

Topic: Modern technology is often credited for connecting people. Technological advances such as computers, the Internet, and smart phones allow people to communicate in ways that they never have before. However, the rise of technology has also meant a decrease in the time people spend together face to face. Overall, technology has encouraged people to spend more time alone and less time building communities.

Assignment: Do technological advances bring people together or make people more isolated? Plan and write an essay in which you develop your point of view on this issue. Support your position with reasoning and examples taken from your reading, studies, experience, or observations.

Sample Essay
Because of advances in modern technology, people are less connected to other people than they used to be, and they spend more time alone. I've seen many examples of this, and I've heard examples of this from my mom and other relatives.

One example is the volunteering I've done. When I first started volunteering, I went to meetings at school to learn about volunteer opportunities. Then groups of us volunteered together. Now people learn about volunteering by searching the internet. We volunteered at an animal shelter walking dogs, cleaning cages, and playing with the animals. When there were updates that all of the volunteers needed to know about, we would have a meeting. Now they just send email. Some volunteer work isn't even in person anymore. You volunteer using a computer or over the phone.

My mom has told me many ways that technology has made people more alone. She said that when she was my age and someone wanted a recipe or a recommendation of a car to buy, they would ask their neighbors or get together with friends or call someone on the phone. Now people search the internet or ask a friend on facebook.

Although technology can bring people together in ways, for the most part, more technology means communities that are less close and people who are spending more time alone.

Explanation
This is an example of a good essay. It presents the point of view clearly in the first and last sentence. It also provides examples with some details. It is well organized, with an introductory paragraph that introduces the examples and a paragraph for each example.

This essay could be improved by expanding on the second example and adding another strong example with details. Some of the language could be improved by replacing weak words with stronger ones. Also, some of the sentences are a bit awkward and could be revised to be clearer.

Despite some organizational and language weaknesses, this is a good essay because it presents and supports a strong point of view.

PRACTICE TEST 1

The SAT Advantage

SECTION 1
(WRITING)
Time: 25 minutes
ESSAY

Directions: Write an essay based on the prompts given.

The essay section gives you an opportunity to demonstrate your effectiveness at written communication. A well-written essay will express a clear point of view, present ideas in a logical manner, and use language precisely.

Your essay must be written in your <u>Answer Grid Booklet</u>. Do not write your essay in your test book. Keep your handwriting legible so that readers who are unfamiliar with your handwriting will be able to read it.

DO NOT WRITE ON ANOTHER TOPIC. AN ESSAY ON AN UNRELATED TOPIC WILL RECEIVE A SCORE OF ZERO.

Consider carefully the matter presented in the following paragraph and the assignment below.

Topic: Professionals are people who have special knowledge acquired through a prescribed program of learning and training; their activities are regulated by professional associations; they exercise some degree of control over their own work; and they have an ethical responsibility to the public. This last requirement—an ethical responsibility to the public—is considered the real hallmark of the professional.

Assignment: Do professionals—doctors, lawyers, accountants, engineers, teachers, etcetera—have a special ethical responsibility to the public? Develop and write an essay expounding on your viewpoint on this matter. You may use reasoning and your general knowledge based on your own experiences, observation of society, general reading or specific studies.

Excellent Quality Sample Essay (Score: 6 out of 6)

Professionals have a special ethical responsibility to the public. However, every worker has a special ethical responsibility to the public, whether he or she is a professional or not.

Of course, patients have a right to expect that their doctors will provide them with honest, trustworthy health care. We do not expect that doctors will order unnecessary tests, prescribe harmful drugs, or skimp on our care because we don't have insurance. Doctors hold our lives in their hands.

Although we recognize that our lawyers must defend us within the boundaries of the law, we also expect that they will protect our interests passionately. We expect them to use their special knowledge of the law to find cases like ours in the past that came out with a good outcome for the client.

Accountants have a special responsibility to the public to make sure that people are honest in the reporting of numbers relating to finances. This is important in tax collection, so that government has sufficient revenue to provide the services we all expect.

What would happen if engineers did not behave professionally and decided to skimp on regulations? Many people could be injured or even killed by a collapsing bridge or dysfunctional elevator. We rely on engineers to keep us safe.

The other side of the coin, though, is that we rely on many people who are not professionals in the same sense that doctors, lawyers, and others are. If they are unethical, though, people may be in grave danger.

What if the heating and air-conditioning person or the electrician does a faulty home repair? The people within the home may be injured or killed by leaking gases or electrocution.

If a bus driver does not perform adequately on the road, whole dozens of people may be killed or injured, and he or she is not a "professional." Lives depend on how well he or she performs the job.

We rely on the janitor to keep buildings free of unsanitary conditions that could lead to illness or infection, and yet no one calls the custodian a professional.

Professionals do have a special ethical duty to the public. However, everyone who deals with people also has an ethical duty to do his or her job well. In that sense, everyone is a professional.

Medium Quality Sample Essay (Score: 3 – 4 out of 6)

I believe that professionals have a special ethical responsibility to the public. After all, when we close our eyes under the surgeon's knife, we hope and pray that the surgeon is good. When we listen to our lawyer's arguments in front of a jury, we hope that the lawyer knows his or her stuff. We certainly hope that our teachers have good knowledge when they are conducting their classes.

We don't know how to measure a doctor's knowledge and skills, or a lawyer's knowledge and skills, or an engineer's knowledge and skills. Our teachers have much more knowledge than we do, and they should have this special knowledge. Because the general public can't measure how good these professionals are, they have a special ethical responsibility to the public. We have to trust them, so they should know and practice their fields very well.

When I went to the dentist, I read his qualifications very carefully. They were posted on the wall. I was impressed by all the credentials and certifications he had. Then I could trust him. I knew he would take good care of my teeth, unless the documents were forged. I had no way of knowing that, but they looked official. I thought from that he would take good care of me, and he did. He proved himself trustworthy, but the first step was the certificates on the wall. That way, I knew he was a professional. Once someone becomes a professional, he or she needs to keep the public's trust.

Low Quality Sample Essay (Score: 1 – 2 out of 6)

There is no argument here. Professionals owe us a responsibility to be their best.

I would not want to be operated on by a doctor who didn't know what he or she was doing. I would not want to be defended by a lawyer who did not care about whether I got off jail or not. I would not want to walk across a bridge that an engineer who would have flunked engineering school but faked his grades. I would not want to be taught by a teacher who didn't like kids or their parents or care about imparting knowledge to the younger generations. Such people should not be allowed.

Professionals make a lot of money. This means they should be very good at what they do. We should be able to trust them for the amount of money they make.

SECTION 2
(CRITICAL READING)
Time: 25 minutes
24 questions

SENTENCE COMPLETION

Directions: For each of the following questions, choose the best answer and fill in the corresponding oval on the answer sheet to indicate your selection.

Each sentence contains one or two blanks indicating that something has been omitted from the sentence. Choose the word or set of words, labeled A through E, that when inserted into the sentence, best fits the meaning of the sentence as a whole.

1. The tragic story of the *RMS Titanic* is one of the most haunting and fascinating disasters in history, possibly because of its -------- passenger list, which reads almost like a *Who's Who* of the rich and famous of the time.

    (A) glamorous
    (B) infamous
    (C) modest
    (D) anonymous
    (E) ludicrous

2. The Internet has revolutionized the way the world does business, as information has become easy to -------- from place to place.

    (A) blog
    (B) pulsate
    (C) translate
    (D) estimate
    (E) convey

3. -------- to common misconceptions, the Lincoln-Douglas debates did not take place during Abraham Lincoln's successful run for the presidency; they took place during his unsuccessful run for a Senate seat in 1858, two years before the presidential election.

    (A) Soldered
    (B) Inevitable
    (C) Contrary
    (D) Common
    (E) Agreeably

4. Experts say that the world is growing more peaceful; -------- the turn of the nineteenth century, six or seven international conflicts were waged per year, but since the advent of the new -------- , only one or two international conflicts take place in a year's time.

   (A) preceding ... millennium
   (B) precursing ... thousand-year reign
   (C) predestined ... era
   (D) heralding ... centurion
   (E) succeeding ... predecessor

5. Televised debates between candidates for political office have become very popular means of examining candidates, for under the bright hot lights and time constraints of television, candidates must get their points across -------- , think well on their feet, and keep their emotions under control when -------- .

   (A) verbosely ... amenable
   (B) craftily ... insulted
   (C) succinctly ... challenged
   (D) serendipitously ... accused
   (E) pointedly ... praised

6. Hoping to prove how priceless the human body is, Yale University molecular biologist Dr. Harold J. Morowitz -------- a synthetic chemical catalogue from a biochemical company to estimate the cost of all the chemicals -------- the human body.

   (A) provided ... compromising
   (B) procured ... comprising
   (C) acquired ... promising
   (D) acclimated ... procuring
   (E) borrowed ... compelling

7. Administering cardio-pulmonary resuscitation, performing the Heimlich Maneuver or applying a tourniquet serve to restore a person's breathing or heart rate, liberate a person from choking, and tie off -------- arteries that are causing blood loss, -------- .

   (A) choked ... profusely
   (B) ruptured ... lightly
   (C) empty ... unconsciously
   (D) flowing ... congealing
   (E) severed ... respectively

8. Because of his -------- finances, Devon was forced to be -------- with his current expenditures.

   (A) ample ... miserly

   (B) banal ... prodigious

   (C) meager ... parsimonious

   (D) minimal ... profligate

   (E) spurious ... magnanimous

The SAT Advantage

> **READING BASED QUESTIONS**
>
> **Directions**: For each of the following questions, choose the best answer and fill in the corresponding oval on the answer sheet to indicate your selection.
>
> The reading passages below are followed by questions based on their content. Questions that follow a pair of related passages may be based on both the content of the passages and/or the relationship between the passages. Answer the questions based on what is <u>stated</u> or <u>implied</u> in the passages.

Questions 9 – 12 are based on the following two passages:

Passage 1

On April 14, 1912, over a thousand people went into the icy waters off Nova Scotia and died there as the *Titanic* sank. Common wisdom, much of it based on the accuracy of the popular movie made by James Cameron, is that surviving the *Titanic* disaster depended upon wealth and class. The fence-like doors that kept the third class passengers penned in
5 were part of the real ship, and they appeared many times in the movie. Bruce Ismay, the self-centered owner of the *Titanic*, cared more about breaking speed records and keeping the promenade decks cleared on his ship than he did about the welfare of the passengers. In the movie, third class women and their children are shown going down with the ship or else frozen dead in the icy waters.

Passage 2

10 According to British parliamentary papers, the largest group of survivors of the April 14, 1912 *Titanic* disaster were women and children of all classes. Third class women and children survivors outnumbered first class male survivors because of the noble sentiment of "Women and children first." The third-class gates did exist, but they were there because health regulations required immigrants, who made up much of the third class, to be
15 restricted to one part of the ship. Bruce Ismay, the owner of the ship, had deliberately designed his ship so that third class accommodations were like second class on other ships, and second class accommodations were like first class. The "heartless" Ismay did this to give immigrants hope that they would have a better life ahead of them.

9. **The author of Passage 1 would probably criticize the author of Passage 2 for:**

   (A) recommending that modern ships also quarantine immigrants for health reasons

   (B) being an apologist for the classism and sexism of the *Titanic* era

   (C) using an unreliable data source about survivor statistics

   (D) failing to understand ship construction in the *Titanic* era

   (E) not seeing the *Titanic* movie

10. **The tone of lines 11 – 13 may be said to be:**

    (A) emphatic

    (B) admiring

    (C) ambiguous

    (D) ambivalent

    (E) condemnatory

11. **It can be inferred from the use of quotation marks in line 17 that the author of Passage 2 would most likely:**

    (A) critique Passage 1 for fomenting class warfare

    (B) disagree with the characterization of Bruce Ismay in Passage 1

    (C) agree with the characterization in Passage 1 of Bruce Ismay

    (D) endorse the James Cameron movie as accurate

    (E) concur with the main points of Passage 1

12. **Both authors acknowledge which of the following facts:**

    (A) most women and children survived the *Titanic* disaster

    (B) the *Titanic* sank on April 14, 1913

    (C) Bruce Ismay was co-pilot of the *Titanic*

    (D) No one ever said the *Titanic* was unsinkable

    (E) there were gates in the third class passenger area

Questions 13 – 24 are based on the following passage:

She couldn't stare directly at the art connoisseur who was gazing at her in the gallery; that would be impolite for a court lady of her standing. She was stationed in profile in the portrait anyway. Yet her eyes spoke. They seemed to say, "Look into my eyes and see the light of genius in the expression painted there. Who could have painted me with such vitality
5 that you can feel the very heat of the blush on my cheek?"

The art connoisseur was Peter Silverman, and it was January 1, 1998 where a sale at the New York auction house Christie's was in progress. The name given to the portrait was *Young Girl in Profile in Renaissance Dress.* The auction catalog said that it was of early nineteenth century German origin. Silverman sensed differently, but he trusted the
10 prestigious auction house's accuracy. He passed up on buying the portrait, which sold for $19,000.

Yet the portrait haunted him. It had an uncanny vibrancy to it. Silverman's trained eye sensed that it was neither German nor nineteenth century. Silverman knew that a German school of artists had produced such Renaissance-style paintings in the nineteenth century,
15 but he had lived in Munich and knew this school of art. His feel for art told him that the painting was a Renaissance find, dating back to fifteenth or sixteenth century Italy.

Then he happened upon her again. He and his wife nearly skipped going to the gallery on a rainy afternoon, but they decided to forge on anyway. There she was—the Renaissance beauty who had haunted him so. What was the likelihood of running into her
20 again and for the same price she had sold for several years ago? This time the portrait almost put Silverman into a trance. He said that his heart start pounding a million times a minute.

A name was resounding in his brain. Silverman began to consult art historians, art forensics experts, classic hairstyle and fashion experts, and drawing experts to try to
25 establish the origins of the portrait. Using high-resolution multispectral scans of Lumiere Technology in Paris, the portrait's deepest layers were revealed to Martin Kemp, Emeritus professor of art history at Oxford University. A name had occurred to him too.

A drawing expert commented on what a master of drawing the original artist had been. The artist's shading revealed that he was left-handed. The artist had profound knowledge of
30 anatomy. There was one artist of the late fourteenth and early fifteenth centuries who had those qualifications: Leonardo da Vinci. The left-handed master of drawing had actually dissected cadavers to learn how to structure human portraits.

Martin Kemp is a renowned Leonardo da Vinci expert. Upon first seeing the portrait, he shared Silverman's thrilled impulse, yet he had reservations. He had received many claims
35 by people saying they had discovered a Leonardo. The art world was a conservative place too. Attributing the portrait would be a long, drawn-out, controversial process, calling upon the combined expertise of the art and scientific worlds.

Carbon-dating showed that the material the portrait was done on was vellum (calfskin) dating back to 1440 and 1650. Leonardo's life span was 1452 to 1519, so the material was
40 contemporary with him. Wardrobe and costume experts pinpointed the hairstyle and dress of the portrait's subject as being specific to the court of Milan in the 1490s. During the 1490s, Leonardo lived in Milan and was often commissioned to draw court portraits.

The art world exploded in controversy. World-renowned experts lined up on both sides: it was an authentic, undiscovered and undocumented Leonardo da Vinci; it was an elaborate,
45 excellent forgery. Experts like Kemp thought the almost spiritual vitality of the portrait spoke of the genius of Leonardo. Other Leonardo experts said the portrait looked nothing like the work of one of the world's greatest artists.

Then Kemp learned that there was a commemorative volume for the marriage of a young princess living in Milan in the 1500s with a missing page where her portrait should
50 have been. When the three faint binding marks on the portrait matched the book perfectly, Kemp renamed the portrait "The Beautiful Princess." The portrait is now attributed to Leonardo da Vinci, although not all art experts agree. It is worth over $100,000,000.

13. **In lines 1 – 5 the portrait is described using this literary device:**

    (A) onomatopoeia

    (B) rhyme and reason

    (C) personification

    (D) simile

    (E) analogy

14. **The purpose of lines 6 – 11 is to:**

    (A) create an aura of mystery

    (B) provide facts and background information

    (C) discredit the auction house of Christie's

    (D) emphasize the exclusiveness of the fine art world

    (E) set forth a theory

15. **Lines 12 – 16 serve to establish Peter Silverman's:**

    (A) abilities as an artist

    (B) historical roots

    (C) vintage veracity

    (D) art expertise

    (E) fallibility

16. **The best words to describe the atmosphere evoked in lines 17 – 22 are:**

    (A) excited discovery

    (B) bemused skepticism

    (C) mere coincidence

    (D) distant disdain

    (E) fateful misfortune

17. **Lines 23 – 27 are designed to create:**

    (A) irony

    (B) a sense of destiny

    (C) a sense of history

    (D) collusion

    (E) suspense

18. **In lines 29 – 30, the use of the word "profound" most likely means:**

    (A) medical

    (B) phonetic

    (C) in depth

    (D) illicit

    (E) preparatory

19. **What facts about Leonardo da Vinci's life are given in lines 28 – 32 to support the idea that he had a profound knowledge of human anatomy?**

    (A) he was such a well-known portraitist because his portraits were so realistic

    (B) he was a court-commissioned painter, and court standards demanded no less

    (C) he had studied the dissection of dead bodies to understand the skeletal and muscular structure of the human being

    (D) he was a master at drawing from a young age, showing strong powers of observation

    (E) he was left-handed and had striven to understand why his body was structured so

20. **Lines 33 – 37 express that when it comes to attributing new discoveries to well-known artists, the art world can be described as:**

    (A) gullible

    (B) stimulated

    (C) credible

    (D) skeptical

    (E) disingenuous

21. **Lines 38 – 42 cite evidence of the portrait's origin that is:**

    (A) irrefutable

    (B) theoretical

    (C) circumstantial

    (D) methodological

    (E) infallible

22. **Lines 43 – 47 strive to:**

    (A) present both points of view

    (B) advocate the portrait's authenticity

    (C) discredit the portrait's Leonardo advocates

    (D) be conclusive

    (E) provoke controversy

23. **Lines 51 – 52 use the words "although not all art experts agree." These words are an attempt to be:**

    (A) adversarial

    (B) impartial

    (C) commemorative

    (D) ironic

    (E) iconic

24. **The essay's perspective may be said to:**

    (A) advocate the portrait as an authentic Leonardo da Vinci

    (B) decry the art world's snobbery and high prices

    (C) maintain that Leonardo da Vinci is overrated as an artist

    (D) be biased in favor of the portrait being a forgery

    (E) advocate that all paintings be carbon-dated to establish authenticity

SECTION 3
(MATHEMATICS)
Time: 25 minutes
20 questions

MULTIPLE CHOICE

Directions: For the questions in this section, solve each problem and decide which of the given answer choices is the best choice. Fill in the corresponding oval on the answer sheet to indicate your selection. You may use any available space for scratchwork.

Note:

1. Calculator use is permitted.
2. All numbers used are real numbers.
3. All figures provided are drawn to scale and lie in a plane unless otherwise indicated.
4. Unless otherwise specified, the domain of any function f is assumed to be the set of all real numbers x for which $f(x)$ is a real number.

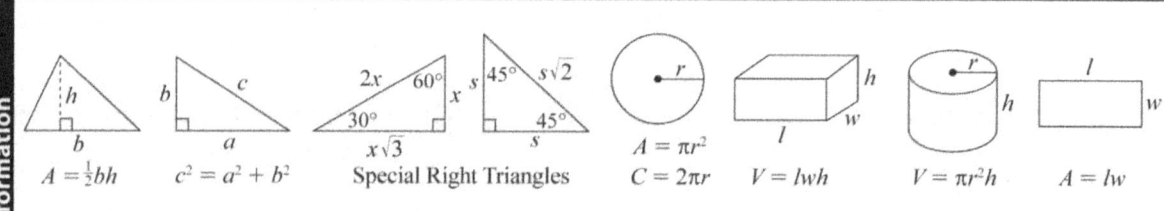

The sum of the degree measures of the angles in a triangle is 180.
The number of degrees of arc in a circle is 360.
A straight angle has a degree measure of 180.

1. A bag contains 25 pieces of candy. If the probability of reaching into the bag without looking and getting milk chocolate candy is $\frac{3}{5}$, how many pieces of milk chocolate candy are in the bag?

   (A) 3

   (B) 6

   (C) 9

   (D) 15

   (E) 18

2. The pie chart below represents the majors of the incoming freshman class at a small college. What is the measure of the central angle formed by the fraction of students who will be Sociology majors?

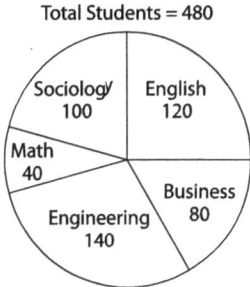

(A) 90°

(B) 75°

(C) 72°

(D) 64°

(E) 60°

3. What is the equation, in standard form, of the line pictured in the graph?

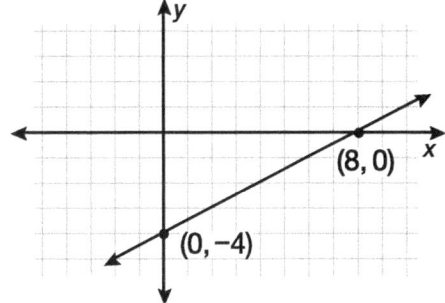

(A) $2x - y = 8$

(B) $x - 2y = 8$

(C) $2x + y = 8$

(D) $x + 2y = 8$

(E) $y = \dfrac{1}{2}x - 4$

4. On the throw of a six-sided die, what is the probability that you will roll a number less than 3?

(A) $\dfrac{1}{6}$

(B) $\dfrac{1}{3}$

(C) $\dfrac{1}{2}$

(D) $\dfrac{2}{3}$

(E) $\dfrac{5}{6}$

5. If n is a positive integer and $\dfrac{3^n}{6n} = \dfrac{3}{4}$, then $n =$

    (A) 1
    (B) 2
    (C) 3
    (D) 4
    (E) 5

6. $3x+y=19$ and $4x=2+y$. What is the value of x?

    (A) -2
    (B) 3
    (C) 7
    (D) 17
    (E) 21

7. Harry's school organized a fundraiser for a charity and raised $4300. One-fifth of that amount was spent in renting the venue for the event and 5% of that amount was spent on other expenses. How much money did they have left over to contribute to the charity?

    (A) $860
    (B) $1075
    (C) $3225
    (D) $3440
    (E) $3655

8. Lines DC and BF intersect in the point A. ABC is a right triangle with angle ABC = 60°. EA bisects the angle DAF. What is the value of angle x?

    Note: Figure not drawn to scale.

    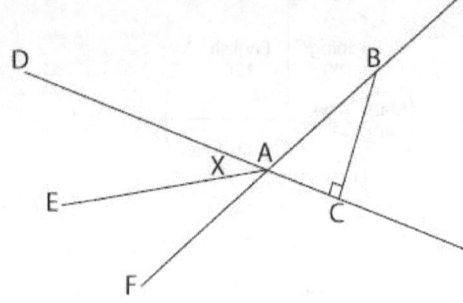

    (A) 10°
    (B) 15°
    (C) 20°
    (D) 30°
    (E) 60°

9. $3^{2k} \times 3^k = 81^3$. What is the value of k?

    (A) 1
    (B) $\dfrac{7}{3}$
    (C) $\dfrac{7}{2}$
    (D) 4
    (E) 6

The SAT Advantage

10. $x^2 - y^2 = 15$ and $x - y = 3$. What is $x + y$?

(A) 1

(B) 4

(C) 5

(D) 12

(E) 18

11. $[x] = x^2$ when x is odd and $[x] = \sqrt{x}$ when x is even. What is the product of $[3] \times [4]$?

(A) $[324]$

(B) $[288]$

(C) $[18]$

(D) $[12]$

(E) $[6]$

12. The triangle below is rotated 90° clockwise and reflected in the given line. Which of the following show its new orientation?

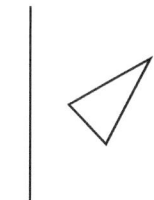

(A)

(B)

(C)

(D)

(E)

81   SAT Practice Test 1

13. $f(x) = 3x^2 + 5x + 1$ and $f(u) = 3$.
    Which of the following could be a value of u?

    (A) 3

    (B) 2

    (C) $\dfrac{-5 - \sqrt{13}}{6}$

    (D) $\dfrac{-5 + \sqrt{13}}{6}$

    (E) -2

Questions 14-16 are based on the data displayed below. Time is shown in minutes and seconds (min:s):

Girls	Age: 11/12		Age: 13/14	
	Average	Best	Average	Best
100m Freestyle	1:16.09	1:12.02	1:09.09	0:55.02
200m Freestyle	2:49.19	2:40.00	2:33.79	2:10.21
100m Backstroke	1:27.79	1:19.60	1:19.79	1:09.54
200m Backstroke	3:14.69	2:30.54	2:56.99	2.30.31

Boys	Age: 11/12		Age: 13/14	
	Average	Best	Average	Best
100m Freestyle	1:15.29	1:00.04	1:08.39	0:56.25
200m Freestyle	2:49.39	2:12.13	2:33.99	2:13.90
100m Backstroke	1:29.39	1:12.09	1:21.19	1:10.11
200m Backstroke	3:36.89	3:20.12	2:47.19	2:31.13

14. In how many of the 8 events did the girls do better than the boys on the average?

    (A) 2

    (B) 3

    (C) 4

    (D) 5

    (E) 6

15. The competitor with the best time in the competition for 100m freestyle was a

    (A) 11-12 year old girl

    (B) 11-12 year old boy

    (C) 13-14 year old girl

    (D) 13-14 year old boy

    (E) A girl of unspecified age

16. In which of the boy's events was the difference between the average time and the best time the highest?

    (A) 11-12, 100m freestyle

    (B) 11-12, 200m freestyle

    (C) 13-14, 100m freestyle

    (D) 13-14, 100m backstroke

    (E) 13-14, 200m backstroke

17. The population of a species in a certain habitat is typically limited by the carrying capacity of the habitat. The population of a new species of fish found in an area as a function of time is given by $P(t) = \dfrac{A}{1+Be^{-t}}$ where t is the time in years. A and B are both constants greater than zero. The population will never exceed

   (A) A

   (B) B

   (C) $\dfrac{A}{B}$

   (D) $\dfrac{A}{1+B}$

   (E) 1 + B

18. For how many ordered pairs of non-zero integers (x, y) is the following true?

   $|x| + |y| < 5$

   (A) 6

   (B) 12

   (C) 24

   (D) 48

   (E) 96

19. The mean and median for 5 distinct positive integers is 16. What is the highest value the biggest integer can have?

   (A) 24

   (B) 32

   (C) 44

   (D) 54

   (E) 80

20. Paint is sprayed to cover a 2m x 8m x 16m rectangular box with two cylinders placed on it. Each cylinder has a radius of 1.5m and a height of 8m. If the side of the box with the largest area is in contact with the ground, what area of the box and cylinders is covered in paint?

   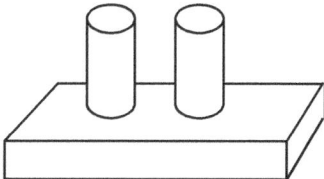

   (A) $176 + 33\pi$ m^2

   (B) $128 + 48\pi$ m^2

   (C) $96 + 28.5\pi$ m^2

   (D) $224 + 33\pi$ m^2

   (E) $224 + 48\pi$ m^2

The SAT Advantage

SECTION 4
(CRITICAL READING)
Time: 25 minutes
24 questions

SENTENCE COMPLETION

Directions: For each of the following questions, choose the best answer and fill in the corresponding oval on the answer sheet to indicate your selection.

Each sentence contains one or two blanks indicating that something has been omitted from the sentence. Choose the word or set of words, labeled A through E, that when inserted into the sentence, best fits the meaning of the sentence as a whole.

1. In her speech, Lisa's use of the word "really" was considered --------; she used it to describe every noun she used.

   (A) excessive
   (B) recessive
   (C) generic
   (D) wistful
   (E) introspective

2. In her novel *The House of Mirth*, Edith Wharton explores the -------- of a woman without means in the provincial world of late nineteenth century high society; the heroine must marry or become someone's mistress in order to survive economically.

   (A) empowerment
   (B) powerlessness
   (C) provincialism
   (D) prudishness
   (E) scrutiny

3. -------- the ultimately unhappy affair of Count Vronsky and Anna in the book *Anna Karenina*, author Tolstoy presents many chapters on the happy marriage of Kostya and Kitty.

   (A) In comparison to
   (B) Going along with
   (C) While accounting for
   (D) In contrast to
   (E) In reference to

4. The -------- of talking to her counselor was a renewed sense of vitality; Sarah had not realized how -------- she had been by her mother's long illness.

   (A) effect ... effected
   (B) effort ... effected
   (C) affect ... effected
   (D) affect ... affected
   (E) effect ... affected

5. The colorful chute conveying marbles was so elaborately -------- with its many -------- passages, the adults were fascinated by the child's toy.

   (A) designed ... simple

   (B) executed ... straight

   (C) elaborate ... elegant

   (D) purported ... complex

   (E) contrived ... labyrinthine

The SAT Advantage

READING BASED QUESTIONS

Directions: For each of the following questions, choose the best answer and fill in the corresponding oval on the answer sheet to indicate your selection.

The reading passages below are followed by questions based on their content. Questions that follow a pair of related passages may be based on both the content of the passages and/or the relationship between the passages. Answer the questions based on what is <u>stated</u> or <u>implied</u> in the passages.

Questions 6 – 7 are based on the following short passage:

Two young Frenchmen, Alexis de Tocqueville and Gustave de Beaumont, traveled to the United States in 1831. Their passion was to discover how democracy worked. When they noticed how often Americans got together in groups, they thought they had discovered the key as to how and why government by the people flourished.

5   Alexis de Tocqueville said, "Americans of all ages, all stations of life, and all types of disposition are forever forming associations…In towns it is impossible to prevent men from assembling, getting excited together and forming sudden passionate resolves. Towns are like great meeting houses with all the inhabitants as members. In them the people wield immense influence over their magistrates."

6. **Based on the information in the passage, Alexis de Tocqueville's attitude toward America and Americans can best be described as:**

   (A) enthusiastic and intrigued

   (B) bored and cynical

   (C) reserved and doubtful

   (D) judgmental and condescending

   (E) sentimental and foppish

7. **The word "flourished" in line 4 likely means:**

   (A) flushed out

   (B) fleshed out

   (C) fulfilled expectations

   (D) collected many funds

   (E) grew and thrived

Questions 8 – 9 are based on the following short passage:

Dr. William Horatio Bates (1860 to 1931) was an American ophthalmologist who developed the Bates Method of eye exercises to improve vision. Dr. Bates attended Cornell University and got his medical certification from Columbia University's College of Physicians and Surgeons.
5   Dr. Bates thought that eyeglasses actually impaired long-term vision, and he called them "eye crutches" that should be eschewed in favor of strengthening eyesight through exercise. The effectiveness of Dr. Bates's eye exercises is unknown. We only have anecdotal evidence from some of his patients that his methods actually improved eyesight. The Bates Method is considered a scientifically unproven alternative therapy and is not endorsed by
10 the medical, ophthalmological, or optical communities.

8. **The tone of the passage may be said to be:**

    (A) one of advocacy

    (B) factual and impartial

    (C) condemnatory toward the Bates Method

    (D) celebratory toward the Bates Method

    (E) highly critical of the Bates Method

9. **In lines 7 – 8 "anecdotal evidence" may be discerned to mean:**

    (A) evidence from diaries

    (B) evidence from scientific journals

    (C) evidence from the words and accounts of patients

    (D) evidence from research by ophthalmologists

    (E) evidence from archives about eye surgery

Questions 10 – 19 are based on the following passage:

Ethics are values which are derived in part from the culture in which people live. Such values are internalized by people from their cultural surroundings. Values are imparted by religion, society's laws, mores, norms, community standards of right and wrong, and various other cultural vehicles. Schools also teach values, either explicitly or implicitly. For example,
5 a teacher may not explicitly teach the value of equality to children, yet each time a pencil is given to each child, with no one being left out, the value of all being equal is demonstrated.

    Ethicists and other people concerned with right and wrong have noted that the smooth functioning of society depends upon people's willing obedience to standards of right and wrong even when they have no fear of "getting caught." The human conscience or moral
10 sense is instructed from without but also is thought by some ethicists to arise naturally from within. Political scientist James Q. Wilson was one thinker whose observations of society made him believe that people have a "moral sense" that arises from within when confronted with issues of right and wrong. This moral sense holds most people back from breaking into the neighbor's house while he or she is on vacation, or from assaulting the lone person in

15 the parking garage, or from slashing other people's tires in the dark of night, even if they could engage in those actions without being caught. People's basic decency is what keeps a society safe and functioning. Indeed, one definition of ethical behavior is what a person does when no one is looking, on the basis of his or her moral convictions alone.

Even with all the cultural institutions that influence the way people think about right and
20 wrong, people face many ethical dilemmas that come up in everyday life and call for decisions. These decisions are not always obvious or easy. Fortunately, there are some handy ethical questions a person can ask himself or herself in order to ascertain whether a proposed action is ethical or not.

Handy ethical questions include: What if everyone did what I am thinking of doing? What
25 kind of a society would we have? Would I want to live in such a society? Who else will be affected by what I am thinking of doing? Will any innocent person suffer because of my actions? What would the people I care about and respect think about what I am thinking of doing? How will I feel inside if I do this? Would I want a video of this action broadcast on YouTube and going viral?

30 The simplest of ethical tests is the Golden Rule: do to others as you would have them do to you. This ethical rule of thumb can be very helpful, and every moral system and religion in the world has had some version of the Golden Rule in place as a foundational ethical test of any action.

Many professions have ethical oaths spelled out for practitioners. Physicians and
35 lawyers take oaths of ethics before they are granted practitioner status in their professions. Part of the training to become a Certified Public Accountant involves understanding ethics in regard to financial reporting. Journalists are expected to pursue truth, confirm and corroborate sources, and give proper credit when they quote or source another person's work. Harvard Business School now offers a voluntary student oath of ethics for students
40 who will be graduating into the business world so that they can practice their professions honorably.

10. In line 4, "either explicitly or implicitly" likely means values are taught:

(A) either openly or covertly

(B) either by the teacher or by someone internal to the school

(C) either clearly or unclearly

(D) either in a clearly spoken way or else by example

(E) either with explanation or with implosion

11. In the context of lines 9 – 11, the word "without" is most likely to mean:

(A) lacking

(B) outside of the person

(C) in some but not in others

(D) with no doubt

(E) indubitably

12. **Lines 11 – 18 cite an expert, James Q. Wilson, for what likely purpose?**

    (A) to establish the credibility of the ideas presented

    (B) to impress people with the idea that they should only do wrongful things when no one is looking

    (C) to make a moral distinction between people who get caught and people, who do not, based on political science

    (D) to show that expert opinion is sometimes used in trials of people who have committed wrong

    (E) to demonstrate that ethics and morality are not necessarily the same thing

13. **Lines 7 – 18 suggest the following view of human nature:**

    (A) a positive view

    (B) a neutral view

    (C) a negative view

    (D) a cynical view

    (E) a sunny, naïve view

14. **In line 20, the word "dilemmas" most likely means:**

    (A) solutions

    (B) conundrums

    (C) compunctions

    (D) crises

    (E) anticipations

15. **In line 22, "to ascertain" most likely means to:**

    (A) ascribe

    (B) certainty

    (C) certitude

    (D) ascription with certitude

    (E) discover or make certain

16. **In line 28, the question "How will I feel inside if I do this?" may be said to be referring to which of these elements mentioned earlier in the passage:**

    (A) values taught from without

    (B) the moral sense or conscience

    (C) political science

    (D) implicit ethical teachings

    (E) explicit ethical teachings

17. **In line 31, the words "ethical rule of thumb" most likely refers to:**

    (A) the rule of reciprocal relationships

    (B) The Golden Rule

    (C) the rules taught in school

    (D) the conscience or moral sense

    (E) all the ethical "test" questions cited in the previous paragraph

18. Lines 34 – 41 may be summarized as being about:

    (A) the efficacy of oath-taking
    (B) professionalism and ethics
    (C) professional ethical oaths
    (D) the ethics of professional oaths
    (E) ethicists' opinions of oaths in the professions

19. In lines 37 – 38, the words "confirm" and "corroborate" are most likely examples of:

    (A) antonyms
    (B) dissonance
    (C) synonyms
    (D) consonantly
    (E) assonantly

Questions 20 – 24 are based on the following passage:

    Franz Liszt (1811 – 1886) was a Hungarian composer who was also a virtuoso at the piano. His father was a court musician, and Liszt began to show interest and aptitude for the piano at a very young age. A prodigy, Liszt began composing and performing before he was ten years old. He was acquainted with Ludwig Van Beethoven and was taught by one of
5 Beethoven's students.
    Liszt's piano concerts were sensational, and he performed all over Europe. He was an extremely skilled pianist—a virtuoso. In fact, Liszt's compositions for piano show that he had incredible physical reach. People of the time joked that he must have had four hands and twenty fingers to play with such virtuosity. Several of Liszt's compositions call for crossing
10 the hands and stretching the fingers to cover multiple octaves. Liszt composed this way because he could perform with this versatility and command.
    Liszt's life was not without controversy, including questionable political associations and his live-in relationship with a princess who sponsored him and urged him to devote himself to composition. Contemporaries also sometimes thought of Liszt as a sort of "trick pony"
15 who gave virtuoso performances as money-making entertainment but who was not to be taken seriously as a composer.
    However, Liszt's virtuosity as a pianist and his unsurpassed mastery of the piano and of music led him to explore new harmonics, which led to his ground-breaking anticipation of twentieth century music. Liszt was prolific, producing a prodigious body of works of passion
20 and originality that establishes him as one of the world's great classical composers.

20. The purpose of lines 1 – 5 is most likely to:

    (A) sketch some highlights of Liszt's youth

    (B) compare Liszt to Beethoven

    (C) decry the treatment of prodigies

    (D) show that musical ability is genetic and therefore inherited

    (E) establish that Liszt was a serious musician because he studied under a student of Beethoven

21. In line 7, the word "virtuoso" likely means:

    (A) a good person who has many virtues

    (B) a person who is excellent in reality and in virtual reality

    (C) someone who is extraordinarily skilled

    (D) someone capable of giving a piano concert

    (E) a person who continually uses the cross-hand technique on the piano

22. The words "virtuosity" and "versatility" in the passage may be said to be used almost:

    (A) syllogistically

    (B) symphonically

    (C) symbolically

    (D) synthetically

    (E) synonymously

23. Lines 12 – 16 outline controversies of these three natures in Liszt's life:

    (A) political, socio-economic, musical

    (B) progressive, marital, compositional

    (C) political, sexual, professional

    (D) political, sexual, professorial

    (E) political, sexual, compositional

24. In line 19, the word "prodigious" most likely means:

    (A) showing talent at an early age

    (B) extraordinary in scope and quality

    (C) especially famous

    (D) leading to prosperity for Liszt

    (E) impressive to heads of state

The SAT Advantage

SECTION 5
(MATHEMATICS)
Time: 25 minutes
18 questions

MULTIPLE CHOICE

Directions: For the questions in this section, solve each problem and decide which of the given answer choices is the best choice. Fill in the corresponding oval on the answer sheet to indicate your selection. You may use any available space for scratchwork.

Note:

1. Calculator use is permitted.
2. All numbers used are real numbers.
3. All figures provided are drawn to scale and lie in a plane unless otherwise indicated.
4. Unless otherwise specified, the domain of any function f is assumed to be the set of all real numbers x for which $f(x)$ is a real number.

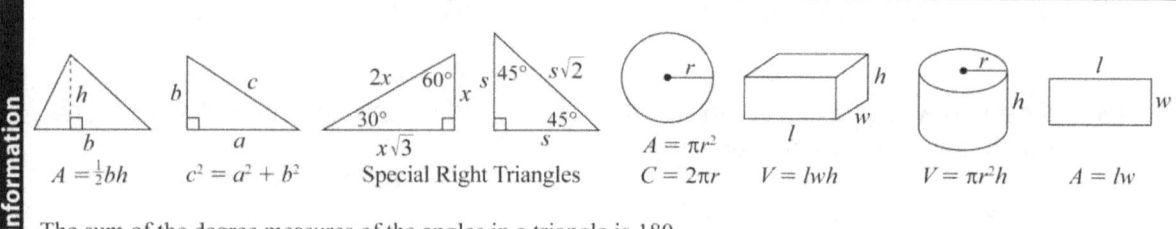

The sum of the degree measures of the angles in a triangle is 180.
The number of degrees of arc in a circle is 360.
A straight angle has a degree measure of 180.

1. A school garden has been divided into $\frac{7}{8}$ square meter plots for students. If the area of the garden is 210 square meters, how many students can get plots?

   (A) 240
   (B) 210
   (C) 184
   (D) 78
   (E) 30

2. What regular polygon has an exterior angle that measures 45°?

   (A) Decagon
   (B) Octagon
   (C) Heptagon
   (D) Hexagon
   (E) Pentagon

3. Which of the following CANNOT be the graph of the f(x)?

(A)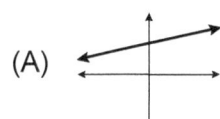

(B)

(C)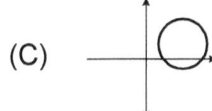

(D)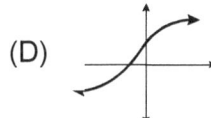

(E)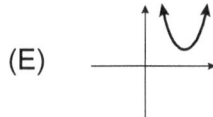

4. Three of the vertices of a rectangle have the coordinates (3,-3), (-8,3), and (3,3). What are the coordinates of the fourth vertex?

(A) (-8,-3)

(B) (-3,-8)

(C) (-3,-3)

(D) (8,-3)

(E) (3,8)

5. Which of the following is equivalent to $\dfrac{3a^b - (4a^2)^{3b}}{9a}$?

(A) $\dfrac{1}{3}a^{b-1} - (4a^2)^{3b}$

(B) $a^{b-1}\left(\dfrac{1}{3} - \dfrac{(4a)^{5b}}{9}\right)$

(C) $\dfrac{1}{3}a^b - \dfrac{(4a^2)^{3b}}{9}$

(D) $\dfrac{3a^{b-1} - (4a^2)^{3b-1}}{9}$

(E) $\dfrac{1}{3}a^{b-1} - \dfrac{4^{3b}a^{6b-1}}{9}$

6. $-\dfrac{4}{5} < x < \dfrac{9}{5}$ is equivalent to

(A) $-11 < 5x + 2 < 2$

(B) $|10x - 5| > 13$

(C) $|10x - 5| < 13$

(D) $4 < 5x < 9$

(E) $-4 < 5x < -9$

7. A 45-45-90 right triangle has the same area as a square. What is the ratio of the hypotenuse of the triangle to the side of the square?

   (A) 2

   (B) $\sqrt{2}$

   (C) 1

   (D) $\dfrac{1}{\sqrt{2}}$

   (E) $\dfrac{1}{2}$

8. If p > 0 and m > 0, which of the following could be the graph of $y = |x - p| + m$?

   I.
   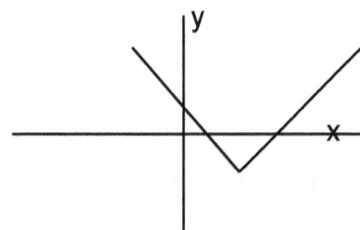

   II.
   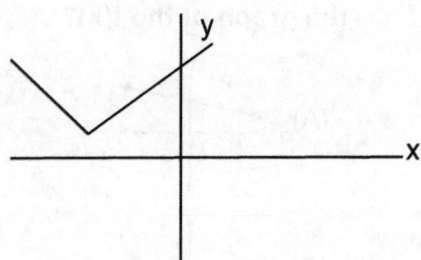

   III.
   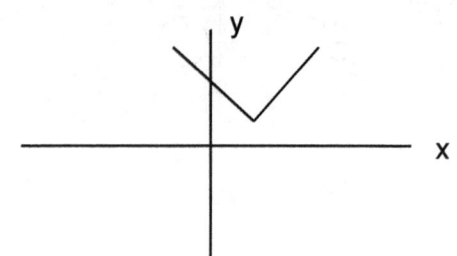

   (A) I and II

   (B) II and III

   (C) III only

   (D) II only

   (E) I only

STUDENT-PRODUCED RESPONSE

Directions: For the Student-Produced Response questions 9 – 18, use the grids at the bottom of the same answer sheet page on which you answered questions 1 – 8. You may use any available space for scratchwork.

The 10 Student-Produced Response questions require you to solve the problem and enter your answer into special grids by filling in the appropriate ovals, as shown below.

Example: 2.25 or $\frac{9}{4}$ or 9/4. Write the answer in the boxes and grid-in the answers by filling in the ovals.

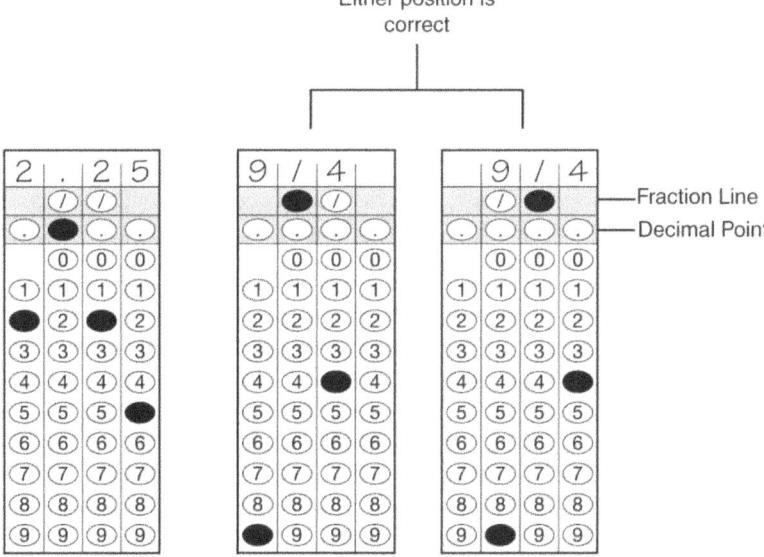

You may start your answers in any column, as shown above, as long as the answer fits. Columns not needed should be left blank. Only fill in one oval per column.

You are not required to write your answer in the boxes at the top of the columns, but it is recommended that you do so. Note, however, you will only receive credit for filling in the ovals correctly.

Only grid in one answer, even if a question has more than one correct answer.

No answers are negative.

Mixed numbers cannot be gridded. For example: the number $1\frac{1}{2}$ must be gridded as 1.5 or 3/2.

If it is gridded as 1 1 / 2, it will be interpreted as 11/2, not $1\frac{1}{2}$.

Enter decimal answers as accurately as possible. For example: the repeating decimal 0.1666... should be gridded as .166 or .167 (less accurate answers such as .16 or .17 are not acceptable). Examples of acceptable ways to grid 1/6 or .1666...

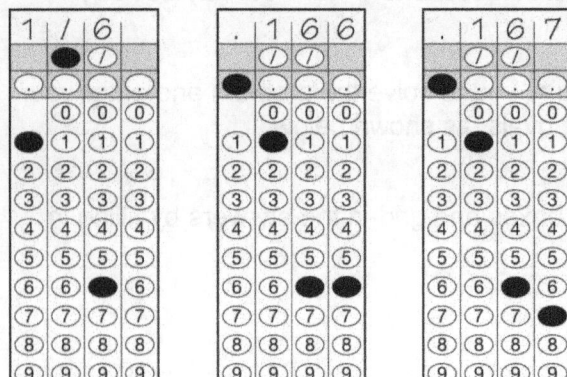

9. The scale of the model of a car is 1:24. If the full-size car is 12 ft long, how long is the model in inches?

10. What number can you add to the numerator and denominator of $\frac{11}{17}$ to get $\frac{3}{4}$?

11. What is the supplement of the complement of an angle measuring 64°?

12. Two bicycle tires with diameters of 30 inches and 24 inches make four revolutions. To the nearest foot, how much farther does the larger wheel travel compared to the smaller wheel?

13. In a particular class, one-half of the students dropped the class after the first test. After the second test, one-third of the remaining students dropped the class. If 16 students went on to take the third test, how many students were originally enrolled in the class?

14. 55 divided by an integer x produces a remainder of 3. What is the smallest possible value of x?

15. The circle shown below is centered at A. If AD = BC, what is the value of angle ABC in degrees?

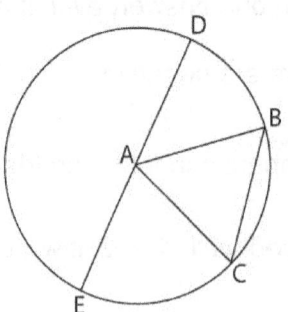

16. Paul and Mina are in two cities 5 miles apart. They start walking towards each other. Paul's speed is 4 miles per hour and Mina's speed is 3 miles per hour. How far (in miles) has Paul walked when they meet?

17. The figure below shows the network of streets connecting 3 towns A, B, and C. If a person walks only east and north, in how many ways can they travel from A to C while passing through B?

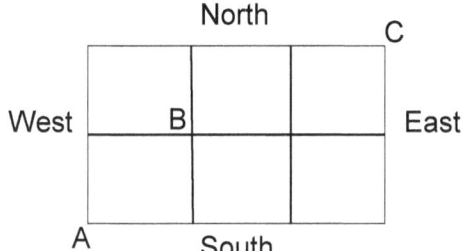

18. What is the units digit of the sum $6^{23} + 4^{23}$?

SECTION 6
(WRITING)
Time: 25 minutes
35 questions

IMPROVING SENTENCES

Directions: For each of the following questions, choose the best answer and fill in the corresponding oval on the answer sheet to indicate your selection.

Part of each sentence (or the entire sentence) is underlined. The five answer choices present five ways of phrasing the underlined portion. Choice A repeats the original phrasing and the other four choices offer alternative phrasings. If you think the original phrasing is best, select choice A; if not, select one of the other options.

In choosing your answer, follow the requirements of standard written English. Pay attention to grammar, choice of words, sentence construction, and punctuation; your selection should result in the most effective, clear, and precise sentence—free of awkwardness or ambiguity.

1. Many retail stores strive to reduce labor costs by hiring only a few workers earning low wages, <u>stores with many well-paid employees are often more profitable</u>.

   (A) stores with many well-paid employees are often more profitable
   (B) although stores with many well-paid employees are often more profitable
   (C) stores with many well-paid employees were often more profitable
   (D) despite the better profitability of hiring more employees and paying them better wages
   (E) however, stores with many well-paid employees are often more profitable

2. There are many challenges <u>which confront whomever</u> wants to succeed at this company.

   (A) which confront whomever
   (B) that confront whomever
   (C) which confront those whom
   (D) that confront whoever
   (E) that confront anyone, including those who

3. According to a recent study, fewer than 2 percent of Americans <u>that meet all the criteria</u> for maintaining a healthy heart.

   (A) that meet all the criteria
   (B) who meet all the criteria
   (C) meeting all the criteria
   (D) that meet all the criterias
   (E) meet all the criteria

4. After hiding thousands of pinyon pine seeds each autumn, a scrub jay forgets some of the places where it stashes the seeds, thus allowing the seeds to sprout.

    (A) where it stashes the seeds
    (B) where they had been stashing the seeds
    (C) where the seeds are being stashed
    (D) where it has stashed the seeds
    (E) where the seeds would have been stashed

5. Discovered by treasure hunters using state-of-the-art technology, a reporter claimed that a seventeenth-century shipwreck off the Cornish coast was the most valuable trove of gold and silver coins ever found.

    (A) Discovered by treasure hunters using state-of-the-art technology
    (B) Having been discovered by treasure hunters using state-of-the-art technology
    (C) Describing a discovery made by treasure hunters using state-of-the-art technology
    (D) Because it had been discovered by treasure hunters using state-of-the-art technology
    (E) Although it had been discovered by treasure hunters using state-of-the art technology

6. One guiding principle of a capitalist economy is that markets flourish only under conditions of unfettered competition.

    (A) only under conditions of unfettered competition
    (B) unless conditions of competition are unfettered
    (C) except for those in which competition is being unfettered
    (D) under conditions in which only competition is unfettered
    (E) but also competition is being unfettered under conditions

7. Many senators objected with the President's plan to protect consumers from high interest rates.

    (A) objected with the President's plan to protect consumers from high interest rates
    (B) objected to the President's plan to protect consumers from high interest rates
    (C) objected with the President's plan, protecting consumers of high interest rates
    (D) objecting, the President's plan to protect consumers with high interest rates
    (E) who objected to the President's plan to protect consumers from high interest rates

8. Viewing the paintings and prints of the legendary Japanese artist Hokusai <u>is like when you are entering a new world that is both exotic and familiar.</u>

   (A) is like when you are entering a new world that is both exotic and familiar
   (B) is similar to when you enter a new world that is both exotic and familiar
   (C) is akin to the experience of entering a world that is new, but both exotic and familiar
   (D) is both exotic and familiar, like when you are entering a new world
   (E) is like entering a new world that is both exotic and familiar

9. While I was on vacation in Colorado, I hiked in the Elk Mountains and <u>rafted on the Taylor River, which</u> is near the Continental Divide.

   (A) rafted on the Taylor River, which
   (B) rafting on the Taylor River, which
   (C) I was also going rafting on the Taylor River, being as it
   (D) had also rafted on the Taylor River that
   (E) have also been rafting on the Taylor River, which

10. Although his flight lasted only 15 minutes, Alan Shepard, the first American in space, became an instant national hero <u>owing to the eagerness of Americans wanting to show their ability of competing with the Soviet Union during the period of the Cold War</u>.

    (A) owing to the eagerness of Americans wanting to show their ability of competing with the Soviet Union during the period of the Cold War
    (B) because Americans were eager to show they could compete with the Soviet Union during the Cold War
    (C) on account of Americans were eager to show their ability to compete with the Soviet Union during the period of the Cold War
    (D) as a result of Americans who were eager to show their ability to compete with the Soviet Union during the Cold War
    (E) since Americans had a eagerness to show their ability of competing with the Soviet Union during the Cold War

11. **Psychologists who study learning and behavior focus on <u>two kinds of conditioning, one called classical and the other operant, the former of which replaces a natural stimulus with a learned one, the latter of which works on the principle of reward and punishment</u>.**

    (A) two kinds of conditioning, one called classical and the other operant, the former of which replaces a natural stimulus with a learned one, the latter of which works on the principle of reward and punishment

    (B) classical and operant conditioning; classical replaces a natural stimulus with a learned one, while operant uses the principle of reward and punishment

    (C) classical conditioning and operant conditioning, contrasting classical conditioning, which is based on replacing a natural stimulus with a learned one, as opposed to operant conditioning, which is based on the principle of reward and punishment

    (D) classical and operant conditioning; classical is based on the process of replacing a natural stimulus with a learned one, while operant is based on the principle of reward and punishment

    (E) classical conditioning, which is based on the process of replacing a natural stimulus with a learned one, contrasted to operant conditioning, which is based on the principle of reward and punishment

IDENTIFYING SENTENCE ERRORS

Directions: For each of the following questions, choose the best answer and fill in the corresponding oval on the answer sheet to indicate your selection.

The following sentences test your ability to recognize grammar and usage errors. In making your selection, follow the requirements of standard written English.

Each sentence contains either a single error or no error at all; none of the sentences contain more than one error. If the sentence contains an error, select the underlined portion A through D that must be changed in order to fix the sentence. If the sentence is correct and contains no errors, select choice E.

12. Researchers speculate that the attempt to limit <u>children's</u> exposure to
                         A
    germs <u>often have</u> the <u>effect</u> of
          B   C
    preventing the optimal development of
    the <u>youngsters'</u> immune systems.
          D
    <u>No error</u>
     E

13. To have <u>spoken</u> so <u>eloquently</u>, the
           A   B
    leader of the committee <u>would have to</u>
                             C
    think <u>deeply about</u> the position she
          D
    advocated. <u>No error</u>
              E

14. After <u>arriving at Ellis Island</u>, <u>exhausted</u>
            A   B
    <u>immigrants</u> answered questions to
    pass inspection and then <u>began to</u>
                             C
    <u>build</u> new lives <u>with their families</u>.
                         D
    <u>No error</u>
     E

15. Before the <u>development of</u> efficient
                A
    steamships in the nineteenth century,
    <u>transporting goods</u> on graceful, three-
         B
    masted clipper ships <u>were</u> the <u>fastest</u>
                   C   D
    <u>way</u> to conduct transatlantic trade.
    <u>No error</u>
     E

16. Many of Robert Rauschenberg's
    collages <u>include</u> iconic images <u>that</u>
           A   B
    <u>serve as</u> striking <u>illusions to</u> significant
                          C
    <u>events and concerns of</u> the twentieth
             D
    century. <u>No error</u>
              E

17. Every one of the tenants were locked
                              A
    out of the apartment building last night
    because the landlord had forgotten to
                          B   C
    issue new keys after changing the
                       D
    locks. No error
          E

18. Last weekend my brother-in-law flew
                    A   B
    to Plainview, the small town where his
    A   C
    ancestors had settled a hundred years
              D
    ago. No error
        E

19. The growing popularity of social
                           A
    networking sites, as well as the
    proliferation of hand-held electronic
    devices, have dramatically affected
            B   C
    the way people live today. No error
            D   E

20. The question facing the committee
                 A
    was whether to allow the team
    B
    members which were present at the
            C
    meeting to air their grievances.
                    D
    No error
    E

21. When you feel anxious, taking a deep
    breath allows one's body to recover
           A   B   C
    from the physiological changes that
                                      D
    are involved in the fear response.
    No error
    E

22. Any precipitation that contain sulfuric
                      A
    or nitric acid is known as acid rain, a
                   B
    major factor in the destruction of lakes,
                    C
    as well as the death of plants and
               D
    animals. No error
             E

23. Among the many customs people
    around the world have for welcoming
    the New Year are skiing with torches
                  A   B
    in Scandinavia, honoring ancestors in
                    C
    Korea, and to eat a dish of black-eyed
              D
    peas in the Southern United States.
    No error
    E

24. The city of Atlanta <u>is</u> not only a <u>thriving</u>
                             A   B

<u>center of</u> American commerce, but

also the home of many important

<u>cultural and educational</u> institutions <u>as</u>
            C   D

<u>well</u>. <u>No error</u>
           E

25. The employees <u>who's</u> jobs <u>were</u> at
                      A   B

stake <u>had grown</u> disenchanted with
         C

what <u>they saw</u> as empty promises
        D

made by management. <u>No error</u>
                                  E

26. The <u>sunnier</u> the days and the <u>cooler</u>
          A   B

the nights, the <u>more colorfully</u> the fall
                 C

foliage <u>appears</u>. <u>No error</u>
      D   E

27. John Hersey's masterpiece *Hiroshima*

<u>includes</u> <u>chillingly detailed</u> interviews
    A   B

and vivid descriptions of the suffering

<u>afflicted upon</u> the citizens of Hiroshima
     C

<u>by the dropping of</u> an atomic bomb.
              D

<u>No error</u>
  E

28. <u>Commonly known as</u> caterpillars,
            A

butterfly larvae, struggling to survive,

<u>consumes</u> a vast quantity of plant
  B

material, shedding <u>their</u> exoskeletons
                       C

several times <u>during the growth</u>
                       D

<u>process</u>. <u>No error</u>
           E

29. The contents of the <u>elderly</u> man's
                       A

house <u>was</u> sold <u>at auction</u> and <u>raised</u>
     B   C   D

several thousand dollars for his heirs.

<u>No error</u>
  E

IMPROVING PARAGRAPHS

Directions: The following passage is an early draft of an essay that may need parts rewritten.

Read the passage provided and select the best answer choice for each question. Some questions are about individual sentences or parts of individual sentences and ask you to improve the sentence structure or word choice. Some questions are about multiple sentences and ask you to consider the overall organization of the passage as a whole. In making your selection, follow the requirements of standard written English.

For each of the following questions, choose the best answer and fill in the corresponding oval on the answer sheet to indicate your selection.

(1) People's fascination with cats has withstood time, place, culture, language, foibles, and proclivities. (2) Cats are among the most popular of modern pets. (3) The images of cats grace advertising and cartoons. (4) The Ancient Egyptians worshipped the cat as a god once cats saved Egypt from famine by preventing mice from eating stored grain in granaries. (5) An African folk tale has it that the reason cats are allowed to sleep indoors is because a cat was the only one to help the first man build his house. (6) The man granted the feline a timeless reward.

(7) In modern times, in addition to cats rivaling dogs in popularity as pets, cats are used in advertising and as characters in cartoons. (8) "Morris," the advertising cat, was a large, orange cat that snubbed most food offered to him by his owners. (9) Morris, however, was always enticed by the cat food being advertised. (10) For years, people would refer to any orange cat as "Morris" or would make jokes about a finicky eater: "He's like Morris the cat—he won't eat!" (11) Garfield, a cartoon cat, also a big, orange tabby. (12) Orange tabbies are among the most popular breed among cat owners. (13) Garfield is famous for being a cynical, lazy, scheming cat that usually gets the better of the people around him. (14) This up-to-date cat sometimes pays a price for his cunning nature, though.

30. A simpler and clearer way to phrase sentence 1 (reproduced below) would be:

    People's fascination with cats has withstood time, place, culture, language, foibles, and proclivities.

    (A) People's fascination with cats has withstood the assault of time.

    (B) People's fascination with cats is universal.

    (C) People's fascination with cats has withstood the examination of time.

    (D) People's fascination with cats has withstood the aura of time.

    (E) Fascinated by cats, people have time and again chosen cats as pets.

31. **In sentence 6 which word used as an adjective would make it clear the sentence is a natural progression from sentence 5?**

    (A) abominable

    (B) modern

    (C) malevolent

    (D) malicious

    (E) grateful

32. **A good revision of sentence 11 (reproduced below) would be:**

    Garfield, a cartoon cat, also a big, orange tabby.

    (A) To add a dependent clause

    (B) To remove an adjective

    (C) To insert a verb

    (D) To remove the subordinate clause

    (E) To change the preposition beginning the prepositional phrase

33. **In the second paragraph of the essay, what sentence should be removed in order to maintain unity and clarity?**

    (A) Sentence 8

    (B) Sentence 10

    (C) Sentence 12

    (D) Sentence 13

    (E) Sentence 14

34. **In sentence 9 (reproduced below), the following rewording would be an improvement:**

    Morris, however, was always enticed by the cat food being advertised.

    (A) The cat food being advertised, however, always enticed Morris.

    (B) Morris, the cat, however, always enticed the cat food advertised.

    (C) However, Morris was always enticed by the cat food he advertised.

    (D) Morris was always enticed by the cat food being advertised.

    (E) Enticed by the cat food being advertised, Morris would always eat.

35. **Given the development of the essay so far, a logical subject for the next paragraph to be written would be:**

   (A) Some geographical details about Egypt and Africa

   (B) More details about cats in ancient and folk history

   (C) References to cats in encyclopedias

   (D) Statistics on cat ownership in modern-day Egypt and Africa

   (E) Traditional ways to reward well-behaving cats

SECTION 7
(CRITICAL READING)
Time: 20 minutes
19 questions

SENTENCE COMPLETION

Directions: For each of the following questions, choose the best answer and fill in the corresponding oval on the answer sheet to indicate your selection.

Each sentence contains one or two blanks indicating that something has been omitted from the sentence. Choose the word or set of words, labeled A through E, that when inserted into the sentence, best fits the meaning of the sentence as a whole.

1. Ernest Hemingway was praised for his -------- prose, which sometimes says more by what is left out than what is said.

   (A) voluminous
   (B) verbose
   (C) taut
   (D) pedantic
   (E) didactic

2. After dropping in the polls, the political candidate experienced a -------- of popularity after several stellar performances in televised debates.

   (A) dearth
   (B) cessation
   (C) bursting
   (D) resurgence
   (E) ebb

3. Because the changes in the reform administration were slow, supporters labeled it an -------- rather than a -------- administration.

   (A) evolutionary ... revolutionary
   (B) emergence ... performance
   (C) anomaly ... policy
   (D) effect ... affect
   (E) alteration ... sprint

4. The beginning of the alternative medical book began with a strong --------

   (A) distender
   (B) extension
   (C) crustacean
   (D) disclaimer
   (E) proponent

5. Although Jill's friends and family considered her -------- , her co-workers found her to be aloof.

   (A) unsociable
   (B) pretentious
   (C) gregarious
   (D) impartial
   (E) laconic

6. "I cannot alter those figures," the bookkeeper told his co-worker. "That would be -------- the rules of --------."

   (A) unethical according to ... accountancy
   (B) wrong by ... any standards
   (C) accounting for ... ledgers
   (D) unimpeachable to ... addition
   (E) impeccable to ... ethics

The SAT Advantage

READING BASED QUESTIONS

Directions: For each of the following questions, choose the best answer and fill in the corresponding oval on the answer sheet to indicate your selection.

The reading passages below are followed by questions based on their content. Questions that follow a pair of related passages may be based on both the content of the passages and/or the relationship between the passages. Answer the questions based on what is <u>stated</u> or <u>implied</u> in the passages.

Questions 7 – 19 are based on the following passages:

Passage 1

Mothers Against Drunk Driving (MADD) is an effective and important organization driven by the passion of its volunteers. MADD was founded by a mother, Candy Lightner, when her 13-year-old daughter was struck and killed by a drunk driver in 1980. Vowing to her dead daughter that she would do something to prevent this from happening to someone else,
5 Lightner learned that more than half of all fatal car crashes were alcohol-related. Although she had no political or legislative experience, Lightner began reaching out to others who had been victimized by someone's choice to drink and drive.

MADD quickly caught on as the victims left behind by drunk driving—car crash victims and those who love them—at last had a forum. Mothers holding up pictures of their dead
10 children and sharing their grief, survivors in wheelchairs or with scars or permanent brain damage helped society see the human impact of drunk driving. Through giving car-crash victims faces and voices, MADD heightened the nation's awareness about drunk driving and worked for the passage of laws that would protect everyone.

MADD's main activity is to help victims of drunk driving car crashes. Among other ways,
15 MADD helps victims through Victim Impact Panels (VIPs). Through VIPs, drunk drivers meet the victims of their poor decision-making and hear them recount the impact of the drivers' actions of their lives. These offenders are people with Driving Under the Influence (DUI) charges or Driving While Intoxicated (DWI) charges. Sometimes Victim Impact Panels are mandated by the court as part of the offenders' sentencing.
20 VIPs are cathartic for people living with the impact of car crashes due to someone else's choice to drink and drive. VIPs help to heal the psychological and emotional wounds of the physical consequences to one's self or to one's loved ones due to the bad choices of someone who could have prevented the losses by acting in a more responsible manner. VIPs also evoke empathy and remorse in the hearts of offenders so that they will change
25 their behavior in the future and not drive while under the influence. VIPs encourage drunk drivers to make better choices; thus it is likely that they reduce drunk driver recidivism.

Passage 2

Mothers Against Drunk Driving (MADD) is credited with cutting fatalities from alcohol-related car crashes from about 30,000 per annum in 1980 to less than 17,000 per annum today. Society's consciousness about drinking and driving has changed from winking and
30 turning a blind eye to little tolerance for the practice of driving while under the influence. MADD estimates that it has saved roughly 300,000 lives by its activism to promote awareness and pass legislation that ensure that drunk driving is strictly limited by law. Many of us may owe our lives to MADD without knowing it. MADD is one of the most powerful and effective grassroots movements in history.

35 Yet one aspect of MADD—Victim Impact Panels—has not been shown to be particularly effective as far as preventing drunk driver recidivism. Although Victim Impact Panels can serve as an important release valve for the feelings of the victims of alcohol-related car crashes, unless they are paired with intervention programs that treat the underlying disease in the offenders—alcoholism—they are not really effective in helping drunk drivers make
40 better choices. In many cases, DUI and DWI offenders are repeat offenders due to addiction to alcohol.

The definition of addiction is that a person continues to engage in the addictive behavior regardless of the negative consequences. That means that no matter what—Victim Impact Panels, fines, incarceration, loss of license, etcetera—the addict will get in trouble again. It
45 may be a DUI or DWI. It may be job loss. It may be divorce. It may be desertion by friends and family. All these things are potential consequences of alcohol addiction, and consequences don't register with an addict until he or she "hits bottom" and has no choice but to face up to the addiction.

Perhaps Victim Impact Panels can be a part of helping someone "hit bottom" but
50 perhaps not. Most studies done on the subject show that VIPs have little effect on whether a drunk driver chooses to drive while under the influence again or not.

Alcoholics Anonymous says that many alcoholics are already riddled with guilt over their addiction and its consequences. Letting a victim vent at a perpetrator may just result in a guilt trip that hardens the offender's attitude and makes him or her seek escape through
55 alcohol once again. Public shaming is not necessarily the best way to make someone change his or her behavior. After all, drunk drivers don't set out to commit vehicular homicide or to hurt anyone. They themselves are victims of an addiction.

Anyone who drives on America's roads owes a debt of gratitude to MADD for their concerted and effective efforts to reduce drunk driving. Yet Victim Impact Panels, while
60 offering victims important cathartic benefits and useful in their own right, may not be one of MADD's more effective strategies for actually reducing drunk driving.

7. **The authors of Passage 1 and Passage 2 agree on which of the following points?**

   (A) MADD's Victim Impact Panels are effective in reducing drunk driving

   (B) MADD is an important and effective group that has had a huge impact on society's awareness of the dangers of drunk driving

   (C) MADD is affiliated with Alcoholics Anonymous

   (D) MADD has effective treatment programs for alcoholics

   (E) MADD should not promote Victim Impact Panels

8. **In line 20 "cathartic" most likely means:**

   (A) using a catheter because of injury

   (B) allowing for release of and relief from negative emotions

   (C) paralytic

   (D) allowing for emotional vengeance through verbalization

   (E) allowing for repression and containment of feelings

9. **The statistics in lines 27 – 34 most likely serve to:**

   (A) establish the efficacy of MADD

   (B) prove that MADD is legislatively inactive

   (C) give credibility to MADD's VIP programs

   (D) refute Passage 1 and its negative view of MADD

   (E) provide statistics showing that MADD's VIPs are an effective deterrent to drunk driving

10. **The author of Passage 2 would most likely say that the information presented in lines 8 – 13 serves to:**

    (A) evoke the reader's sympathy for victims so as to win the reader over to VIP panels

    (B) demonstrate that this particular public role of victims of alcohol-related car crashes has been effective

    (C) convince the reader that drunken driving has a human face

    (D) show that MADD emotionally manipulated legislators into passing anti-drunk driving laws

    (E) show that MADD was a bunch of people too emotional about their losses to achieve any effective results

11. **Which of the following can be found in both passages?**

    (A) belief in the effectiveness of VIPs

    (B) statistics on drunk driving in one specific state

    (C) examples of legislation that MADD has helped pass, such as the BAC laws

    (D) support and praise for MADD's overall effectiveness

    (E) references to Alcoholics Anonymous

12. **Which of the following best describes the relationship between the two passages?**

    (A) Passage 1 and Passage 2 are completely opposed in viewpoint

    (B) Passage 1 and Passage 2 both support MADD but Passage 2 has grave misgivings about the organization

    (C) empathy for victims of alcohol-related car crashes in Passage 1; empathy for alcoholics in Passage 2

    (D) Passage 1 supports MADD; Passage 2 decries it

    (E) Passage 1 and Passage 2 both support MADD but disagree as to the efficacy of VIPs in reducing drunk driving recidivism

13. **Lines 1 – 13 serve primarily to:**

    (A) show the role of professional counselors and political agitators in the formation of MADD

    (B) show the strength of victim-ology

    (C) show the grassroots origins of Mothers Against Drunk Driving

    (D) demand reparations to victims of alcohol-related car crashes

    (E) encourage people that they too can make a difference

14. **The author of Passage 2 would most likely respond to lines 24 – 26 by:**

    (A) saying that offenders' hearts are so hard, they will not be moved

    (B) saying that, although studies show VIPs reduce drunk driver recidivism, they are too emotional for all involved

    (C) noting that VIPs require victims to appear in court, which can be traumatic

    (D) noting that saying "it is likely" is proof enough that VIPs do reduce drunk driver recidivism

    (E) noting that sometimes offenders experience debilitating guilt from VIPs and that studies show little effect of VIPs on recidivism

15. **In Passage 1, the author suggests that MADD's primary mission is:**

    (A) to recruit passionate volunteers

    (B) to help victims of alcohol-related car crashes and prevent others from becoming victims

    (C) to effect legislation

    (D) to promote VIPs

    (E) to condemn, blame, and punish drunk drivers

16. **The author of Passage 2 sees alcoholics as:**

    (A) perpetrators of unforgivable crimes

    (B) victims of addiction

    (C) in need of crisis intervention techniques

    (D) synonymous with drunk drivers

    (E) punishable by death

17. **Which of the following statements about MADD is supported by both passages?**

    (A) Except for comforting victims, MADD is not an effective organization

    (B) MADD was directed by experts in legislation, law, and counseling

    (C) MADD is an amateur organization that has had some lucky wins in legislation

    (D) MADD's Victim Impact Panels decrease drunken driving incidents

    (E) MADD has had far-reaching impact on the nation's laws and attitudes regarding drunk driving

18. **The authors of Passage 1 and Passage 2 agree that VIPs:**

    (A) serve to release and relieve the feelings of victims of alcohol-related car crashes

    (B) are effective preventive measures

    (C) reduce drunk driving recidivism

    (D) serve no purpose whatever

    (E) should be banned

19. **In line 26 "recidivism" most likely means:**

    (A) punishment by law

    (B) returning to criminal activity as a repeat offender

    (C) repentance and remorse

    (D) reactivation of licenses after suspension

    (E) retrograde punishment for offenses committed years earlier

The SAT Advantage

SECTION 8
(MATHEMATICS)
Time: 20 minutes
16 questions

MULTIPLE CHOICE

Directions: For the questions in this section, solve each problem and decide which of the given answer choices is the best choice. Fill in the corresponding oval on the answer sheet to indicate your selection. You may use any available space for scratchwork.

Note:

1. Calculator use is permitted.
2. All numbers used are real numbers.
3. All figures provided are drawn to scale and lie in a plane unless otherwise indicated.
4. Unless otherwise specified, the domain of any function f is assumed to be the set of all real numbers x for which $f(x)$ is a real number.

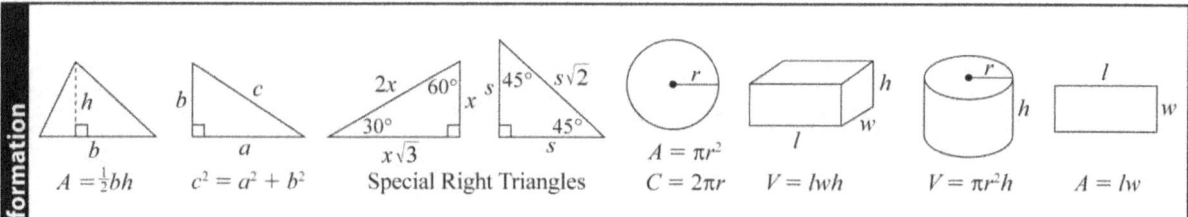

The sum of the degree measures of the angles in a triangle is 180.
The number of degrees of arc in a circle is 360.
A straight angle has a degree measure of 180.

1. Rosita buys 300 feet of yarn for a craft project. If the yarn costs 12 cents a yard, how much does Rosita spend?

   (A) $12.00
   (B) $36.00
   (C) $108.00
   (D) $360.00
   (E) $1200.00

2. Solve for a: $7a + 2 = 3a - 5 + 2a$

   (A) $3\frac{1}{4}$
   (B) 2
   (C) $-\frac{7}{6}$
   (D) -2
   (E) $-3\frac{1}{2}$

3. Two positive integers have a greatest common factor (GCF) of 4 and a least common multiple of 40. Which pair of positive integers satisfies these conditions?

   (A) 6 and 10
   (B) 8 and 10
   (C) 8 and 20
   (D) 10 and 20
   (E) 10 and 40

4. A jacket originally costing $40 is discounted by 20%. When the jacket fails to sell, the new cost is reduced by 30%. What is the cost of the jacket after the 30% reduction?

   (A) $18.60
   (B) $20.00
   (C) $22.40
   (D) $26.80
   (E) $28.00

5. Which of the following is greater than $\frac{6}{7}$?

   (A) 0.625
   (B) $\frac{17}{25}$
   (C) 0.78
   (D) $\frac{19}{23}$
   (E) 0.86

6. If $(2^x)^3 = 64$, what is the value of x?

   (A) 0
   (B) 1
   (C) 2
   (D) 3
   (E) 4

7. Which of the following must be true about △ pictured below?

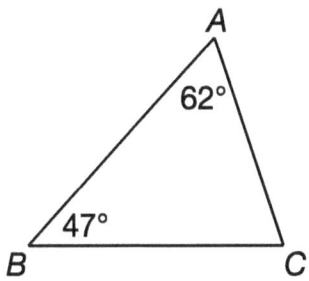

   (A) $\overline{BC} > \overline{AB} > \overline{AC}$
   (B) $\overline{AC} > \overline{AB} > \overline{BC}$
   (C) $\overline{BC} > \overline{AC} > \overline{AB}$
   (D) $\overline{AB} > \overline{BC} > \overline{AC}$
   (E) $\overline{AC} > \overline{BC} > \overline{AB}$

8. If the two lines represented by the two equations below do NOT intersect, what is the value of k?

   $2x + 3y = 7$

   $y = kx - 1$

   (A) 3
   (B) 2
   (C) $\frac{3}{2}$
   (D) $-\frac{2}{3}$
   (E) $-\frac{3}{2}$

9. In the diagram below $\overline{AB}$ is a radius of ⊙ and $\overline{BC}$ is tangent to the circle at point B. What is the value of x?

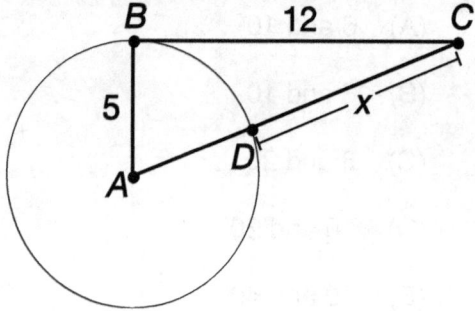

   (A) 5
   (B) 6
   (C) 6.5
   (D) 8
   (E) 13

Questions 10-11 are based on the height and weight data for a group of people displayed below:

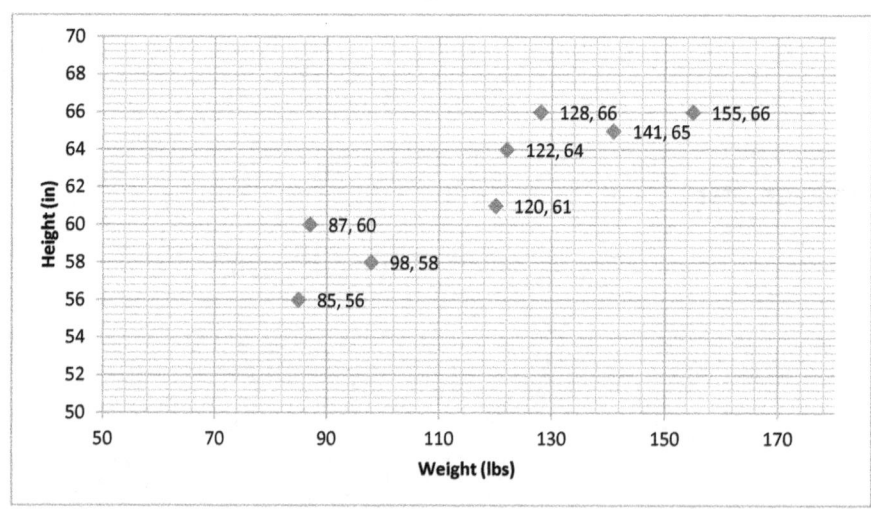

The (weight, height) is displayed next to each data point.

10. The mode for the height data

    (A) is equal to the median
    (B) is less than the median
    (C) is greater than the median
    (D) is sometimes greater and sometimes less than the median
    (E) cannot be found from the given data

11. The median weight is

    (A) 113 lbs
    (B) 119 lbs
    (C) 120 lbs
    (D) 121 lbs
    (E) 122 lbs

12. What is the greatest possible value of the function $f(x) = -(x-2)(x+3)$?

    (A) 13.0
    (B) 6.25
    (C) 0.5
    (D) -0.5
    (E) -6.25

13. A line passes through the points (p, 2q) and (-q, -2p). A line perpendicular to it has the slope

    (A) 2
    (B) -0.5
    (C) p + q
    (D) $\dfrac{-1}{p+q}$
    (E) $\dfrac{2p}{q}$

14. A box is filled with gold, silver, and red beads. If one bead is picked at random, the probability of getting a gold bead is $\dfrac{1}{4}$. If there are as many silver beads as red beads, what is the ratio of the number of gold beads to the number of silver beads?

    (A) $\dfrac{1}{3}$
    (B) $\dfrac{1}{2}$
    (C) $\dfrac{2}{3}$
    (D) $\dfrac{3}{2}$
    (E) $\dfrac{2}{1}$

15. The sum of 5 consecutive integers is a multiple of 5. Possible values of the first integer in the sequence include

   I. All even numbers
   II. All numbers ending with 3
   II. All numbers ending with 5

   (A) I only

   (B) I and II

   (C) II and III

   (D) I, II, and III

   (E) none of the above

16. x^2+1, $x-2$ and $x+3$ can be the 3 sides of a triangle

   (A) for $x>2$

   (B) for $x<2$

   (C) for $x>-6$

   (D) for $x>\sqrt{6}$

   (E) for no values of x

SECTION 9
(WRITING)
Time: 10 minutes
14 questions

IMPROVING SENTENCES

Directions: For each of the following questions, choose the best answer and fill in the corresponding oval on the answer sheet to indicate your selection.

Part of each sentence (or the entire sentence) is underlined. The five answer choices present five ways of phrasing the underlined portion. Choice A repeats the original phrasing and the other four choices offer alternative phrasings. If you think the original phrasing is best, select choice A; if not, select one of the other options.

In choosing your answer, follow the requirements of standard written English. Pay attention to grammar, choice of words, sentence construction, and punctuation; your selection should result in the most effective, clear, and precise sentence—free of awkwardness or ambiguity.

1. The rising cost of housing in the metropolitan areas of major Northern cities <u>have discouraged many young families and driven to relocate to other regions of the country</u>.

    (A) have discouraged many young families and driven to relocate to other regions of the country

    (B) have discouraged many young families and drove them to relocate to other regions of the country

    (C) has discouraged many young families and driven them to relocate to other regions of the country

    (D) has discouraged many young families and drove them to relocate to other regions of the country

    (E) has discouraged many young families to drive to other regions of the country to relocate

2. Nathaniel Currier and James Ives were popular nineteenth-century <u>printmakers, their inexpensive prints</u> decorated homes throughout the United States and England.

    (A) printmakers, their inexpensive prints

    (B) printmakers; but their inexpensive prints

    (C) printmakers, yet their inexpensive prints

    (D) printmakers; their inexpensive prints

    (E) printmakers, in as much as their inexpensive prints

3. **One major cause of obesity is when many people spend most of the day sitting at their jobs.**

    (A) One major cause of obesity is when
    (B) One major cause of obesity is that
    (C) Many cases of obesity result from when
    (D) Many cases of obesity are due to the fact that because
    (E) Many cases of obesity are the result of when

4. **In addition to being a Pulitzer Prize-winning novelist, critical acclaim was also received by John Updike for his essays and poems.**

    (A) critical acclaim was also received by John Updike for his essays and poems
    (B) critical acclaim for his essays and poems was also received by John Updike
    (C) John Updike's essays and poems also received critical acclaim for him
    (D) his essays and poems were also a source of critical acclaim received for John Updike
    (E) John Updike also received critical acclaim for his essays and poems

5. **Even people who claim to be perfectly logical and objective base many of their choices on logical reasons less than they do on their emotional responses to the options available.**

    (A) base many of their choices on logical reasons less than they do on
    (B) base many of their choices less on logical reasons than on
    (C) make many of their choices based on logical reasons less than on
    (D) are basing many choices on less logical reasons than on
    (E) base many of their choices on lesser than logical reasons and more often on

6. **Unlike them in the National League, the teams in the American League of Major League Baseball** choose a designated hitter who replaces the pitcher in the batting order.

   (A) Unlike them in the National League, the teams in the American League of Major League Baseball

   (B) In Major League Baseball, the teams of the National League, when in contrast to those of the American League,

   (C) In Major League Baseball, the teams of the National League, unlike those in the American League,

   (D) The teams of the National League in Major League Baseball contrast to those of the American League in that they

   (E) The teams of the American League, when contrasted to them of the National League in Major League Baseball,

7. Since the passage of the Endangered Species Act in 1973, some endangered species have become extinct, while others, including the bald eagle, have recovered **because of the government's banning strictly the hunting of these species and protecting carefully their habitats**.

   (A) because of the government's banning strictly the hunting of these species and protecting carefully their habitats

   (B) because the government strictly was banning their hunting and carefully was protecting their habitats

   (C) because of the hunting ban and habitat protection that the government was strict and careful about

   (D) because the hunting ban on the species and the protection of their habitats had been strict and careful by the government

   (E) because of the government's strict ban on hunting these species and careful protection of their habitats

8. Jonas Salk, who discovered the first polio vaccine, <u>sought no patent for his medicine and received no profits from its distribution</u>.

   (A) sought no patent for his medicine and received no profits from its distribution
   (B) sought neither a patent for his medicine nor received any profits from its distribution
   (C) sought no patent for his medicine nor received any profits from its distribution
   (D) sought no patent for his medicine and receiving no profits from its distribution
   (E) neither sought nor received a patent or profits from its discovery and distribution

9. If you maintain a positive attitude, <u>one may achieve many of one's objectives in life</u>.

   (A) one may achieve many of one's objectives in life
   (B) one may achieve many of his or her objectives in life
   (C) one may achieve many of your objectives in life
   (D) you may achieve many of your objectives in life
   (E) you may achieve many of one's objectives in life

10. To qualify for the next round of the competition, contestants were required both to write a personal essay <u>and their performing of community service must be ongoing</u>.

    (A) and their performing of community service must be ongoing
    (B) and to perform ongoing community service
    (C) as well as performing ongoing community service
    (D) and their community service performance being ongoing
    (E) while performing ongoing community service

11. **The first safe and effective antibiotic, produced in 1939, <u>saved millions of lives during World War II by protecting wounded soldiers from deadly infections</u>.**

    (A) saved millions of lives during World War II by protecting wounded soldiers from deadly infections

    (B) saving millions of lives during World War II and thus effective in protecting wounded soldiers from deadly infections

    (C) was responsible for the saving of millions of lives during World War II because it was useful for the protecting of wounded soldiers from infections that would have been deadly

    (D) which saved millions of lives during World War II, had done so by protecting wounded soldiers from deadly infections

    (E) was saving millions of lives during World War II because of the fact that it had been protecting wounded soldiers from deadly infections

12. **In the 1800s, the Northern economy included farms that provided food and factories that produced other necessities, <u>and this was not true of the South, whose economy was based on</u> a plantation system that produced cash crops such as tobacco and cotton.**

    (A) and this was not true of the South, whose economy was based on

    (B) not the case in the South, where the economy had been based on

    (C) as opposed to the South, which had an economy which was based on

    (D) unlike the Southern economy, being based on

    (E) but the Southern economy was based on

13. **A continent twice the size of Australia and covered by ice, over 70 percent of the world's fresh water is located in Antarctica.**

    (A) A continent twice the size of Australia and covered by ice, over 70 percent of the world's fresh water is located in Antarctica.

    (B) A continent that is twice the size of Australia and that is covered by ice, over 70 percent of the world's fresh water is located in Antarctica.

    (C) Over 70 percent of the world's fresh water is located in Antarctica, a continent twice the size of Australia and covered by ice.

    (D) Over 70 percent of the world's fresh water being located in it, Antarctica is a continent, it is covered by ice, and it is twice the size of Australia.

    (E) Being twice the size of Australia and being covered by ice, over 70 percent of the world's fresh water is located in Antarctica.

14. Despite evidence to the contrary, Nicholas **believed not only that his system was foolproof but he could teach it to others**.

    (A) believed not only that his system was foolproof but he could teach it to others

    (B) not only believed that his system was foolproof but also he could teach it to others

    (C) believed not only that his system was foolproof, but also that he could teach it to others as well

    (D) believed not only that his system was foolproof but also that he could teach it to others

    (E) not only believed that his system was foolproof, but also believed that he could teach it to others as well

PRACTICE TEST 1 ANSWER KEY

Section 1 (Writing)

Section 2 (Critical Reading)

1. A
2. E
3. C
4. A
5. C
6. B
7. E
8. C
9. B
10. B
11. B
12. E
13. C
14. B
15. D
16. A
17. E
18. C
19. C
20. D
21. C
22. A
23. B
24. A

Section 3 (Mathematics)

1. D
2. B
3. B
4. B
5. B
6. B
7. C
8. B
9. D
10. C
11. A
12. D
13. E
14. D
15. C
16. B
17. A
18. C
19. C
20. E

Section 4 (Critical Reading)

1. A
2. B
3. D
4. E
5. E
6. A
7. E
8. B
9. C
10. D
11. B
12. A
13. A
14. B
15. E
16. B
17. B
18. C
19. C
20. A
21. C
22. E
23. C
24. B

Section 5 (Mathematics)

1. A
2. B
3. C
4. A
5. E
6. C
7. A
8. C
9. 6
10. 7
11. 154
12. 6
13. 48
14. 4
15. 60
16. 20/7
17. 6
18. 0

Section 6 (Writing)

1. B
2. D
3. E
4. D
5. C
6. A
7. B
8. E
9. A
10. B
11. B
12. B
13. C
14. E
15. C
16. C
17. A
18. E
19. B
20. C
21. B
22. A
23. D
24. D
25. A
26. C
27. C
28. B
29. B
30. B
31. E
32. C
33. C
34. A
35. B

Section 7 (Critical Reading)

1. C
2. D
3. A
4. D
5. C
6. A
7. B
8. B
9. A
10. B
11. D
12. E
13. C
14. E
15. B
16. B
17. E
18. A
19. B

Section 8 (Mathematics)

1. A
2. E
3. C
4. C
5. E
6. C
7. D
8. D
9. D
10. C
11. D
12. B
13. B
14. C
15. D
16. E

Section 9 (Writing)

1. C
2. D
3. B
4. E
5. B
6. C
7. E
8. A
9. D
10. B
11. A
12. E
13. C
14. D

PRACTICE TEST 1
ANSWER RATIONALES

The SAT Advantage

SECTION 1 (WRITING)

ESSAY

Excellent Quality Sample Essay (Score: 6 out of 6) Rationale

The writer exhibits critical thinking by agreeing with the premise and yet expanding upon it to include other applications and reach an original conclusion. The writer develops agreement with the premise that professionals do have an ethical duty by exploring ways in which professionals such as doctors, lawyers, accountants, and engineers and their work affect people if they do not perform well. The writer also gives attention to expansion of the premise—that all workers have ethical responsibility—with examples of non-professional workers who have a duty to public safety.

The writer uses a variety of sentence structures from simple sentences "We rely on engineers to keep us safe" to compound "If a bus driver does not perform adequately on the road, whole dozens of people may be killed or injured, yet he or she is not a 'professional.'" to complex "Although we recognize that our lawyers must defend us within the boundaries of the law, we also expect that they will protect our interests passionately".

The writer uses appropriate and specific vocabulary, for example: A "collapsing bridge" and a "dysfunctional elevator" are vivid examples using appropriate and specific vocabulary words that help the reader understand the enormity of the engineer's professional responsibility.

The writer uses concrete rather than abstract examples. If the writer merely said "Many people could be injured or even killed by bad engineering" it would not be as strong or effective as the statement "Many people could be injured or even killed by a collapsing bridge or dysfunctional elevator." "Bad engineering" is more abstract than the concrete examples the writer uses.

The writer uses the active voice: "Doctors hold our lives in their hands" rather than "Our lives are in the hands of our doctors," for example. The active voice is stronger and shows better writing.

The essay shows progression as it develops its statements through examples of the ethical responsibilities of professionals. It then develops its statement that "everyone has an ethical responsibility..." made in the first paragraph by using examples of non-professionals who nevertheless affect public safety.

The writer of the essay has successfully proven the point made in the introductory paragraph, which stated the thesis of the essay. The writer reinforces the thesis with a restatement of it in the concluding paragraph and also adds in an original and thought-provoking concluding sentence. The writer shows mastery of the writing process.

Medium Quality Sample Essay (Score: 3 – 4 out of 6) Rationale

The writer exhibits some critical thinking by finding ways to support the thesis that professionals have a special ethical responsibility to the public. The writer gives examples of times when the public entrusts themselves to professionals. A particularly vivid example is "when we close our eyes under the surgeon's knife, we hope and pray that the surgeon is good."

The writer also develops the idea that professionals have special knowledge, which is one of the points made about what distinguishes professionals in the excerpt the students read. The writer develops this idea by saying that the public has no way to measure this special knowledge and therefore must trust the professionals. It is in this, possessing special knowledge, that professionals have a special ethical responsibility to the public, the writer concludes insightfully.

The writer uses a variety of sentence structures from simple sentences "They were posted on the wall" to compound "Our teachers have much more knowledge than we do, and they should have this special knowledge" to complex "Because the general public can't measure how good these professionals are, they have a special ethical responsibility to the public." However, overuse of "We" and "When we" to begin sentences makes for repetitious reading.

The writer uses appropriate and specific vocabulary in many cases. Examples are "conducting their classes" and "credentials and certifications."

However, the essay loses progression in the third paragraph. It does not show progression from one reasonable point or set of points to the next. In fact, it is digressive; it is almost off topic. The essay trails off in development at this point. Digressive and distracting points such as "unless the documents were forged" lead the reader off on tangents. The third paragraph is only loosely tied to the theme and puts too much emphasis on the credentials on the wall rather than the topic, which is whether professionals have special ethical responsibilities toward the public.

Because of these issues, this essay is a medium quality essay.

Low Quality Sample Essay (Score: 1 – 2 out of 6) Rationale

The critical thinking is limited in this essay. The writer relies on flat assertions of opinion but does not demonstrate the points with good examples or develop the ideas. The writer does not consider other points of view, allow for them, or rebut them. The phrase "There is no argument here" shows that critical thinking is not in play.

The repetition of the phrase "I would not want to" in the second paragraph shows a lack of facility with ideas and language. There is little creative or original expression. There is also little variety in sentence composition. Many of the sentences in the essay are simple sentences. There are grammatical errors such as "Such people should not be allowed."

The essay does not show progression. It is simply an array of undeveloped points, relying on assertion of opinion rather than examples and/or reasonable development of an argument. In order to gain a higher score, the author would have to develop more points in better ways and show more critical thinking skills by appealing to reason with well-expressed ideas and arguments. What is more, the writer would have to work on more creative expression and variety of sentence composition.

SECTION 2 (CRITICAL READING)

SENTENCE COMPLETION

1. Answer: (A) glamorous
The missing adjective to modify "passenger list" must have the same characteristics as the clause that follows it, which further describes the passenger list: "which reads almost like a *Who's Who* of the rich and famous of the time." The word "glamorous" (A) is associated with "the rich and famous" and is the best fit.

2. Answer: (E) convey
The sentence asks the reader to look for a word that describes the transfer of information from place to place. Only one word among the five means to "transfer" or "transmit": that word is "convey" (E), which means to transfer or cause to move from one place to another.

3. Answer: (C) Contrary
The statement is contradicting common misconceptions that the debates took place during Lincoln's run for the presidency, so it is proper to use the word most closely related to contradicting, which is "Contrary" (C). Contrary has the same Latin root as contradiction: *contra* meaning "against" or "in opposition or contrast."

4. Answer: (A) preceding … millennium
To answer this question, the logical flow of ideas in the sentence must be followed. The sentence starts out in the present "the world is" and then refers to the past: "the turn of the nineteenth century." Therefore, the first word to best fit the meaning of the sentence must be a word that means something happened in the past, such as "before." The only word among the choices that means something that went before is "preceding" (A). The "turn of the nineteenth century" as used in the sentence refers to the advent of the year 2000 or the new millennium (one thousand years). The combination in answer (A) preceding … millennium is the correct one.

5. Answer: (C) succinctly … challenged
The part of the sentence that requires words is a list of the things candidates must achieve during televised debates. The phrase "time constraints of television" implies that candidates must answer in short, targeted ways, which is the meaning of the word "succinctly" (C). People often respond emotionally when they are challenged, and the "bright hot lights" implies that their emotions are on display for scrutiny during the debates. It is the nature of debate that a debater will be challenged to defend his or her positions; therefore, the combination of "succinctly … challenged" is the best answer.

6. Answer: (B) procured … comprising
The opening phrase "Hoping to prove how priceless the human body is," describes why the doctor would want to get possession of a synthetic chemical catalogue. "To get possession of" something means to "procure" or "acquire" it. To "comprise" something means to make up or constitute its parts or elements, and the doctor wishes to estimate the costs of all the chemicals making up the human body, so the combination of "procured … comprising" (B) is the most fitting for the meaning of the sentence.

The SAT Advantage

7. Answer: (E) severed ... respectively
The first word must be an adjective describing "arteries that are causing blood loss." Only "severed" or "ruptured" arteries cause blood loss, so the first answer is either (E) or (B). The sentence is constructed of a list of first aid maneuvers followed by a list of what each of the maneuvers actually does, arranged in an order that corresponds with or matches the list of first aid maneuvers. The adverb "respectively" means "in the order given," and since the two lists do correspond perfectly in order, "respectively" is the best choice.

8. Answer: (C) meager ... parsimonious
The missing words must somehow agree with each other due to the linking word "because". Either Devon had a large quantity of money and could be generous with his expenditures or he had very little money and would need to be thrifty (the word "forced" would lead us to assume the latter). Choice (C) provides "meager", which means "a small amount" and "parsimonious", which means frugal or economical. Choices (A) and (D) offer opposite meanings and choices (B) and (E) are simply not related to one another.

READING BASED QUESTIONS

9. Answer: (B) being an apologist for the classism and sexism of the *Titanic* era
This question is an extended reasoning question, which means the answer must be inferred from the passage rather than being directly stated within it. There is more probability that criticism would come in regard to answer (B) because Passage 2 addresses issues of sexism and classism. The author of Passage 2 uses the word "noble" to describe the sentiments expressed in the order to allow women and children to go first, which shows the author admires some of the attitudes of an era now classified as sexist. Passage 2 directly states that the purpose of the third class area gates was for health reasons rather than to separate the ship into classes. It also refutes the idea that Bruce Ismay was not a democratic man by citing his benevolent reasons for making third and second class accommodations on the *Titanic* above grade. Passage 2 thus indirectly addresses sexism and directly addresses classism and could be criticized for that.

10. Answer: (B) admiring
The use of the word "noble" to describe the sentiment that moved men to put their own lives in jeopardy to protect women and children shows that the author admires the sentiment.

11. Answer: (B) disagree with the characterization of Bruce Ismay in Passage 1
The author of Passage 2 puts the word "heartless" in quotations marks to show that this is something that is said about Bruce Ismay, particularly based upon the movie's depiction of him as a self-centered man, but which may not be true. Passage 1 accepts the movie's depiction of Bruce Ismay, calling him "self-centered" and decrying his lack of concern for his passengers, whereas Passage 2 does not agree with this characterization. Passage 2 directly refutes the idea that Bruce Ismay did not care about the well-being of his passengers, including the third class ones, by citing his motives for building higher grade accommodations.

12. Answer: (E) there were gates in the third class passenger area
Passage 1 states that, "The fence-like doors that kept the third class passengers penned in were part of the real ship." Passage 2 states, "The third-class gates did exist," so, the authors both acknowledge that fact.

The SAT Advantage

13. Answer: (C) personification
Imparting human characteristics to an inanimate object is the definition of the literary device of personification. Lines such as, "She couldn't stare directly at the art connoisseur who was gazing at her in the gallery; that would be impolite for a court lady of her standing" imply that the woman in the portrait has human feelings rather than being an inanimate object. Likewise, later lines imply that the woman has thoughts about her own creation, such as, "Look into my eyes and see the light of genius in the expression painted there. Who could have painted me with such vitality that you can feel the very heat of the blush on my cheek?" An inanimate object cannot think; therefore, this is an example of imparting human characteristics to an inanimate object, called personification.

14. Answer: (B) provide facts and background information
Since these lines provide factual background information such as a person's name (Peter Silverman) and a date (January 1, 1998) of a sale at an actual place (New York auction house Christie's) as well as quotations from the auction catalog and a specific price ($19,000), the purpose of the lines is clearly to provide facts and give background information.

15. Answer: (D) art expertise
Phrases like "Silverman's trained eye" and "Silverman knew that a German school of artists had produced such Renaissance-style paintings in the nineteenth century" and "His feel for art" establish that Silverman had expertise in art. The information that "he had lived in Munich" also gives him credibility in his judgment that the work was not of German origin.

16. Answer: (A) excited discovery
The fact that Silverman and his wife "nearly skipped going to the gallery" adds to the sense that this discovery might not have happened at all, which makes it all the more exciting that it did. The question asking, "What was the likelihood of running into her again?" also adds to the sense of excited discovery by implying this is more than coincidence. When the portrait "almost put Silverman into a trance" and "his heart started pounding a million times a minute" the reader knows that Silverman feels a strong sense of excited discovery.

17. Answer: (E) suspense
The author does not say the name Silverman was thinking of. This creates suspense, for the fact that the name "was resounding in his brain" means the name must have been of some significance. The citing of a list of experts ("Silverman began to consult art historians, art forensics experts, classic hairstyle and fashion experts, and drawing experts") culminating in the penetrating "high-resolution multispectral scans of Lumiere Technology" adds to the suspense of who might have painted the portrait. Lastly, we have an "Emeritus professor of art history at Oxford University" to whom an unnamed "name had occurred" also. By this time, the reader is in suspense, wanting to know who the experts think drew the portrait.

18. Answer: (C) in depth
The definition of the word "profound" is "extending far below the surface." Therefore, "in depth" is the proper meaning.

19. Answer: (C) he had studied the dissection of dead bodies to understand the skeletal and muscular structure of the human being
The lines state, "The left-handed master of drawing had actually dissected cadavers to learn how to structure human portraits," showing that (C) is the most accurate answer according to the facts cited about Leonardo da Vinci's life.

The SAT Advantage

20. Answer: (D) skeptical
The statement that Martin Kemp "had received many claims by people saying they had discovered a Leonardo" implies that Kemp himself had to be skeptical of such claims. The statements that "The art world was a conservative place" and that attributing the portrait to Leonardo da Vinci "would be a long, drawn-out, controversial process calling upon the combined expertise of the art and scientific worlds" implies the art world is not easily persuaded or convinced. "Skeptical" means "doubtful" or not easily given to belief and is the suitable answer here.

21. Answer: (C) circumstantial
Circumstantial evidence is evidence where surrounding circumstances point to a possibility but offer no conclusive proof. Although the material the portrait was done on dated back to 1440 and 1650 and Leonardo's life span was 1452 to 1519, there was no proof that Leonardo used the material. Though the fashion in the portrait was found to be "specific to the court of Milan in the 1490s" and Leonardo "lived in Milan and was often commissioned to draw court portraits" that is still not conclusive proof that Leonardo drew the portrait. Circumstances were right for him to have drawn the portrait, so the evidence was circumstantial.

22. Answer: (A) present both points of view
These lines include language such as "it was an authentic, undiscovered and undocumented Leonardo da Vinci" and "it was an elaborate, excellent forgery" to show different perspectives on the portraits. "Experts like Kemp" are said to believe that the portrait "spoke of the genius of Leonardo" while it is acknowledged that "other Leonardo experts" said it "looked nothing like the work" of Leonardo. The lines provide a balanced presentation of both points of view.

23. Answer: (B) impartial
To be impartial means to not take a side and to be objective and fair. Although the passage cites the portrait as being worth a large sum of money (a sum commanded only by an artist of Leonardo's stature) and that the portrait "is now attributed to Leonardo da Vinci," in fairness, the author admits that acceptance by art experts is not universal, leaving the possibility open that the portrait is not by Leonardo.

24. Answer: (A) advocate the portrait as an authentic Leonardo da Vinci
The opening paragraph mentions "the light of genius" and has the portrait ask who could have painted her so realistically, implying that the portraitist was a great artist. The build-up of suspense and the eventual announcement of the artist's name show that the author has a strong sense that this discovery is dramatic. The statements that the portrait "matched the book perfectly" and "is now attributed to Leonardo da Vinci" and "is worth over $100,000,000" imply that the author believes that the portrait is an authentic Leonardo.

SECTION 3 (MATHEMATICS)

MULTIPLE CHOICE

1. Answer: (D) 15

The $\frac{3}{5}$ probability of getting milk chocolate implies that $\frac{3}{5}$ of the total number of pieces of candy in the bag are made of milk chocolate. So the number of pieces of milk chocolate candy = $\frac{3}{5}$ x 25 = $\frac{75}{5}$ = 15.

2. Answer: (B) 75°

A central angle in a circle is any angle with its vertex on the center. In the pie chart shown, all of the chart's components are created by using central angles.

A circle measures 360°. Find the fraction of the circle that is composed of Sociology majors.

$$\frac{sociology\ majors}{all\ students} = \frac{100}{480} = \frac{5}{24}$$

The Sociology majors represent $\frac{5}{24}$ of the circle's 360°. Multiply $\frac{5}{24}$ by 360 to find the measure of the central angle.

$$(\frac{5}{24})(360) = 75°$$

3. Answer: (B) $x - 2y = 8$

Find the equation of the line in slope-intercept form, $y = mx + b$, and then transform the equation into standard form, $Ax + By = C$ (remember A, B, and C must be integers and A > 0).

Find the slope using the formula $\frac{y_2 - y_1}{x_2 - x_1}$:

$$\frac{0 - (-4)}{8 - 0} = \frac{1}{2}$$

Inspecting the graph, we see the y-intercept is (0,-4), so we replace b with -4:

$$y = \frac{1}{2}x - 4$$

Transform the equation into standard form:

$$y = \frac{1}{2}x - 4$$

$$-\frac{1}{2}x + y = -4$$

$$-2(-\frac{1}{2}x + y = -4)$$

$$x - 2y = 8$$

4. Answer: (B) $\frac{1}{3}$

To find the probability, divide the number of acceptable outcomes by the total number of possible outcomes. The acceptable outcomes are 1 and 2, so there are 2 of them. The total number of possible outcomes is 6. So the probability of rolling a number less than 3 is $\frac{2}{6}$ which reduces to $\frac{1}{3}$.

5. Answer: (B) 2

This problem is unsolvable without using a plug-and-check strategy. The conventional method of answering this question is to cross-multiply the proportion and set the products equal to one another:

$$4(3^n) = 18n$$

However, the problem cannot be resolved without more information. Thus, begin substituting the values that are provided in the answer choices. Begin with choice C, 3, and evaluate the results.

$$\frac{3^3}{6(3)} = \frac{27}{18} = \frac{3}{2}$$

Substituting 3 provides an answer that is too large. Move down to choice B and substitute 2 for *n*.

$$\frac{3^2}{6(2)} = \frac{9}{12} = \frac{3}{4}$$

6. Answer: (B) 3

Adding the two equations together, we get $7x + y = 21 + y; \Rightarrow 7x = 21; \Rightarrow x = 3$.

7. Answer: (C) $3225

Amount spent for renting the venue = $\frac{4300}{5}$ = $860.

Amount spent on other expenses = 5% of 4300 = $\frac{4300}{20}$ = $215

Total expenses = $860 + $215 = $1075
Amount left for contribution to charity = $4300 − $1075 = $3225.

8. Answer: (B) 15°
Since ABC is a right triangle, angle BAC = 90° − ABC = 90° − 60° = 30°.
Angle DAF = Angle BAC = 30° (Vertical angles).
Since EA bisects the angle DAF, x = DAF/2 = 15°.

9. Answer: (D) 4
$3^{2k} \times 3^k = 81^3$

$\Rightarrow 3^{2k+k} = 81^3$ (combining exponents on the left hand side)

$\Rightarrow 3^{3k} = (3^4)^3$ (writing 81 as a power of 3)

$\Rightarrow 3^{3k} = 3^{12}$ (combining exponents on the right hand side)

$\Rightarrow 3k = 12$ (setting exponents on both sides equal to each other)

$\Rightarrow k = 4$ (dividing both sides by 3)

10. Answer: (C) 5
Since $(x+y)(x-y) = x^2 - y^2$, $x+y = \frac{x^2 - y^2}{(x-y)} = \frac{15}{3} = 5.$

11. Answer: (A) [324]

Notice that in both rules ($[x] = x^2$ and $[x] = \sqrt{x}$) once the operation is performed, *the result is no longer in the brackets.*

$[3] = 3^2 = 9$

$[4] = \sqrt{4} = 2$

$[3] \times [4] = 9 \times 2 = 18$

Selection A, $[324]$, is even, so find its square root.

$\sqrt{324} = 18$

Thus,

$$[3] \times [4] = 18 \qquad [324] = 18$$

so $[3] \times [4] = [324]$.

12. Answer: (D)
After a 90° rotation in the clockwise direction, the orientation of the triangle is

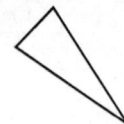

After reflection through the given line, the orientation becomes

13. Answer: (E) -2
$$f(u) = 3u^2 + 5u + 1 = 3$$
$$\Rightarrow 3u^2 + 5u - 2 = 0$$

Factoring the above expression, we get $(3u-1)(u+2) = 0$

So the possible values of u are -2 and $\frac{1}{3}$.

14. Answer: (D) 5
The 8 events are the 100m freestyle, 200m freestyle, 100m backstroke, and 200m backstroke for the two age groups 11/12 and 13/14.

The data shows that girls had shorter average times on 5 of these events: 200m freestyle, 100m backstroke, and 200m backstroke for ages 11/12 and 200m freestyle and 100m backstroke for ages 13/14.

15. Answer: (C) 13-14 year old girl
The best time in the girl's 13-14 category for 100m freestyle was 55.02 s. This is shorter than the other times for 100m freestyle: 1:12.02, 1:00.04 and 0:56.25.

The SAT Advantage

16. Answer: (B) 11-12, 200m freestyle
In the boys' 11-12 200m freestyle event, the difference between the best and average times was 2:49.39 − 2:12.13 = 37.26 s. This was higher than the difference for any of the other boys' events.

17. Answer: (A) A
Looking carefully at the population equation $P(t) = \dfrac{A}{1 + Be^{-t}}$, note that the population increases when e^{-t} decreases and vice versa.

The highest possible value of e^{-t} is 1, when t = 0 (since t is never negative). This corresponds to the lowest possible population value $\dfrac{A}{1+B}$.

The lowest possible value of e^{-t} is asymptotically 0 when t becomes very large. This corresponds to the highest possible population value A.

18. Answer: (C) 24
First consider only positive integers. The ordered pairs that satisfy the condition $|x| + |y| < 5$ are (1,1), (1,2), (1,3), (2,1), (2,2) and (3,1). Including negative integers, it is clear that for each of these 6 ordered pairs, there are 4 possible combinations of positive and negative numbers that also satisfy the condition. For instance (1,1) corresponds to (1,1), (-1,1), (1,-1) and (-1,-1). Therefore, the total number of ordered pairs that satisfy the given condition is 6 x 4 = 24.

19. Answer: (C) 44
Since 16 is the median, it must be the middle number in the sequence. If the last number in the sequence x is the highest possible number, the other 3 numbers must have the lowest possible values. So the sequence must look like this: 1, 2, 16, 17, x.

The mean of these 5 numbers is also 16. So

$$\frac{1+2+16+17+x}{5} = 16; \Rightarrow \frac{36+x}{5} = 16; \Rightarrow 36+x = 80; \Rightarrow x = 44.$$

20. Answer: (E) $224 + 48\pi$ m^2
The following areas are covered in paint:
- The lateral surface of the box = $2(16 \times 2 + 8 \times 2) = 96$ m^2
- The top surface of the box not covered by the cylinders = $16 \times 8 - 2\pi(1.5)^2$ m^2
- The lateral surface of the two cylinders = $2 \times (2\pi \times 1.5) \times 8 = 48\pi$ m^2
- The top surface of the two cylinders = $2\pi(1.5)^2$ m^2

Adding them all together we get $96 + 128 - 2\pi(1.5)^2 + 48\pi + 2\pi(1.5)^2$ m^2 = $224 + 48\pi$ m^2

SECTION 4 (CRITICAL READING)

SENTENCE COMPLETION

1. Answer: (A) excessive
In the second independent clause in this sentence, Lisa's use of the word "really" is elaborated upon. From this second independent clause we can see that Lisa overused the word "really." She used it too much because "she used it to describe every noun she used." The definition of the word "excessive" is to do something beyond normal limits, so answer (A) fits by definition.

2. Answer: (B) powerlessness
The second part of the sentence, which is an independent clause, explains more about the "woman" referred to in the first part of the sentence. She is the heroine of the book and she has only two choices to survive economically. This means she was powerless. She was completely dependent upon a man wanting her as a wife or a lover or she would not survive.

3. Answer: (D) In contrast to
The words "unhappy" and "happy" in the sentence are especially important in establishing the answer to this question. An unhappy couple and a happy couple clearly are (D) in contrast. Contrast means putting things that are very different, even opposites, next to one another in order to make a vivid comparison. The fact that one couple is having an affair and one couple is in a marriage also draws a contrast between the couples' situations.

4. Answer: (E) effect ... affected
The frequently confused and misused words of "effect" and "affect" are the subject of this question. An "effect" is the result brought about by some event or cause. However, when a person is under an effect, he or she is "affected." In this sentence, the first event or cause is Sarah's talk with her counselor; this has the "effect" of renewing a sense of vitality in her. Sarah was under the effect of her mother's long illness; she was "affected" by it.

5. Answer: (E) contrived ... labyrinthine
The word needed for the first blank refers to the way the chute is made, so answer (A) "designed", answer (B) "executed", and (E) "contrived" are all possibilities. However, the companion word for answer (A), which is "simple," does not match in meaning the fact that the chute was "elaborately" made. Similarly, the companion word for answer (B), which is "straight," does not match in meaning the fact that the chute was "elaborately" made. Only the combination of answer (E), "contrived" and "labyrinthine," which means complex, many-layered, and with many passages, matches the need for words that explain how "elaborately" the child's toy was designed.

READING BASED QUESTIONS

6. Answer: (A) enthusiastic and intrigued
The fact that Alexis de Tocqueville and Gustave de Beaumont traveled to America to study its institutions indicates a certain amount of intrigue with the system of democracy in the relatively young nation. The word "passion" indicates "enthusiasm" and a strong desire to understand which denotes being "intrigued". Using the words "excited together" and "passionate" as well as noting that "it is impossible to prevent men from assembling together" and the last words in the passage "the people wield immense influence" through these assemblies also conveys a certain amount of enthusiasm and intrigue.

The SAT Advantage

7. Answer: (E) grew and thrived
The word "flourish" means to grow a great deal and to do well. The two young Frenchmen would not have traveled to the United States to see an institution such as democracy if it was not doing well and commanding attention and admiration from the world. The passage says they wanted to "discover how democracy worked," which implies that democracy was known to be working well or flourishing.

8. Answer: (B) factual and impartial
The passage provides many facts. It gives the birth and death dates of Dr. Bates as well as his full name and educational background. The fact that his methods are not endorsed by various associations related to eye health care is also noted in an impartial way. It is also noted that there is anecdotal evidence from patients of Dr. Bates that his methods worked, so there is a certain degree of impartiality in this recognition. The opinion of Dr. Bates about eyeglasses and eye exercises is stated factually, without comment. Because of the facts presented and because the passage does not state one way or the other whether the author believes in the Bates Method or not, the tone may be said to be factual and impartial.

9. Answer: (C) evidence from the words and accounts of patients
An "anecdote" is a little story, or a short account of an experience. The article specifically states that "anecdotal evidence" from some of his patients" is all we have to go on as to the efficacy of the Bates Method, so the words "of patients" match closely the words in Answer (C). The statements "The effectiveness of Dr. Bates's eye exercises is unknown" and it is "a scientifically unproven alternative therapy" that is "not endorsed" by any eye health association or community" show that the Answers (B), (D), and (E) are not accurate as they involve scientific proof. There is no mention in the passage about "diaries," so Answer (A) also is wrong.

10. Answer: (D) either in a clearly spoken way or else by example
"Explicit" means that something is clearly outlined, spoken out about, or spelled out. "Implicitly" means that something is unexpressed in words but is understood anyway. The wording of the next sentence helps to show that some things are taught by example (implicitly) rather than expressed clearly in words (explicitly) when it says that a teacher, by giving a pencil to each child, is demonstrating a value by example even if the teacher has not taught the value directly with words.

11. Answer: (B) outside of the person
The use of the word "without" and the word "but" transitioning from one thought to another, shows that "without" is most likely being used in contrast to "within." Since "within" is referring to "within the human person" in the sentence, "without" is most likely referring to "without the human being" or (B) outside of the person; that is, through instruction from people and institutions outside of the person, as the first paragraph of the passage indicates ethical values are transmitted.

12. Answer: (A) to establish the credibility of the ideas presented
Experts, authors, and famous people are often cited to give an argument or idea more credibility. James Q. Wilson, the text tells us, was a "political scientist" whose "observations" of society led him to believe in a moral sense. Citing a political scientist who has observed and commented on society gives credibility to the ideas of the rest of the paragraph which deal with an inner sense of right and wrong.

13. Answer: (A) a positive view
The language about a "moral sense" that "arises from within" indicates a positive view of human nature. This positive view is further explained when the author talks about "the moral sense" and how it "holds most people back" from criminality, even when they will not get caught. The author also says that, "People's basic decency is what keeps a society safe and functioning" and expresses a positive view of human nature in that people are said to have "basic decency."

14. Answer: (B) conundrums
The student will most likely need to use process of elimination to arrive at this answer choice. The word "dilemmas" means a situation in which a person is facing a difficult choice. The definition of the word rules out answer (A) "solutions", because a solution does not call for people to make decisions. "Compunctions" (C) happen after a fact, when a person feels a twinge of guilt or conscience over something enacted. Answer (D) "crises" is too strong a word for the kinds of situations people face "in everyday life." Answer (E) "anticipations" are something people would look forward to, and many situations that call for ethical decision-making are not anticipated; they simply "come up in everyday life."

15. Answer: (E) discover or make certain
The infinitive form "to ascertain" means that the meaning of the phrase should also be in the infinitive form: "to (do something)" which calls for a verb. Since answers (B), (C), and (D) are nouns, those answers are incorrect. "To ascribe" (A) means to attribute to, so by definition it is incorrect even though it is an infinitive. "To discover" or "to make certain" fits in the context of the sentence, makes sense by definition and form, and is the correct answer.

16. Answer: (B) the moral sense or conscience
The words "feel inside" point to an inner sense of right and wrong. The author talks about "the human conscience" arising "naturally from within." He or she also speaks of a "moral sense" that "arises from within." Therefore, "the moral sense of conscience" (B) is the most appropriate answer for elements that were mentioned earlier in the passage, because these words relate to how a person feels inside.

17. Answer: (B) The Golden Rule
Both the topic sentence of the paragraph and the last sentence of the paragraph refer to The Golden Rule as "the simplest of ethical tests" and "a foundational ethical test for any action," respectively. Since the language "ethical rule of thumb" is sandwiched between these two references to the effectiveness of The Golden Rule as a measure of moral actions, "ethical rule of thumb" may be said most likely to refer to The Golden Rule.

18. Answer: (C) professional ethical oaths
The topic sentence of the paragraph begins by talking about how "professions" have "ethical oaths." That is a strong indicator that the subject of these lines is answer (C), professional ethical oaths. There is nothing in these lines that indicates anything about the efficacy of oath-taking (A), professionalism itself plus ethics (B), whether professional oaths are ethical (D), or ethicists' opinions of oaths in the professions (E). After the topic sentence, the paragraph goes on to name the ethical oaths professionals such as "physicians," "lawyers," CPAs, "journalists", and potential business people take, making it clear that this paragraph is about (C) professional ethical oaths.

19. Answer: (C) synonyms
Although "confirm" and "corroborate" share consonants and might be said to have consonance, the form "consonantly" is an adverb and the way question 19 is worded, it calls for a noun as an

answer. This makes answer (D) inaccurate. The same is true for answer (E) assonantly. Although the words do repeat vowel sounds and might be said to be examples of assonance, they are not examples of "assonantly," an adverb. "Antonyms" (A) is inaccurate, as the words are close in meaning and antonyms are opposite in meaning. Answer (B) dissonance is also inaccurate because the words are not in disharmony and do not sound wrong together. The words "confirm" and "corroborate" are close in meaning, making them synonyms.

20. Answer: (A) sketch some highlights of Liszt's youth
These lines give a brief sketch of a few major points of Liszt's life, including his birth and death dates, his nationality, his father's involvement with music, Liszt's early attraction to and talent for music, and his acquaintance with Beethoven, as well as his apprenticeship under one of Beethoven's students. These are some very brief outlines of Liszt's youth, so they may qualify as sketching some highlights of that time period.

21. Answer: (C) someone who is extraordinarily skilled
"Virtuoso" is related to the word "virtuous," but the meanings are different. A virtuoso has great strength or skills in a certain area, usually in a performance area. A good person who has many virtues has great character strength and is virtuous. Therefore, answer (C) is more accurate than answer (A). Since the passage says Liszt lived in the nineteenth century, the idea of "virtual reality" as in (B) could not be said to apply to him. Answers (D) and (E) would indicate someone who has considerable talent on the piano, but they would not necessarily be "virtuosos." The use of the word "virtuoso" is associated in the passage with Liszt's "sensational," that is extraordinary, concerts, so (C) someone who is extraordinarily skilled is the best answer.

22. Answer: (E) synonymously
Since "virtuosity" is shown to mean extraordinary skill, and "versatility" has as its meaning "able to turn in many directions smoothly and perform a variety of actions well," the two words are almost synonymous.

23. Answer: (C) political, sexual, professional
The author uses the language "questionable political associations" to explain one of the controversies in Liszt's life. His "live-in relationship" with a sponsor is mentioned as well, which may be interpreted as a sexual controversy. It is noted that some contemporaries hold a dim view of Liszt's performances, which would be a professional controversy as it involved members of Liszt's profession.

24. Answer: (B) extraordinary in scope and quality
The word "prolific" implies that Liszt produced a great deal of work, so a "prodigious" body of work likely means one that was extraordinary in scope. However, the words "passion and originality" show that his works also had quality. The fact that his prodigious body of works "establishes him as one of the world's great classical composers" shows that Liszt's work was extraordinary in scope and quality, answer (B).

The SAT Advantage

SECTION 5 (MATHEMATICS)

MULTIPLE CHOICE

1. Answer: (A) 240

Since the 210 square meter garden has been divided into plots of area $\frac{7}{8}$ square meter each, the number of plots is 210 divided by $\frac{7}{8}$. To divide by $\frac{7}{8}$, flip the fraction to $\frac{8}{7}$ and multiply. $210 \times \frac{8}{7} = 240$. So there are 240 plots.

2. Answer: (B) Octagon

A regular polygon is a figure with equal sides and equal angles. Regardless of the number of sides in a regular polygon, the sum of the exterior angles is always 360°. To find the number of sides in a regular polygon with an exterior angle that measures 45°, divide 360 by 45:

$360 \div 45 = 8$

An eight-sided regular polygon is called an octagon.

3. Answer: (C)

The f(x), called "the function of x", is a special relation of numbers that allow for only one input per output. In the standard coordinate plane (x,y), x is considered the input and y the output.

An easy way to discern if a graph is of a function is to use the vertical line test. Pass several vertical lines through a graph; if each vertical line intersects the graph at only one point, then the graph is of a function. If a vertical line intersects the graph at more than one point, the graph is not of a function.

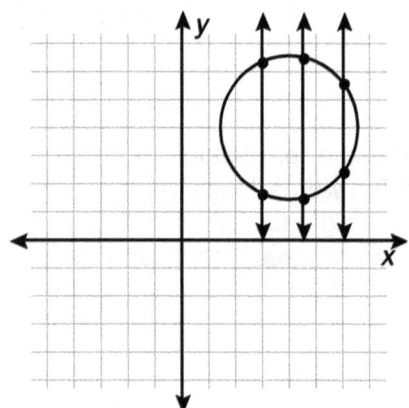

Vertical lines intersect the circle at more than one point so it cannot be the graph of a function.

146   SAT Practice Test 1 Answer Rationales

4. Answer: (A) (-8,-3)

Rectangles are quadrilaterals that have opposite sides congruent and parallel and have four right angles. Graph the three known vertices to find the coordinates of the missing vertex.

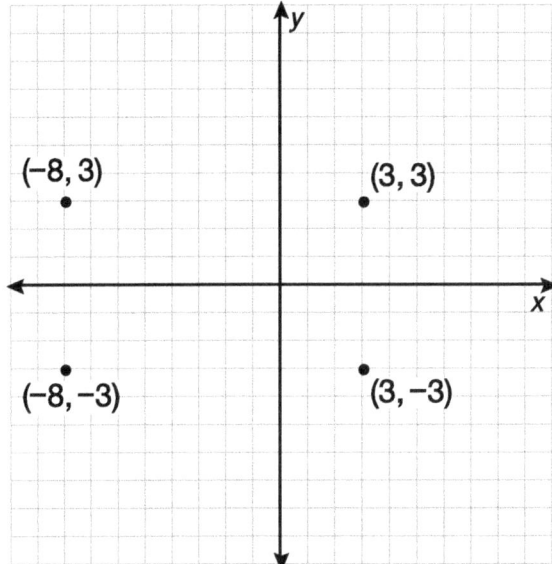

By inspection, we find the length of the rectangle, from (-8,3) to (3,3) is 11 units. Thus, the coordinates of a point that is 11 units away from (3,-3) is (-8,-3). Alternatively, we see the distance from (3,3) to (3,-3) is 6 units. Therefore, the width of the rectangle is 6 units. Count down 6 units from (-8,3) to arrive again at the coordinates (-8,-3).

5. Answer: (E) $\frac{1}{3}a^{b-1} - \frac{4^{3b}a^{6b-1}}{9}$

$$\frac{3a^b - (4a^2)^{3b}}{9a} = \frac{3a^b - 4^{3b}a^{6b}}{9a} = \frac{3a^b}{9a} - \frac{4^{3b}a^{6b}}{9a} = \frac{1}{3}a^{b-1} - \frac{4^{3b}a^{6b-1}}{9}$$

6. Answer: (C) $|10x - 5| < 13$

$|10x - 5| < 13$ implies $10x - 5 < 13$ and $10x - 5 > -13$.

So $10x < 18$ and $10x > -8$ or $x < \frac{18}{10}$ and $x > -\frac{8}{10}$.

This is equivalent to $-\frac{4}{5} < x < \frac{9}{5}$.

7. Answer: (A) 2

Let a leg of the 45°-45°-90° triangle be a. The hypotenuse of the triangle = $\sqrt{2}\,a$ and the area of the triangle = $\frac{1}{2}a^2$.

Let the side of the square be s. The area of the square = s^2.

Setting the two areas equal to each other we get $\frac{1}{2}a^2 = s^2$; $\Rightarrow a^2 = 2s^2$; $a = \sqrt{2}s$.

The ratio of the hypotenuse of the triangle to the side of the square = $\frac{\sqrt{2}a}{s} = \frac{\sqrt{2}(\sqrt{2}s)}{s} = \frac{2s}{s} = 2$.

8. Answer: (C) III only

The vertex of the V graph represented by $y = |x - p| + m$ is at (p, m). This is because the lowest value of y occurs when $x = p$ and $x - p = 0$. The value of y at this x point is m.

Since both p and m are positive, the vertex of the V graph must be in the first quadrant. Only graph III satisfies this condition.

STUDENT-PRODUCED RESPONSE

9. Answer: 6

Set up the proportion $\frac{1}{24} = \frac{x}{12}$. To solve for x, multiply both sides of the equation by 24 to get 1 = 2x. So $x = \frac{1}{2}$ ft = 6 inches.

10. Answer: 7

Let x = the unknown number to be added to the numerator and denominator of the fraction.

$$\frac{11+x}{17+x} = \frac{3}{4}$$

Cross-multiply the fractions and set the products equal to one another.

$3(17 + x) = 4(11 + x)$

$51 + 3x = 44 + 4x$

$7 = x$

The SAT Advantage

To check, replace x with 7 in the equation.

$$\frac{11+7}{17+7} = \frac{18}{24} = \frac{3}{4}$$

11. Answer: 154
Two angles are supplementary if their sum is 180°. Two angles are complementary if their sum is 90°. Find the complement of an angle measuring 64° by subtracting 64 from 90.

90 – 64 = 26

Find the supplement of an angle measuring 26° by subtracting 26 from 180.

180 – 26 = 154

12. Answer: 6
One revolution of each wheel is equivalent to the circumference of each circle. Find the circumference of each circle by using the formula Circumference = diameter x π. (π is approximately equal to 3.14).

Find the circumference of the larger circle.

30 x 3.14 = 94.2

Multiply 94.2 by 4 to find the total inches the tire traveled in 4 revolutions.

4 x 94.2 = 376.8

Divide 376.8 by 12 to find the number of feet in 376.8 inches.

$$376.8 \div 12 = 31.4 \approx 31$$

Multiply 24 by 3.14 to find the circumference of the tire with the 24 inch diameter.

24 x 3.14 = 75.36

Multiply 75.36 by 4 to find the total inches the tire traveled in 4 revolutions.

75.36 x 4 = 301.44

Divide 301.44 by 12 to find the number of feet in 301.44 inches.

$$301.44 \div 12 = 25.12 \approx 25$$

Subtract 25.12 feet from 31.4 feet to find out how much farther the larger tire traveled compared to the smaller tire.

31.4 – 25.12 = 6.12 ft

Note that the question asks for the answer to the nearest foot. So be sure to grid in 6 and not 6.12.

13. Answer: 48

Let x = the number of students originally enrolled in the class. Those who dropped the class after the first test were one-half of x, or $\frac{1}{2}x$. If one-half of the class dropped the class at this point, then $\frac{1}{2}x$ went on take the second test.

$$x - \frac{1}{2}x = \frac{1}{2}x$$

Of the number of students who took the second test, one-third of that number dropped the class after the second exam.

$$\frac{1}{2}x - (\frac{1}{3})(\frac{1}{2})x = \frac{1}{2}x - \frac{1}{6}x = \frac{1}{3}x$$

After two exams, 16 students remained in the class. Set 16 equal to $\frac{1}{3}x$ to find how many students were originally enrolled in the class.

$$\frac{1}{3}x = 16$$
$$(3)(\frac{1}{3})x = (3)(16)$$
$$x = 48$$

14. Answer: 4

Since the remainder is 3, x must be larger than 3 and also a factor of 55 − 3 = 52. Factors of 52 that are larger than 3 are 4, 13, 26, and 52. Hence the smallest possible value of x is 4.

15. Answer: 60

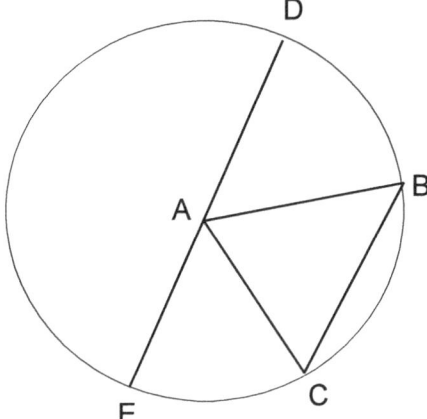

Since the circle is centered at A, AD is a radius of the circle. BC = AD is also equal to the radius of the circle. AC and AB are both radii of the circle. Hence ABC is an equilateral triangle and each of its angles is equal to 60°.

16. Answer: $\frac{20}{7}$

Let Paul and Mina meet after t hours. Paul walked 4t miles and Mina walked 3t miles. Since the distance between the two towns is 5 miles, 4t + 3t = 5; 7t = 5; t = $\frac{5}{7}$ hr. So the distance Paul walks = 4t = 4 x $\frac{5}{7}$ = $\frac{20}{7}$ miles.

17. Answer: 6

We first find out how many ways the person can walk from A to B and then how many ways they can walk from B to C. The total number of ways from A to C through B will be the product of both these numbers.

To go from A to B, the person must walk one block north and one block east. This can be done in two ways; first north then east (NE) or first east then north (EN).

To go from B to C, the person must go two blocks east and one block north. This can be done in three ways: NEE, ENE and EEN.

Hence the total number of routes from A to C through B = 2 x 3 = 6.

18. Answer: 0

The powers of 6 are: $6^1 = 6, 6^2 = 36, 6^3 = 216, ...$

The powers of 4 are: $4^1 = 4, 4^2 = 16, 4^3 = 64, ...$

All the powers of 6 end in the units digit 6. The odd powers of 4 end in the units digit 4 and then even powers of 4 end in the units digit 6.

So 6^{23} ends in 6 and 4^{23} ends in 4. Hence the sum of the two numbers ends in the units digit 0 since 6 + 4 = 10.

SECTION 6 (WRITING)

IMPROVING SENTENCES

1. Answer: (B) although stores with many well-paid employees are often more profitable
The original sentence incorrectly joins two independent clauses, using only a comma between them. Choice (B) correctly joins the two clauses, using the conjunction *although* to show the relationship between the ideas in the two clauses. Choice (C) is incorrect because it does not include a conjunction and because it introduces an incorrect past-tense verb. Choice (D) includes a conjunction but is too wordy. Choice (E) adds the conjunction *however*, which should be preceded by a semicolon, rather than the comma in the original sentence.

2. Answer: (D) that confront whoever
The clause *whomever wants to succeed* is the object of the verb *confronts*. However, the word *whomever* is actually the subject of the verb *wants* in the clause, so it should be in the subjective case: *whoever*. That means you can automatically eliminate choices (A), (B), and (C). Choice (E) uses a pronoun in the correct case, but the subject *those* would require the plural verb *want*, rather than the singular verb *wants* in the existing sentence.

3. Answer: (E) meet all the criteria
The original sentence is actually a fragment because the word *that* turns it into a dependent clause lacking a main verb. Choices (B), (C), and (D) also create fragments, and choice (D) introduces the incorrect plural form *criterias* as well.

4. Answer: (D) where it has stashed the seeds
To show the correct sequence of events, choice (D) uses the present-perfect tense verb *has stashed*. The stashing occurred before the forgetting, so choice (A) is incorrect. Choice (B) uses the wrong verb tense and also introduces the plural pronoun *they* to refer to the singular noun *jay*. Choices (C) and (E) use the wrong verb tense and introduce the passive voice, which is not appropriate here.

5. Answer: (C) Describing a discovery made by treasure hunters using state-of-the-art technology
The introductory phrase must describe the nearest noun, *reporter*. Since the reporter was not discovered by the treasure hunters, choices (A), (B), (D), and (E) are incorrect. Only the phrase in choice (C) can describe the reporter.

6. Answer: (A) only under conditions of unfettered competition
The word *only* logically explains the relationship between markets and competition. The connecting words *unless*, *except*, and *but also* in choices (B), (C), and (E) are not logical. Choice (D) uses the word *only* in a way that changes the meaning of the sentence.

7. Answer: (B) objected to the President's plan to protect consumers from high interest rates
Choice (B) correctly uses the preposition *to*, rather than *with*, after the verb *objected*. Choices (D) and (E) also include the preposition *to*, but using either *objecting* or *who objected* turns the sentence into a fragment that lacks a main verb.

8. Answer: (E) is like entering a new world that is both exotic and familiar
Two things that are being compared should have the same grammatical structure: You can logically compare *viewing* and *entering*. Including the word *when* is always incorrect in this kind of comparison, so choice (A) is incorrect. Choice (B) is incorrect because *when you enter* is not in the same grammatical form as *viewing*. Choice (C) includes the grammatical form *entering*, but adds the redundant phrase *the experience of*, which ruins the parallel structure of the comparison. Choice (D) is incorrect because it includes the incorrect combination *like when*, does not use parallel structure, and slightly changes the meaning of the sentence. Choice (E) correctly expresses the comparison in a simple, direct way.

9. Answer: (A) rafted on the Taylor River, which
The original sentence correctly uses the parallel past-tense verbs *hiked* and *rafted* to clearly express two actions that occurred during the same time period. Choice (B) is incorrect because the verb form *rafting* does not match the verb form *hiked*. Choice (C) creates a run-on, contains a verb form that does not match *hiked*, and introduces the wordy, illogical phrase *being as it*. Choices (D) and (E) use verb forms that do not match the past-tense verb *hiked*, and choice (D) also uses the word *that*, which creates an incorrect essential clause.

10. Answer: (B) because Americans were eager to show they could compete with the Soviet Union during the Cold War
Choice (A) uses the incorrect form *ability of competing*, rather than *ability to compete*. It also adds the unnecessary words *owing to*, *eagerness of*, and *wanting to*. Choice (C) uses the wordy and unidiomatic phrase *on account of*, rather than the simple, clear word *because*. Choices (D) and (E) take many more words to express an idea that is more simply and clearly stated in choice (B).

11. Answer: (B) classical and operant conditioning; classical replaces a natural stimulus with a learned one, while operant uses the principle of reward and punishment
Choices (A), (C), (D), and (E) are long and confusing, adding lots of extra words that confuse the definitions, rather than clarify them.

IDENTIFYING SENTENCE ERRORS

12. Answer: (B) often have
The subject of the sentence is the singular word *attempt*, which requires the singular verb *has*, rather than *have*.

13. Answer: (C) would have to think
The sentence uses the wrong form of the conditional mood. The verb should be *would have to have thought*.

14. Answer: (E) No error
The original sentence is correct. It uses the correct forms of nouns, pronouns, and verbs.

15. Answer: (C) were
The subject of the sentence is the gerund *transporting*, which is singular and requires the singular verb *was*.

16. Answer: (C) illusions to
This sentence incorrectly uses the word *illusions*, meaning "deceptive appearances," instead of the correct word, *allusions*, meaning "indirect references."

17. Answer: (A) were locked
The subject of the sentence is *Every one*, which is singular and requires the singular verb *was*.

18. Answer: (E) No error
The original sentence is correct. It uses a correct sequence of verb tenses and also uses the connecting word *where* correctly to introduce a descriptive clause.

19. Answer: (B) have
The subject of the sentence is *popularity*, which is singular and requires the singular verb *has*. The phrase beginning with *as well as* is parenthetical and does not give the sentence a compound subject.

20. Answer: (C) which were present
The pronoun *which* should never be used in a clause that describes people. The correct pronoun is *who*.

21. Answer: (B) one's body
Since the subject in the introductory clause is *you*, the pronoun in the subject of the sentence should also be *you*, rather than the third-person pronoun *one*.

22. Answer: (A) that contain
The word *precipitation* is singular, so the descriptive clause *that contain* should use the singular verb *contains*.

23. Answer: (D) to eat a dish
Items in a series should all have the same grammatical structure. To match the gerund phrases *skiing with torches* and *honoring ancestors*, the final phrase should be *eating a dish of black-eyed peas*.

24. Answer: (D) as well
Since the sentence already contains the paired conjunctions *not only…but also*, the phrase *as well* is redundant.

25. Answer: (A) who's
The word *who's* is a contraction meaning "who is." The correct possessive form needed here is *whose*.

26. Answer: (C) more colorfully
The modifier here describes the noun *foliage*. The adjective form *more colorful* would be correct.

27. Answer: (C) afflicted upon
The verb *afflicted* is most often used in a passive form: Someone is *afflicted* with a disease. The correct word in the context of the sentence is *inflicted*. Someone *inflicts* pain or suffering upon other people.

28. Answer: (B) consumes
The word *larvae*, a synonym for *caterpillars*, is plural. It requires the plural verb *consume*.

29. Answer: (B) was
The word *contents* is plural and requires the plural verb *were*.

IMPROVING PARAGRAPHS

30. Answer: (B) People's fascination with cats is universal.
Answers (A), (C), and (D) offer the phrases "assault of time," "examination of time," and "aura of time," respectively. None of these phrases are exact in meaning and present more confusion than clarity. Answer (E) changes the meaning of the sentence and adds in more ideas than are present in sentence 1. Sentence 2 would then become redundant. Sentence 1 also could not be the topic sentence of the paragraph if (E) were the answer, as the paragraph covers much more ground than people's choice of cats as pets. Answer (B) is simple and clear. The meaning of the word "universal" is something that applies to people transcendent of places, times, and cultures, which is the point of the sentence in the context of the paragraph. Language is part of culture, and "foibles" and "proclivities" are small particularities that would be encompassed by something universal as well.

31. Answer: (E) grateful
Since the tone of the paragraph and sentence is an upbeat one, there is nothing (A) abominable, (C) malevolent or (D) malicious going on, so those answers may be eliminated. Since the sentence continues to refer to an African folk tale, the word "modern" (B) does not indicate that sentence 6 is a progression from sentence 5; in fact, the word "modern" would disrupt the flow of thought. However, using "grateful" as an adjective in front of the word "man" would connect the two sentences, 5 and 6, and also show progression. In sentence 5 the cat was the "only one to help the first man build his house," so a "grateful man" in sentence 6 would be very likely, based on the action in sentence 5, to give the cat a "timeless reward."

32. Answer: (C) To insert a verb
Sentence 11 is an incomplete sentence because it lacks a verb. The addition of a verb would make it a complete sentence. This would make the sentence: Garfield, a cartoon cat, *is* also a big, orange tabby.

33. Answer: (C) Sentence 12
The paragraph is about the use of cats in advertising and cartoons, as introduced in the topic sentence, sentence 7. Sentences 8, 10, 13, and 14 discuss the characteristics of a cat used in commercials and a cartoon character cat. Sentence 12, though, goes off on another subject, which is about a breed of cat and its popularity with cat owners. Although it is related to the other sentences in that the cat in commercials and the cartoon cat are large orange cats or tabbies, this factual sentence about the breed does not fit in with the flow of the paragraph and should be removed.

34. Answer: (A) The cat food being advertised, however, always enticed Morris.
The original sentence 9 is in the passive voice; that is, the subject of the sentence (Morris) is being acted upon rather than doing the acting. By changing the subject of the sentence to "the cat food," Morris is still being acted upon, but the sentence is now in the active voice, where the subject is doing the acting. Writing in the active voice is almost always considered better writing.

35. Answer: (B) More details about cats in ancient and folk history
The second paragraph of the existing essay develops ideas introduced in the first paragraph, but it does not develop all of the ideas introduced there. The second paragraph develops the images of cats in modern societies via advertising and cartoons in more detail and gives examples. Logically, then, the third paragraph would develop the ideas in the rest of the first paragraph by providing more details and examples about cats in ancient and folk history. This would possibly include more information from ancient Egypt and African folk tales, but it would include geographical details about Egypt and Africa (A), encyclopedia information about cats (C), statistics on cat ownership in modern-day Egypt and Africa (D) or traditional ways to reward well-behaving cats (E).

SECTION 7 (CRITICAL READING)

SENTENCE COMPLETION

1. Answer: (C) taut
"Taut" (C) means firm and strong without looseness or excess. A taut structure is one that is tight and economical, without any unnecessary details. The clause of the sentence, starting with the word "which" indicates that in his prose, Hemingway used few words yet still conveyed strong meaning. "Voluminous" (A) and "verbose" (B) mean that there was excess; "pedantic" (D) means a usual, stodgy style; and "didactic" (E) means teaching or instructing directly. None of the meanings other than "taut" would be consistent with prose that requires the reader's mind to fill in the blanks through implied meaning.

2. Answer: (D) resurgence
The first phrase in the sentence "After dropping in the polls" implies that the candidate was once high in the polls but then experienced a lower period. Then the candidate seems to come back to a position of popularity in the polls because of "several stellar performances." The movement of the candidate in the sentence is from a higher place to a lower place and then back up to a higher place. The sentence is structured such that a noun, modified by "of popularity" must be placed in the blank. "Bursting" (C) is not a noun. The other choices are all nouns, but "dearth" (A), "cessation" (B), and "ebb" (E) all mean low points or even stoppage. "Resurgence" (D), on the other hand, means a second wave, swell, or rising once again. "Re" usually means to do something once more or again, so if the candidate is rising once again in the polls, he or she is experiencing (D) resurgence.

3. Answer: (A) evolutionary ... revolutionary
The use of the word "reform" to describe the administration means that changes were coming about; things were being "re-formed." The use of the word "slow" in the sentence means that the changes were not coming all at once. "Evolutionary rather than revolutionary" (A) fits both the meaning of the sentence and the sentence structure. The words chosen must be adjectives describing the administration, and all of the other word choices are nouns, not adjectives, and cannot be used to describe "administration."

4. Answer: (D) disclaimer
A disclaimer is a formal denial of any legal responsibility for the results of using, in this instance, a book for treatment rather than seeking treatment with a licensed practitioner. Most medical books begin with a disclaimer. An "alternative" medical book would have an even stronger disclaimer than a traditional medical book because alternative medicine is less trusted; therefore, "disclaimer" (D) goes with the word "strong." A book could not begin with an "extension" (B) as an extension makes something longer than it already is; it does not begin something. A "distender" (A) does not make sense either, as a book does not distend anything. "Crustacean" (C), of course, is a kind of animal, and a "proponent" (E) is an advocate. While a book could begin with a strong "proponent" advocating something, "proponent" would need further modification to explain what the proponent was advocating.

5. Answer: (C) gregarious
The linking word "although" suggests the idea expressed in each clause of the sentence will be different. "Aloof" means standoffish or reserved, so we need a word that means sociable or approachable. "Gregarious" (C) means sociable, so it is the best selection. Both (E) "laconic"

and (A) "unsociable" are near synonyms for aloof and (B) "pretentious" and (D) "impartial" are not related to the meaning of the sentence.

6. Answer: (A) unethical according to … accountancy
In this sentence, a bookkeeper is apparently being asked by a co-worker to change recorded figures in a business. The bookkeeper refuses and explains why he or she cannot do what he or she considers a negative or wrongful thing. In answers (D) and (E), "unimpeachable" and "impeccable" mean positive things: unimpeachable means something is above legal or moral question; and impeccable means something is flawless, so neither (D) nor (E) can be the answer. Answer (B) which includes the word "wrong" and answer (A) which includes the word "unethical" are the best candidates. Since the sentence is about bookkeeping, the second word would likely relate to accounting or accountancy. When we plug in answer (B) it does not make the best sense. "Wrong by the rules of any standards" is repetitious: "rules" and "standards" are the same thing, and the answer does not refer to accounting to accountancy. Answer (A) is the best answer.

READING BASED QUESTIONS

7. Answer: (B) MADD is an important and effective group that has had a huge impact on society's awareness of the dangers of drunk driving
Passage 1 says "Mothers Against Drunk Driving (MADD) is an effective and important organization," which shows the author's position on that point. This is the same wording as in answer (B): describing MADD as "an important and effective group." Passage 2 says, "MADD is one of the most powerful and effective grassroots movements in history," showing that the authors agree on this point. Passage 1 says that MADD has "helped society see the human impact of drunk driving." This shows that the author of Passage 1 believes MADD has impacted "society's awareness of the dangers of drunk driving," which is the phrasing of answer (B). Passage 2 affirms that the author considers MADD to have had a "huge impact on society's awareness", stating that "MADD estimates that it has saved roughly 300,000 lives by its activism to promote awareness and pass legislation that ensure that drunk driving is strictly limited by law." Both authors agree about MADD's importance, effectiveness, and social impact (B).

8. Answer: (B) allowing for release of and relief from negative emotions
The definition of "cathartic" is to experience the purge, release, or elimination of emotional tension and blockage. Passage 1 explains more about the catharsis mentioned: "VIPs help to heal the psychological and emotional wounds of the physical consequences to one's self or to one's loved ones." Therefore, VIPs being "cathartic for people living with the impact of car crashes due to someone else's choice to drink and drive" most likely means that the people experience "release and relief from negative emotions" as in answer (B).

9. Answer: (A) establish the efficacy of MADD
Since the rest of Passage 2 is critical of the use of Victim Impact Panels as an attempt to reduce drunk driving (although it is not critical of the use of the Panels for other purposes), the author most likely uses these introductory lines to establish MADD's considerable efficacy in other areas, as in answer (A). Since Passage 2 acknowledges that MADD has been effective in passing legislation, answer (B) is wrong. Passage 2 cites studies that show that VIPs are not effective deterrents to drunk driving, so answers (C) and (E) are wrong. Passage 1 does not have a negative view of MADD, so answer (D) is also wrong. By reasoning and by process of elimination, answer (A) is correct.

10. Answer: (B) demonstrate that this particular public role of victims of alcohol-related car crashes has been effective
The key to this answer is that it must come from the perspective of the author of Passage 2. The author of Passage 2 believes that MADD is an effective organization. The author states in Passage 2, "Many of us may owe our lives to MADD without knowing it. MADD is one of the most powerful and effective grassroots movements in history." These lines show that the author of Passage 2 believes in MADD's effectiveness. However, the author of Passage 2 does not feel that VIPs are effective in reducing drunk driving and mentions studies to support this position in: "Most studies done on the subject show that VIPs have little effect on whether a drunk driver chooses to drive while under the influence again or not." However, since the power of MADD's program is that it helps society see the human costs of drunk driving, the author of Passage 2 would likely see these lines as demonstrating how effective this particular public role of victims of alcohol-related car crashes has been, answer (B).

11. Answer: (D) support and praise for MADD's overall effectiveness
Passage 1 shows support and praise for MADD's overall effectiveness (D): "Mothers Against Drunk Driving (MADD) is an effective and important organization" and "MADD heightened the nation's awareness about drunk driving and worked for the passage of laws that would protect everyone." Passage 2 shows support and praise for MADD's overall effectiveness (D) in the lines which state statistics about MADD's accomplishments and in statements such as, "Many of us may owe our lives to MADD without knowing it. MADD is one of the most powerful and effective grassroots movements in history." Therefore, we can say that support and praise for MADD's overall effectiveness can be found in both passages, answer (D).

12. Answer: (E) Passage 1 and Passage 2 both support MADD but disagree as to the efficacy of VIPs in reducing drunk driving recidivism
Both Passage 1 and Passage 2 show support for MADD. Passage 2 does not "have grave misgivings" about MADD as in answer (B) nor does Passage 2 "decry" MADD as in answer (D), so those answers can be eliminated. Answer (C) accurately shows that Passage 1 exhibits empathy for victims of alcohol-related car crashes whereas Passage 2 exhibits empathy for alcoholics; however, the question calls for the *best description* of the relationship. As was said above, both Passages support MADD. However, Passage 1 asserts that VIPs are effective in reducing drunk driving recidivism: "it is likely that they reduce drunk driver recidivism," but Passage 2 asserts that "Most studies done on the subject show that VIPs have little effect on whether a drunk driver chooses to drive while under the influence again or not," showing that answer (E) best describes the relationship between the two passages.

13. Answer: (C) show the grassroots origins of Mothers Against Drunk Driving
Statements such as that MADD is "driven by the passion of its volunteers," and "MADD was founded by a mother" show the grassroots origins of Mothers Against Drunk Driving, answer (C). Passage 1 says of the founder of MADD that "she had no political or legislative experience," which shows MADD was a grassroots effort. The author also tells of how MADD grew through "victims left behind by drunk driving—car crash victims and those who love them" who "at last had a forum." He or she also speaks of mothers and survivors of car wrecks who "helped society see the human impact of drunk driving. Through giving car-crash victims faces and voices, MADD heightened the nation's awareness about drunk driving." These lines show that ordinary people affected by someone else's drunk driving came forward in a grassroots effort to increase national awareness, answer (C).

The SAT Advantage

14. Answer: (E) noting that sometimes offenders experience debilitating guilt from VIPs and that studies show little effect of VIPs on recidivism
The author of Passage 2 does not appear to consider offenders' hearts hard; indeed, the author shows some empathy for those addicted to alcohol and notes that alcoholics already feel guilty in the line, "Letting a victim vent at a perpetrator may just result in a guilt trip that hardens the offender's attitude and makes him or her seek escape through alcohol once again," so answer (A) does not make sense. The author of Passage 2 notes that "Most studies done on the subject show that VIPs have little effect on whether a drunk driver chooses to drive while under the influence again or not," so answer (B) is not a good fit. There is no mention of VIPs being required to appear in court or how traumatic that might be as in answer (C), and since the author of Passage 2 talks about actual studies done, the author is unlikely to agree that "it is likely" is proof enough of VIPs efficacy, as in answer (D). Answer (E) is the best choice.

15. Answer: (B) to help victims of alcohol-related car crashes and prevent others from becoming victims
The author of Passage 1 says, "MADD's main activity is to help victims of drunk driving car crashes," which supports answer (B). Although MADD attracts passionate volunteers (A), that is a natural by-product of MADD's mission rather than a purpose for it, as evidenced by the statement, "MADD quickly caught on as the victims left behind by drunk driving—car crash victims and those who love them—at last had a forum. Mothers holding up pictures of their dead children and sharing their grief, survivors in wheelchairs or with scars or permanent brain damage helped society see the human impact of drunk driving." Although MADD effects legislation (C) and uses VIPs (D), neither of those activities speak to the primary mission of MADD, which springs from its founder's motivation when she vowed "to her dead daughter that she would do something to prevent this from happening to someone else." This shows that preventing others from becoming victims is MADD's primary mission.

16. Answer: (B) victims of addiction
The author of Passage 2 calls for intervention for alcoholics but says that "unless they are paired with intervention programs that treat the underlying disease in the offenders—alcoholism—they are not really effective in helping drunk drivers make better choices," yet the author does not call for the "crisis intervention" mentioned in answer (C). Nor does the author of Passage 2 condemn alcoholics as "perpetrators of unforgivable crimes" (A) or (E) "punishable by death." The author does not seem to equate alcoholics with drunk drivers, as alcoholism is, as the author says, a "disease." The author of Passage 2 says, "In many cases, DUI and DWI offenders are repeat offenders due to addiction to alcohol" and that "drunk drivers don't set out to commit vehicular homicide or to hurt anyone. They themselves are victims of an addiction," showing that answer (B) victims of addiction, is the best answer.

17. Answer: (E) MADD has had far-reaching impact on the nation's laws and attitudes regarding drunk driving
Passage 1 says, "Through giving car-crash victims faces and voices, MADD heightened the nation's awareness about drunk driving and worked for the passage of laws that would protect everyone," which supports answer (E). Passage 2 says, "Society's consciousness about drinking and driving has changed from winking and turning a blind eye to little tolerance for the practice of driving while under the influence. MADD estimates that it has saved roughly 300,000 lives by its activism to promote awareness and pass legislation that ensure that drunk driving is strictly limited by law." These lines from both passages show that they agree that MADD has had "far-reaching impact on the nation's laws and attitudes regarding drunk driving," answer (E).

18. Answer: (A) serve to release and relieve the feelings of victims of alcohol-related car crashes

In Passage 1, the author says, "VIPs are cathartic for people living with the impact of car crashes due to someone else's choice to drink and drive. VIPs help to heal the psychological and emotional wounds of the physical consequences to one's self or to one's loved ones due to the bad choices of someone who could have prevented the losses by acting in a more responsible manner." In Passage 2, the author says, "Yet Victim Impact Panels, while offering victims important cathartic benefits and useful in their own right, may not be one of MADD's more effective strategies for actually reducing drunk driving" and that "Victim Impact Panels can serve as an important release valve for the feelings of the victims of alcohol-related car crashes." These lines show that the authors of Passage 1 and Passage 2 agree that VIPs "serve to release and relieve the feelings of victims of alcohol-related car crashes," answer (A).

19. Answer: (B) returning to criminal activity as a repeat offender

The definition of "recidivism" is to return or relapse into previous, usually criminal, behavior. Answer (B) includes this definition. Since part of MADD's avowed mission is to prevent people from becoming victims of drunk driving car crashes, it is likely that MADD would want to alter behavior on the part of drunk driving offenders and prevent them from doing the same thing again. The author says, "VIPs encourage drunk drivers to make better choices; thus it is likely that they reduce drunk driver recidivism." If drunk drivers are encouraged to "make better choices" and the goal is to "reduce drunk driver recidivism," it can be gleaned from the context of the sentence that "drunk driver recidivism" is a return to unhelpful choices and slipping back into repeat criminal activity, as in answer (B).

SECTION 8 (MATHEMATICS)

MULTIPLE CHOICE

1. Answer: (A) $12.00
Since the cost of the yarn is given in yards, first convert the length of yarn Rosita bought into yards. Since 3 feet = 1 yard, 300 feet = $\frac{300}{3}$ = 100 yards. Rosita spent 100 × 12 cents = 1200 cents = $12.00.

2. Answer: (E) $-3\frac{1}{2}$
First subtract 7*a* from both sides to get all the *a* terms on one side. Then 2 = 3*a* – 5 + 2*a* – 7*a*. Combine all the *a* terms: 2 = –2*a* – 5. Add 5 to both sides to get 7 = –2*a*. Dividing both sides by –2, *a* = $-\frac{7}{2}$ = $-3\frac{1}{2}$.

3. Answer: (C) 8 and 20
The greatest common factor (GCF) of two or more numbers is the largest factor that divides evenly into the numbers. Find the factors of 8 and 20.

8: 1, 2, 4, 8
20: 1, 2, 4, 5, 10, 20

The greatest common factor of 8 and 20 is 4.

The least common multiple (LCM) of 8 and 20 is the smallest number that has 8 and 20 as factors. Since 8 and 20 are relatively small numbers, an easy way to find the LCM is by listing the multiples of each number. You can find the multiples of any number simply by multiplying by 1, then 2, and so on.

8: 8, 16, 24, 32, 40
20: 20, 40

The least common multiple of 8 and 20 is 40.

The easiest way to approach this problem is to note that all the other answer choices include the number 10 which does not have 4 as a factor. Hence none of them can be correct.

4. Answer: (C) $22.40

Find the cost of the jacket after the 20% reduction. Expressing the percent as a decimal, 0.20, facilitates calculation.

$40.00 − (0.20)(40) = $32.00

Discount the new cost, $32.00, by an additional 30%.

$32.00 − (0.30)(32.00) = $22.40

5. Answer: (E) 0.86

Convert all the fractions, including $\frac{6}{7}$, to decimals to make them uniform.

$\frac{6}{7} = 0.857$

$\frac{19}{23} = 0.826$

$\frac{17}{25} = 0.68$

Selection A is correct because 0.86 > 0.857

6. Answer: (C) 2

When raising a power to another power, multiply the exponents.

$(2^x)^3 = 2^{(3)(x)} = 2^{3x}$

In the example $a^x = a^4$, x must be 4 because the base, a, is the same on both sides of the equation. However, in the expression $(2^x)^3 = 64$, the bases are different. Therefore, change 64 into a power of 2.

$64 = 2^6$

Now set $2^{3x} = 2^6$.

$2^{3x} = 2^6$

3x = 6

x = 2

7. Answer: (D) $\overline{AB} > \overline{BC} > \overline{AC}$

In any triangle, there is a correspondence between the angles and their opposite sides. The largest angle will always be opposite the largest side and the smallest angle will always be opposite the smallest side.

In ⬜, it is necessary to calculate the measure of $\angle C$ so the relative sizes of the sides can be found. The sum of the measures of the angles in a triangle is 180°, so subtract the known angles, 47° and 62°, from 180.

180 – (47 + 62) = 180 – 109 = 71.

The measure of $\angle C$ is 71°, so $m\angle C > m\angle A > m\angle B$. $\angle C$ is opposite $\overline{AB}$, $\angle A$ is opposite $\overline{BC}$, and $\angle B$ is opposite $\overline{AC}$. Therefore, $\overline{AB} > \overline{BC} > \overline{AC}$.

8. Answer: (D) $-\dfrac{2}{3}$

Lines that do not intersect are parallel lines. Lines that are parallel have the same slope but different y-intercepts. The line y = kx – 1 is in slope-intercept form. Use the general formula, y = mx + b, where m represents the slope and b the y-intercept, to find the slope and y-intercept of the line. In the line y = kx – 1, the slope is k and the y-intercept is -1.

The line 2x + 3y = 7 is in standard form. The standard form of a line is in the form of Ax + By = C, where A, B, and C are all integers and A is positive. Transform the equation into slope-intercept form to examine its slope and y-intercept.

$2x + 3y = 7$
$3y = -2x + 7$
$\dfrac{3}{3}y = \dfrac{-2}{3}x + \dfrac{7}{3}$
$y = -\dfrac{2}{3}x + \dfrac{7}{3}$

Since parallel lines have the same slope, k must equal $-\dfrac{2}{3}$.

9. Answer: (D) 8

A segment that is tangent to a circle is perpendicular to the radius of the circle. Therefore, $\angle B$ is a right angle and ⬜ is a right triangle. Given that AB = 5, and BC = 12, use the Pythagorean Theorem to find the length of AC.

$a^2 + b^2 = c^2$

$5^2 + 12^2 = c^2$

$25 + 144 = c^2$

$169 = c^2$

$\sqrt{169} = \sqrt{c^2}$

$13 = c$

Note that $\overline{AD}$ is a radius of ⬜. All radii in a circle have equal measures so AB = AD = 5.

Find x by subtracting the length of AD from the length of AC.

13 – 5 = 8

10. Answer: (C) is greater than the median
Height data in inches: 56, 58, 60, 61, 64, 65, 66, 66
- The median height is 62.5, the average of the two middle numbers 61 and 64.
- The mode, or the most frequently occurring number, is 66.

Hence the mode is greater than the median for the height data

11. Answer: (D) 121 lbs
Arraying the weights from least to greatest, we get:

85, 87, 98, 120, 122, 128, 141, 155

The median is the value in the middle. In this case, there are two values, 120 and 122, that are in the middle, so find their average:

(120 + 122) ÷ 2 = 121

12. Answer: (B) 6.25
$f(x) = -(x-2)(x+3)$ is a quadratic equation and is, therefore, represented by a parabola. Note that the coefficient of x^2 is negative, hence it is a parabola that opens downwards. So the greatest value of the function corresponds to the vertex of the parabola.

Putting the above expression in standard form (i.e., in the form $ax^2 + bx + c$) we get:
$-(x-2)(x+3) = -(x^2 - 2x + 3x - 6) = -(x^2 + x - 6) = -x^2 - x + 6$

The vertex of parabola $ax^2 + bx + c$ is located at $x = -\dfrac{b}{2a}$.

In this case, $-\dfrac{b}{2a} = -\left(\dfrac{-1}{-2}\right) = -\dfrac{1}{2}$. Hence the vertex of the parabola is at $x = -\dfrac{1}{2}$.

Another way to look at this is to consider that the function $f(x) = -(x-2)(x+3)$ has zeros (i.e., crosses the x-axis) at $x = 2$ and $x = -3$. Based on the symmetry of the parabola, one can argue that the vertex must be at the halfway point between these two numbers. That point is $x = -\frac{1}{2}$.

The value of the function $f(x) = -(x-2)(x+3)$ at $x = -\frac{1}{2}$ is $-\left(-\frac{1}{2}-2\right)\left(-\frac{1}{2}+3\right) = -\left(-\frac{5}{2}\right)\left(\frac{5}{2}\right) = \frac{25}{4} = 6.25$

Note that this problem could also be solved quickly and easily by using the graphing and table functions in a simple graphing calculator.

13. Answer: (B) -0.5

The slope of the line that passes through (p, 2q) and (-q, -2p) = $\frac{-2p-2q}{-q-p} = \frac{-2(p+q)}{-1(p+q)} = \frac{-2}{-1} = 2$.

The slope of a line perpendicular to it is the negative reciprocal = $-\frac{1}{2}$ = -0.5.

14. Answer: (C) $\frac{2}{3}$

Let the total number of beads in the box be x. Since the probability of getting a gold bead at random is $\frac{1}{4}$, the number of gold beads in the box = $\frac{x}{4}$.

The remainder of the $\frac{3x}{4}$ beads in the box is equally divided into silver and red. Hence there are $\frac{3x}{8}$ silver beads and $\frac{3x}{8}$ red beads in the box.

So the ratio of gold beads to silver beads = $\frac{x/4}{3x/8} = \frac{x}{4} \times \frac{8}{3x} = \frac{8}{12} = \frac{2}{3}$.

15. Answer: (D) I, II, and III
Let the first integer in the sequence be n. Then the sum of the 5 consecutive integers is n + (n+1) + (n+2) + (n+3) + (n+4) = 5n + 10 = 5(n + 2).

Therefore, the sum of any 5 consecutive integers is always a multiple of 5. Hence all the choices are valid.

16. Answer: (E) for no values of x
The sum of any two sides of a triangle must be greater than the third.

In this case, the three sides are:

$x^2 +1$, $x-2$ and $x+3$

Setting the sum of the first two to be greater than the third we get:
$x^2 +1+x-2 > x+3; \Rightarrow x^2 -1 > 3; \Rightarrow x^2 > 4$.

Setting the sum of the second two sides to be greater than the first we get:
$x-2+x+3 > x^2 +1; \Rightarrow 2x+1 > x^2 +1; x^2 < 2x; x < 2$.

But there is no value of x for which both $x^2 > 4$ and $x < 2$. Hence there cannot be a triangle with sides related in the given way.

The SAT Advantage

SECTION 9 (WRITING)

IMPROVING SENTENCES

1. Answer: (C) has discouraged many young families and driven them to relocate to other regions of the country
The subject of the sentence is *cost*, which is singular and requires a singular verb. Choices (C), (D), and (E) all include the singular verb *has*. However, choice (D) incorrectly uses the past form *drove* instead of the part participle *driven*, while choice (E) incorrectly uses the infinitive *to drive*.

2. Answer: (D) printmakers; their inexpensive prints
The original sentence incorrectly joins two independent clauses, using only a comma. Choices (B) and (C) join the clauses with conjunctions that are not logical. Choice (D) correctly joins the two clauses with a semicolon. Choice (E) is too wordy.

3. Answer: (B) One major cause of obesity is that
The original sentence incorrectly uses the conjunction *when* instead of the correct conjunction, *that*. Choices (C) and (E) also include the incorrect conjunction *when*. Choice (D) is wordy and redundant.

4. Answer: (E) John Updike also received critical acclaim for his essays and poems
The introductory phrase that opens the sentence should be followed immediately by the noun that the phrase describes: *John Updike*. Only choice (E) rephrases the sentence in this way.

5. Answer: (B) base many of their choices less on logical reasons than on
To be logical, this comparison requires the parallel phrases *less on...than on*, as in choice (B). The other choices use the wrong form of the modifier *less* or place the modifier in the wrong position in the sentence.

6. Answer: (C) In Major League Baseball, the teams of the National League, unlike those in the American League,
Choices (A) and (E) incorrectly use the pronoun *them* instead of *those*. Choices (B) and (D) are wordy and awkward.

7. Answer: (E) because of the government's strict ban on hunting these species and careful protection of their habitats
Choices (A) and (B) place the modifiers *strictly* and *carefully* in the wrong positions. Choices (C) and (D) are awkward and have a slightly different meaning than the original sentence.

8. Answer: (A) sought no patent for his medicine and received no profits from its distribution
The original sentence is correct because it contains two parallel verb phrases: *sought no patent* and *received no profits*. Choice (B) uses the conjunctions *neither...nor* incorrectly. Choice (C) uses the conjunction *nor* incorrectly, without its partner *neither*. Choice (D) contains verb forms that do not match. Choice (E) does not express the ideas as clearly as choice (A).

9. Answer: (D) you may achieve many of your objectives in life
The two parts of this sentence require matching pronouns. Since the first part of the sentence uses the second person pronoun *you*, so should the underlined part. Only choice (D) rewords the underlined clause with the matching pronouns *you* and *your*.

The SAT Advantage

10. Answer: (B) and to perform ongoing community service
This sentence requires matching grammatical forms to follow the paired conjunctions *both…and*. Since the infinitive *to write* follows the word *both*, the infinitive *to perform* should follow the word *and*, as in choice (B). The other choices introduce verb forms that do not match the form of *to write*.

11. Answer: (A) saved millions of lives during World War II by protecting wounded soldiers from deadly infections
The original sentence expresses its ideas clearly and directly. The use of *saving* in choice (B) turns the sentence into a fragment lacking a main verb. Choice (C) is too wordy. Choices (D) and (E) are also wordy and introduce incorrect shifts in tenses by using the verb forms *had done* and *had been protecting*.

12. Answer: (E) but the Southern economy was based on
Choice (E) expresses the contrast between the two regions in the simplest, clearest way. The use of the conjunction *and* in choice (A) does not prepare the reader for a contrast. Choices (B), (C), and (D) use connecting words that express a contrast but introduce errors in verb usage and are too wordy.

13. Answer: (C) Over 70 percent of the world's fresh water is located in Antarctica, a continent twice the size of Australia and covered by ice.
The word *Antarctica* needs to directly precede or directly follow the phrase that describes it: *a continent twice the size of Australia and covered by ice*. Only choice (C) corrects the sentence in this way. Choice (D) is awkward, and it obscures the main point of the sentence.

14. Answer: (D) believed not only that his system was foolproof but also that he could teach it to others
Only choice (D) explains the two things that Nicholas believed in way that is both logical and grammatically correct: *believed not only that…but also that*. Choice (A) leaves out the needed words *also that*. Choice (B) incorrectly places the words *not only* and leaves out the word *that*, which needs to follow *but also*. Choice (C) structures the comparison correctly, but adds the redundant words *as well* at the end. Choice (E) places *not only* in the wrong position, redundantly repeats the word *believed*, and adds the redundant phrase *as well*.

PRACTICE TEST 2

The SAT Advantage

SECTION 1
(WRITING)
Time: 25 minutes
ESSAY

Directions: Write an essay based on the prompts given.

The essay section gives you an opportunity to demonstrate your effectiveness at written communication. A well-written essay will express a clear point of view, present ideas in a logical manner, and use language precisely.

Your essay must be written in your <u>Answer Grid Booklet</u>. Do not write your essay in your test book. Keep your handwriting legible so that readers who are unfamiliar with your handwriting will be able to read it.

DO NOT WRITE ON ANOTHER TOPIC. AN ESSAY ON AN UNRELATED TOPIC WILL RECEIVE A SCORE OF ZERO.

Consider carefully the matter presented in the following paragraph and the assignment below.

Topic: Adolescents are told to "resist peer pressure," to "think for themselves" and to stand up for their own beliefs. Yet Henry David Thoreau, the famous nonconformist who wrote *Walden*, said, "Public opinion is a weak tyrant compared with our own private opinion."

Assignment: Do we do things out of peer pressure or do we do things because we ourselves agree with them in "our own private opinion"? Develop and write an essay expounding on your viewpoint on this matter. You may use reasoning and your general knowledge based on your own experiences, observation of society, general reading or specific studies.

Excellent Quality Sample Essay (Score: 6 out of 6)

Nearly everyone has experienced peer pressure. People care very much what other people think. If someone urges us to do something and it seems like that person and/or others will not like us if we don't do it, we feel a strong pressure. At the same time, some part of our inner self is going along with it, telling us that we need to do this in order to make friends or keep them, so we are agreeing inside. This is our own private opinion; we think friends are so important or that other people's opinions are so important, we must go along. That means it is true that the real tyrant is our own private opinion.

For example, when I was ten, one of my girlfriends sneaked a cigarette out of her parents' house. She said we should go to the park and smoke it. We swiped a book of matches from the convenience store (it wasn't really swiping, because they were there for people to take, near the cigarettes), and we went to the park and lit the cigarette up. It was so awful, I didn't want to take a second drag. I thought my friends would laugh at me and think I was weak, so I took the second drag, almost against my own will. I made the decision, though, and it was my hand that reached for the cigarette a second time. So my private opinion really was a tyrant.

We never know what people really are thinking. My friends might have admired me for saying I didn't want any more—especially after they took a first drag themselves! We were all dizzy and coughing. I had to force myself to take a second drag, and I did it so I could look tough to them. They probably did the same thing for the same reason. Maybe if I had said, "That tastes nasty" and refused, they would have respected me more for my courage and honesty.

We do what we choose to do. No one makes us do things. Even other people's words or opinions and what they think about us (and we can never control or even know what they really think) can't make us do something. We have to choose to do it. If we choose wrongly, we have only ourselves to blame. That is why I would say that our own private opinion is the most powerful tyrant.

Someone once said that conquering yourself is the hardest battle you will ever fight. I agree with that. We all have to fight the powerful inner tyrant of our own private opinions.

Medium Quality Sample Essay (Score: 3 – 4 out of 6)

I, for one, am tired of hearing adults telling adolescents to resist peer pressure and think for themselves. I do not notice many adults resisting peer pressure and thinking for themselves. In my neighborhood, all the houses look alike except for the color. Everyone goes to work at a 9 to 5 job on weekdays, and they all drive cars that look alike except for the color. Then everyone mows their lawn on Saturdays. They are all in lockstep. They should practice what they preach. The only reason for this large scale conformity that I can think of is that people really are slaves to the tyrant of public opinion. They feel they must do things the way everyone else does them.

I think public opinion is the tyrant of conformity. It is true that if we did not agree with public opinion—if we resisted the pressure to be and do like everyone else—we would take a stand and be different. But even if most people do not agree with public opinion they still go along, because public opinion is a stronger tyrant than private opinion.

In history, it has been the people who did not go along with the system who made a difference, like Dr. Martin Luther King. He stood up to injustice courageously. He did not accept things the way they were, because they were not fair. Rosa Parks and other black people should not have been shoved to the back of the bus on the basis of the color of their skin. It's ironic—different colored houses and cars are acceptable but different colored people are not? How wrong is that?

Sometimes we have to go against public opinion in order to get something done right. I think then people's own private opinion secretly agrees with us, and then they go along. Now, for example, public opinion says that blacks and whites can eat in the same restaurants, use the same bathrooms and drinking fountain, etcetera, and guess what? It's no problem. Dr. King was right. At the time, though, public opinion didn't seem to think so.

I think few people have the courage of a Dr. Martin Luther King, Jr. Almost everyone goes along with public opinion, conforming even when their private opinion disagrees. So I think the worst tyrant is still public opinion until someone very brave comes along.

Low Quality Sample Essay (Score: 1 – 2 out of 6)

People do things out of their own private opinion. They want to do what they do. Even if someone puts pressure on them, they still do it because they want to inside. No one is forcing them. No one is holding a gun to their head.

Everyone knows what peer pressure is. We wouldn't know it if it wasn't true. Most people have been victims of peer pressure. Someone calls us "chicken" if we don't do something or laughs at us, so we do it. Adolescents feel peer pressure a lot. I have felt peer pressure.

My brother crashed his car because of peer pressure. People kept telling him to speed up. He knew he shouldn't speed up. He was on a rainy, slick street at night and it was dark. But he sped up because of the tyranny of public opinion, peer pressure, in other words. Then he crashed because he couldn't handle it.

People shouldn't pressure people to do things they shouldn't. We should all be left to make our own decisions. Other people's ideas about what we should do should not be ours. We should have our own. People shouldn't be in other people's heads. They don't pay rent to be in our brains, so they shouldn't be there.

SECTION 2
(CRITICAL READING)
Time: 25 minutes
24 questions

SENTENCE COMPLETION

Directions: For each of the following questions, choose the best answer and fill in the corresponding oval on the answer sheet to indicate your selection.

Each sentence contains one or two blanks indicating that something has been omitted from the sentence. Choose the word or set of words, labeled A through E, that when inserted into the sentence, best fits the meaning of the sentence as a whole.

1. The panel of judges at the music competition awarded first place to a vocalist whose technique was not perfect but whose -------- livened up the whole contest.

    (A) precision
    (B) spontaneity
    (C) constraint
    (D) restraint
    (E) deficiency

2. It stretches our -------- to realize that someone born in 1900 had a life expectancy of just 47 years, while a person born in the year 2000 has an average life expectancy of 76 years.

    (A) fantasy
    (B) credulity
    (C) clarity
    (D) credibility
    (E) credentials

3. Before grocery stores became the norm, rural Americans shopped at general stores, which sold everything from feed for livestock to calico for dresses; those yearning for a(n) -------- atmosphere in their decorating schemes might use antique wooden general store bins in their kitchens.

    (A) modern
    (B) art deco
    (C) bucolic
    (D) abstract
    (E) cubistic

4. Because literary agents are the gatekeepers to the traditional publishing world, the -------- author was told that she needed to write an intriguing agent -------- letter and a great synopsis.

   (A) veteran ... acquirement
   (B) beginning ... repulsion
   (C) seasoned ... attraction
   (D) experienced ... propulsion
   (E) aspiring ... acquisition

5. Rachel had to give her rebellious dog medicine; she -------- to grinding up the pill and pressing it into the dog's food as a -------- .

   (A) resorted ... subterfuge
   (B) plotted ... disguise
   (C) planned ... blind
   (D) converted ... ruse
   (E) assayed ... trick

6. In Jane Austen's *Pride and Prejudice*, the title refers to Mr. Darcy's aristocratic -------- and Miss Bennett's judgmental opinion that his -------- means he is incapable of love or compassion.

   (A) disdain ... arrogance
   (B) *noblesse oblige* ... wealth
   (C) humility ... snobbery
   (D) excesses ... asceticism
   (E) abscesses ... prudery

7. Water is -------- ; in addition to its life-nourishing properties as a beverage for humans, plants, and animals, it is also used everywhere as a cleanser and as the most basic of -------- .

   (A) beneficial ... thirst-slakers
   (B) ubiquitous ... solvents
   (C) scarce ... saline solutions
   (D) malign ... solutions
   (E) benefactor ... chemicals

8. In the world of international business, Western businesspeople tend to rely on detailed, negotiated contracts between strangers to cover all business --------; Eastern businesspeople tend to -------- relationships of trust over time by getting to know one another, and through the exchange of gifts, visits, and other symbols of good will that will help to weather any storms once the parties have entered into a business relationship.

   (A) possibilities ... negotiate

   (B) contracts ... create

   (C) permissions ... fracture

   (D) eventualities ... cultivate

   (E) acumen ... prosecute

The SAT Advantage

> **READING BASED QUESTIONS**
>
> **Directions**: For each of the following questions, choose the best answer and fill in the corresponding oval on the answer sheet to indicate your selection.
>
> The reading passages below are followed by questions based on their content. Questions that follow a pair of related passages may be based on both the content of the passages and/or the relationship between the passages. Answer the questions based on what is <u>stated</u> or <u>implied</u> in the passages.

Questions 9 – 14 are based on the following passage:

On October 24, 1861, Western Union completed the Pacific Telegraph line in Salt Lake City. This signaled the end of a short-lived legend: the Pony Express. The network of communications wires bearing telegraph messages now stretched fully from East to West and all over the West itself. Dispatches could be sent almost instantaneously across and
5 within the American continent, whereas the Pony Express took ten days to bring transcontinental news.

    The Pony Express was something like a relay race, although riders only raced against time and not against one another. Pony Express riders were usually small in height and light in weight like jockeys so as to achieve maximum speed on their horses. They rode at a
10 breakneck speed between Pony Express stations, which were usually about ten miles apart. Braving Indian territory, bad weather, and tricky terrain, Pony Express riders delivered the priceless mail pouch from station to station undeterred.

    Besides the mail, each rider carried important items in his pouch. He carried a horn to blow in advance of arriving at a Pony Express station to alert authorities that horse and rider
15 were coming and that a fresh horse should be at the ready. He carried a water sack to carry him through dusty, dry rides. Added to this were a Bible and a revolver. These were considered sufficient to surmount any emergencies a Pony Express rider might run into. Some Pony Express riders might have carried food. In emergencies, riders were known to stay in the saddle at their breakneck pace for twenty hours or more, only pausing every ten
20 miles or so to change horses (or ponies).

    Technically, the weight and height of the horses used for the Pony Express put them in the category of ponies. Like their riders, the ponies were small but doughty.

    The American West seemed naturally to give rise to legends: cowboys singing by campfires on the cattle drive, gunslingers and gamblers shooting up wild Western towns,
25 battles with Indians, and brave settlers crossing the continent in wagons pulled by oxen. The Pony Express is one of those legends. Although it only lasted a couple of years before it was replaced by the telegraph, the pounding hoof beats of the Pony Express still echo in the nation's history.

The SAT Advantage

9. **Lines 1 – 6 imply that the fate of the Pony Express was:**

    (A) unrelated to other technological developments of the time

    (B) steeped in legend and therefore assured

    (C) inextricably linked with the development of the telegraph system

    (D) in natural decline due to economic and climate factors

    (E) doomed from the start

10. **In line 12, the use of the word "undeterred" most likely means:**

    (A) Pony Express riders were not afraid of Indians

    (B) Pony Express riders did not turn back or fail in their delivery missions in spite of adversity

    (C) Pony Express riders sometimes bypassed stations to ride on for another relay to save time

    (D) Pony Express riders knew they were often carrying large amounts of money and other valuables, so they forged through no matter what

    (E) Pony Express riders used scouts to go ahead of them to spot bad weather, hostile Indian activity, and to give them geographical tips on the lay of the land

11. **The tone of lines 16 – 17 might be said to be:**

    (A) sarcastic

    (B) supercilious

    (C) admiring

    (D) disapproving

    (E) tongue-in-cheek

12. **In line 22 the word "doughty" most likely means:**

    (A) intrepid

    (B) plump

    (C) persevering, like dough that sticks to the bowl

    (D) bandy-legged

    (E) speedy

13. **Legends of the West cited in lines 23 – 28 include all but which of the following:**

    (A) pioneers

    (B) the Pony Express

    (C) Western towns

    (D) the law enforcement of famous sheriffs like Wyatt Earp

    (E) gunfighters

14. The tone of lines 23 – 28 may be said to be:

(A) repudiating the past

(B) evocative of a bygone era

(C) reflective on a bygone era

(D) antagonistic toward a bygone era

(E) nostalgic for a bygone era yet critical of it too

Questions 15 – 24 are based on the following passages:

Passage 1

A major case about toxic waste dumping took place in 1982 when six families from Woburn, Massachusetts sued corporate giants Beatrice Foods and W. R. Grace & Company. The six families charged that their children had gotten leukemia from drinking polluted water from wells the corporations had contaminated with toxic chemical wastes.

5   The case captured the public's imagination. Its story was told in a bestselling non-fiction book by Jonathan Harr entitled *A Civil Action*. A movie of the same title was made, starring John Travolta.

In a controversial move, Judge Walter Jay Skinner ruled that the case should be divided into three phases. In the first phase, the attorney for the plaintiffs attempted to show that the
10 wells serving the families had been contaminated by Grace and Beatrice (another company, UniFirst, also became a defendant). If the jury did not find the corporations responsible for polluting the water, the trial would end. If they did find the corporations responsible, the trial would go on to the second segment, in which the plaintiffs' side needed to prove to the jury that the children's leukemia was caused by drinking the polluted water. Again, if the jury
15 found that to be true, the third segment of the trial would begin, which would set compensatory payment.

The attorney for the families, Jan Schlichtmann, argued that breaking the trial into three phases deprived him of the opportunity to put the suffering and grief-stricken families on the witness stand. They would not even be present for the first segment of the trial. Their
20 poignant and sympathy-inducing stories would not be told. It would be a boring, technical first phase about well water pollution, groundwater movement, dates, and chemicals with long names.

Schlichtmann was also uncomfortable with the fact that Judge Skinner told the defendants' attorney, Jerome Facher, that the break-up into three phases meant he would
25 not have to memorize the material all at once. Facher had complained about that.

In the book, Schlichtmann is depicted as having ongoing concerns as to the judge's relationship with Jerome Facher. The judge and the attorney were about the same age, they respected each other, and they seemed to think alike. Schlichtmann worried about the judge's impartiality.

30   The case against Jerome Facher's client, Beatrice Foods, was dismissed when the jury found the corporation not responsible for the pollution. However, W. R. Grace & Company was found responsible, and they paid eight million dollars in settlement before the trial went further. UniFirst also settled for one million dollars. The trial ended after the first phase.

    Although the settlement amounts sound sizable, millions of dollars were spent in
35 scientific tests of groundwater movement, soil, and well contamination as well as on expert witnesses. Although each family received a sizable settlement, their attorney, Jan Schlichtmann, was forced to declare bankruptcy.

    His bank account was not the only thing broken by the case. His faith in the justice system was damaged too.

Passage 2

40   The controversial and intriguing case of six families of leukemia victims versus big corporations is still debated in law journals. Transcripts from the trial and varying perspectives on it are readily available on the Internet. The case is also often the basis of mock trials.

    In a dramatic movie about the case, *A Civil Action*, the defendants' counsel, Jerome
45 Facher, is depicted as a corrupt creature of the system. He says that the families must never be allowed to take the witness stand. He fears that their emotional stories about the deaths of their children could cost him the case. The movie implies that Facher was unfeeling and that Judge Skinner went along with him, in part by breaking the trial into three phases. Facher and Skinner are "the bad guys" in the movie.

50   In real life, Jerome Facher and others thought breaking the trial into three phases was only fair: after all, if the corporations had not polluted the wells, what relevance did the grieving families have to the case? Emotional appeals could sway the jury away from the facts.

    It actually might have been fortunate for Jan Schlichtmann and the plaintiffs to have the
55 trial proceed in three phases. Settlements were reached before the second phase when Schlichtmann would have to prove that pollution caused the children's leukemia. Other "leukemia clusters" had been found in other towns, unrelated to pollution. What was more, scientists did not know what caused leukemia. The corporations offered settlement money after Schlichtmann won the first phase of the trial, saving him from having to prove the
60 unprovable.

    Judge Skinner did have a long-term relationship of mutual respect with Jerome Facher. Both men were considered examples of integrity in the law profession. Yet Judge Skinner did not enter the case on anyone's side. At one point early on, Skinner reflected to Schlichtmann that he had the potential to win an "astronomical" amount of money in the
65 case and said that this was a very important case indeed.

    One possible reason Schlichtmann's firm went bankrupt was because he had expensive tastes. He entertained settlement offers from opponents in fancy hotels with elaborate spreads of food and wines. Two families thought he had overspent on the case and should compensate the families for his extravagance, which Schlichtmann did.

15. The attitudes toward Schlichtmann of the authors of Passage 1 and Passage 2, respectively, are:

    (A) sympathetic and dismissive
    (B) sympathetic and impartial
    (C) unsympathetic and supportive
    (D) empathetic and compassionate
    (E) empathetic and impassioned

16. Lines 3 – 4 imply that:

    (A) the children got leukemia from drinking polluted water
    (B) the families believed their children got leukemia from drinking polluted water
    (C) the corporations deliberately polluted the water
    (D) the families knew they could get a lot of money out of the large corporations
    (E) large corporations do not care about families

17. The three phases of the trial as described in lines 8 – 16 were to:

    (A) prove the corporations did not pollute the water, prove that pollution is unrelated to leukemia, and award damages to the defendants for loss of reputation surrounding the trial
    (B) prove the corporations violated toxic waste statutes, prove toxic waste is linked with cancers including leukemia, and award damages to the plaintiffs and the town
    (C) prove the corporations polluted the water, prove the pollution caused leukemia in the children, and award damages to the plaintiffs
    (D) prove the corporations were environmentally responsible, prove the leukemia came from X-rays, and award significant amounts of corporate money to cancer research
    (E) prove Judge Skinner was prejudiced against Schlichtmann's case, prove he and Jerome Facher were in cahoots, and assign punishment such as disbarment

18. **In line 20 the word "poignant" most likely means:**

    (A) emotionally manipulative

    (B) touching the heart; affecting the emotions profoundly

    (C) psychologically disturbing

    (D) morally compelling

    (E) gripping

19. **According to Passage 1 and Passage 2, Schlichtmann's and Facher's attitudes toward Judge Skinner breaking the trial into three phases were, respectively, that:**

    (A) it hurt Schlichtmann's case by denying him the jury's sympathy; it helped focus on the facts rather than emotions

    (B) it denied the families their right to testify; it destroyed the plaintiff's case

    (C) it was fair because of the vast amount of material in the case; it was unfair because the jury would be directed to disregard their emotions about the case

    (D) it violated the plaintiff's right to a fair trial; it denied the corporations their day in court

    (E) it made the plaintiff's case a "slam dunk"; it hurt the corporations' case

20. **In line 57, the term "leukemia clusters" is not defined because it is:**

    (A) not important

    (B) self-explanatory

    (C) not factual

    (D) not a scientific term

    (E) not relevant to the case or the test

21. **In lines 59 – 60 "prove the unprovable" refers to:**

    (A) proving that leukemia does not occur in people under age twenty

    (B) proving that the families had never sued anyone before

    (C) proving that leukemia sometimes occurs in clusters

    (D) proving that Jerome Facher and Judge Skinner conspired to defeat Schlichtmann

    (E) proving that chemical pollution causes leukemia

22. **Passage 2 depicts the relationship between Judge Skinner and Jerome Facher as being one of mutual:**

    (A) loathing based on a long history of antagonistic cases

    (B) regard based on a long history of personal interaction as friends

    (C) liking based on common interests

    (D) respect based on one another's integrity

    (E) mistrust as the judge knew the lawyer was wily and had vast knowledge of case law

23. **According to Passage 1, the following factors led Schlichtmann to be concerned about the judge's impartiality:**

    (A) the judge breaking the trial into three parts; the judge having gone to the same law school as Facher; the judge mentioning an invitation to Facher's home

    (B) the judge's history of being on the side of business in toxic waste cases; the judge's conservative history; Facher's political affiliations

    (C) the judge's empathy with Facher's age-related limitations because they were the same age; the judge's ruling that no witnesses from the families would be allowed to take the stand throughout the trial; the judge's ruling that Beatrice Foods was not liable

    (D) Facher's joking relationship with the judge; the fact that all of Facher's motions were affirmed by the judge; the fact that Facher's objections were always sustained

    (E) the judge's sympathy with Facher's complaint about the amount of material to be memorized; the judge's and Facher's mutual respect; and how much they thought alike

24. **What would the author of Passage 2 most likely say about the sentiments expressed in lines 34 – 39?**

    (A) Jan Schlichtmann should have been held in contempt of court for his actions during and after the trial

    (B) Jan Schlichtmann made noble sacrifices out of his devotion to the families of Woburn, Massachusetts

    (C) Jan Schlichtmann's clients received a fair trial and Schlichtmann was profligate of funds, which may possibly have led to his bankruptcy

    (D) Jan Schlichtmann's devotion to the Woburn families did not really pay off for him personally, but that is a risk a lawyer takes

    (E) Jan Schlichtmann subverted the legal system to command huge settlements from giant corporations he knew could afford them

SECTION 3
(MATHEMATICS)
Time: 25 minutes
20 questions

MULTIPLE CHOICE

Directions: For the questions in this section, solve each problem and decide which of the given answer choices is the best choice. Fill in the corresponding oval on the answer sheet to indicate your selection. You may use any available space for scratchwork.

Note:

1. Calculator use is permitted.
2. All numbers used are real numbers.
3. All figures provided are drawn to scale and lie in a plane unless otherwise indicated.
4. Unless otherwise specified, the domain of any function f is assumed to be the set of all real numbers x for which $f(x)$ is a real number.

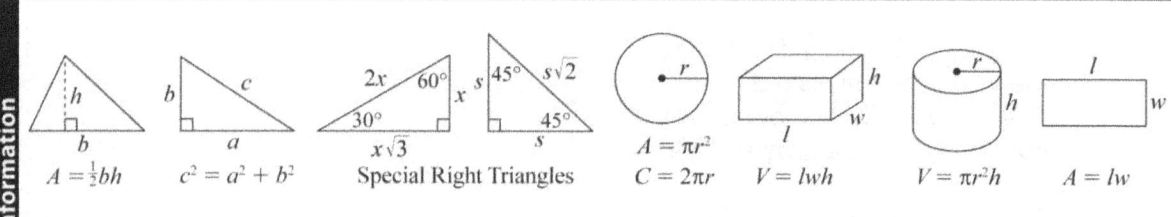

The sum of the degree measures of the angles in a triangle is 180.
The number of degrees of arc in a circle is 360.
A straight angle has a degree measure of 180.

1. In 10 seconds, Sharon can run 71 yards, Mary can run 83 yards, and Nancy can run 18 yards more than Sharon. How many more yards can Nancy run than Mary in 10 seconds?

    (A) 6
    (B) 18
    (C) 30
    (D) 53
    (E) 65

2. Manuel joined the Stay Fit Gym for a special rate of $19.95 per month. He also had to pay the yearly registration fee of $30.65. Which of the following represents the total payment that Manuel made to the gym for the first two years?

    (A) $30.65 + (12 x $19.95)
    (B) $30.65 + (24 x $19.95)
    (C) $19.95 + (12 x $30.65)
    (D) $61.30 + (12 x $19.95)
    (E) $61.30 + (24 x $19.95)

3. If $4x-3=13$, then $5x+7=?$

(A) 4
(B) 13
(C) 19.5
(D) 27
(E) 31.5

4. If $9^{3x+6} = 27^{x-4}$, what is the value of x?

(A) 8
(B) 2
(C) -4.5
(D) -5
(E) -8

5. In parallelogram ABCD, if m $\angle DAB = (2x+10)°$, and m $\angle ABC = (4x+20)°$, what is the value of x?

(A) 120
(B) 80
(C) 60
(D) 45
(E) 25

6. If c cans of mixed vegetables cost d dollars, in terms of c and d, what would be the cost of 7 cans of vegetables?

(A) $\dfrac{cd}{7}$

(B) $\dfrac{7d}{c}$

(C) $\dfrac{c}{7d}$

(D) $7dc$

(E) $7(d-c)$

Use the following information to answer questions 7 and 8.

The parents and alumnae of Bristol Western High School are completing their Spring semester charity drive for 2011. The chart below compares the results in 2011 with the Spring semester results in 2010.

Charity Report for Bristol Western High School
($ in thousands)

	2011	2010
Jan	5.38	6.01
Feb	7.11	7.13
Mar	6.75	4.26
Apr	3.88	4.74
May	7.56	6.86

7. Which percentage represents the increase in donations in 2011 compared to 2010?

   (A) 5.5%

   (B) 5.8%

   (C) 7.3%

   (D) 7.5%

   (E) 16.8%

8. If the charity drive increases at the same percentage as it did in 2011, what would be the projected collections for 2012?

   (A) $32.46

   (B) $333.08

   (C) $5,119.30

   (D) $32,459.00

   (E) $47,414.00

9. Marcie bought some 45 cent stamps and some 22 cent stamps for $3.79. If she bought 12 stamps in all, how many 45 cent stamps did she buy?

   (A) 5

   (B) 7

   (C) 9

   (D) 10

   (E) 11

10. The vertices of rectangle ABCD in a standard coordinate plane are (3,7), (3,0), (7,0), and (7,7). What are the coordinates of the point where the diagonals intersect?

    (A) (3.5, 5)

    (B) (3, 5.5)

    (C) (5, 3.5)

    (D) (2.5, 2.5)

    (E) (-2, 2.5)

11. A number is 1 less than twice it's reciprocal. Which of the following is a possible value of the number?

    (A) -2

    (B) $-\sqrt{2}$

    (C) -1

    (D) $\sqrt{2}$

    (E) 2

12. If $A\Phi B = \dfrac{1}{\sqrt{AB}}$, what is the value of $3\Phi(9\Phi 4)$

    (A) $\dfrac{1}{3\sqrt{2}}$

    (B) $\dfrac{1}{\sqrt{2}}$

    (C) $\sqrt{2}$

    (D) 2

    (E) 3

13. A sock drawer has 6 red, 13 blue, 5 green, 8 white, and 12 black socks. If a person is pulling socks out of the drawer without looking, how many socks must she pull out to make sure she has at least one pair of the same color?

    (A) 2
    (B) 5
    (C) 6
    (D) 13
    (E) 14

14. A function f(x) is defined as

    $f(x) = 4x^2 - 3$ for $|x| < 1$
    $f(x) = -|x| + 2$ for $|x| \geq 1$

    How many times does the function cross the x-axis?

    (A) 1
    (B) 2
    (C) 3
    (D) 4
    (E) 5

15. The median value of a set of numbers is x and the mean is 2x + 1. Which of the following is a possible set of numbers that satisfies this condition?

    (A) 1, 2, 3, 5, 5, 9
    (B) 6, 22, 6, 29, 7, 6, 29
    (C) 3, 7, 1, 4, 4, 2, 2
    (D) 0, 0, 5, 2, 2, 1, 18, 1
    (E) 2, 3, 4, 20, 21, 23

16. $f(x) = g(x^2 - 4)$. If $g(x) = 1$ for all $x > 0$ which of the following could be a graph of $f(x)$?

    I.

    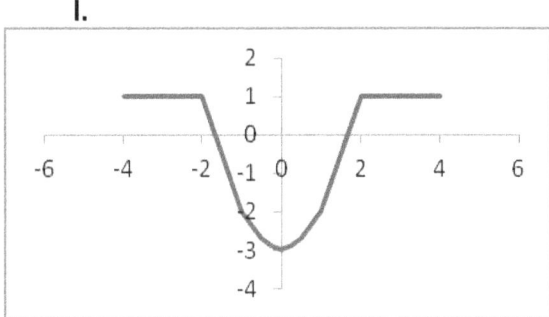

    II.

    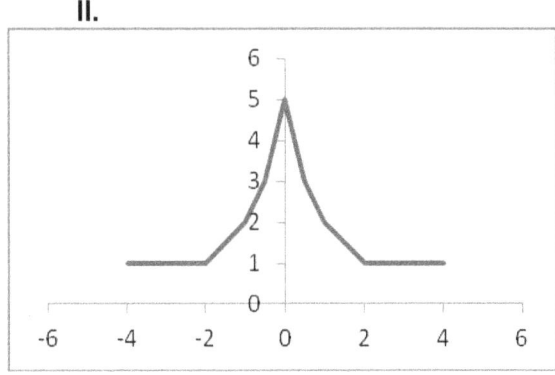

III.

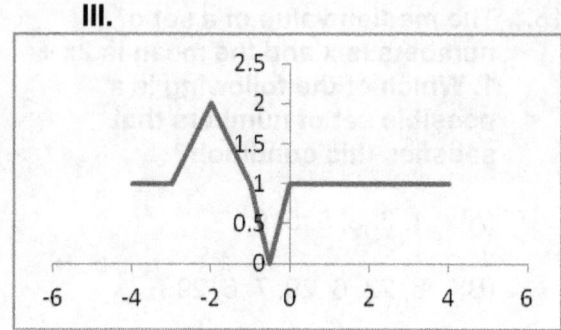

(A) I only

(B) II only

(C) III only

(D) I and II

(E) II and III

17. In triangle ABC, point D is placed on side BC such that $BD = \frac{1}{3} DC$. What is the ratio of the areas of triangles ABD and ABC?

(A) 1:1

(B) 1:3

(C) 1:4

(D) 2:3

(E) 3:4

18. Two numbers are picked at random from the set {1, 3, 5, 6, 7}. What is the probability that their product will be an even number?

(A) 0.2

(B) 0.33

(C) 0.4

(D) 0.7

(E) 0.85

19. Squares ABCD and CEFG are adjacent. If ABCD has an area measuring 16 square units and CEFG has an area measuring 8 square units, what is the perimeter of the figure below?

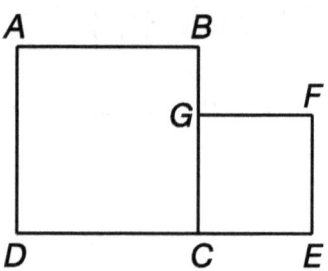

(A) $16 + 8\sqrt{2}$

(B) 24

(C) $16 + 4\sqrt{2}$

(D) $12 + 6\sqrt{2}$

(E) 12

20. Three tennis balls are packed in a cylindrical tube one on top of the other. If the balls fit snugly inside the tube so that the sides of the tube touch each ball all the way around and the ball on top touches the cover on the tube, what fraction of the cylinder's volume is taken up by the tennis balls?

(A) $\dfrac{3}{5}$

(B) $\dfrac{2}{3}$

(C) $\dfrac{3}{4}$

(D) $\dfrac{5}{6}$

(E) $\dfrac{7}{8}$

The SAT Advantage

SECTION 4
(CRITICAL READING)
Time: 25 minutes
24 questions

SENTENCE COMPLETION

Directions: For each of the following questions, choose the best answer and fill in the corresponding oval on the answer sheet to indicate your selection.

Each sentence contains one or two blanks indicating that something has been omitted from the sentence. Choose the word or set of words, labeled A through E, that when inserted into the sentence, best fits the meaning of the sentence as a whole.

1. Met by a -------- of criticism, the new play closed within a week.

    (A) barrage

    (B) barricade

    (C) barrister

    (D) baggage

    (E) banister

2. The -------- employees refused to strike, but they nevertheless murmured among themselves about how poorly important information was -------- throughout the organization.

    (A) rebellious ... distributed

    (B) defiant ... purveyed

    (C) submissive ... distributive

    (D) obedient ... mesmerized

    (E) docile ... disseminated

3. The detectives recommended the charges be dropped as a -------- of evidence meant no jury would convict the accused.

    (A) plethora

    (B) barrage

    (C) puny

    (D) paucity

    (E) acme

4. The politician was considered wily and -------- in her positions; she always seemed to -------- the press when they tried to pin her down to firm statements.

    (A) evasive ... satisfy

    (B) supple ... circumvent

    (C) disingenuous ... satisfy

    (D) consistent ... fool

    (E) obscure ... vilify

5. During negotiations, the representatives of the two families were told to -------- the issues and agree to -------- one another's annoying foibles.

    (A) ignore ... endorse

    (B) depersonalize ... condone

    (C) exacerbate ... adopt

    (D) resolve ... condemn

    (E) exaggerate ... imitate

READING BASED QUESTIONS

Directions: For each of the following questions, choose the best answer and fill in the corresponding oval on the answer sheet to indicate your selection.

The reading passages below are followed by questions based on their content. Questions that follow a pair of related passages may be based on both the content of the passages and/or the relationship between the passages. Answer the questions based on what is <u>stated</u> or <u>implied</u> in the passages.

Questions 6 – 9 are based on the following passage:

Those interested in giving first aid to others do well to learn the first principle of the Hippocratic Oath: "Do no harm." Hippocrates (460 - 375 B.C.) is considered the founder of medicine and the first doctor. His primary dictum to aspiring doctors remains part of the modern versions of the Hippocratic Oath that doctors take today before entering the medical
5 profession.

Perhaps remembering the "first principle of the first doctor when giving first aid" can serve as a mnemonic device for anyone who is caught in an emergency situation and wants to give succor to others. For example, it is not wise to move someone who has been injured in an accident unless the person is in imminent danger of being injured in the environment.
10 Moving an injured person can harm him or her further.

It is natural to want to help someone who has been compromised by an accident or other kind of injury or by a spontaneous physical problem such as a heart attack. First aid may include performing the life-saving methods of cardio-pulmonary resuscitation, the Heimlich Maneuver, or applying a tourniquet.

15 However, it is important to be trained before trying to perform first aid. Restoring a person's breathing or heart rate through cardio-pulmonary resuscitation, liberating a person from choking through the Heimlich Maneuver, and stopping blood loss by applying a tourniquet all require some understanding. The good news is that these life-saving techniques are easily learned. Training in first aid is often available for free through the Red
20 Cross or local health agencies, and a basic understanding may be gained through searching for the topics on the Internet.

6. **The purpose of lines 1 – 5 is to:**

   (A) inspire those interested in giving first aid to join the medical profession

   (B) inspire the taking of oaths of ethics among all professionals, including first aid workers

   (C) show the irrelevancy of the Hippocratic Oath to the modern medical profession

   (D) show how the taking of ethical oaths among doctors has declined

   (E) introduce a classical precept of ethics in medicine to the practice of first aid

7. **What is the reader to infer from the statement in lines 3 – 5 that aspiring doctors still take some version of the Hippocratic Oath today?**

   (A) the ancient Hippocratic Oath retains some meaning and value in modern times

   (B) the Hippocratic Oath has been altered irrevocably over the centuries

   (C) the taking of the Hippocratic Oath is largely symbolic these days

   (D) few modern doctors take any version of the Hippocratic Oath

   (E) by and large, the Hippocratic Oath has been set aside as irrelevant to modern medicine

8. **What in line 7 is meant by a "mnemonic device"?**

   (A) it is another first aid method similar to the Heimlich Maneuver

   (B) it is a principle of ethics that is part of the Hippocratic Oath

   (C) it is a mental device used to aid in remembering something

   (D) it means putting first things first

   (E) it is a device used to move someone who is injured without further hurting him or her

9. **The tone of lines 15 – 21 may be described as:**

   (A) cautionary yet encouraging

   (B) strongly admonitory yet oddly sanguine

   (C) mildly warning yet ultimately careless

   (D) authoritarian yet permissive

   (E) careful yet lax

Questions 10 – 11 are based on the following passage:

Musician Dave Carroll was traveling with his band from Nova Scotia to Chicago. At Chicago's O'Hare Airport, Carroll witnessed baggage handlers tossing baggage around carelessly. When Carroll opened the case of his $3,500 Taylor guitar, the guitar's neck was broken. When he tried to complain to airport personnel, Carroll was brushed off.

5   Carroll then used his musical talents to make a YouTube video with a song called "United Breaks Guitars." The video humorously showed baggage personnel tossing baggage around as if they were playing catch and laughing when they missed.

The video went viral. The first day over 100,000 people viewed it. Four days later, United Airlines' stock price declined by 10%, costing its investors an estimated $180 million in
10 value.

United changed its tune. They offered Carroll monetary compensation (he told them to donate the money to charity) and asked his permission to use "United Breaks Guitars" as a customer service training video. Now Carroll often serves various companies as a corporate consultant on customer service.

10. Which of the following best characterizes Dave Carroll?

(A) brooding, angry, vengeful

(B) powerless, depressed, disinterested

(C) creative, resourceful, good-humored

(D) wistful, wimpy, woeful

(E) sardonic, cynical, surly

11. The passage suggests that the video ultimately:

(A) caused United Airlines to make a musical counter video because Carroll's video made United "change its tune."

(B) caused all the major airlines to review their baggage handling standards

(C) caused United Airlines to offer Carroll a job as a corporate consultant on customer service

(D) caused United Airlines to take a stock hit and thus compelled it to try to compensate Carroll

(E) caused United Airlines to face multiple lawsuits

Questions 12 – 14 are based on the following passage:

A few years ago, I visited Beijing, China. I was amazed to see people of all kinds on bikes. Men in suits and women in silk dresses pedaled by, intent on getting to work on time. Young and old, rich and poor—everyone was on a bike.

Plazas were thick forests of parked bicycles. Amazingly, there were no chains or locks
5 on the bikes. Even in this big city, people trusted one another not to steal, and the trust was well-founded. There was very little thievery of bikes.

I've heard that influential citizens in Beijing are beginning to notice that people in European and American cities use cars. These citizens are beginning to look down on bicycles and urge Chinese people toward the use of automobiles. That is a shame, because
10 riding bikes cuts down on pollution and increases people's health through exercise. It also would be a shame to lose the camaraderie of a culture where people trust each other enough to leave their bikes unlocked in public. If the car replaces the bike in Beijing, I hope that the neighborliness and unity of the bike culture is not lost as well.

12. **The author of the passage expresses the hope that:**

   (A) if the bike culture is lost, the car culture will aid the Chinese economy

   (B) Beijing will pass anti-pollution laws when cars become prevalent

   (C) lost camaraderie and trust are not part of the price of "modernization"

   (D) China does not imitate American and European cities in their lack of city plazas

   (E) thievery does not become more common in the bike culture of Beijing

13. **The author thinks the bike culture of Beijing should be preserved because:**

   (A) bikes are less expensive than cars

   (B) Beijing should not compete with European and American cities

   (C) the public plazas would be empty if there were no bikes there

   (D) thievery would increase in a car culture

   (E) bikes cause less pollution and are good for people's health through the exercise they afford

14. **In lines 5 – 6 the statement "the trust was well-founded" likely means:**

    (A) there was a good reason and basis for this trust

    (B) trust had been built on an historical foundation of political gains

    (C) the bikes were too thickly packed in the plazas—they were like forests—so it was hard to steal a bike

    (D) no one had a choice to lock their bikes because manufacturers could not produce combination locks

    (E) the rigid social and political system made stealing a capital offense

Questions 15 – 24 are based on the following passage:

Hunter Scott was only twelve years old when he watched the movie *Jaws*. Full of horrifying attacks by a great white shark, the movie had audiences gasping and fearing to go swimming in the ocean.

Yet the shark attacks weren't the part of the movie that most intrigued Hunter Scott. He
5 was interested in the scene where Quint, the captain of a fishing boat, gives an account of being shipwrecked during World War II and surrounded by sharks in the open ocean. In the movie, the character Quint mentions that the name of the ship was *The U.S.S. Indianapolis*.

A little research showed Scott that there was indeed a ship named *The U.S.S. Indianapolis* which sank near the Philippines after being torpedoed by the Japanese in
10 World War II. The ship was not rescued right away, possibly to avoid drawing attention to its secret mission of delivering components of a nuclear bomb. Many of the men were killed and eaten by sharks. Scott asked his teacher if he could do a research project on *The U.S.S. Indianapolis* for credit, and he was given permission to do so.

Fortunately for Scott, some of the original crew members were still alive and had formed
15 a survivors' group, so they could easily put him in touch with the other survivors. What was more, their proud descendants had formed a support group called The Second Watch to remember the sacrifice and bravery of their ancestors. There was plenty of material for a history project.

Scott found out that of the over one thousand crew members of *The U.S.S. Indianapolis*,
20 only a third of them lived to tell the tale of being stranded in the ocean for four or five days. These three hundred or so men had plenty of memories to share with Scott. They remembered watching comrades grow delirious from sun exposure or drinking seawater and swimming off, only to be swallowed by the deep. They remembered beating the water and screaming when they saw sharks circling their numbers and prowling on the attack. They
25 remembered watching unfortunate comrades bitten and eaten by sharks. They watched other comrades slowly succumb to the wounds they had received during the torpedo attack.

Yet this group had a camaraderie and unity that inspired Scott. Over half of the 28 survivors had been in Ensign Harlan Twible's group. Ensign Twible had heroically enjoined them to help one another. This group tied themselves together with ropes so that no one
30 could drift off or drown if his face slipped into the water during sleep. They shared lifejackets and helped one another into ones they took off the dead. They exhorted one another not to give up hope and to keep fighting for survival. It was their group that hallooed and waved to a low-flying plane and caught the attention of the pilot, who then arranged for their rescue. Twible was later awarded Navy and Marine Corps medals for his heroism in keeping the
35 group together and enhancing their chances of survival.

Surprisingly, Scott found that the survivors were not as haunted by their horrific days in the water as they were by the knowledge that their captain had suffered charges over the incident. He was accused of not properly zig-zagging the ship in order to avoid torpedo fire. The men who had gone into the water did not think their captain was to blame for the
40 incident, and they wanted to clear his name.

With Scott's help and encouragement, they supported one another as they had during the most awful incident of their lives. The veterans won that battle as they won the battle for

survival in the frightening, powerful, and shark-ridden sea—by sticking together and supporting one another. They began a campaign, and in the year 2000 these intrepid
45 survivors appeared as a group before Congress to ask for the exoneration of their deceased captain—and they got it.

15. **The fact that Hunter Scott picked up on the name of the ship the character Quint describes in the movie *Jaws* and then did some research to corroborate that the ship was not fiction shows that:**

    (A) the twelve year old had a morbid interest in bloody shark attacks

    (B) the twelve year old did not know that World War II was over

    (C) the twelve year old had a quick and inquiring mind with a proclivity toward history

    (D) the twelve year old was bored during the film because of its plastic animatronics

    (E) the twelve year old was too interested in the past to enjoy the present

16. **Lines 10 – 11 imply that the ship was not rescued promptly because:**

    (A) the publicity surrounding its rescue might reveal the secretive nature of its mission

    (B) anti-nuclear forces in the United States demonstrated against its rescue

    (C) not even the Navy knew of the existence of the *U.S.S. Indianapolis* due to the top secret nature of its mission

    (D) the Japanese blocked all distress signals from it, knowing the ship contained "the bomb"

    (E) a nuclear bomb was about to be set off

17. Lines 14 – 18 demonstrate that:

    (A) the descendants of the survivors of the *U.S.S. Indianapolis* were proud of the sacrifices their ancestors had made and wanted to keep their memories alive

    (B) the descendants of the survivors of the *U.S.S. Indianapolis* had to organize to keep their ancestors' sacrifices from being forgotten since the Navy was still sensitive about the nuclear mission

    (C) the descendants of the survivors of the *U.S.S. Indianapolis* held their ancestors in low honor and esteem

    (D) the descendants of the survivors of the *U.S.S. Indianapolis* were indignant over the length of time it took the Navy to rescue their ancestors

    (E) the descendants of the survivors of the *U.S.S. Indianapolis* were ashamed of their ancestors' role in delivering nuclear bomb components

18. In line 23 the phrase "swallowed by the deep" is likely used for the purpose of:

    (A) dramatic imagery

    (B) personalization of the ocean

    (C) a statement of fact; the ocean bottom was two miles below

    (D) a grammatical error; "deep," as an adjective, should have a noun to modify as in "deep ocean."

    (E) a reference to the second book the author of *Jaws* wrote, which is entitled *The Deep*

19. In lines 21 – 25, three sentences start with the words "They remembered." The author likely did this because:

    (A) there were many questions about what really happened, so the facts had to be distinguished from unreliable memories and the eyewitness accounts of injured and frightened men

    (B) the author wanted to make sure the reader understood that the *U.S.S. Indianapolis* incident happened in the past

    (C) the sentences should not start out that way; the author is being repetitious

    (D) the repetition puts the emphasis on the survivors and their accounts to Hunter Scott of their painful memories of the *U.S.S. Indianapolis* incident

    (E) the author could not think of any synonyms for the word "remember"

20. In line 26 the word "succumb" most likely means:

    (A) close in meaning to the word "succor," it means they slowly tended to their wounds

    (B) recover

    (C) heal

    (D) watch the wounds become infected by the bacteria-filled ocean waters

    (E) to yield; to give in to stronger forces

21. The following can be surmised from the fact that over half of the men who survived were in Ensign Twible's group:

    (A) Ensign Twible was a man of good fortune and it rubbed off on those around him

    (B) nothing; it is simply a factual figure that most of the survivors came from Ensign Twible's group

    (C) very little; it was probably coincidence that most of the survivors came from Ensign Twible's group

    (D) Ensign Twible must have shown leadership skills that enabled many in his group to survive

    (E) Because he was an Ensign, Twible was probably the best trained man on the ship when it came to survival situations

22. The message of lines 27 – 35 might be summed up as:

    (A) men against nature will always win

    (B) even an Ensign can become a hero

    (C) in unity there is strength

    (D) every man for himself

    (E) the survival of the fittest

23. In line 27 the word "camaraderie" most likely means:

    (A) a formal military comradeship

    (B) drunken fellowship; the men drank together to forget their horrifying experience

    (C) mutual good will, familiar friendliness

    (D) hilarity, forgetfulness

    (E) escapist tendencies

24. **Lines 36 – 46 deal less with the incident itself and more with:**

   (A) the psychological aftermath for the survivors and their families

   (B) new regulations in the Navy which would make it impossible for this to happen again

   (C) the descendants of the survivors and their ongoing efforts as The Second Watch

   (D) Hunter Scott's history project and the reception it got at his school

   (E) the survivors' feelings about the charges against their captain and their efforts to exonerate their captain officially from any wrongdoing

SECTION 5
(MATHEMATICS)
Time: 25 minutes
18 questions

MULTIPLE CHOICE

Directions: For the questions in this section, solve each problem and decide which of the given answer choices is the best choice. Fill in the corresponding oval on the answer sheet to indicate your selection. You may use any available space for scratchwork.

Note:

1. Calculator use is permitted.
2. All numbers used are real numbers.
3. All figures provided are drawn to scale and lie in a plane unless otherwise indicated.
4. Unless otherwise specified, the domain of any function f is assumed to be the set of all real numbers x for which $f(x)$ is a real number.

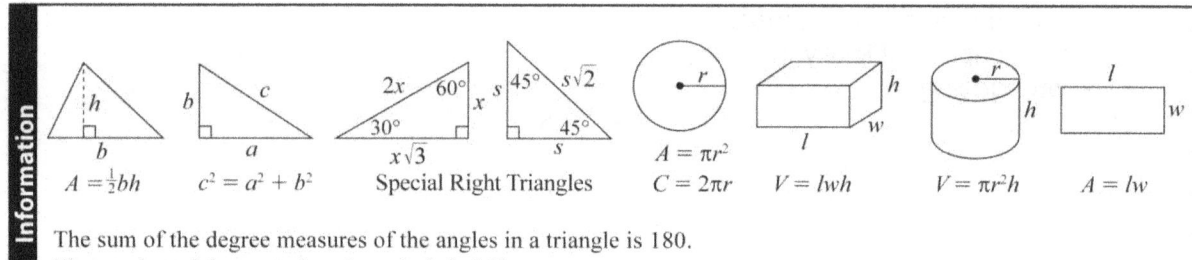

The sum of the degree measures of the angles in a triangle is 180.
The number of degrees of arc in a circle is 360.
A straight angle has a degree measure of 180.

1. In 2009 there were 255 girls and 153 boys at Warren Middle School. What percent of the students were girls?

    (A) 166%

    (B) 65%

    (C) 62.5%

    (D) 54%

    (E) 37.5%

2. Miranda reaches into her sock drawer and pulls out a sock. There are 10 black socks, 6 white socks, and 4 blue socks. What is the probability that she will pull out a white sock?

(A) $\dfrac{1}{5}$

(B) $\dfrac{3}{10}$

(C) $\dfrac{1}{2}$

(D) $\dfrac{7}{10}$

(E) 1

3. If m > 0, then $\dfrac{2}{m} + \dfrac{1}{7} = ?$

(A) $\dfrac{3}{7+m}$

(B) $\dfrac{14+m}{7m}$

(C) $\dfrac{2}{7m}$

(D) $\dfrac{2m}{7}$

(E) 2

4. The histogram below shows the number of students who attend a certain elementary school. What is the median number of students?

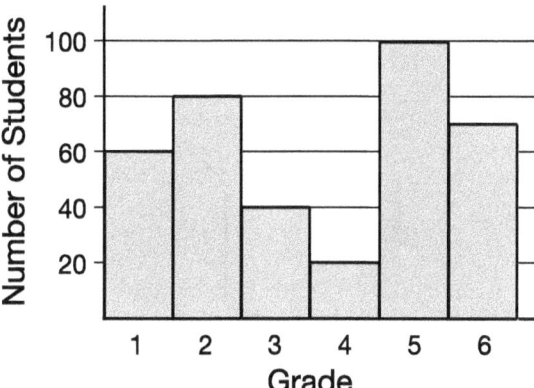

(A) 80

(B) 65

(C) $61\dfrac{2}{3}$

(D) 40

(E) 25

5. One afternoon, Jenny ran at a rate of 5 miles per hour, rode her bicycle at a rate of 17 miles per hour, and rested. The graph below indicates that the order of resting, riding her bicycle, and running was:

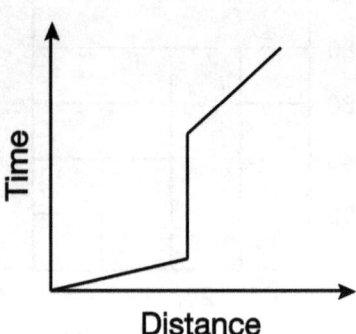

(A) Rested, ran, rode

(B) Rested, rode, ran

(C) Ran, rested, rode

(D) Rode, rested, ran

(E) Ran, rode, rested

6. Which of the following CANNOT be the slope of $\overrightarrow{OM}$?

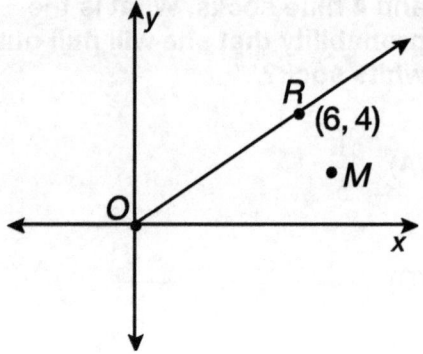

(A) $\dfrac{1}{4}$

(B) $\dfrac{1}{2}$

(C) $\dfrac{3}{5}$

(D) $\dfrac{5}{8}$

(E) $\dfrac{17}{25}$

7. Which of the following values of k will make the expression $8x^3 + 25k$ factorable?

I. 5
II. 1
III. 1/25

(A) I only

(B) II only

(C) III only

(D) I and II

(E) I and III

8. $|y(x) - h(x)| > 2$ for all values of x.
   Which of these graphs could represent the two functions?

   I.
   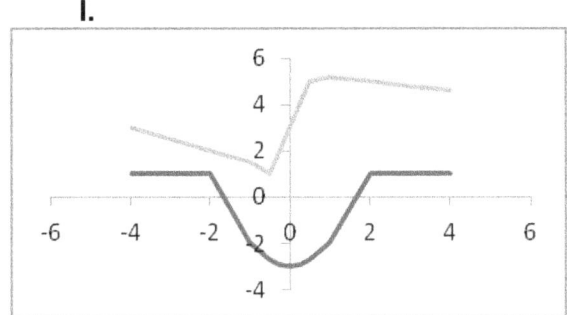

   II.
   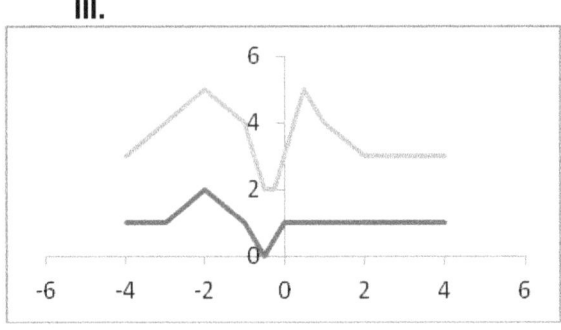

   III.

   (A) I only
   (B) II only
   (C) III only
   (D) I and II
   (E) I and III

The SAT Advantage

STUDENT-PRODUCED RESPONSE

Directions: For the Student-Produced Response questions 9 – 18, use the grids at the bottom of the same answer sheet page on which you answered questions 1 – 8. You may use any available space for scratchwork.

The 10 Student-Produced Response questions require you to solve the problem and enter your answer into special grids by filling in the appropriate ovals, as shown below.

Example: 2.25 or $\frac{9}{4}$ or 9/4. Write the answer in the boxes and grid-in the answers by filling in the ovals.

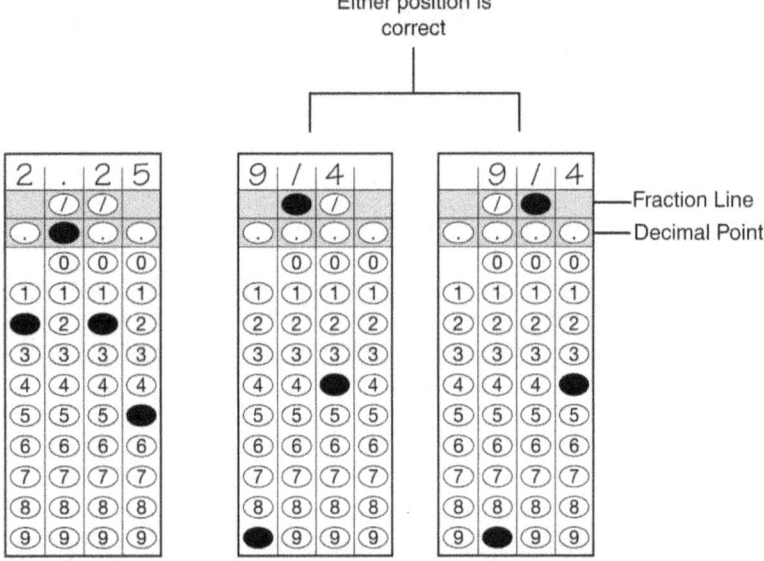

You may start your answers in any column, as shown above, as long as the answer fits. Columns not needed should be left blank. Only fill in one oval per column.

You are not required to write your answer in the boxes at the top of the columns, but it is recommended that you do so. Note, however, you will only receive credit for filling in the ovals correctly.

Only grid in one answer, even if a question has more than one correct answer.

No answers are negative.

Mixed numbers cannot be gridded. For example: the number $1\frac{1}{2}$ must be gridded as 1.5 or 3/2.

If it is gridded as 1 1 / 2, it will be interpreted as 11/2, not $1\frac{1}{2}$.

Enter decimal answers as accurately as possible. For example: the repeating decimal 0.1666... should be gridded as .166 or .167 (less accurate answers such as .16 or .17 are not acceptable). Examples of acceptable ways to grid 1/6 or .1666...

9. Maria earns $8.60 per hour and works 35 hours each week. Her employer gave her a raise, increasing her weekly pay to $315. On an hourly basis, how much was Maria's raise in dollars?

10. What is the measure of m + n in degrees?

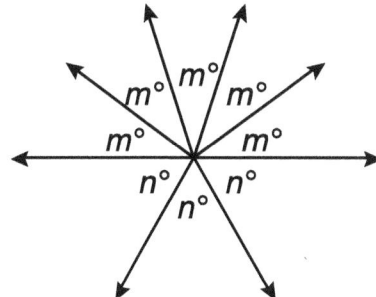

11. A monkey slithers up a slippery pole. He climbs 3 ft in 3 seconds and then slides down 2 ft in the next second. If the pole is 12 ft long and the monkey continues this pattern of alternately climbing up for 3 seconds and sliding down for 1 second, after how many seconds will the monkey reach the top of the pole?

12. Five times the square of an integer is five more than 24 times the integer. What is the number?

13. If one picks a random number between 100 and 150 (including both 100 and 150), what is the probability that it is the square of an integer?

14. ABC is a triangle. D is a point on AB and E is a point on AC such that angle ADE = angle ABC. If AD/AB = $\frac{3}{4}$ and BC = 12 cm, what is DE?

15. The function $f(x) = (x-h)^2 + k$ touches the x-axis at only one point. What is the value of k?

16. A square is inscribed within a circle and another circle is inscribed within the square. What is the ratio of the area of the large circle to that of the small circle?

17. What is the remainder when 7^{109} is divided by 5?

18. At temperatures close to dewpoint, there is a linear relationship between relative humidity RH and temperature t:
$RH = 100 - 5(t - t_d)$ where t_d is the dewpoint which is assumed to be constant.

If the dewpoint $t_d = 40°$ F, by what percentage does relative humidity increase when the temperature changes from $1.2t_d$ to $1.1t_d$?

(Round off your answer to the nearest degree Fahrenheit.)

SECTION 6
(WRITING)
Time: 25 minutes
35 questions

IMPROVING SENTENCES

Directions: For each of the following questions, choose the best answer and fill in the corresponding oval on the answer sheet to indicate your selection.

Part of each sentence (or the entire sentence) is underlined. The five answer choices present five ways of phrasing the underlined portion. Choice A repeats the original phrasing and the other four choices offer alternative phrasings. If you think the original phrasing is best, select choice A; if not, select one of the other options.

In choosing your answer, follow the requirements of standard written English. Pay attention to grammar, choice of words, sentence construction, and punctuation; your selection should result in the most effective, clear, and precise sentence—free of awkwardness or ambiguity.

1. The photographer Lyonel Feininger <u>having trained as a painter, he became</u> a successful cartoonist and caricaturist in Berlin and taught painting at the renowned Bauhaus school before turning to photography at age 57.

   (A) having trained as a painter, he became
   (B) training as a painter, he became
   (C) was also a trained painter, having become
   (D) was also a trained painter, becoming
   (E) was also a trained painter who became

2. Students of American history learn that the decade 1840–1850 was one of startling technological progress, geographical expansion, <u>and they discover controversies in politics caused by rapid changes in society</u>.

   (A) and they discover controversies in politics caused by rapid changes in society
   (B) as they discover that controversies in politics are caused by rapid changes in society
   (C) and controversial discoveries about politics caused by changes in society that were rapid
   (D) and political controversy caused by rapid social change
   (E) discovering political controversies and causing rapid social change

3. Experts say most citizens are not prepared for <u>disasters, fewer than 10 percent of Americans have created</u> a disaster relief kit containing water, food and spare batteries.

   (A) disasters, fewer than 10 percent of Americans have created
   (B) disasters; fewer than 10 percent of Americans have created
   (C) disasters and fewer than 10 percent of Americans have created
   (D) disasters; fewer than 10 percent of Americans having created
   (E) disasters; fewer than 10 percent of whom had created

4. American women who entered the labor force during World War II <u>not only produced weapons and kept vital industries alive, but also changed perceptions of what women could do</u>.

   (A) not only produced weapons and kept vital industries alive, but also changed perceptions of what women could do
   (B) not only produced weapons and kept vital industries alive, they changed perceptions of what women could do as well
   (C) while not only producing weapons and keeping vital industries alive, they also were changing perceptions of what women could do
   (D) being not only productive of weapons and keeping vital industries alive, also changing perceptions of what women could do
   (E) produced not only weapons that kept vital industries alive, but also changed perceptions of what women could do

5. After the desertion of his father and the death of his mother, **the Allan family of Richmond, Virginia, became the foster parents of young Edgar Poe.**

    (A) the Allan family of Richmond, Virginia, became the foster parents of young Edgar Poe

    (B) the Allan family of Richmond, Virginia becoming his foster parents, young Edgar Poe grew up in a new family

    (C) young Edgar Poe's foster parents were the Allans of Richmond, Virginia

    (D) the foster parents of young Edgar Poe became the Allan family of Richmond, Virginia

    (E) young Edgar Poe became the foster child of the Allan family of Richmond, Virginia

6. Some studies show that adding ginger to your diet can aid digestion, relieve pain, **and for reducing cholesterol levels.**

    (A) and for reducing cholesterol levels

    (B) reducing cholesterol levels as well

    (C) and reduce cholesterol levels

    (D) and the reduction of cholesterol levels

    (E) and level the reduction of cholesterol

7. **In 1954, the U.S. Supreme Court overturned the doctrine of "separate but equal," until then** states could legally maintain segregated schools for children of different races.

    (A) In 1954, the U.S. Supreme Court overturned the doctrine of "separate but equal," until then

    (B) Because the U.S. Supreme Court overturned the doctrine of "separate but equal" in 1954,

    (C) Before 1954, when the U.S. Supreme Court overturned the doctrine of "separate but equal,"

    (D) Finally, the U.S. Supreme Court overturned the doctrine of "separate but equal" in 1954; but until then

    (E) Even though the U.S. Supreme Court overturned the doctrine of "separate but equal" in 1954, until which time

8. Louis Pasteur, the French chemist who invented the pasteurization process for killing bacteria in **milk, he also developed treatments** for cholera, rabies, and anthrax.

    (A) milk, he also developed treatments

    (B) milk, also developing treatments

    (C) milk, also developed treatments

    (D) milk, after developing treatments

    (E) milk, although he also developed treatments

9. **To be successful, <u>residents must willingly participate in our town's trash reduction policy by recycling paper and plastic.</u>**

   (A) residents must willingly participate in our town's trash reduction policy by recycling paper and plastic

   (B) residents' willing participation in the recycling of paper and plastic is needed in our town's trash reduction policy

   (C) our town depends on the willing participation of residents in its trash reduction policy to recycle paper and plastic

   (D) our town's trash reduction policy depends on the willing participation of residents in the recycling of paper and plastic

   (E) our town depends on residents to willingly participate in the trash reduction policy by recycling paper and plastic

10. <u>Because the day before Ash Wednesday is traditionally a time of indulgent eating, the Mardi Gras festival in New Orleans derives its name from the French words meaning "fat Tuesday."</u>

   (A) Because the day before Ash Wednesday is traditionally a time of indulgent eating, the Mardi Gras festival in New Orleans derives its name from the French words meaning "fat Tuesday."

   (B) Because the day before Ash Wednesday is traditionally a time of indulgent eating is why the Mardi Gras festival in New Orleans derives its name from the French words meaning "fat Tuesday."

   (C) The French words for "fat Tuesday" give their name to the Mardi Gras festival in New Orleans because, with it being the day before Ash Wednesday, its time of indulgent eating is traditional.

   (D) It being traditionally a time of indulgent eating, the day before Ash Wednesday in New Orleans, therefore, is given the name of the Mardi Gras festival, derived from the French words meaning "fat Tuesday."

   (E) Being traditionally a time of indulgent eating, that is why the Mardi Gras festival in New Orleans, which occurs on the day before Ash Wednesday, derives its name from the French words meaning "fat Tuesday."

11. **Jane Goodall observed and interacted with chimpanzees for many years and she** has become known as the world's foremost experts on these apes.

   (A) Jane Goodall observed and interacted with chimpanzees for many years and she

   (B) Jane Goodall, who observed and interacted with chimpanzees for many years,

   (C) Jane Goodall, observing and interacting with chimpanzees for many years, and she

   (D) While observing and interacting with chimpanzees for many years, Jane Goodall

   (E) Her having observed and interacted with chimpanzees for many years, Jane Goodall

IDENTIFYING SENTENCE ERRORS

Directions: For each of the following questions, choose the best answer and fill in the corresponding oval on the answer sheet to indicate your selection.

The following sentences test your ability to recognize grammar and usage errors. In making your selection, follow the requirements of standard written English.

Each sentence contains either a single error or no error at all; none of the sentences contain more than one error. If the sentence contains an error, select the underlined portion A through D that must be changed in order to fix the sentence. If the sentence is correct and contains no errors, select choice E.

12. <u>Of all</u> the acts of heroism that occurred
      A
    during the tornado, the rescue of the
    three children <u>who</u> were trapped under
            B
    fallen rafters <u>were</u> certainly the <u>most</u>
              C   D
    <u>impressive</u>. <u>No error</u>
                E

13. Neither the company president <u>nor</u> the
                                 A
    treasurer <u>was</u> blamed <u>for</u> the
            B   C
    unfortunate <u>effects</u> of the budget cuts.
              D
    <u>No error</u>
     E

14. Although <u>their</u> wages <u>are seen</u> as an
            A   B
    important factor, the average worker
    considers pleasant working conditions
    <u>to be</u> <u>more crucial</u> to the achievement
     C   D
    of job satisfaction. <u>No error</u>
                          E

15. Because the number of social
    networking sites <u>are</u> <u>rising</u>, many
                A   B
    people now belong to several online
    communities <u>in which</u> <u>they spend</u>
                  C   D
    hours each day. <u>No error</u>
                    E

16. A jockey who <u>has ridden</u> horses for
              A
    several owners on the same day <u>will</u>
                                 B
    have <u>wore</u> jackets and caps of
          C
    <u>distinctly different</u> colors and patterns
              D
    as emblems of the different owners.
    <u>No error</u>
      E

17. None of these legal issues <u>wouldn't</u>
                                  A
    <u>have</u> arisen if the committee leader

    <u>had only</u> abided <u>by</u> the rules and <u>let</u>
       B   C   D
    the members vote on the proposal.

    <u>No error</u>
       E

18. Most of the athletes <u>who</u> <u>were</u>
                           A   B
    <u>penalized</u> <u>because of</u> the scuffle on
        C   C(cont)
    the field disagreed <u>to</u> the referee's
                          D
    decision. <u>No error</u>
                 E

19. The haiku form, although <u>considerably</u>
                                   A
    <u>shorter than most other</u> poetic
           B
    structures, <u>is</u> <u>remarkably expressive</u>.
                 C   D
    <u>No error</u>
       E

20. Connecting with people face-to-face in
    our everyday lives <u>is</u> <u>potentially both</u>
                        A   B
    more difficult and more rewarding than
    <u>to respond</u> <u>to them</u> electronically.
         C   D
    <u>No error</u>
       E

21. <u>Fewer</u> people were <u>immigrating</u> from
       A   B
    the impoverished nation <u>as a result of</u>
                                 C
    the travel restriction policies <u>adopted</u>
                                        D
    <u>by</u> the new regime. <u>No error</u>
                                 E

22. J. D. Salinger was <u>among</u> the <u>most</u>
                          A   B
    <u>reclusive</u> writers in literary history,
        C(should be C label on reclusive)
    <u>although</u> he was known <u>as frequenting</u>
        C   D
    local businesses in his community.

    <u>No error</u>
       E

23. No matter how convinced we are of
    the wisdom and correctness of our
    views, there <u>are</u> surely a social
                   A
    obligation to respect the choices of
    people <u>whose</u> opinions <u>differ from</u>
              B   C
    <u>ours</u>. <u>No error</u>
       D   E

24. <u>During World War I</u>, the *Britannic*, a
           A
    sister ship of the *Titanic*, <u>sunk</u> <u>off the</u>
                                     B   C
    <u>coast of</u> a Greek island while on its
        C(cont)
    way <u>to rescue</u> wounded soldiers in the
          D
    Balkans. <u>No error</u>
                 E

25. The preschool children <u>with which</u> the
                                    A
    teacher's aide was working <u>grew</u>
                                  B
    <u>increasingly</u> more restless and less
          C
    interested <u>in listening</u> to a story.
                      D
    <u>No error</u>
        E

26. New <u>sources of</u> rare earth metals are
             A
    <u>being sought</u> as their use in high-
          B
    technology devices grows and as
    China, <u>which</u> supplies most of the
                 C
    market, <u>will begin</u> to limit exports of
                   D
    these substances. <u>No error</u>
                            E

27. There is no sense <u>in complaining</u>
                              A
    <u>about</u> the new rules now that the
       B
    reason for them <u>had been</u> explained <u>to</u>
                          C   D
    <u>everyone's</u> satisfaction. <u>No error</u>
                                      E

28. A new study urged <u>that</u> people <u>with a</u>
                           A   B
    <u>history</u> of heart disease <u>exercise</u>

    extreme caution <u>not to combine</u>
                          D
    certain medications. <u>No error</u>
                               E

29. Food safety is a high priority in the
    United States, but thousands of
    Americans <u>are still taken</u> ill each year
                     A
    when <u>they</u> fail <u>to inspect and monitor</u>
             B   C
    food processing plants <u>carefully</u>.
                                 D
    <u>No error</u>
        E

IMPROVING PARAGRAPHS

Directions: The following passage is an early draft of an essay that may need parts rewritten.

Read the passage provided and select the best answer choice for each question. Some questions are about individual sentences or parts of individual sentences and ask you to improve the sentence structure or word choice. Some questions are about multiple sentences and ask you to consider the overall organization of the passage as a whole. In making your selection, follow the requirements of standard written English.

For each of the following questions, choose the best answer and fill in the corresponding oval on the answer sheet to indicate your selection.

(1) Although Tennessee Williams's play *The Glass Menagerie* is often performed more often than is *The Night of the Iguana* and although I find all of Tennessee Williams's work fascinating, I prefer *The Night of the Iguana.*
(2) It would be hard to miss the symbolism of the tied-up iguana. (3) Shannon, the defrocked priest who is losing his job and perhaps his mind, is tied up to a hammock in the Mexican resort to prevent him from committing suicide. (4) It is interesting that both the iguana and Shannon are eventually set free to live their lives unfettered.
(5) The character of Hannah is fascinating. (6) Shannon is clearly attracted to her. (7) She very gently refuses to have anything to do with him romantically. (8) She is a spiritual person, a spinster who has spent years bonding with and taking care of her aged grandfather. (9) She has fought her own "blue devils" to a standstill and is more than capable of helping Shannon drive out his demons of incipient alcoholism and full-blown despair. (10) She saves his sanity and guides him into a relationship with Maxine, the resort-owner, which seems like an unlikely pairing. (11) One conclusion the reader or watcher of the play can come to about Hannah's refusal is that Hannah is wise enough to know that a relationship between two such people as themselves would never last. (12) There is a possible second reason as well. (13) Shannon would probably become dependent on her for emotional sustenance. (14) She probably does not want that, having just been liberated from her loving bondage to her grandfather. (15) The elderly gentleman dies at the Mexican resort while gazing at the sea, which he calls the "Cradle of Life."

30. What would be the best revised version of sentence 1 (reproduced below)?

    Although Tennessee Williams's play *The Glass Menagerie* is often performed more often than is *The Night of the Iguana* and although I find all of Tennessee Williams's work fascinating, I prefer *The Night of the Iguana*.

    (A) Although most audiences find *The Glass Menagerie* more fascinating and interesting, so it is performed more often, I prefer to see *The Night of the Iguana*.

    (B) Although Tennessee Williams's fascinating *The Glass Menagerie* is performed more often than *The Night of the Iguana*, I prefer the latter play.

    (C) Although both *The Glass Menagerie* and *The Night of the Iguana* are both by playwright Tennessee Williams, the latter is performed more often than the former by popular demand.

    (D) A viewing of both *The Glass Menagerie* and *The Night of the Iguana* will show that audiences prefer *The Glass Menagerie* by applause.

    (E) The sentence is fine as it is.

31. Which of the following sentences is best to insert between sentences 2 and 3?

    (A) Caught, bound, and held captive for eating, the iguana symbolizes people who are trapped in despair.

    (B) Shannon is at the end of his rope.

    (C) A tied-up iguana is not free.

    (D) The doomed creature tries and tries to escape captivity.

    (E) Although I am not sure that the iguana is a national symbol of Mexico, I think it might be.

32. What is the best way to deal with sentence 7 (reproduced below)?

    She very gently refuses to have anything to do with him romantically.

    (A) Leave it as it is

    (B) Change "she very gently" to "she extremely gently"

    (C) Connect it to sentence 6 with the word "yet," put "She" into the lower case, and eliminate the period at the end of sentence 6 to make the two sentences into one thought

    (D) Place it before sentence 6

    (E) Omit it

33. Where would be a logical place to break the lengthy last paragraph into two paragraphs?

    (A) Starting with sentence 8

    (B) Starting with sentence 10

    (C) Starting with sentence 14

    (D) It should not be broken up

    (E) Starting with sentence 11

34. What is the best way to deal with sentence 13 (reproduced below)?

    Shannon would probably become dependent on her for emotional sustenance.

    (A) Leave it as it is

    (B) Omit it

    (C) Move it in front of sentence 12

    (D) Move it to the end of the paragraph

    (E) Move it to the beginning of the paragraph

35. Which of the following, if placed after sentence 14, would be the most effective concluding sentence for the essay?

    (A) The *Night of the Iguana* is a good play.

    (B) Lonely, troubled people are like iguanas.

    (C) Perhaps Hannah is an "iguana" too, glad to be set free and not about to be tied down again.

    (D) People often go to the sea, the "Cradle of Life," to die.

    (E) Maxine and Shannon will go on to a new life together.

SECTION 7
(CRITICAL READING)
Time: 20 minutes
19 questions

SENTENCE COMPLETION

Directions: For each of the following questions, choose the best answer and fill in the corresponding oval on the answer sheet to indicate your selection.

Each sentence contains one or two blanks indicating that something has been omitted from the sentence. Choose the word or set of words, labeled A through E, that when inserted into the sentence, best fits the meaning of the sentence as a whole.

1. Although he had fought to get it, once he had been offered the new job, the young man was -------- about leaving his desirable old one.

    (A) irresolute

    (B) certain

    (C) adamant

    (D) indubitable

    (E) militant

2. Worldly-wise and -------- , the courtesan seemed to experience less and less pleasure in life.

    (A) bejeweled

    (B) jaded

    (C) naïve

    (D) humorous

    (E) optimistic

3. You cannot be -------- about practice if you want to win an Olympic medal; you must be -------- in your determination to keep yourself in top condition.

    (A) lax ... doubtful

    (B) erratic ... tenacious

    (C) diligent ... unbending

    (D) vigilant ... resolute

    (E) careless ... volatile

4. Charles Dickens often features -------- heroes in his books, reflecting his own poverty-stricken childhood.

    (A) wealthy

    (B) profligate

    (C) pre-eminent

    (D) impecunious

    (E) middle-class

5. The politician intoned to his opponent, "You cannot -------- me one -------- by all the lies you have told about me in the course of your campaign, as the truth will always win out."

   (A) diminish ... modicum

   (B) exalt ... particle

   (C) honor ... atom

   (D) belittle ... behemoth

   (E) deride ... iota

6. The young woman was --------, modest, and shy in front of her -------- to the award, as she felt the one who had gone before her was so much better than she was.

   (A) humble ... successor

   (B) blatant ... antecedent

   (C) blasé ... forerunner

   (D) self-effacing ... precursor

   (E) arrogant ... predecessor

READING BASED QUESTIONS

Directions: For each of the following questions, choose the best answer and fill in the corresponding oval on the answer sheet to indicate your selection.

The reading passages below are followed by questions based on their content. Questions that follow a pair of related passages may be based on both the content of the passages and/or the relationship between the passages. Answer the questions based on what is <u>stated</u> or <u>implied</u> in the passages.

Questions 7 – 19 are based on the following passage:

Surveys show that public speaking is the number one fear people experience in life. In fact, fear of public speaking ranks higher than the fear of death! A comedian quipped that on the way to a funeral, the majority of people would rather be in the casket than have to give the eulogy. We're that scared of public speaking!

5   One way to talk yourself out of "stagefright" before a public speaking engagement is to ask yourself, "Would I really rather be dead than have to do this?" Imagine facing a firing squad and how awful that would be. Imagine being in a fatal car accident on the way to the speech. Would you really rather have those things happen than have to give your speech? Of course not! Count yourself lucky that you only have to give a speech.

10   Another way to talk yourself out of stagefright is to tell yourself, "This will all be over in a few hours. I'll be home again, in my jeans, watching TV, eating, and relaxing. Nothing will change. Everything will go back to the way it was."

There are many remedies for stagefright, even if you are the kind of person who cowers behind the curtain while waiting to go onstage. Even if you are the most timorous little
15 mouse you can become a mighty lion by using a few techniques to reduce and/or control stagefright.

Tried and true advice is to arrive early and stand in the place where you are going to be making the presentation. When you actually do go to the place, your subconscious mind will feel comfortable with a sense of "I've already been here and done this before," and you will
20 automatically feel more at ease.

The subconscious mind does not distinguish between what is imagined and what really happens. If you imagine yourself going up to the podium in a relaxed and confident way, and imagine yourself giving the speech with clarity and calm, when it comes time to actually do so, your subconscious mind will be relaxed, knowing that you've already achieved this.

25   Related to training your subconscious mind so that it works *for* you and *against* fear is the process of "desensitizing" yourself to fear. Psychologists help patients with extreme fears desensitize themselves to anxiety through training them in a process of deep relaxation coupled with gradual exposure to the fearful situation. Fear and relaxation cannot co-exist, so if you "desensitize" yourself to fear-filled situations by relaxing during
30 visualization and gradual exposure, you will come automatically to associate the fear-filled situations with relaxation.

To de-sensitize yourself, psychologists suggest tightening and loosening muscles, concentrating on the feeling of release as you let go. For example, make a tight fist; then relax it. While concentrating on the feeling of relaxation, visualize yourself walking onstage and standing behind the microphone, about to begin your speech. Do this many times, and you will automatically associate being onstage with a deep feeling of relaxation rather than any feeling of fear.

Visualizing a relaxing setting helps too. As you prepare to give your speech, say something to yourself like: "I am on a hot beach on a lazy day with no challenges in front of me. The ocean is lapping gently at the shore, the sand is warm beneath my shoulders, and the sun is baking all the tension out of me. There is nothing but a clear sky overhead, and I am completely serene and safe." Picturing such a scene vividly can carry you all the way up to the microphone with a smile on your face. Your muscles and body will feel relaxed too. Keeping the imaginary experience in the back of your mind as you give your presentation can keep you calm the whole time.

Speaking of deep and steady breathing, taking twenty long deep breaths as you are waiting to go onstage also helps to relax you. Count them. Breathe all the way to the pit of your stomach, inhaling and exhaling. It does not have to be obvious to others.

It is comforting to know that many singing and other stars have confessed to terrible anxiety before going on stage. One Broadway star said that she would go to the theatre when it was empty and shout out loud, "I love you!" to a pretend audience. When she walked onstage, she walked into all those invisible 'I love you!' vibrations and she felt more confident. Another well-known singer repeated to herself something her agent had told her: "There's no advantage in fear. There's no advantage in fear."

You can also tell yourself helpful things about fear. You can tell yourself that you have a choice: you can choose not to be afraid. You will be getting up in front of all those people regardless. You can get up in fear or you can get up in confidence. It is your choice whether you are afraid or not, and you can choose not to be afraid. You can choose to enjoy yourself. You can choose to have an experience of great communal understanding between yourself and a group of people. You can choose to be funny and charming and one of them or you can scare yourself off and make everyone uncomfortable.

Practice deep breathing, engage in the vivid visualization of relaxing scenes, perform desensitization exercises, and assert affirmations like "I love you," "There's no advantage in fear," and "I can choose not to be afraid." Visit the presentation stage early and stand there in a relaxed way prior to giving your speech in order to feel warm familiarity with the place. You can do this. You can perform without fear.

The SAT Advantage

7. The word "eulogy" in line 4 most likely means:

   (A) a speech of high praise for a person's character and accomplishments in life

   (B) a speech about a dead person's failures in life

   (C) a soliloquy as in *Hamlet*

   (D) a song dedicated to the deceased

   (E) a reading aloud of the deceased person's letters to friends

8. The last sentence in the second paragraph (line 9) contains what is known in English as:

   (A) a declarative sentence

   (B) an interrogative sentence

   (C) an imperative sentence

   (D) an exclamatory sentence

   (E) an explanatory sentence

9. The word "cowers" in line 13 most likely means:

   (A) hides

   (B) shrinks away

   (C) cowards

   (D) clings

   (E) wagers

10. In lines 14 – 16 the author is speaking:

    (A) metaphorically

    (B) categorically

    (C) imperatively

    (D) realistically

    (E) cynically

11. "Tried and true" in line 17 is consistent with the passage's tone of:

    (A) reassurance that stagefright can be conquered

    (B) warning that stagefright never goes away and that most methods are not permanently effective against it

    (C) doubtfulness that the reader will ever conquer stagefright

    (D) lack of sympathy for people who experience stagefright

    (E) scoffing at people who experience stagefright

12. Lines 17 – 24 approach managing stagefright from a perspective of:

    (A) on the level of consciousness Freud called the "superego"

    (B) on the foremost level of the conscious mind

    (C) on deep levels of human consciousness

    (D) on deep levels of human conscience

    (E) on the foremost level of the conscience mind

13. **Lines 25 – 31 describe:**

(A) a psychological process of reprogramming a person's responses to fear-inducing situations

(B) a psychological process of fooling the subconscious mind into thinking it is in a threatening situation

(C) a psychological procedure that "surgically" removes fears through autosuggestion

(D) a psychological breakthrough in relaxation technology

(E) a psychological process of hypnotizing a person into overcoming his or her fears and anxieties

14. **Lines 32 – 37 may be described as:**

(A) deep muscle re-training

(B) "how to" instructions in de-sensitization

(C) a layman's guide to psychology

(D) hands-on training in massage therapy

(E) do-it-yourself therapy for beginners in psychology

15. **Line 38 introduces the idea of visualization, but a related idea is also presented in lines 39 – 42. This idea is:**

(A) confirmation of nerves

(B) affirmation of nature

(C) affirmation of the ego

(D) affirmative self-talk

(E) visualization coupled with virtual reality

16. **The implication of lines 49 – 54 is:**

(A) performers who suffer from stagefright soon lose their fame and fortunes

(B) famous entertainers got that way because they rarely experience stagefright

(C) even well-known performers suffer from stagefright and must overcome it through using various techniques

(D) some well-known performers have lost their careers because of stagefright

(E) the self-designed techniques some stars use to overcome stagefright are not valid

17. **Lines 55 – 61 may be said to be emphasizing:**

    (A) human agency and the power of choice

    (B) a "can do" approach to public speaking or performing

    (C) an admonishment that public speaking and performing are only for those who experience little to no stagefright

    (D) a warning to stay emotionally distant from the audience

    (E) a method of affirming to yourself that you can do this

18. **The assurances "You can do this. You can perform without fear," in line 66 is based upon:**

    (A) doing all the practices listed in lines 62 – 66

    (B) the author's knowledge of the reader's mind and heart

    (C) the author's understanding that all people are good public speakers

    (D) assumptions about the readers because they are college-bound

    (E) misappropriation of certain psychological techniques

19. **A good title for this passage might be:**

    (A) Public Speaking for Beginners

    (B) Fear and Anger on the Public Speaking Circuit

    (C) Outwit Your Fear of Public Speaking through Proven Methods

    (D) Conquering Stagefright through Psychoactive Drugs

    (E) Everyone a Public Speaker

SECTION 8
(MATHEMATICS)
Time: 20 minutes
16 questions

MULTIPLE CHOICE

Directions: For the questions in this section, solve each problem and decide which of the given answer choices is the best choice. Fill in the corresponding oval on the answer sheet to indicate your selection. You may use any available space for scratchwork.

Note:

1. Calculator use is permitted.
2. All numbers used are real numbers.
3. All figures provided are drawn to scale and lie in a plane unless otherwise indicated.
4. Unless otherwise specified, the domain of any function f is assumed to be the set of all real numbers x for which $f(x)$ is a real number.

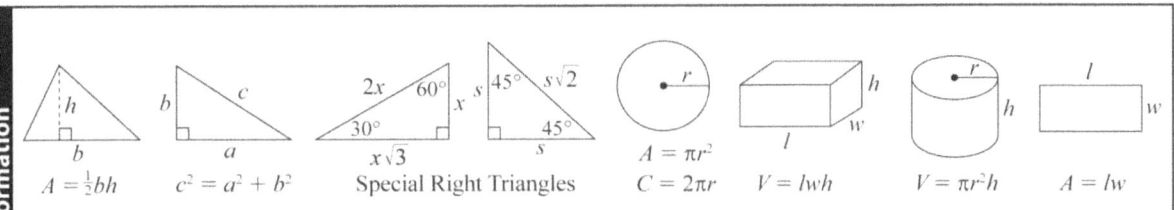

The sum of the degree measures of the angles in a triangle is 180.
The number of degrees of arc in a circle is 360.
A straight angle has a degree measure of 180.

1. A winter coat that costs $155.00 is marked up. The new price is $186.00. What is the percent increase?

   (A) 16.7%

   (B) 20%

   (C) 25%

   (D) 31%

   (E) 35%

2. Solve: $2 + 5(x-1) \leq 9$

   (A) $x \geq \dfrac{12}{7}$

   (B) $x \leq \dfrac{12}{5}$

   (C) $x \leq 12$

   (D) $x \geq 7$

   (E) $x \geq \dfrac{12}{5}$

3. Four times the sum of three and some number is the same as the number squared. What is the unknown number?

    (A) -12 only
    (B) 6 only
    (C) -4 only
    (D) 6 or -2
    (E) 2 or -6

4. If the ratio of the angles in a quadrilateral is 2:3:5:8, what is the measure of the largest angle?

    (A) 20°
    (B) 40°
    (C) 60°
    (D) 100°
    (E) 160°

5. What is the area of a triangle with vertices at (-2,0), (4,0), and (3,10)?

    (A) 60
    (B) 30
    (C) 20
    (D) 12
    (E) 5

6. If x > 0 and y < 0, which of the following must be FALSE?

    (A) $\dfrac{x}{y^2} > 0$

    (B) $\dfrac{x^2}{y^3} < 0$

    (C) $\dfrac{2x^3}{y^2} > 0$

    (D) $(\dfrac{x^2}{y^3})^2 < 0$

    (E) $2xy < 0$

7. If the following system of equations has an infinite number of solutions, what is the value of m?

    $2x - 4y = 13$
    $-4x + 8y = m$

    (A) 26
    (B) 13
    (C) 0
    (D) -13
    (E) -26

8. A trail mix is made with 2 pounds of peanuts, 1 pound of raisins, and 1.5 pounds of pretzels. Peanuts cost $1.50 a pound and raisins cost $2.10 a pound. If the mixture sells for $1.80 a pound, what is the cost of pretzels per pound?

    (A) $0.60
    (B) $1.50
    (C) $2.00
    (D) $3.50
    (E) $8.80

9. A dart board has a rectangle inscribed within a circle. If the length of the rectangle is 1.5 times the radius of the circle, what is the probability of a dart thrown at the board landing inside the rectangle?

    (A) $\dfrac{3\sqrt{7}}{4\pi}$

    (B) $\dfrac{3\sqrt{7}}{8\pi}$

    (C) $\dfrac{4\pi}{3\sqrt{7}}$

    (D) $\dfrac{8\pi}{3\sqrt{7}}$

    (E) $\dfrac{3\sqrt{7}}{16\pi}$

10. In the cube shown, the dashed line joins the midpoints of side BC and DH. If the side of the cube is of length s, what is the length of the dashed line?

    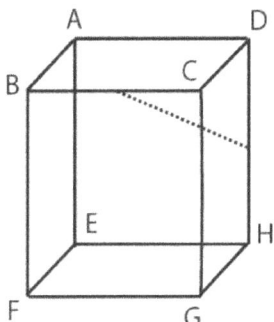

    (A) $\sqrt{\dfrac{2}{3}}s$

    (B) $\sqrt{3}s$

    (C) $\sqrt{2}s$

    (D) $\dfrac{s}{\sqrt{2}}$

    (E) $\sqrt{\dfrac{3}{2}}s$

11. In the equations below, r < 0 and w < 0. What is the value of r − w?

    $|r - 3| = 12$
    $|w + 7| = 22$

    (A) -20
    (B) -10
    (C) 0
    (D) 10
    (E) 20

12. A model of a cylindrical building is built at a scale 1:50. The area of the circular base of the building is how many times larger than the circular base of the model?

    (A) 50
    (B) 125
    (C) 250
    (D) 2500
    (E) 125000

13. Which of these could be the angle between the hands of a clock at 3:20 p.m.?

    (A) 330°
    (B) 270°
    (C) 30°
    (D) 20°
    (E) 15°

14. Two dice are rolled. What is the probability that the sum of the numbers on the two dice is greater than 10?

    (A) $\dfrac{1}{36}$
    (B) $\dfrac{1}{18}$
    (C) $\dfrac{1}{12}$
    (D) $\dfrac{1}{10}$
    (E) $\dfrac{1}{9}$

15. A rectangular building site 400 ft x 1000 ft has a triangular park attached to one end as shown. If the area of the park must be at least one-fifth that of the building site, what is the minimum length of the hypotenuse of the park?

    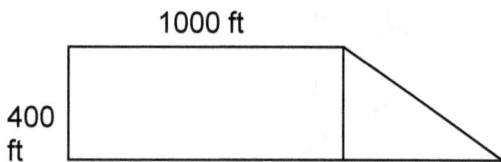

    (A) 566 ft
    (B) 400 ft
    (C) 200 ft
    (D) 144 ft
    (E) 80 ft

16. A function is given by $f(x) = x^2 2^x$. Which of the following is the graph of f(x+2)?

(A)
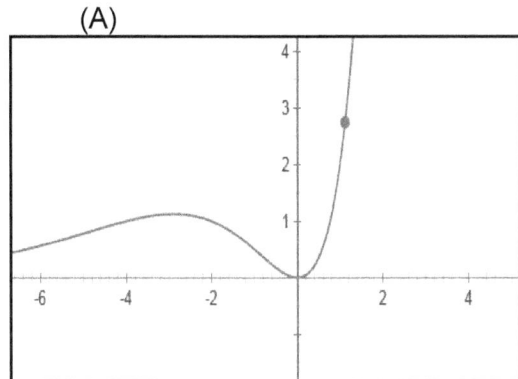

(B)
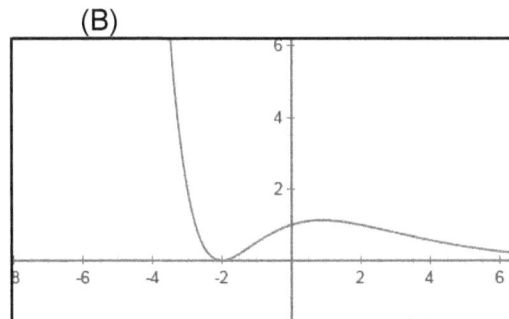

(C)
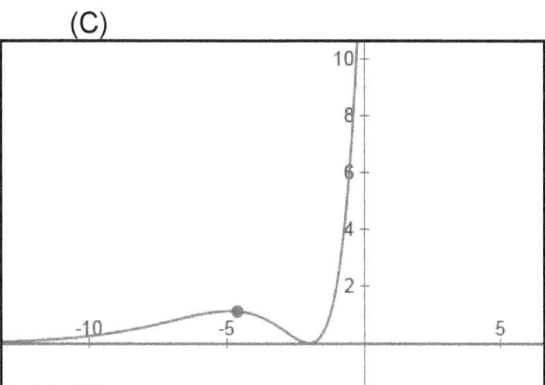

(D)
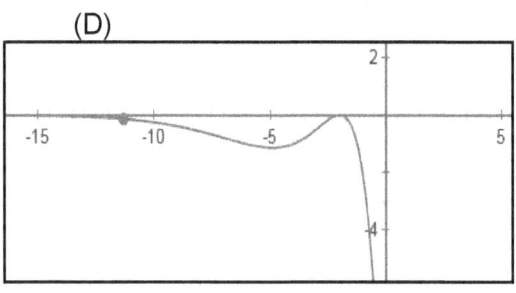

(E)
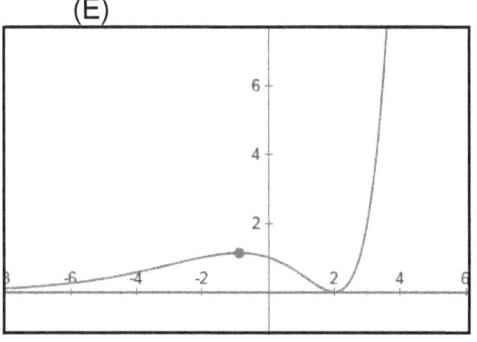

SECTION 9
(WRITING)
Time: 10 minutes
14 questions

IMPROVING SENTENCES

Directions: For each of the following questions, choose the best answer and fill in the corresponding oval on the answer sheet to indicate your selection.

Part of each sentence (or the entire sentence) is underlined. The five answer choices present five ways of phrasing the underlined portion. Choice A repeats the original phrasing and the other four choices offer alternative phrasings. If you think the original phrasing is best, select choice A; if not, select one of the other options.

In choosing your answer, follow the requirements of standard written English. Pay attention to grammar, choice of words, sentence construction, and punctuation; your selection should result in the most effective, clear, and precise sentence—free of awkwardness or ambiguity.

1. Mark performed an act of heroism during the fire but declined to be honored by the mayor <u>nor being considered for</u> any other form of recognition.

    (A) nor being considered for
    (B) nor considering
    (C) or considering
    (D) or to be considered for
    (E) or to have been considered for

2. Lily goes to the recreation center more often <u>than we do because of having a membership</u>.

    (A) than we do because of having a membership
    (B) than us because of having a membership
    (C) than we do, this is the result of her having a membership
    (D) than us as a result of her having a membership
    (E) than we do because she has a membership

3. Attending concerts is more exciting than listening to recorded music, but <u>prohibitively expensive is the cost of concert tickets for many people</u>.

   (A) prohibitively expensive is the cost of concert tickets for many people

   (B) the cost of concert tickets is prohibitively expensive for many people

   (C) concert tickets have a prohibitively expensive cost for many people

   (D) in the cost of concert tickets it is prohibitively expensive

   (E) there are prohibitively expensive costs for many people who want to buy concert tickets

4. Fearing that the new highway would cause traffic congestion and dangers for pedestrians in their neighborhood, <u>a protest was filed by the residents to persuade state officials to relocate the route</u>.

   (A) a protest was filed by the residents to persuade state officials to relocate the route

   (B) a protest to persuade state officials to relocate the route was filed by the residents

   (C) the residents filed a protest to persuade state officials to relocate the route

   (D) the residents, filing a protest to relocate the route, had persuaded the state officials

   (E) state officials were persuaded by a protest filed by the residents to relocate the route

5. <u>Some employees manage to justify stealing office supplies from their employers, in most respects they are scrupulously honest, however.</u>

   (A) Some employees manage to justify stealing office supplies from their employers, in most respects they are scrupulously honest, however.

   (B) Although being scrupulously honest in other respects, some employees, however, manage to justify stealing office supplies from their employers.

   (C) Some of the employees which manage to justify stealing office supplies from their employers are in other respects scrupulously honest.

   (D) Some employees who are otherwise scrupulously honest manage to justify stealing office supplies from their employers.

   (E) Some employees manage to justify stealing office supplies from their employers and are scrupulously honest in other respects.

6. The "white matter" that occupies nearly half the human brain <u>controls the shared signals of different neurons and coordinates</u> the activities of different brain regions.

   (A) controls the shared signals of different neurons and coordinates

   (B) controlling the shared signals of different neurons and coordinating

   (C) has controlled the shared signals of different neurons and coordinating

   (D) that controls the shared signals and different neurons and coordinates

   (E) is controlling the shared signals of different neurons and coordinates

7. One of the most popular crafts in America today is making elaborate scrapbooks of family <u>photos, another craft that many Americans enjoy</u> is making quilts to commemorate important family events.

   (A) photos, another craft that many Americans enjoy

   (B) photos; another craft that many Americans enjoy

   (C) photos, another craft, and it is one that many Americans enjoy

   (D) photos; another craft which is being enjoyed by many Americans

   (E) photos and also a craft being enjoyed by many Americans

8. Free equipment for the school's media center, including computers and DVD players, <u>provided by</u> local businesses.

   (A) provided by

   (B) it was provided by

   (C) they were provided by

   (D) were provided by

   (E) was provided by

9. The independent filmmaker could not make her movie unless she <u>can find producers and actors who are as dedicated and adventurous as she is</u>.

   (A) can find producers and actors who are as dedicated and adventurous as she is

   (B) would be able to find producers and actors who are as dedicated and adventurous as she is

   (C) could find producers and actors with a dedication and a sense of adventure that are equal to her own

   (D) could find producers and actors who were as dedicated and adventurous as she was

   (E) can find producers and actors with a dedication and a sense of adventure that were equal to her own

10. Graduating with honors and receiving a basketball scholarship, Armand is almost as gifted a student as he is an athlete.

    (A) almost as gifted a student as he is an athlete
    (B) gifted as an athlete and almost so gifted as a student
    (C) of almost equal gifts, whether as a student or an athlete
    (D) of the same gifts as a student and as an athlete, almost
    (E) a gifted athlete, with almost as many gifts as a student

11. Explaining what we would learn in Introduction to Art, do not get discouraged too quickly was the advice our teacher gave us.

    (A) do not get discouraged too quickly was the advice our teacher gave us
    (B) the advice our teacher gave us was not to get discouraged too quickly
    (C) our teacher advised us not to get discouraged too quickly
    (D) our class was advised by the teacher not to get discouraged too quickly
    (E) not getting discouraged too quickly was what our teacher advised us

12. Because the director of the daycare center emphasizes individualized attention, it is a staff of five childcare workers for each age level who supervise the children's activities at all times.

    (A) it is a staff of five childcare workers for each age level who supervise the children's activities at all times
    (B) the children at each age level being supervised in their activities at all times by a staff of five childcare workers
    (C) a staff of five childcare workers for each age level are the ones supervising the children's activities at all times
    (D) a staff of five childcare workers for each age level supervise the children's activities at all times
    (E) a staff of five childcare workers supervise, for each age level and at all times, the children's activities

13. Studying carefully the end of the movie, the heroes celebrate their ability to live in freedom and dignity with their neighbors.

    (A) Studying carefully the end of the movie,
    (B) Considering how the movie ends,
    (C) If one attempts to study the end of movie,
    (D) At the end of the movie,
    (E) If one were to attempt an analysis of the movie's ending,

14. **As a diabetic patient, the American Diabetes Association advises you that you must strictly control your diet.**

   (A) As a diabetic patient, the American Diabetes Association advises you that you

   (B) As a diabetic patient, the American Diabetes Association advise you that you

   (C) You, as a diabetic patient, are advised by the American Diabetes Association, and you

   (D) The American Diabetes Association, who advise you that you, as a diabetic patient

   (E) The American Diabetes Association advises you that as a diabetic patient you

PRACTICE TEST 2 ANSWER KEY

Section 1 (Writing)

Section 2 (Critical Reading)

1. B
2. B
3. C
4. E
5. A
6. A
7. B
8. D
9. C
10. B
11. E
12. A
13. D
14. B
15. B
16. B
17. C
18. B
19. A
20. B
21. E
22. D
23. E
24. C

Section 3 (Mathematics)

1. A
2. E
3. D
4. E
5. E
6. B
7. B
8. D
9. A
10. C
11. A
12. C
13. C
14. D
15. B
16. D
17. C
18. C
19. C
20. B

Section 4 (Critical Reading)

1. A
2. E
3. D
4. B
5. B
6. E
7. A
8. C
9. A
10. C
11. D
12. C
13. E
14. A
15. C
16. A
17. A
18. A
19. D
20. E
21. D
22. C
23. C
24. E

Section 5 (Mathematics)

1. C
2. B
3. B
4. B
5. D
6. E
7. E
8. C
9. 0.40
10. 96
11. 39
12. 5
13. 1/17
14. 9
15. 0
16. 2
17. 2
18. 33

Section 6 (Writing)

1. E
2. D
3. B
4. A
5. E
6. C
7. C
8. C
9. D
10. A
11. B
12. C
13. E
14. A
15. A
16. C
17. A
18. D
19. E
20. C
21. B
22. D
23. A
24. B
25. A
26. D
27. C
28. B
29. B
30. B
31. A
32. C
33. E
34. A
35. C

Section 7 (Critical Reading)

1. A
2. B
3. B
4. D
5. A
6. D
7. A
8. C
9. B
10. A
11. A
12. C
13. A
14. B
15. D
16. C
17. A
18. A
19. C

Section 8 (Mathematics)

1. B
2. B
3. D
4. E
5. B
6. D
7. E
8. C

9. A
10. E
11. E
12. D
13. D
14. C
15. A
16. C

Section 9 (Writing)

1. D
2. E
3. B
4. C
5. D
6. A
7. B

8. E
9. D
10. A
11. C
12. D
13. D
14. E

PRACTICE TEST 2
ANSWER RATIONALES

SECTION 1 (WRITING)

ESSAY

Excellent Quality Sample Essay (Score: 6 out of 6) Rationale

The writer has chosen to agree with Thoreau's saying about the tyranny of our own private opinions as opposed to what other people may think. The writer shows critical thinking by considering the strength of peer pressure and some of the reasons for that, including "People care very much what other people think." After acknowledging this different point of view objectively and admitting that it has some validity, the writer asserts agreement with Thoreau's thesis. The writer then develops an argument in support of that agreement by providing an example and examining the writer's own reasoning process during the incident of the example and in retrospect.

The essay shows progression of thought. After the example, the writer delves into alternative responses in the incident, including possible alternative reactions of the peers involved. This serves to show that the writer did have a choice as to what action to take and lays a foundation for the next paragraph and point, which is "We do what we choose to do. No one makes us...We have to choose to do it." The writer finishes this paragraph by restating the thesis: that our own private opinion is the most powerful tyrant, in agreement with Thoreau's assertion.

The writer uses appropriate and specific vocabulary. "Our inner self" is a good way to express one's "private opinion" without repeating the language used in the excerpt. When the writer does repeat the language in the excerpt, he or she does it at the end of a paragraph, as if summing up the paragraph and reminding the reader of the original point. This is an effective use of language. Since the essay is about ethical choices, using the language of virtues such as courage, honesty, and respect is appropriate.

The writer brings in information that goes beyond the information provided in the excerpt. The writer provides an appropriate and relevant personal example that shows he or she is engaged in the topic, understands it, and is addressing it appropriately and responsibly. He or she also paraphrases a related and thoughtful idea in the last paragraph that supports the thesis: "Someone once said that conquering yourself is the hardest battle you will ever fight." The writer has successfully followed the directions to "use reasoning and your general knowledge based on your own experiences, observation of society, general reading or specific studies."

The writer varies sentence structure. He or she uses simple sentences such as "We do what we choose to do" and "I agree with that." The writer also uses compound sentences such as "This is our own private opinion; we think friends are so important or that other people's opinions are so important, we must go along" and "I had to force myself to take a second drag, and I did it so I could look tough to them." The writer also uses complex sentences such as "Maybe if I had said, 'That tastes nasty' and refused, they would have respected me more for my courage and honesty." The writer also uses the device of an "em dash" to add variety and humor to the text: "My friends might have admired me for saying I didn't want any more—especially after they took a first drag themselves!"

Two flaws in the essay are a slightly unclear opening paragraph and the detail about the "swiping" of the matches, which is distracting and unnecessary. However, due to its critical thinking, progressive reasoning and development, appropriate example, thoughtful tone, and variety of sentence structures, this essay classifies as an excellent one.

Medium Quality Sample Essay (Score: 3 – 4 out of 6) Rationale

This essay takes a strong stance and uses examples, rhetorical questions, and irony to make its points. These are strengths of the essay.

The essay shows some development of thought as the writer provides an example of nonconformity (Dr. King), develops it, and ties it to the examples of conformity (houses and cars) that the writer brought up in the first paragraph, providing a contrast.

The development of thought is a little muddled, though. Although the essay writer seems to be saying that people go along with public opinion even when their own private opinion is different, this is not really clear. The writer says, "Sometimes we have to go against public opinion in order to get something done right. I think then people's own private opinion secretly agrees with us, and then they go along." At the end of the paragraph, the writer says, "Dr. King was right. At the time, though, public opinion didn't seem to think so." It is not clear whether the writer believes that people's private and public opinions were the same or different. The writer seems to imply that private opinion was different, but this point is not really developed.

The writer uses some appropriate vocabulary, such as "lockstep" "conformity" "injustice" and "ironic." The writer uses a variety of sentence structures, from simple sentences like "They are all in lockstep" to compound sentences like "Everyone goes to work at a 9 to 5 job on weekdays, and they all drive cars that look alike except for the color" to complex sentences like "But even if most people do not agree with public opinion they still go along, because public opinion is a stronger tyrant than private opinion."

The essay does not consider another point of view, so it is lacking in objectivity. The tone is strident. Although the writer applies critical thinking to society and shows logical development of his or her points in relation to that, the writer does not properly develop the difference or relationships as he or she sees it between public and private opinion.

For all these reasons, this is a medium quality essay.

Low Quality Sample Essay (Score: 1 – 2 out of 6) Rationale

This is a low quality essay. It asserts a position in the first paragraph that "People do things out of their own private opinion" and "No one is forcing them." However, the rest of the essay discusses the power of peer pressure. There is no development of the idea that people do things out of their own private opinion. What little development of thought there is supports the idea that people do things out of peer pressure, in contradiction to the position the writer takes in the first paragraph.

The thinking and logic is not clear. In the first paragraph, the writer says "they still do it" without saying what "it" is. In the second paragraph, the writer says "We wouldn't know it if it wasn't true." The reader assumes the writer is talking about peer pressure, but the thought is not clear and is poorly developed.

There is little logical progression in the essay. Although the writer provides an example of peer pressure, this example supports the opposite of what the writer has asserted as his or her stance in the first paragraph. The last paragraph supports the idea that other people's ideas are what direct our actions; this too is in direct contradiction to the position the writer took in the first paragraph.

There are many simple sentences in the essay, giving it an abrupt, staccato feel: "People do things out of their own private opinion," "They want to do what they do," "We should have our own," etcetera.

The writing is repetitious. For example, the sentences "No one is forcing them. No one is holding a gun to their head" repeat the same point and in an unoriginal way, using a cliché. The sentence "He was on a rainy, slick street at night and it was dark" is repetitious and unnecessarily wordy: if he was on a street at night, there is no need to say that it was dark. In the last paragraph, the sentences "People shouldn't be in other people's heads. They don't pay rent to be in our brains, so they shouldn't be there" are repetitious of the same thought, even though the second sentence is probably trying to introduce humor or sarcasm. It is not done effectively and falls flat.

Instead of logical argumentation, the writer supports his or her points with these common phrases: "No one is holding a gun to their head" and "They don't pay rent in our brains, so they shouldn't be there." These simple and unoriginal assertions do not develop or support logical points.

The SAT Advantage

SECTION 2 (CRITICAL READING)

SENTENCE COMPLETION

1. Answer: (B) spontaneity
Because the vocalist's technique "was not perfect," it is unlikely that his or her (A) "precision" would win the contest. Because the vocalist "livened up the whole contest" it is hard to believe that his or her "constraint" or "restraint" (holding back in some ways) would win the contest, so answers (C) and (D) are incorrect. The only way answer (E) "deficiency" would liven up a contest would be if people laughed at the person's inadequacy; and it is unlikely such a person would be "awarded first place." "Spontaneity" (B) means proceeding from natural feelings without constraint, rising up out of a momentary impulse, doing something without much plan or forethought, often resulting in something fresh and new. "Spontaneity" might make up for a lack of perfect technique and it would also "liven up" a contest, so answer (B) is the correct answer.

2. Answer: (B) credulity
Since this is statistical, factual information, answer (A) "fantasy" would not be appropriate. Answer (C) "clarity" means how clear something is, so, by process of elimination, that answer is also incorrect. We have three answers, then, with the Latin root "credere," meaning "to believe." This makes sense in the context of the sentence; the facts stretch our ability to believe in them because they are so remarkable. "Credibility" means the power to inspire belief, so answer (D) is inappropriate. "Credentials" give credibility by some sort of affirmation or confirmation, so answer (E) does not fit the sentence. "Credulity" means a person's or people's readiness or willingness to believe something. The pronoun "our" implies "people's," so in meaning and context, answer (B) "credulity" is the correct answer.

3. Answer: (C) bucolic
The sentence is about items "rural" Americans shopped for in general stores, and "antique wooden general store bins" are the decorating items recommended that must be modified by the missing adjective. Since such bins were part of "rural" life, the missing adjective would relate to rural life. "Bucolic" means out in the country, rural, often with an air of nostalgia or yearning for simpler times and lifestyles. Answer (C) "bucolic", then, is an excellent answer. All the other answers refer to more modern and sophisticated forms of design that would not fit in with the references in the sentence to previous times, antiques, and a rural world.

4. Answer: (E) aspiring … acquisition
The sense of the sentence is that the information in it is instructional to authors seeking publication. This would imply that the authors are "beginning" (B) authors or "aspiring" (E) authors (authors who hope to be published). "Veteran," "seasoned," and "experienced" do not fit with this sense of the sentence (answers (A), (C), and (D)). "Beginning" authors, answer (B), would not want their letters to result in the "repulsion" of an agent, but rather in agent "acquisition," so (E) is the correct answer.

5. Answer: (A) resorted … subterfuge
Since Rachel had to do something to get the medicine into her "rebellious" dog, the first space calls for a verb that will fit with the phrase "to grinding up." "Plotted" (B), "planned" (C), and "assayed" (E) would not fit the gerund form "grinding," which is a verbal serving as a noun. For example, "she planned" would have to go with "to grind up…" This means answers (B), (C), and (E) are incorrect. "Converted" (D) would fit grammatically with "to grinding up the pill" if the rest of the sentence said that she had tried many other methods so had to convert to the one she

used, but it does not. "Ruse" means a disguise or a trick, so that meaning would fit. However, Sentence Completion calls for the best fit, and "resorted to grinding up" is an excellent fit as it means she used her resources to find a course of action. "Subterfuge" also fits well as the second word in the sentence, as it means a stratagem or means of hiding something or allowing something to escape notice. Thus, (A) is the best choice.

6. Answer: (A) disdain ... arrogance

Since the first word to fit into the sentence is modified by "aristocratic," a noun that would work well with that adjective is best. In general, "aristocratic" is not associated with "humility," so answer (C) is incorrect. "Abscesses" in answer (E) are wounds or pus-filled or pus-surrounded openings in the skin, so answer (E) is nonsensical: "abscesses" cannot be "aristocratic." We can associate "disdain," answer (A), which means to look down upon, with "aristocratic"; we can also associate "*noblesse oblige*," answer (B), which means the obligation of the wealthy or the nobility to help the less fortunate; and "excesses," answer (D), could also be associated with "aristocratic" as it could refer to indulgences or luxuries of the wealthy or aristocratic. However, in answer (D), "excesses" does not go with "asceticism," which means self-sacrifice and rigid control of appetites. In answer (B), "*noblesse oblige*" does not make sense in conjunction with "incapable of love or compassion," as the concept implies compassion for the less fortunate. Answer (A), because of the similarities in meaning between "disdain" and "arrogance" is the best fit.

7. Answer: (B) ubiquitous ... solvents

The key to the first word to fill in the sentence is found later in the sentence: water, the sentence tells us is used "everywhere." "Everywhere" is the same as "ubiquitous", so answer (B) is definitely a candidate for the best answer. The fact that water is used by "humans, plants, and animals" also hints at the word ubiquitous for certainly these beings are ubiquitous. Although water is definitely "beneficial," as in answer (A), to use "thirst-slakers" for the second word would be redundant as the sentence has already made the point that humans, animals, and plants use water as a beverage and the sentence has moved on to water's other uses, such as a cleanser. "Solvents" in answer (B) would work well as the second word, because of its relation to the earlier part of the thought: cleansers and solvents are related but not exactly the same, so pairing "solvents" with "cleanser" works well in the sentence.

8. Answer: (D) eventualities ... cultivate

The relationship between the two parts of the sentence, which are separated into independent clauses by the semi-colon, is to describe the differences between the Western and Eastern approaches to business relationships. Both independent clauses refer to the business relationships forged (either through contracts or through trust) as needing strengthening to help the business relationship survive if "storms" or other things happen. Since "eventualities" means "things that may happen" or "events that may occur," the first part of answer (D) is a good answer. The second part of answer (D), "cultivate," means to help something grow by taking beneficial action toward it. Exchanging gifts, visits, and symbols of good will, as well as getting to know one another, would definitely classify as cultivating "relationships of trust over time," so (D) is the best answer.

READING BASED QUESTIONS

9. Answer: (C) inextricably linked with the development of the telegraph system

The author says, "This signaled the end of a short-lived legend: the Pony Express." The "This" referred to is the completion of the telegraph line. The first paragraph compares the speed of dispatches, which was "almost instantaneous" with the telegraph and mention that it took "ten days to bring transcontinental news" with the Pony Express. These words and phrases show that the fate of the Pony Express was inextricably linked with the development of the telegraph system, answer (C).

10. Answer: (B) Pony Express riders did not turn back or fail in their delivery missions in spite of adversity
To "deter" means to turn away or discourage or be discouraged. To be "undeterred" then means to not turn away in spite of discouraging circumstances. Since the sentence lists discouraging circumstances or circumstances of adversity such as crossing Indian territory where there might be hostiles, riding in bad weather and riding over rough land, "undeterred" most likely means that, in spite of adversity, Pony Express riders did not turn back or fail in their delivery missions, which is the language of answer (B).

11. Answer: (E) tongue-in-cheek
The juxtaposition of "a Bible" and "a revolver" as two pieces of equipment in a Pony Express rider's sack right away brings about a sense of irony. The irony is not cutting, though, as in being sarcastic, answer (A). The irony is further brought out by the line that these opposite pieces of equipment "were considered sufficient to surmount any emergencies a Pony Express rider might run into." Tongue-in-cheek humor makes use of irony, so (E) tongue-in-cheek is the best answer.

12. Answer: (A) intrepid
"Intrepid" means to be resolute, fearless, and enduring. "Doughty" is a synonym for "intrepid." Although the word "doughty" seems to be related to "dough" and therefore may seem to imply plumpness, its meaning is unrelated to answers (B) and (C). The riders themselves were not speedy, so comparing the ponies to the riders in speed is invalid in answer (E). Bandy-legged or bow-legged, answer (D), would be irrelevant to the passage and would not necessarily make for speed or efficiency of transit.

13. Answer: (D) the law enforcement of famous sheriffs like Wyatt Earp
These lines make no mention of law enforcement or Wyatt Earp, answer (D), but they do mention "settlers," which may be used as a synonym for "pioneers," answer (A); they mention the Pony Express, answer (B), and they mention wild "Western towns," answer (C). Although the word "gunfighters," answer (E), is not used, the term "gunslingers" which may be considered a synonym, is mentioned, so the only answer not mentioned is indeed answer (D).

14. Answer: (B) evocative of a bygone era
The tone of these lines may contain some nostalgia as in answer (E), but it contains no criticism of the era of the American West. Answers (A) and (D), then, are also incorrect, because there is no repudiation or antagonism toward the past. The tone is not reflective as in answer (C), because the author is not trying to gain meaning by looking back on the past. Rather, the bygone era is evoked by the words and ideas themselves, taking the reader's mind back to the time when these legends were actively shooting, gambling, pioneering, battling, and cattle-driving their way into the national consciousness, making (B) evocative of a bygone era, the correct answer.

15. Answer: (B) sympathetic and impartial
In Passage 1, Schlichtmann's perspective on the case is depicted with some sympathy. It is carefully explained that Schlichtmann felt the first phase of the trial would be "boring" and "technical," and the list of topics to be covered in the first phase corroborates this: "well water

The SAT Advantage

pollution," "groundwater movement," "dates," and "chemicals with long names." The author tells of how the "suffering" of the "grief-stricken families" with their "poignant and sympathy-inducing stories" would not be presented to the jury, showing sympathy with Schlichtmann's side. Good reasons are given for Schlichtmann's "concerns about the judge's impartiality"; reasons which are presented as being credible and understandable. The fact that Schlichtmann was forced to declare bankruptcy after winning such large settlements and the language that says his bank account was "broken" and that "his faith in the justice system was damaged too" make Schlichtmann a sympathetic figure, so answer (A) or (B) is the correct one.

Passage 2 is not dismissive of Schlichtmann though, so answer (A) can be eliminated. The author offers impartial and reasonable arguments why the case being split into three parts was "fair," which is in itself a word indicating impartiality: "after all, if the corporations had not polluted the wells, what relevance did the grieving families have to the case? Emotional appeals could sway the jury away from the facts." It is stated that the break-up might have benefitted Schlichtmann by preventing him from having to "prove the unprovable". That last paragraph provides the fact that two families "thought he had overspent on the case and should compensate the families for his extravagance." However, it is noted that Schlichtmann did compensate the families. This indicates that Passage 2 is "impartial" toward Schlichtmann as it states reasons and facts that show that his viewpoint might not be the whole picture yet it also provides facts to his credit as well.

16. Answer: (B) the families believed their children got leukemia from drinking polluted water

In bringing about a lawsuit, the families obviously believed that their children got leukemia from drinking polluted water. The families "charged that their children had gotten leukemia from drinking polluted water," so they clearly believed it. However, in a lawsuit, a defendant may be proven innocent in the course of the trial. Therefore, in describing the lawsuit, Passage 1 does not state as a fact that the children got leukemia from drinking polluted water, so answer (A) is wrong. No conclusions are drawn about whether the corporations acted deliberately or carelessly, so answers (C) and (E) are wrong. No mention is made of a monetary motivation on the part of the families, either, so answer (D) is also wrong.

17. Answer: (C) prove the corporations polluted the water, prove the pollution caused leukemia in the children, and award damages to the plaintiffs

The author states that, "In the first phase, the attorney for the plaintiffs attempted to show that the wells...had been contaminated by Grace and Beatrice," showing that the first phase of the trial was to "prove the corporations polluted the water," as in answer (C). The second segment of the trial was needed "to prove to the jury that the children's leukemia was caused by drinking the polluted water" or "prove the pollution caused leukemia in the children" as in answer (C). The third segment of the trial "would set compensatory payment," which is another way of saying "award damages to the plaintiffs," as is stated in answer (C).

18. Answer: (B) touching the heart; affecting the emotions profoundly

The words "suffering and grief-stricken families" indicate that the stories the families might tell on the witness stand would be emotionally affecting and would touch the heart. They would certainly not be "emotionally manipulative," answer (A), and although they might be "gripping" (E) and "morally compelling" (D), the instructions call for the best fit. Coming from "suffering and grief-stricken families," the stories the families would tell about their children's deaths would most likely touch the heart and affect the emotions profoundly, which is the language of answer (B).

19. Answer: (A) it hurt Schlichtmann's case by denying him the jury's sympathy; it helped focus on the facts rather than emotions

In Passage 1, Schlichtmann's attitude about the three-phased trial is made clear. He "argued that" it "deprived him" of the opportunity to impress the jury with the "suffering and grief-stricken families" and their testimonies on the witness stand as well as their presence in the courtroom. "Their poignant and sympathy-inducing stories" would simply "not be told." From these lines, we can see that Schlichtmann's perspective was that his case was hurt because he was denied the jury's sympathy, as in answer (A).

Facher's attitude about the three-phased trial is covered in Passage 2. Facher thought the three-phased trial was "only fair". "After all," if the corporations were not guilty of polluting the wells, "what relevance did the grieving families have to the case?" "Emotional appeals" could "sway" the jury away from the "facts". We can see from these quotations from Passage 2 that Facher thought the judge's action in breaking the trial into three stages helped focus on the facts rather than emotions, as in answer (A).

20. Answer: (B) self-explanatory

In the context of the two passages, the term "leukemia clusters" is self-explanatory. The passages talk about six families, each with a child who was a victim of leukemia, who were all from the same town of Woburn, Massachusetts. It would be unusual under any circumstances for six children from the same small area to die of the same disease. The term is definitely important, making answer (A) wrong, because the prevalence of leukemia among Woburn families drinking from the same wells was what caused the lawsuit in the first place. The term is definitely relevant to the case, making answer (E) wrong, because the leukemia cluster was what alerted parents that the problem might be in the water. Since the author talks about scientists having found other leukemia clusters and not knowing what causes leukemia, we know that the term "leukemia clusters" is a scientific term, so answer (D) is wrong. As a scientific term, "leukemia clusters" is also a factual term, so answer (C) is wrong too. By process of elimination, answer (B) is the correct answer.

21. Answer: (E) proving that chemical pollution causes leukemia

The paragraph in which this line appears deals with how breaking the case into three parts might have helped Schlichtmann win his settlement. The second phase, as the author tells us, was "when Schlichtmann would have to prove that pollution caused the children's leukemia." Since it is stated that "scientists did not know what caused leukemia", having to prove that chemical pollution causes leukemia would have been "having to prove the unprovable."

22. Answer: (D) respect based on one another's integrity

The author states that, "Judge Skinner did have a long-term relationship of mutual respect with Jerome Facher." The lines go on to state that, "Both men were considered examples of integrity in the law profession." There is no mention of a personal relationship or friendship, such as in answers (B) and (C). (There is a reference to the two men thinking similarly, but that is in Passage 1). Based on the statement that they had a relationship of "mutual respect", answers (A) and (E) are also eliminated, leaving answer (D).

23. Answer: (E) the judge's sympathy with Facher's complaint about the amount of material to be memorized; the judge's and Facher's mutual respect; and how much they thought alike

The judge's sympathy with Facher's complaint about the amount of material is shown: "Judge Skinner told the defendant's attorney, Jerome Facher, that...he would not have to memorize the material all at once." The author mentions that Facher "had complained about that." It is mentioned, in the context of Schlichtmann's concern about the judge's impartiality, that the two men "respected each other" and that "they seemed to think alike." These quotes all support answer (E).

24. Answer: (C) Jan Schlichtmann's clients received a fair trial and Schlichtmann was profligate of funds, which may possibly have led to his bankruptcy
Passage 1 expresses that Schlichtmann went bankrupt, and that his bank account and his faith in the justice system were both broken by the case. This implies that Schlichtmann felt the way the case was handled was unfair. What would the author of Passage 2 say about this? The author of Passage 2 makes some specific comments on how fair the trial was, especially the breaking up of it into three parts.

Passage 2 states that "it actually might have been fortunate" for Jan Schlichtmann that the trial was divided up into three phases, because "settlements were reached before the second phase" wherein Schlichtmann would have to "prove the unprovable". From this, it can be inferred that the author of Passage 2 would find any assertions that the trial had broken Schlichtmann's faith in the justice system debatable.

In Passage 2, the author specifically addresses Schlichtmann's "expensive tastes" and describes his use of "fancy hotels" and "elaborate spreads of food and wines." Passage 2 also mentions the fact that two families he was representing in the case "thought he had overspent" and that he "should compensate the families for his extravagance" The author of Passage 2 also uses the words "one possible reason" for Schlichtmann's bankruptcy, which is similar to the word "possibly" in answer (C).

The SAT Advantage

SECTION 3 (MATHEMATICS)

MULTIPLE CHOICE

1. Answer: (A) 6
This is a two-step problem. First find out how many yards Nancy runs. Then, determine how many more yards she runs than Mary. Since Nancy runs 18 more yards than Sharon and Sharon runs 71 yards in 10 seconds, Nancy runs 71 + 18 = 89 yards in 10 seconds. Mary runs 83 yards and Nancy runs 89 yards in 10 seconds. So Nancy runs 89 − 83 = 6 yards more than Mary in 10 seconds.

2. Answer: (E) $61.30 + (24 x $19.95)
The registration fee is yearly. So for two years Manuel pays $30.65 x 2 = $61.30. The monthly payment of $19.95 for two years adds up to 24 x $19.95. Hence the total amount Manuel pays for two years is given by $61.30 + (24 x $19.95).

3. Answer: (D) 27
Solve for x in the first equation and then substitute that value in the subsequent expression:

$4x - 3 = 13$

$4x = 16$

$x = 4$

$5(4) + 7 = 27$

4. Answer: (E) -8
If $7^x = 7^4$, we know x = 4 because the bases, 7, are the same. In the problem $9^{3x+6} = 27^{x-4}$, we cannot set the exponents equal to one another because the bases, 9 and 27, are not equivalent. Thus, we need to convert each expression to base 3:

$9^{3x+6} = 27^{x-4}$

$(3^2)^{3x+6} = (3^3)^{x-4}$

$3^{6x+12} = 3^{3x-12}$

$6x + 12 = 3x - 12$

$3x = -24$

$x = -8$

5. Answer: (E) 25

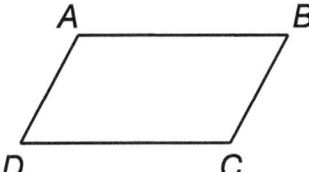

Consecutive angles in a parallelogram are supplementary which means their sum is 180°.

Add the measures of the angles and set that sum equal to 180:

$4x + 20 + 2x + 10 = 180$
$6x + 30 = 180$
$6x = 150$
$x = 25$

6. Answer: (B) $\frac{7d}{c}$

If c cans cost d dollars, then 1 can costs $\frac{d}{c}$ dollars. So 7 cans cost $\frac{d}{c} \times 7 = \frac{7d}{c}$.

Another way to think about this: Substitute values for the variables and see which selection makes sense. Let the number of cans, c, equal 6 and the cost for the cans, d, be $12.00. By dividing the cost for the cans by the number of cans, we arrive at a cost of $2.00 per can. Multiply the number of cans desired, 7, by $2.00 per can, and we arrive at a cost of $14.00. In terms of the variables, we get:

$7(\frac{d}{c}) = \frac{7d}{c}$

7. Answer: (B) 5.8%

To find a percent increase, use the formula $\frac{increase}{original} = \frac{n}{100}$.

To find the increase in 2011 over 2011, find the sum of both and subtract the smaller figure from the larger.

2011: 5.38 + 7.11 + 6.75 + 3.88 + 7.56 = 30.68
2010: 6.01 + 7.13 + 4.26 + 4.74 + 6.86 = 29

Increase: 30.68 − 29 = 1.68

Input the data into the formula to find the percent increase.

$$\frac{1.68}{29} = \frac{n}{100}$$

Cross-multiply the fractions and solve for n.

29n = 168
n = 5.79

Selection B, 5.8%, is the closest to the answer.

8. Answer: (D) $32,459.00
The increase in donations in 2011 compared to 2010 was about 5.8%. Find 5.8% of $30,680 and add it to $30,680. Expressing 5.8% as a decimal will facilitate calculations.

$30,680 + (0.058)(30,680) =
$30,680 +1779 = $32,459

9. Answer: (A) 5
Let the number of 45 cent stamps be x.

The number of 22 cent stamps = 12 − x.

45x + (12 − x)22 = 379
45x + 264 − 22x = 379
23x = 379 − 264 = 115
$$x = \frac{115}{23} = 5$$

10. Answer: (C) (5, 3.5)
Like all parallelograms, the diagonals of a rectangle bisect each other. That means the diagonals intersect at their midpoints.

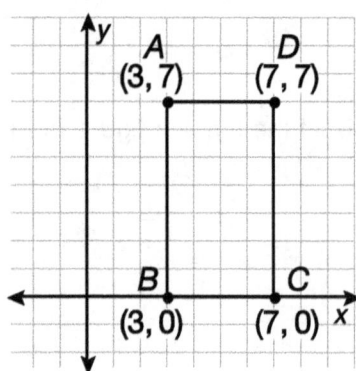

To find the midpoint of either segment, use the midpoint formula.

Midpoint formula: $\dfrac{x_1+x_2}{2}, \dfrac{y_1+y_2}{2}$

Find the midpoint of $\overline{AC}$ with endpoints located at (3,7) and (7,0)

$\dfrac{3+7}{2}, \dfrac{7+0}{2} = (5, 3.5)$

You can check your answer by seeing whether the midpoint of $\overline{BD}$ is also (5,3.5).

$\dfrac{3+7}{2}, \dfrac{0+7}{2} = (5, 3.5)$

11. Answer: (A) -2
Let the number be n. Then we have:

$n = 2\left(\dfrac{1}{n}\right) - 1$

Multiplying both sides by n:

$n^2 = 2 - n;\ n^2 + n - 2 = 0$

Factoring:

$(n+2)(n-1) = 0;\quad n = -2 \text{ or } 1$

12. Answer: (C) $\sqrt{2}$

$9\Phi 4 = \dfrac{1}{\sqrt{9 \times 4}} = \dfrac{1}{\sqrt{36}} = \dfrac{1}{6}.$

$3\Phi(9\Phi 4) = 3\Phi \dfrac{1}{6} = \dfrac{1}{\sqrt{3 \times \dfrac{1}{6}}} = \dfrac{1}{\sqrt{\dfrac{1}{2}}} = \sqrt{2}.$

13. Answer: (C) 6
The maximum number of socks a person can pull out of the drawer without repeating a color is 5 since there are 5 different colors. The 6th sock pulled out of the drawer must be one of the 5 previous colors. So a person pulling 6 socks out of the drawer can be sure she has at least one pair of the same color.

14. Answer: (D) 4

$$f(x) = 4x^2 - 3 \text{ for } |x| < 1$$
$$f(x) = -|x| + 2 \text{ for } |x| \geq 1$$

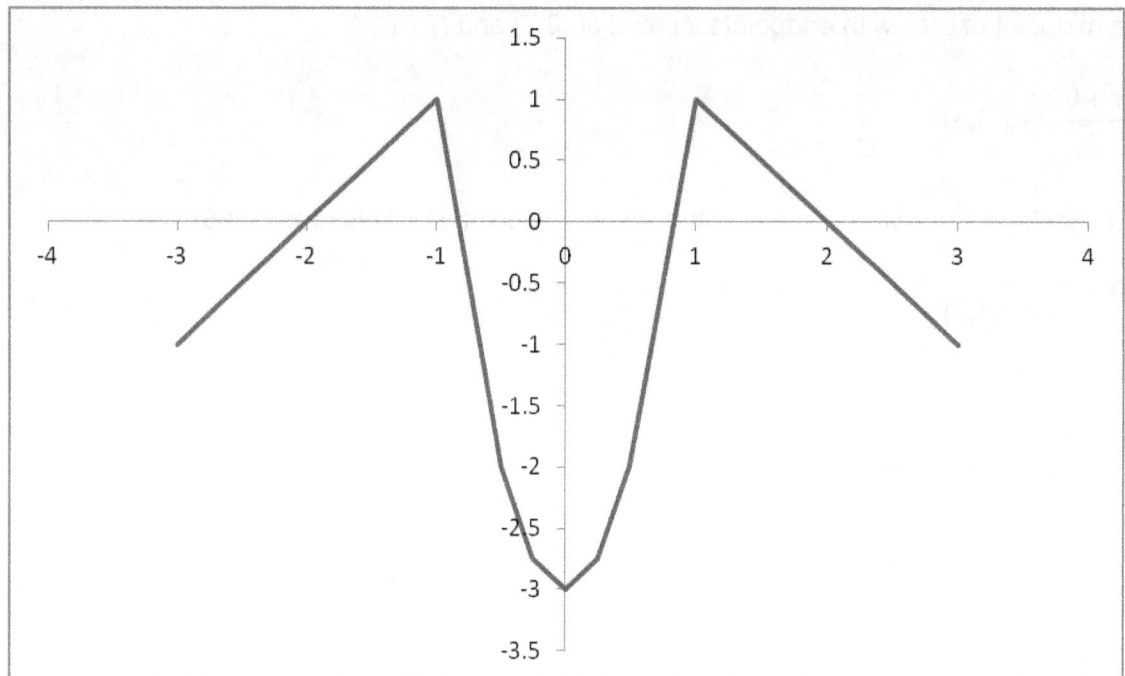

A quick plot of the function with a few points shows that between x = -1 and x = 1, the graph is an upward-opening parabola with a vertex at -3. Since f(x) has the positive value 1 at both x = -1 and x = 1, the graph crosses the x axis twice in this range. For values of x > 1 and x < -1, the graph is a straight line on either side of the origin and crosses the x-axis once on each side. So, in all, the graph crosses the x-axis 4 times.

Looking at the problem analytically, between x = -1 and x = 1, rewrite the equation as
$$(y+3) = 4(x-0)^2$$

This is the equation of an upward-opening parabola in vertex form with the vertex at (0,-3). Since f(x) has positive values at x = 1 and x = -1, even without plotting it is clear that the graph must cross the x-axis twice within this range.

For values of x > 1 or < -1, the graph of the given absolute value function is an inverted V (since the |x| term has a negative sign) with the vertex at (0,2). So clearly the arms of the V will cross the x-axis in two places.

15. Answer: (B) 6, 22, 6, 29, 7, 6, 29
The median for choice B is 7 and the mean is 15. Note that, in order for the mean to be so much larger than the median, the numbers must have a large range. This should make it easy to eliminate choices A and C.

16. Answer: (D) I and II
Since $g(x) = 1$ for all $x > 0$, the graph must satisfy the condition
$f(x) = 1$ for all $x^2 - 4 > 0; \Rightarrow x^2 > 4; \Rightarrow |x| > 2$.

For both graphs I and II, $f(x) = 1$ for all $|x| > 2$

17. Answer: (C) 1:4

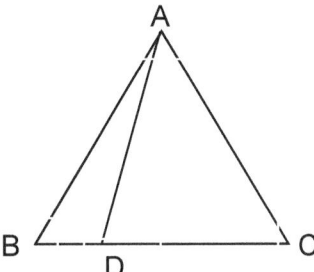

Triangles ABD and ABC both have the same height. So their areas are in the same ratio as their bases since the area of a triangle = $\frac{1}{2}$ x base x height.

Since BD = $\frac{1}{3}$ DC, DC = 3BD and BC = 4BD.

Area of triangle ABD = $\frac{1}{2}$ x BD x height

Area of triangle ABC = $\frac{1}{2}$ x BC x height = $\frac{1}{2}$ x 4BD x height

So the ratio of the areas of triangles ABD and ABC = 1:4.

18. Answer: (C) 0.4
The total number of ways 2 numbers can be picked from the set of 5 numbers is:

$\{1, 3, 5, 6, 7\}$ = $_5^{}C_2 = \frac{5!}{2!3!} = 10.$

Since 6 is the only even number, only the pairs that include 6 will have an even product.

There are 4 possible combinations that include 6: 1 6, 3 6, 5 6, and 7 6.

So the probability of picking a pair with an even product = $\frac{4}{10}$ = 0.4.

19. Answer: (C) $16 + 4\sqrt{2}$

The perimeter of a figure is its measure around the exterior. To find this, we need to know the side of each square.

The formula for the area of a square is Area = s². Use this formula to find the side of each square.

For square ABCD,

$16 = s^2$
$\sqrt{16} = \sqrt{s^2}$
$4 = s$

For square CEFG,

$8 = s^2$
$\sqrt{8} = \sqrt{s^2}$
$2\sqrt{2} = s$

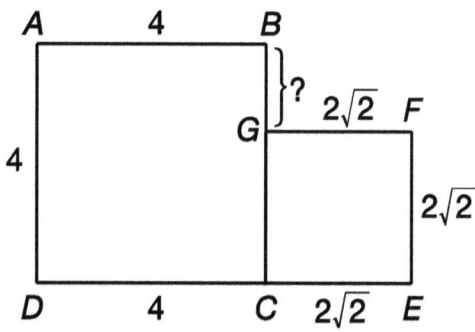

$\overline{GC}$ is in the interior of the figure and should not be included in the perimeter of the entire figure. Since $\overline{GC}$ is eliminated from the perimeter, add solely the length of $\overline{BG}$ into the final sum. Find $\overline{BG}$ by subtracting the length of $\overline{GC}$, $2\sqrt{2}$, from the length of $\overline{BC}$, which is 4.

$\overline{BC} - \overline{GC} = 4 - 2\sqrt{2}$

Add all the sides that are part of the perimeter of the figure.

$4 + 4 + 4 + 2\sqrt{2} + 2\sqrt{2} + 2\sqrt{2} + (4 - 2\sqrt{2}) = 16 + 4\sqrt{2}$

The SAT Advantage

20. Answer: (B) $\frac{2}{3}$

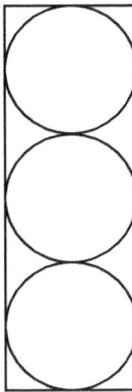

Let the radius of each ball be r. It is clear from the above figure that the radius of the cylinder = r and the height of the cylinder = $3 \times 2r = 6r$.

The volume of the cylinder = $\pi r^2 h = \pi r^2 \times 6r = 6\pi r^3$.

The total volume of the three tennis balls = $3 \times \frac{4}{3}\pi r^3 = 4\pi r^3$.

Hence, the fraction of the cylinder's volume occupied by the balls = $\frac{4\pi r^3}{6\pi r^3} = \frac{2}{3}$.

SECTION 4 (CRITICAL READING)

SENTENCE COMPLETION

1. Answer: (A) barrage
A "barrage" (A) is an outpouring of many things at once, so it is the best fit for the sentence. A "barricade" is an obstruction set up to block entrance, so answer (B) does not fit. A "barrister" is a lawyer, so answer (C) does not fit. "Baggage," of course, is luggage, so answer (D) does not fit, and a "banister," answer (E), is a handrail near a staircase. By process of elimination and also by definition of the word, answer (A) fits best in the context of the sentence.

2. Answer: (E) docile … disseminated
Because the employees "refused to strike" we can eliminate "rebellious" or "defiant" as adjectives to describe them, as in answers (A) and (B). The second word to fill in the blanks in answer (C) refers to a principle of mathematics, so answer (C) is incorrect. In answer (D) the second word is "mesmerized," which means to be put under a spell or put into a trance, so (D) is incorrect. Answer (E) best fits into the sentence, for the employees were "docile," meaning submissive, obedient, and tame, but they did object to how "poorly" information flowed through the organization. "Disseminated" means to spread or disperse so it fits with the spread or dispersing of information.

3. Answer: (D) paucity
"Paucity" (D) means scarcity or only a few, so it fits into the context of the sentence. The charges were to be "dropped" because "no jury would convict the accused" based on the evidence. This wording suggests that there was very little evidence or a scarcity of evidence. "Plethora" means a great many, "barrage" means an outpouring of many things at once, and "acme" means a height of something, so answers (A), (B), and (E) don't fit. The way the sentence is structured, the blank must be filled in by a noun, and that noun must start with a consonant, because the preceding word is "a" rather than "an." "Puny," answer (C), starts with a consonant but it is an adjective not a noun and so it does not fit grammatically into the sentence, so answer (C) is also not correct.

4. Answer: (B) supple … circumvent
Because the first word is paired with "wily" it is likely that it relates to being clever and skilled in outwitting others. This would eliminate "consistent" in answer (D). "Evasive" in answer (A) is a good candidate, but its pair for the second blank is "satisfy," and does not fit with the meaning of the sentence as she clearly did not satisfy the press by being "wily" and not easy to pin "down to firm statements". An evasive politician would not satisfy the press, so answer (A) is incorrect. Likewise, a "disingenuous" politician as in answer (C) would also fail to satisfy the press. Being "obscure" in her answers, as in answer (E), would fit the first part of the sentence, however, the second part of the sentence does not fit with the second word, as to "vilify" means to excoriate or verbally abuse. While an obscure politician might blame and vilify the press, the two parts of the sentence are tied together by a semi-colon. That means they must be very closely related, and with the word "vilify" in the second position, a very different thought is introduced. If the semi-colon were an "and," then "vilify" would fit because it would mean "in addition" and a new thought could be introduced. A "supple" or "flexible" politician can always "get around" the press, which is the meaning of "circumvent," so answer (B) is the best fit.

5. Answer: (B) depersonalize … condone

During negotiations, no one would advise the opposing parties to "ignore" the issues and "endorse" the other's foibles, so answer (A) does not make sense. Being told to "depersonalize" the issues, as in answer (B), however, is a common negotiations technique and agreeing to put up with or go along with "one another's annoying foibles" would be good advice as well, for "foibles" are generally small faults or tendencies. The parties could very well be asked to "agree to condone one another's annoying foibles." If the parties were advised to "exacerbate" or make worse the issues, as in answer (C), it is unlikely that they would also be told to "adopt" the other's foibles, as one action is provocative and the other action is pacifying. Being told to "resolve" their issues, as in answer (D) makes sense, but it would be difficult to do if the parties were also advised to "condemn" the other's foibles, so answer (D) is incorrect. To "exaggerate" the issues would also not be helpful in negotiations, as in answer (E), and to "imitate" the other's annoying foibles would not make sense in the context of negotiations either. Answer (B) is the one that makes the most sense.

READING BASED QUESTIONS

6. Answer: (E) introduce a classical precept of ethics in medicine to the practice of first aid

The short essay is about the importance of knowing what one is doing before attempting to apply first aid. First aid methods such as the Heimlich Maneuver are mentioned as requiring some training in order to be administered properly. By introducing the idea of doing no harm, as part of the classical Hippocratic Oath, the author is instructing the reader in the cautious application of first aid, so (E) is the correct answer.

7. Answer: (A) the ancient Hippocratic Oath retains some meaning and value in modern times

The phrase "remains part of the modern versions of the Hippocratic Oath" indicates that modern versions of the Hippocratic Oath retain some of the Oath's original components, presumably because they have meaning and value in modern times, as stated in answer (A). The similarity between the words "remains" and "retains" in answer (A) is also a hint that (A) is the best answer. The fact that doctors still take some versions of the Oath "today before entering the medical profession" indicates that the oath "retains some meaning and value in modern times" as stated in answer (A).

8. Answer: (C) it is a mental device used to aid in remembering something

"Mnemonic" devices are mental methods of remembering something, so answer (C) is correct by definition of the term. The author suggests that perhaps "remembering the first principle of the first doctor when giving first aid," with its repetitions of the word "first" can serve as a reminder to would-be helpers to "Do no harm." The author is recommending a helpful memory device, which is a "mnemonic" device.

9. Answer: (A) cautionary yet encouraging

The author states, "it is important to be trained before trying to perform first aid" and mentions specific first aid techniques and that "they all require some understanding." These phrases can be understood to be cautionary in tone. They are not "strongly admonitory" as in answer (B) or "authoritarian" as in answer (D). The paragraph changes tone with the phrase "The good news is…." The life-saving techniques, asserts the author, are "easily learned" and places to learn the techniques are readily "available" and "free", including at "the Red Cross or local health agencies." Since this is responsible advice, we cannot say that the tone becomes "lax" as in answer (E) or "ultimately careless" as in answer (C). Rather, the tone goes from being cautionary to being encouraging, as in answer (A).

10. Answer: (C) creative, resourceful, good-humored
Since Carroll "used his musical talents to make a YouTube video", he may be said to be creative, as in answer (C). Far from being "powerless" as in answer (B) or "wimpy" as in answer (D), he used the resources available to him to make his statement when his guitar was broken by the airline's carelessness. He may then be said to be "resourceful" as in answer (C). Although it would be natural to be angry at the loss of a $3,500 guitar, the author describes that the video treated the incident "humorously" with comic acting-out of "baggage personnel tossing baggage around as if they were playing catch and laughing when they missed." This is a good-humored way to treat the incident, showing Carroll is "good-humored" as in answer (C). The passage states that Carroll tells United to donate the compensatory money "to charity," showing he does not have the characteristics of being "sardonic, cynical, surly" as in answer (E).

11. Answer: (D) caused United Airlines to take a stock hit and thus compelled it to try to compensate Carroll
The author states that "four days" after the video went viral "United Airlines' stock price declined by 10%, costing its investors an estimated $180 million in value." This means that it "caused United Airlines to take a stock hit" as in answer (D). There is no mention of United making a musical counter video as in answer (A), and the expression "change its tune" means a change in attitude, not a literal piece of music. Nothing in the passage suggests that "all the major airlines" were impacted as in answer (B). Later lines specifically state that "Carroll often serves various companies as a corporate consultant on customer service," not just United, as in answer (C). There is no mention of "multiple lawsuits" as in answer (E) either.

12. Answer: (C) lost camaraderie and trust are not part of the price of "modernization"
Since the author thinks that Beijing changing to a car culture rather than staying a bike culture would be "a shame" because of pollution and exercise concerns, putting "modernization" in quotes is a good tip off that this answer reflects the author's skeptical viewpoint about some technological "improvements." The passage specifically mentions the "camaraderie of a culture" where people "trust each other" and hopes that those features of the bike culture of Beijing will not be lost. Therefore, answer (C) is the best answer.

13. Answer: (E) bikes cause less pollution and are good for people's health through the exercise they afford
The author specifically states that replacing the bike with the car would be "a shame" and goes on to list the reasons as "biking cuts down on pollution" and biking "increases people's health through exercise." Because of this wording, it is clear that answer (E) is the best answer.

14. Answer: (A) there was a good reason and basis for this trust
"Well-founded" means standing on a firm foundation or derived from trustworthy sources. From this definition of the word, answer (A) is the most sensible answer. The statement that "people trusted one another not to steal" and that that trust was well-founded is supported by the line which says, "there was very little thievery of bikes." This statement gives the "good reason and basis for this trust" as in answer (A) and shows that the trust was "well-founded."

15. Answer: (C) the twelve year old had a quick and inquiring mind with a proclivity toward history
Hunter Scott attentively noted the name of the ship and got it right from a passing mention in a movie. He had the name right because he was able to corroborate the ship's factual existence

and use it as a basis to get in touch with real survivors of the incident. This shows he had a quick mind. He also had an inquiring mind, because not all twelve year olds would leave the movies and look up a historical incident. He also made the connection between his interest in the *U.S.S. Indianapolis* and a history project. Scott's contacting of the survivors of the actual incident show that he had a strong tendency or proclivity toward history. All this shows that answer (C) is the correct answer.

16. Answer: (A) the publicity surrounding its rescue might reveal the secretive nature of its mission

The wording of these lines is that the ship was not rescued right away "possibly to avoid drawing attention to its secret mission of delivering components of a nuclear bomb." The matching of the words "secretive" in answer (A) and "secret" in the language in these lines is a hint that (A) is the correct answer. The wording of "to avoid drawing attention" shows that officials wanted to avoid any publicizing of the incident, so "the publicity" in answer (A) also fits. Delivering nuclear bomb components would naturally be a security concern, especially during war time, so it would be disastrous "to reveal the secretive nature" of the ship's mission, as is part of the language of answer (A).

17. Answer: (A) the descendants of the survivors of the *U.S.S. Indianapolis* were proud of the sacrifices their ancestors had made and wanted to keep their memories alive

These lines specifically state that the "proud descendants" had formed the support group "to remember the sacrifice and bravery" of their relatives. This language ties in closely with the language of answer (A): "the descendants…were proud of the sacrifices" and "wanted to keep their memories alive." No mention is made of the Navy's attitude as in answer (B); the descendants were "proud" of their ancestors, so they did not hold them in "low honor and esteem" as in answer (C). No mention is made of descendants' anger as in answer (D), and the fact that the descendants were "proud" negates answer (E) that they were "ashamed of their ancestors' role."

18. Answer: (A) dramatic imagery

Using process of elimination, answer (B) is incorrect, because the literary term for imparting human qualities to an inanimate object is "personification," not personalization. Since there is no measurement cited of the ocean's depths and the paragraph is not about the ocean but the men in it, answer (C) is also incorrect. Answer (D) is incorrect because the ocean is sometimes referred to as "the deep," making it a noun not requiring an adjective. Answer (E) is incorrect because there is no reference to a book upon which the movie *Jaws* is based, nor is there any reason to cite the author's second book. Answer (A) is the best answer because the phrase "swallowed by the deep" evokes the melancholy and tragedy of the incidents out in the ocean, using dramatic imagery.

19. Answer: (D) the repetition puts the emphasis on the survivors and their accounts to Hunter Scott of their painful memories of the *U.S.S. Indianapolis* incident

The context of the paragraph is about the survivors being available to share with Hunter Scott their vivid memories of an incident he was fascinated by. In this context, answer (D) is the best answer. The repetition puts emphasis on the "They," who are the living men (the survivors) and their recalled memories of the incident. The implication is that they are recounting their memories to the interested Scott. The repetition also helps emphasize that these events were unlikely to be forgotten by any of them and were painfully burned into their memories.

20. Answer: (E) to yield; to give in to stronger forces
Since the wording of the sentence shows "they had received" the wounds "during the torpedo attack," this means that the wounds were inflicted before the men were stranded in the water. Once stranded in the water, it is implied that some men are not recovering from the wounds. They are being "slowly" overcome by their injuries and dying of injuries that did not kill them outright but which are slowly sapping their strength, causing them to yield or give in to stronger forces (succumb).

21. Answer: (D) Ensign Twible must have shown leadership skills that enabled many in his group to survive
The author spells out the leadership that Ensign Twible showed in that he "heroically enjoined" the men "to help one another." The paragraph goes on to show that "this group tied themselves together with ropes" to protect themselves and one another from drifting off or drowning. Later lines tell how they "exhorted one another not to give up hope and to keep fighting." The men were clearly following Ensign Twible's example and listening to his leadership. The fact that Twible was later awarded two medals for heroism shows that Twible showed leadership skills, as in answer (D).

22. Answer: (C) in unity there is strength
The very thing that Ensign Twible "heroically enjoined" the men to do was "to help one another" and to act as one united body rather than as isolated individuals. The group literally "tied themselves together with ropes," showing that they acted as a unit, and this was effective in preventing what had happened to others, as recounted by the author that some others simply swam off only to be "swallowed by the deep." They "shared lifejackets" and "helped one another into ones" and by acting as a unit, they "exhorted one another not to give up hope and keep fighting for survival." By banding together in unity, the men were able to strengthen one another to the point that more of them survived, so answer (C) is a proper summary.

23. Answer: (C) mutual good will, familiar friendliness
The definition of the word "camaraderie" is familiarity, friendliness, and good will. By process of elimination, we know that there is no mention of the men drinking together, as in answer (B). They certainly have not forgotten their experience in hilarity, as in answer (D), nor have they tried to escape from the memories as in answer (E). Although they were originally tied by formal, military bonds, the men are voluntarily banding together now, so answer (A) is also able to be eliminated, leaving answer (C).

24. Answer: (E) the survivors' feelings about the charges against their captain and their efforts to exonerate their captain officially from any wrongdoing
The author specifically mentions that the survivors were "not as haunted" by the incident as they were "by the knowledge that their captain had suffered charges." These lines depict "the survivors' feelings about the charges against their captain," which is the wording in the first part of answer (E). This section also deals with the men's thoughts about their captain's responsibility and more of their feelings: "they wanted to clear his name." Later lines describe how "They began a campaign" and "appeared as a group before Congress to ask for the exoneration" of their captain, which shows "their efforts to exonerate their captain officially," as in answer (E).

SECTION 5 (MATHEMATICS)

MULTIPLE CHOICE

1. Answer: (C) 62.5%

The total number of students = 255 + 153 = 408. The percentage of girls = $\frac{255}{408} \times 100 = 62.5$.

2. Answer: (B) $\frac{3}{10}$

To find the probability, divide the number of acceptable outcomes, in this case, the number of white socks, by the total number of possible outcomes. There are 6 white socks and a total of 20 socks. So the probability of getting a white sock is $\frac{6}{20}$ which reduces to $\frac{3}{10}$.

3. Answer: (B) $\frac{14+m}{7m}$

Find the lowest common denominator for both fractions and add the two expressions.

The lowest common denominator for the quantities 7 and m is 7m.

$$\frac{2}{m} \times \frac{7}{7} = \frac{14}{7m}$$

$$\frac{1}{7} \times \frac{m}{m} = \frac{m}{7m}$$

Add the two fractions:

$$\frac{14}{7m} + \frac{m}{7m} = \frac{14+m}{7m}$$

4. Answer: (B) 65

The median of a data set is the middle value. Array the data from least to greatest to find the middle term.

20   40   60   70   80   100

Since 60 and 70 are both in the middle, find their mean (the mean is the average).

$$\frac{60+70}{2} = 65$$

5. Answer: (D) Rode, rested, ran

The first portion of the graph, starting at time 0, indicates much distance was covered in a small amount of time. The vertical component indicates time passed but no distance was covered. The third component indicates that less distance per unit of time was covered when compared to the first component. Since the first component of the graph implies a greater velocity, it represents the bicycle ride. The vertical component that shows the passage of time without any distance covered is the rest period. Finally, the third component, which shows more time passing per unit of distance (compared to the first component), must be the running portion of the graph.

(Note that here the distance is plotted on the x-axis. This could be confusing since it is usually time that is plotted on the x-axis.)

6. Answer: (E) $\frac{17}{25}$

M is in the interior of the region between $\overrightarrow{OR}$ and the x-axis. Therefore, the slope of $\overrightarrow{OM}$ must be less than the slope of $\overrightarrow{OR}$ but greater than the slope of the x-axis. Find the slope of $\overrightarrow{OR}$ by using the slope formula $m = \frac{y_2 - y_1}{x_2 - x_1}$ where m represents the slope. Point R, (6,4) and the origin, (0,0) are both on $\overrightarrow{OR}$, so input their values into the slope formula.

$$\frac{4-0}{6-0} = \frac{4}{6} = \frac{2}{3}$$

The slope of $\overrightarrow{OR}$ is $\frac{2}{3}$.

The slope of the x-axis is 0. You can check this by using any two points on the x-axis. Let's use (3,0) and (0,0).

$$\frac{0-0}{0-3} = \frac{0}{-3} = 0$$

Any value that falls outside the parameters $0 < m < \frac{2}{3}$ cannot be the slope of $\overrightarrow{OR}$. Choice E, $\frac{17}{25}$, is 0.68 when expressed as a decimal. $\frac{2}{3}$, when expressed as a decimal, is 0.666...

Therefore, the slope of $\overrightarrow{OM}$ cannot be $\frac{17}{25}$.

7. Answer: (E) I and III

$8x^3 + 25k$ will be factorable if it can be expressed as the sum of two cubes since $8x^3 = (2x)^3$ and $a^3 + b^3 = (a+b)(a^2 - ab + b^2)$.

Both $k = 5$ and $k = \dfrac{1}{25}$ will make $25k$ expressable as a cube.

If $k = 5$, $8x^3 + 25k = (2x)^3 + 5^3 = (2x+5)(4x^2 - 10x + 25)$.

If $k = \dfrac{1}{25}$, $8x^3 + 25k = (2x)^3 + 1^3 = (2x+1)(4x^2 - 2x + 1)$.

8. Answer: (C) III only

$|y(x) - h(x)| > 2$ implies that the two functions are separated by at least 2 units for all values of x. Choice II can be eliminated at once since the two lines intersect, so the separation between them is reduced to zero at some points. In Choice 1, the functions are mostly separated by at least 2 units but not around the point x = -2. Only Choice III fits the given criterion.

STUDENT-PRODUCED RESPONSE

9. Answer: 0.40
Maria earned $8.60 per hour and worked 35 hours a week. Find Maria's weekly pay before she received her raise by multiplying her hourly rate by the number of hours she worked each week.

$8.60 × 35 = $301

Find out how much Maria's weekly pay increased by subtracting her old weekly pay from her new weekly pay.

$315 − 301 = $14

Divide $14 by 35 to find Maria's hourly increase.

$14 ÷ 35 = $0.40

10. Answer: 96
The number of degrees in a straight line is 180. The sum of the 5 angles that measure m° each is 180. Similarly, the sum of the 3 angles that measure n° each is also 180.

$m + m + m + m + m = 180$

$5m = 180$

$m = 36$

$n + n + n = 180$

$3n = 180$

$n = 60$

$m + n = 36 + 60 = 96$

11. Answer: 39

This problem is a little tricky. It is easy to reason that the monkey climbs 1 ft (3 ft up and 2 ft down) in 4 seconds and so 12 ft in 12 x 4 = 48 s. But this reasoning is wrong since the monkey would reach the top of the pole at 12 ft before sliding down to 10 ft.

The monkey's climbing pattern: 3 ft (3 s), 1 ft (4 s), 4 ft (7 s), 2 ft (8 s), 5 ft (11 s), 3 ft (12 s) …and so on. The monkey is at 9 ft at 36 s. In the next 3 seconds, the monkey climbs up to 12 ft. So, it reaches the top of the pole at 39 seconds.

12. Answer: 5

Let the integer be n. Writing out the equation according to the given information, factoring, and finding the possible values of n we get:

$$5n^2 = 24n + 5$$
$$\Rightarrow 5n^2 - 24n - 5 = 0$$
$$\Rightarrow (5n+1)(n-5) = 0$$
$$\Rightarrow n = 5 \text{ or } -\frac{1}{5}$$

Since the number is an integer, the correct answer is n = 5.

13. Answer: 1/17

There are 51 numbers between 100 and 150, inclusive. Since we are counting number 100 in the set, subtract 100 from 150 and add 1 to the result:
150 - 100 = 50
50 + 1 = 51

The square numbers in the range 100-150 are the following: 100, 121, and 144 (the squares of 10, 11, and 12).

Since 3 out of the 51 possible choices are square numbers, the probability of picking a square number is 3/51, which equals 1/17.

14. Answer: 9

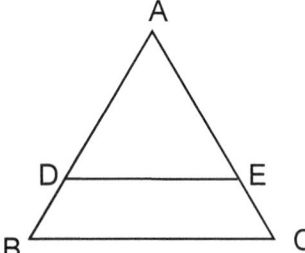

Since angle ADE = angle ABC, DE is parallel to BC (equal corresponding angles).

So we also have angle AED = angle ACB (corresponding angles).

Therefore, triangles ADE and ABC have equal angles and are similar.

The sides of similar triangles are proportional. Therefore

$$\frac{AD}{AB} = \frac{AE}{AC} = \frac{DE}{BC} = \frac{3}{4}.$$

$$DE = BC \times \frac{3}{4} = 12 \times \frac{3}{4} = 9 \text{ cm}$$

15. Answer: 0

$f(x) = (x-h)^2 + k$ is the equation of a parabola in vertex form, i.e., the vertex of the parabola is at (h, k). Since the parabola touches the x-axis at only one point, the vertex is on the x-axis and its y coordinate is zero. Therefore k = 0.

16. Answer: 2

Let the radius of the larger circle be R and the radius of the smaller circle be r. Let the side of the square be s.

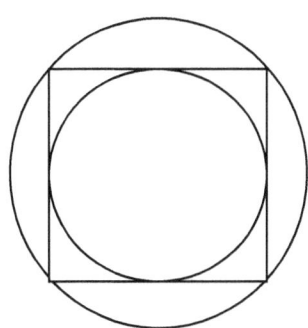

The diameter of the large circle is equal to the diagonal of the square:

$$2R = \sqrt{s^2 + s^2} = \sqrt{2s^2} = \sqrt{2}s; \quad R = \frac{\sqrt{2}s}{2}$$

The radius of the small circle is equal to half the side of the square:

$$r = \frac{s}{2}$$

The ratio of the area of the large circle to that of the small circle:

$$\frac{\pi R^2}{\pi r^2} = \frac{\pi \left(\frac{\sqrt{2}s}{2}\right)^2}{\pi \left(\frac{s}{2}\right)^2} = \frac{2s^2}{s^2} = 2.$$

17. Answer: 2

What is the remainder when 7^{109} is divided by 5?

First note that $7^1 = 7; \; 7^2 = 49; \; 7^3 = 343; \; 7^4 = 2401$.

7^5 will be a number ending in 7 since 7^4 ends with a 1.

So the units digits of the powers of 7 follow the repeating pattern of 4 numbers:
7, 9, 3, 1, 7, 9, 3, 1, ….

So all powers of 7 where the exponent is a multiple of 4 will end in 1.

108 is a multiple of 4. So 7^{108} will end in 1. This means that 7^{109} will end in 7.

Any number that ends in 7, when divided by 5, produces a remainder of 2.

18. Answer: 33

When $t = 1.2t_d$

$$RH = 100 - 5(t - t_d) = 100 - 5(1.2t_d - t_d) = 100 - 5(0.2t_d) = 100 - 5(0.2 \times 40) = 100 - 40 = 60.$$

When $t = 1.1t_d$

$$RH = 100 - 5(t - t_d) = 100 - 5(1.1t_d - t_d) = 100 - 5(0.1t_d) = 100 - 5(0.1 \times 40) = 100 - 20 = 80.$$

Percentage change in relative humidity = $\dfrac{80 - 60}{60} \times 100 = \dfrac{20}{60} \times 100 = 33.3\%$

Rounded off, the percentage change = 33.

SECTION 6 (WRITING)

IMPROVING SENTENCES

1. Answer: (E) was also a trained painter who became
The original sentence is awkward and confuses the relationship between Feininger's training and the rest of his career. It also includes the unnecessary pronoun *he*. Choice (B) confuses the sequence of events, suggesting that Feininger trained as a painter while he was a photographer, which the rest of the sentence contradicts. Choice (C) begins in a logical way, but then suggests that having become a cartoonist and caricaturist was Feininger's training, rather than the result of his training. Choice (D) also begins well, but the verb form *becoming* does not match the form of the verb *taught* to which it is linked with the conjunction *and*. Choice (E) avoids all these problems by clearly expressing the relationship between Feininger's training and accomplishments as a painter, which all occurred before he became a photographer.

2. Answer: (D) and political controversy caused by rapid social change
This sentence begins as a list of things that students learn about the decade 1840–1850. All of the items that follow the words *was one of* should be in the same grammatical form. Choices (A) and (B) interrupt the list by starting a new clause with the subject *they*. Choice (E) interrupts the list with a descriptive phrase. In choice (C), the phrase *controversial discoveries* is in the correct form for the list, but it changes the meaning of the sentence. Choice (D) is correct because it accurately expresses the ideas in the original sentence and because the phrases *political controversy* and *social change* are in the same form as the phrases *technological progress* and *geographical expansion*.

3. Answer: (B) disasters; fewer than 10 percent of Americans have created
In the original sentence, two independent clauses are incorrectly joined with a comma and no conjunction. Choice (B) correctly changes the comma to a semicolon. Choice (C) joins the clauses with the word *and*, but does not include a comma. The word *and* also suggests that two different points are being made in the sentence, when, actually, the second clause is merely an explanation of the first one. Choices (D) and (E) add a semicolon, but the words after the semicolon do not include a correct verb form.

4. Answer: (A) not only produced weapons and kept vital industries alive, but also changed perceptions of what women could do
The original sentence correctly uses the paired conjunctions *not only…but also* to join verb phrases with the same grammatical form: *produced weapons*, *kept vital industries alive*, *changed perceptions*. The other choices introduce errors. Choice (B) incorrectly uses *not only* without its needed partner, *but also*. Choice (C) includes both conjunctions, but incorrectly adds the word *while* to introduce what should be the main verbs of the sentence. Choice (D) creates a fragment because the verb forms *being* and *changing* are not in the correct form. Choice (E) places *not only* in the wrong position, changing the meaning of the sentence.

5. Answer: (E) young Edgar Poe became the foster child of the Allan family of Richmond, Virginia
A descriptive phrase at the beginning of a sentence should be followed immediately by the noun that the phrase describes. The opening phrase in this sentence describes *young Edgar Poe*. Only choice (E) correctly places Poe as the subject of the sentence.

The SAT Advantage

6. Answer: (C) and reduce cholesterol levels
Items in a list should be in the same grammatical form. Choice (C) is correct because the verb phrase *reduce cholesterol levels* matches the grammatical forms of *aid digestion* and *relieve pain*.

7. Answer: (C) Before 1954, when the U.S. Supreme Court overturned the doctrine of "separate but equal,"
Choice (A) incorrectly joins two independent clauses with only a comma. Choice (B) creates a sentence that means the exact opposite of the original, changing the sequence of cause and effect. Choice (C) expresses the original idea in a logical, grammatically correct way, using a prepositional phrase and a subordinate clause to introduce the main clause. Choice (D) incorrectly uses a semicolon with the conjunction *but*. Choice (E) uses awkward grammatical structures and confuses the cause-and-effect relationship between the Supreme Court decision and segregated schools.

8. Answer: (C) milk, also developed treatments
The subject of the sentence is *Louis Pasteur*. Adding the subject *he* after the noun phrase that identifies Pasteur is redundant (A). Simply removing the word *he*, as in Choice (C) creates a correct sentence. To correct a sentence like this, remember that the sentence should make sense when you leave out all the words set off by commas. Choices (B) and (D) do not include a correct verb form to follow the subject *Louis Pasteur*; they create fragments. Choice (E) uses the correct verb form, but introducing the word *although* into what should be the main clause in the sentence also creates a fragment.

9. Answer: (D) our town's trash reduction policy depends on the willing participation of residents in the recycling of paper and plastic
The question you should ask here is "For what to be successful?" the residents? the town? or the town's trash reduction policy? The next word after the opening verb phrase should tell what needs to be successful: *our town's trash reduction policy*. Only choice (D) phrases the sentence in this way.

10. Answer: (A) Because the day before Ash Wednesday is traditionally a time of indulgent eating, the Mardi Gras festival in New Orleans derives its name from the French words meaning "fat Tuesday."
The original sentence is correct because it expresses the idea of the origin of the name Mardi Gras simply and clearly. All of the other choices are long, complicated, and convoluted. Choice (B) redundantly includes both *because* and *is why*.

11. Answer: (B) Jane Goodall, who observed and interacted with chimpanzees for many years,
The original sentence is a run-on that incorrectly joins two main clauses without the proper punctuation. Choice (B) solves this problem in a logical way, by turning one of the main clauses into a descriptive subordinate clause. Choice (C) incorrectly uses the conjunction *and* to join a phrase and a clause. Choice (D) adds the word *While*, which introduces an idea of sequence that was not present in the original sentence. Choice (E) introduces the sentence with an awkward grammatical construction that does not flow logically into the main clause.

The SAT Advantage

IDENTIFYING SENTENCE ERRORS

12. Answer: (C) were
The subject of the sentence is *rescue*, not *children*, *rafters*, or *acts*. Since rescue is singular, it requires the singular verb *was*.

13. Answer: (E) No error
This sentence pairs the conjunctions *neither…nor* correctly. It also uses the singular verb *was* correctly for two subjects joined by *nor*. The preposition *for* is used correctly after the verb *blamed*. The word *effects* is used correctly as a noun.

14. Answer: (A) their
The subject of the sentence is *worker*, which is singular. Therefore, the sentence should begin *Although his or her wages*.

15. Answer: (A) are
The subject of the sentence is the singular word *number*, which requires the singular verb *is*.

16. Answer: (C) wore
The correct verb form to follow the helping verb *have* is *worn*.

17. Answer: (A) wouldn't have
The word *none* is a negative. Combining it with *wouldn't* creates a double negative. The sentence requires the word *would*, rather than *wouldn't*.

18. Answer: (D) to
The correct preposition here should be *with*.

19. Answer: (E) No error
The sentence is correct as is. Choice (A) correctly uses the comparative adjective *shorter*, which is modified by the adverb *considerably*. Choice (B) correctly uses the expression *than most other* to make a comparison. The singular verb *is* agrees with the singular subject *form*. The adjective *expressive* is used correctly to describe *form*, and the adjective itself is correctly modified by the adverb *remarkably*.

20. Answer: (C) to respond
The verb form *to respond* in this comparison should match the form of the subject: *connecting*. The gerund *responding* would be the correct choice. *Connecting* is more difficult and rewarding than *responding*.

21. Answer: (B) immigrating
People *emigrate from* one country and *immigrate to* another. The preposition *from* should alert you that the word emigrate is required here.

22. Answer: (D) as frequenting
In correct idiomatic English, the verb *known* is followed by an infinitive form of the verb, rather than the gerund (-*ing*) form. The correct verb here would be *known to frequent*.

The SAT Advantage

23. Answer: (A) are
The subject of the clause beginning with the word *there* is *obligation*, which requires the singular verb *is*.

24. Answer: (B) sunk
The correct past form of *sink* is *sank*. *Sunk* is the past participle form, which is used only in a participial phrase or after the helping verbs *has*, *have*, or *had*.

25. Answer: (A) with which
The pronoun *which* should never be used with people. The correct form here would be *whom*.

26. Answer: (D) will begin
The verb forms in linked *as* clauses should be in the same tense: as their use *grows* and as China *begins* to limit exports.

27. Answer: (C) had been
Since the sentence begins with the present tense construction *There is*, the next part of the sentence should use the present perfect *has been*, rather than the past perfect *had been*. If the sentence began with *There was*, then *had been* would be correct.

28. Answer: (B) with a history
This sentence would "sound right" to most people. Technically, however, the plural noun *people* requires the plural noun *histories* to follow *with*. Each person has his or her own history of heart disease. People do not have a shared collective history of heart disease.

29. Answer: (B) they
Using the word *they* here seems to suggest that the people who were taken ill were the ones who failed to inspect and monitor the food processing plants. There is no antecedent for the pronoun *they*. Instead of using *they*, the sentence needs a noun such as *government agencies* or *officials at the U.S. Department of Agriculture*.

IMPROVING PARAGRAPHS

30. Answer: (B) Although Tennessee Williams's fascinating *The Glass Menagerie* is performed more often than *The Night of the Iguana,* I prefer the latter play.
Sentence 1 has repetition in it. The word "often" is used twice unnecessarily; "fascinating and interesting" is redundant as the two words are very close in meaning, and the sentence already implies that audiences prefer *The Glass Menagerie* because it is performed more often. Sentence 1 is wordy, so editing out the repetition and redundancy to make a succinct statement, as is done in answer (B), is the best revision.

31. Answer: (A) Caught, bound, and held captive for eating, the iguana symbolizes people who are trapped in despair.
Sentences 2 and 3 do not seem to be connected as they stand in the essay. Sentence 2 talks about the tied-up iguana's symbolism; sentence 3 goes into some detail about Shannon. The only connection is that both Shannon and the iguana are tied up, but a transitional sentence connecting the symbolism of the iguana to Shannon would be helpful. Saying that the iguana is "Caught, bound, and held captive for eating" certainly puts the iguana in a situation of despair. Sentence 3 tells us that Shannon is also in situation of despair. He is "defrocked," about to lose another job, is on the verge of insanity and has apparently been tied up to prevent him from

committing suicide. Answer (A) gives details about the situation of the iguana and why it can serve as a symbol for people in situations like Shannon's.

32. Answer: (C) Connect it to sentence 6 with the word "yet," put "She" into the lower case, and eliminate the period at the end of sentence 6 to make the two sentences into one thought
Connecting sentence 7 to sentence 6 is an improvement because the topic sentence of the paragraph is how fascinating the character of Hannah is. The fact that Shannon is attracted to her (sentence 6) does not make her fascinating, but the fact that she refuses him in spite of his clear attraction to her is interesting. Connecting the two sentences into one thought supports the first sentence about Hannah's fascinating qualities. It makes the fact that Shannon is attracted to her part of all the details about her character that follow.

33. Answer: (E) Starting with sentence 11
Breaking the paragraph up starting with sentence 11 makes sense. Sentences 11 - 15 deal with conclusions one may draw about Hannah's refusal of Shannon. Sentence 11 speaks of "One conclusion" and sentence 12 speaks of "a possible second reason." Then sentences 13 through 15 tell about Hannah's liberation from "her loving bondage" to her grandfather and how she might not want to get into a dependency relationship with someone else. These thoughts are all part of and related to the conclusions one can draw about Hannah's reasons for her refusal. Starting a new paragraph with sentence 11 would make for a cohesive paragraph with all the sentences related to the same topic.

34. Answer: (A) Leave it as it is
Sentence 13 serves as an explanatory sentence connecting sentence 12 to the rest of the paragraph. It states a circumstance that would allow for the "possible second reason" mentioned in sentence 12: that is, that Shannon could become too emotionally dependent on Hannah. It relates to the rest of the paragraph as well, because the reader knows that Hannah has helped Shannon "drive out his demons (sentence 9) and "she saves his sanity" (sentence 10). In the context of the paragraph, sentence 12 makes perfect sense as it connects the ideas within the paragraph well. It is succinct and well-expressed and needs no revision.

35. Answer: (C) Perhaps Hannah is an "iguana" too, glad to be set free and not about to be tied down again.
By process of elimination, answer (A) is not particularly expressive and falls flat as a concluding sentence. Answer (B) would also be a disappointing concluding sentence because it does not sum anything up or lead to any conclusions. Answer (D) is not relevant to the essay and is probably not true either, as many people cannot go to the sea to die. Although Answer (E) is implied in the essay, that sentence would be out of place after sentence 14, as the preceding sentences are about Hannah's character. Answer (C), however, relates Hannah's character to much of the material in an earlier paragraph about the symbolism of the iguana, its relation to despair and situations of entrapment, and even to Shannon's situation. Answer (C) leaves the reader on an interesting line of thought that is based on what has gone before: although Shannon is an obvious candidate to be the "iguana" in the play because he is tied up, it is possible that Hannah is one too, because she has experienced liberation from her own "blue devils" and her aged grandfather. It is thoughtful, provocative, and also sums up much of the material of the preceding paragraphs of the essay, as a concluding sentence should.

The SAT Advantage

SECTION 7 (CRITICAL READING)

SENTENCE COMPLETION

1. Answer: (A) irresolute
The answer to this question is hinted at by the opening phrase "Although he had fought to get it." This phrase implies that the subject of the sentence is going to do or be something that is inconsistent with having fought to get the new job. It turns out his old job was "desirable," and since he is going to do something inconsistent with having fought to get the new one, we may surmise that he was having doubts about leaving his old job. In other words, he was not resolved to leave his old job in spite of fighting for a new one. Answer (A), "irresolute," expresses this state of doubt and inconsistency. All the other answers suggest unbending determination to leave his old job.

2. Answer: (B) jaded
Being "jaded" (that is, dulled in feeling by having had too much of something) is often associated with being "worldly-wise" or "world-weary." The fact that the courtesan is experiencing "less and less pleasure in life" definitely implies that she was dulled in feeling by having had too much of something. Answer (A), "bejeweled", is irrelevant to anything, and answers (C), (D), and (E) suggest positive and/or fresh states of mind that do not match with experiencing "less and less pleasure in life."

3. Answer: (B) erratic ... tenacious
The sense of the sentence is that a person has to be consistent and diligent about practice and strong in determination to "win an Olympic medal." It is a warning that "You cannot be" a certain way "if" you want to win. "Lax" (A), "careless" (E), and "erratic" (B) are all things a person could not be in order to win an Olympic medal. However, the second word to answer (A) is "doubtful." "You must be doubtful in your determination" does not make sense for a winner. Similarly, the second word in answer (E) is "volatile," which means up and down, inconsistent in emotions and explosive. "You must be volatile in your determination" does not make sense for a would-be winner. The combination of "You cannot be erratic about practice" and "You must be tenacious in your determination," answer (B), fits the sentence well in meaning.

4. Answer: (D) impecunious
Since the second part of the sentence gives the hint that the missing word will be related to Dickens's "poverty-stricken childhood," it must have something to do with being poor. That eliminates answers (A), (B), (C), and (E). "Impecunious" means penniless or having very little money on a consistent basis, so answer (D) is the best answer.

5. Answer: (A) diminish ... modicum
A political opponent usually seeks to make his or her rival appear less desirable as a candidate, so the word "diminish," answer (A), or the word "belittle," answer (D), would fit into what a political rival might be trying to do. The partner word in answer (A) also fits, as a "modicum" is a little bit of something. The partner word in answer (D), however, is "behemoth," which means something huge, so it does not make sense in the context of the sentence to "belittle" and to also make something huge.

6. Answer: (D) self-effacing ... precursor
Since "the young woman" was "modest" and "shy" in front of someone, it is likely that the word missing in the first blank is a word that goes along with these qualities. "Humble," answer (A)

277   SAT Practice Test 2 Answer Rationales

and "self-effacing," answer (D), go along with being "modest" and "shy." The words "the one who had gone before her" give us a hint as to what the second word is; it means someone who has gone before. "Successor" in answer (A) means someone who goes or follows after, so answer (A)'s second word does not fit. Answer (D) has as its second word "precursor," which is a synonym for "predecessor" or "one who had gone before."

READING BASED QUESTIONS

7. Answer: (A) a speech of high praise for a person's character and accomplishments in life

The topic sentence introduces the idea of public speaking as the subject of the paragraph. Since public speaking is the topic, the reader can surmise that a "eulogy" is a speech of some sort, not a "song" as in answer (D) or a "reading aloud" of letters as in answer (E). A "soliloquy as in *Hamlet*" (C) is spoken aloud but it is supposed to be an internal reflection, like spoken thought, and would be inappropriate at a public event like a funeral. Only answers (A) and (B) mention a speech, and it is unlikely that a "dead person's failures in life" would be the topic of discussion at his or her funeral. The reader can surmise that most likely a "eulogy" is (A) a speech of high praise for a person's character and accomplishments in life.

8. Answer: (C) an imperative sentence

There are four kinds of sentences in English: those that make a statement (A) a declarative sentence; those that ask a question (B) an interrogative statement; those that give a command or direction (C) an imperative sentence; and those that show emphasis or emotion (D) an exclamatory sentence. Answer (E), an explanatory sentence, applies to many declarative sentences. The last sentence reads: "Count yourself lucky that you only have to give a speech," and it is giving a direction or a command in that it directly addresses the reader and tells him or her to do something. It therefore is an imperative sentence.

9. Answer: (B) shrinks away

Although "cowering" may include wanting to hide behind a curtain (A) or clinging in fear to a curtain (D), "shrinks away" is a more accurate definition of the word "cowers." "Cowards" in answer (C) is a plural noun, whereas the sentence structure calls for a verb. "Wagers" in answer (E) means to make a bet or gamble, and does not fit the meaning of the sentence. By process of elimination, (B) shrinks away, is the best answer.

10. Answer: (A) metaphorically

The author is employing the device of comparing something to something else yet making a statement that the first thing is the same as the thing it is being compared to. This is a metaphor. If the sentence read, "Even if you are like a most timorous little mouse," it would be a simile, but the sentence is worded such that the person is being declared as being the same as "the most little timorous mouse." It is similar to Shakespeare's famous metaphor: "All the world's a stage." Shakespeare is declaring that the world is a stage, which is a metaphor rather than a simile, which would read "All the world is like a stage."

11. Answer: (A) reassurance that stagefright can be conquered

The passage's tone is one of helpful reassurance and advice for overcoming stagefright. Phrases such as, "One way to talk yourself out of "stagefright" before a public speaking engagement" and "Another way to talk yourself out of stagefright" and "There are many remedies for stagefright" reassure the reader that stagefright can be conquered. The author also notes that, "It is comforting to know that many singing and other stars have confessed to terrible anxiety before going on stage," which provides reassurance that many famous people have to cope with stagefright and they manage. The ending comment of, "You can do this. You can perform without fear" is also an example of a tone of (A) reassurance that stagefright can be conquered.

12. Answer: (C) on deep levels of human consciousness
The author refers several times to the "subconscious mind". He or she states, "The subconscious mind does not distinguish between what is imagined and what really happens" and "your subconscious mind will be relaxed, knowing that you've already achieved this." Since "sub" means "under," this would imply that the perspective of managing stagefright is from "deep levels" of "conscious" or "consciousness" as in answer (C). It is a common error to mix up "conscious" with "conscience" as in answers (D) and (E), but it is incorrect. Answer (A) is incorrect because there is no mention of Freud or the "superego." Because of the references to the "subconscious mind," answer (B) is also incorrect.

13. Answer: (A) a psychological process of reprogramming a person's responses to fear-inducing situations
The words "training your subconscious mind" do not imply "fooling the subconscious mind" as in answer (B) nor do they imply a "breakthrough," as in answer (D), so those two answers can be eliminated. The author describes a "process," so the word "process" would likely be in the correct answer, eliminating answer (C). There is no mention of hypnosis, as in answer (E), and answer (A) accurately sums up the process of training the person to associate fear-filled situations with relaxation that is described in the words "you will come automatically to associate the fear-filled situations with relaxation."

14. Answer: (B) "how to" instructions in de-sensitization
The paragraph begins with the words "To de-sensitize yourself," implying that this paragraph is going to show the reader how to apply de-sensitization techniques him- or herself. This would imply that answers (B) and (E) with their wording of "how-to instructions" and "do-it-yourself" respectively are accurate answers. However, answer (E) includes the words "therapy for beginners in psychology" whereas answer (B) sticks to the point of the paragraph, as noted in the topic sentence, with the word "de-sensitization." Psychology is a broad field, so answer (E) is too broad to be accurate.

15. Answer: (D) affirmative self-talk
Affirmations are positive assertions used in positive psychology to help a person improve his or her self-talk. A classic affirmation is invoked by the words "I am completely serene and safe." Later lines make affirmative statements that the person is in a relaxed, positive, soothing, and enjoyable setting. These statements are in the form of "self-talk": "*I am on a hot beach.*" Answer (D) affirmative self-talk is the most accurate answer, as the other answers containing the words "affirmation" have to with nature (B) or the ego (C), which have little to do with the paragraph. Although a natural setting is evoked in these lines, the affirmation has more to do with the relaxation the natural setting provides rather than nature itself.

16. Answer: (C) even well-known performers suffer from stagefright and must overcome it through using various techniques
Since the author states that "it is comforting to know that many singing and other stars have confessed to terrible anxiety," it is clear that the author is trying to assure readers that a person can still perform very well even if he or she experiences stagefright. That would eliminate answers (A), (B), and (D), because these "singing and other stars" are successful; one was a "Broadway star." Since these self-designed techniques worked, answer (E) can also be

eliminated because the techniques are clearly valid. The passage says that after using her technique, the star "felt more confident," which shows that her self-designed technique was indeed valid.

17. Answer: (A) human agency and the power of choice
"Human agency" means that human beings are agents of their own destinies; that is, they can enact their own choices, and human beings have free will or "the power of choice." The wording in these lines puts great emphasis on human agency and the power of choice with such phrases as, "You can tell yourself," "You can choose," and "It is your choice" as the beginning of sentences, making answer (A) the correct answer.

18. Answer: (A) doing all the practices listed in lines 62 – 66
Since the assurances in question are part of the paragraph that summarizes and lists the practices recommended throughout the passage, the thoughts expressed in them, "You can do this," and "You can perform without fear" must be taken in the context of the paragraph. The implication is, "If you do these things…you can do this and perform without fear." By process of elimination, we can say that (B), (C), and (D) are not correct because the author does not know the reader's mind and heart, has not asserted that all people are good public speakers, and shows no assumptions about the readers of the passage being college-bound. In fact, the author makes no promises as to whether the reader or any person is a good public speaker; he or she will simply be able to perform without fear if he or she follows the techniques. Answer (E) implies that psychological techniques have been misappropriated, which means they have been inappropriately used or recommended. This is not the case, as the passage clearly credits psychologists with de-sensitization techniques.

19. Answer: (C) Outwit Your Fear of Public Speaking through Proven Methods
Since the passage refers to the psychological technique of de-sensitization and also refers to "Tried and true advice" and how performing stars handle their stagefright, the phrase "through Proven Methods" seems to be appropriate for a title. In answer (A) the title is very broad, covering all of public speaking, whereas the passage specifically addresses stagefright in public speaking or performing, so answer (A) is incorrect. Answer (B) includes "Anger," and there is nothing in the passage about anger; nor is there anything in the passage about "psychoactive drugs," as in answer (D). Like answer (A), answer (E) is very broad, covering the whole of public speaking instead of the specific aspect of stagefright. Answer (C) is appropriate because the passage does give examples of how to "psych out" or "outwit" the mind and emotions so that the person stays calm and overcomes stagefright through methods that work (Proven Methods).

SECTION 8 (MATHEMATICS)

MULTIPLE CHOICE

1. Answer: (B) 20%
First find the amount that the price changed, and then divide by the original price. The price increased by $31.00. Divide $31.00 by $155.00. The result is 0.2, or 20%.

2. Answer: (B) $x \leq \frac{12}{5}$
Distribute and simplify the left hand side to get $2 + 5x - 5 = 5x - 3$. So the inequality becomes $5x - 3 \leq 9$. Adding 3 to both sides, $5x \leq 12$. Dividing both sides by 5, $x \leq \frac{12}{5}$.

3. Answer: (D) 6 or -2
Let x represent the unknown number.

$$4(x+3) = x^2$$
$$4x+12 = x^2$$

Set the equation equal to 0 and factor the resulting expression.

$$x^2 - 4x - 12 = 0$$

Find two numbers with sum -4 and product -12.

-6 + 2 = -4   (-6)(2) = -12

Use the factors -6 and 2 to solve the equation.

(x − 6)(x + 2) = 0

Since (x − 6)(x + 2) = 0, then x − 6 = 0 or x + 2 = 0
x − 6 = 0   x + 2 = 0
x = 6 or x = -2

4. Answer: (E) 160°
The sum of the measures of the angles in a quadrilateral is 360°. Let x represent the common multiple of: 2, 3, 5, and 8 that has a sum of 360°.

2x + 3x + 5x + 8x = 360
18x = 360
x = 20

In the ratio, 2:3:5:8, 8 represents the largest angle in the quadrilateral. Multiply 8 by 20 to find the measure of the largest angle.

8 x 20 = 160°

5. Answer: (B) 30
Graph the vertices of the triangle.

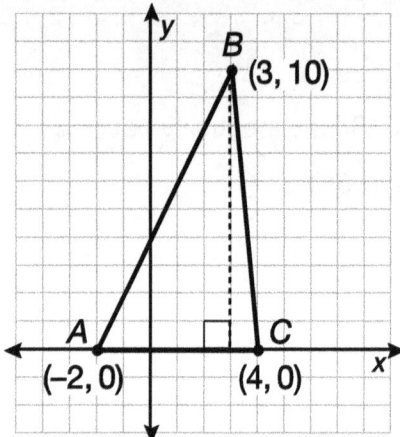

The area of a triangle is found by using the formula Area = $\frac{1}{2}(base)(height)$. By inspection, the length of the base, between (-2,0) and (4,0) is 6 units. The height of a triangle is found by extending a line from a vertex to the opposite side such that the line is perpendicular to the opposite side. Extend a line from $\angle B$; the y-coordinate of B, 10, is the height of the triangle.

Area = $\frac{1}{2}(base)(height)$

Area = $\frac{1}{2}(6)(10) = 30$

6. Answer: (D) $(\frac{x^2}{y^3})^2 < 0$

The square of a number must be positive always. Hence choice D is clearly false.

To check, set x and y equal to manageable numbers that satisfy the inequalities x > 0 and y < 0.

Let x and y equal 2 and -1 respectively. Simplify the quantity $(\frac{x^2}{y^3})^2$ by raising the numerator and the denominator to the second power. When raising one power to another, multiply the exponents.

$$\left(\frac{x^2}{y^3}\right)^2 = \frac{x^{2\times2}}{y^{3\times2}} = \frac{x^4}{y^6}$$

Substitute 2 for x and -1 for y.

$$\frac{2^4}{(-1)^6} = \frac{16}{1} = 16$$

7. Answer: (E) -26

Two lines can intersect at one point, no points, or infinite points. If the two lines have different slopes, they intersect at one point and have one solution. Two lines that have the same slope but different y-intercepts are parallel, do not intersect, and have no solutions. Lines that have the same slope and the same y-intercept are the same line and therefore intersect at every point and have an infinite number of solutions.

If the system of equations has an infinite number of solutions, the lines must be equivalent equations.

$$2x - 4y = 13$$
$$-4x + 8y = m$$

We see that each term in the second equation results from multiplying the top equation by -2. Therefore, m = -26.

$$-2(2x - 4y = 13) = -4x + 8y = -26$$

8. Answer: (C) $2.00

Let the cost of pretzels be x dollars a pound. Then the cost of 4.5 lbs of the mixture made with 2 lbs of peanuts, 1 lb of raisins, and 1.5 pounds of pretzels can be written as:

2(1.50) + 1(2.10) + 1.5(x) = 4.5(1.80)
3.0 + 2.1 + 1.5x = 8.1
5.1 + 1.5x = 8.1
1.5x = 8.1 − 5.1 = 3
x = $\frac{3}{1.5}$ = 2

The cost of pretzels is $2 a pound.

9. Answer: (A) $\dfrac{3\sqrt{7}}{4\pi}$

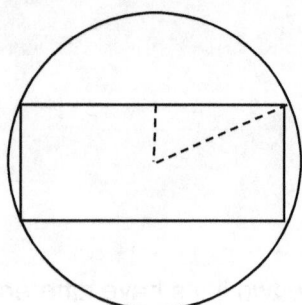

To find the probability of the dart landing in the rectangle, first find the area of the rectangle in terms of the circle's radius.

Let the radius of the circle be r.

The length of the rectangle = 1.5r or $\dfrac{3}{2}$r.

Half the length of the rectangle = 0.75r or $\dfrac{3}{4}$r.

Notice in the figure that half the length of the rectangle, half the width of the rectangle, and the radius of the circle form a right triangle.

Hence, the width of the rectangle =

$$2\left(\sqrt{r^2-\left(\dfrac{3}{4}r\right)^2}\right)=2\left(\sqrt{r^2-\dfrac{9r^2}{16}}\right)=2\left(\sqrt{\dfrac{16r^2-9r^2}{16}}\right)=2\left(\sqrt{\dfrac{7r^2}{16}}\right)=2\left(\dfrac{\sqrt{7}r}{4}\right)=\dfrac{\sqrt{7}r}{2}.$$

The area of the rectangle = $\dfrac{3r}{2}\times\dfrac{\sqrt{7}r}{2}=\dfrac{3\sqrt{7}r^2}{4}$.

The probability that the dart will land in the rectangle is equal to the ratio of the area of the rectangle to the area of the circle = $\dfrac{3\sqrt{7}r^2}{4}\div\pi r^2=\dfrac{3\sqrt{7}}{4\pi}$.

10. Answer: (E) $\sqrt{\dfrac{3}{2}}s$

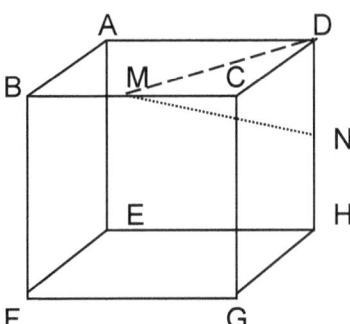

To find the length of MN, first find the length of MD.

Note that MCD is a right triangle. So $MD^2 = MC^2 + CD^2 = \left(\dfrac{s}{2}\right)^2 + s^2 = \dfrac{s^2}{4} + s^2 = \dfrac{5s^2}{4}$

Note that MDN is also a right triangle. So $MN^2 = MD^2 + DN^2 = \dfrac{5s^2}{4} + \dfrac{s^2}{4} = \dfrac{6s^2}{4} = \dfrac{3s^2}{2}$.

Hence MN = $\sqrt{\dfrac{3}{2}}s$.

11. Answer: (E) 20
Solve each absolute value equation:

$|r - 3| = 12$

Therefore:
r – 3 = 12 or r – 3 = -12
r = 15 or r = -9

$|w + 7| = 22$

Therefore:
w + 7 = 22 or w + 7 = -22
w = 15 or w = -29

Since r and w are both less than 0, select -9 and -29 for r and w respectively.

r – w = -9 – (-29) = 20

12. Answer: (D) 2500
Since the model is built at the scale 1:50, the radius of the base of model is 50 times smaller than the radius of the base of the building. If the radius of the base of the model is r, the radius of the base of the building is 50r.

The area of the base of the model = πr^2

The area of the base of the building = $\pi(50r)^2 = 2500\pi r^2$

So the area of the base of the building is 2500 times the area of the base of the model.

13. Answer: (D) 20°
The angle moved by the hands of a clock between consecutive numbers on a clock face (between 12 and 1, 1 and 2, etc.) is 30°. At 3:20 p.m., the minute hand is on 4 and the hour hand is one-third ($\frac{20}{60}$) of the way between 3 and 4, i.e., the hour hand has moved 10° from 3 towards 4. So the angle between the two hands of the clock = 30° − 10° = 20°.

Another value for the angle between the hands of the clock at 3:20 p.m., if we consider the reflexive angle, = 360° − 20° = 340°.

14. Answer: (C) $\frac{1}{12}$

Each die can have 6 possible numbers on it. So the total number of possible combinations of numbers on the two dice = 6 x 6 = 36.

The only possible sums greater than 10 are 11 and 12.

11 can be obtained in 2 ways: 5 on die 1 and 6 on die 2; or 6 on die 1 and 5 on die 2.
12 can be obtained in 1 way: 6 on both dice.

Therefore, there are 3 possible combinations out of the 36 that will produce sums greater than 10. Hence the probability of getting a sum greater than 10 = $\frac{3}{36} = \frac{1}{12}$.

15. Answer: (A) 566 ft

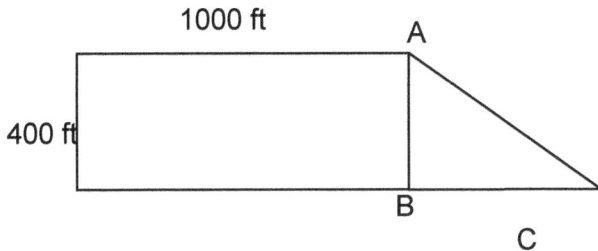

Area of the building site = 400 ft x 1000 ft = 400,000 sq. ft

Minimum area of the park = $\dfrac{400,000}{5}$ = 80,000 sq. ft

Area of the park = $\dfrac{1}{2}$ AB x BC = 80,000.

Since AB = 400 ft,

$\dfrac{1}{2}$ 400BC = 80,000

BC = $\dfrac{80,000}{200}$ = 400 ft

Hence minimum length of the hypotenuse AC = $\sqrt{400^2 + 400^2}$ = $400\sqrt{2}$ = 566 ft.

16. Answer: (C)

Note that the function $f(x) = x^2 2^x$ has the value 0 at x = 0 and that it increases as x increases for all x > 0. Function f(x+2) will have a value of 0 at x + 2 = 0; i.e., at x = -2. Also, function f(x+2) will increase with increasing x for all x > -2. Only choice C satisfies both of these conditions.

The SAT Advantage

SECTION 9 (WRITING)

IMPROVING SENTENCES

1. Answer: (D) or to be considered for
First, you should notice that choices (A) and (B) incorrectly use the conjunction *nor* without its partner, *neither*. So you can eliminate them immediately. Then you need to focus on the two things that Mark declined. In the first part of the sentence, he declined *to be honored*. The verb that follows the conjunction *or* should be in the same tense and grammatical form as *to be honored*. Only choice (D) does that with the verb form *to be considered*.

2. Answer: (E) than we do because she has a membership
There are actually two issues to be decided here: *than us* versus *than we do* and the best way to express why Lily goes to the recreation center so often. If you know that *than we do* is correct, you can immediately eliminate choices (B) and (D). In choice (A), *because of having* is ambiguous and is not correct idiomatic usage. Choice (C) is wordy and creates a run-on by joining two independent clauses with a comma. Choice (E) expresses the situation in a way that is grammatically correct and clarifies who has a membership by using the pronoun *she* to refer to the subject, *Lily*.

3. Answer: (B) the cost of concert tickets is prohibitively expensive for many people
If you ask yourself why more people don't go to concerts, you can use your common sense to identify the correct answer here: because *the cost of concert tickets is prohibitively expensive*. Many questions in this section of the SAT try to trick you by presenting "fancy," complicated ways of stating a simple idea. In most cases, the longer and more complicated the answer choice, the less likely it is to be correct.

4. Answer: (C) the residents filed a protest to persuade state officials to relocate the route
Okay, here is that SAT favorite again, a sentence that begins with a long, introductory phrase or clause. The rule is the same as with previous questions like this: The next word after the long phrase or clause should be the person or thing the phrase describes. Who was doing the fearing in this situation? *the residents*. Only choices (C) and (D) begin with those words, so one of them must be the correct answer. Choice (C) is simpler, and Choice (D) changes the meaning of the sentence, suggesting that the residents had already persuaded the state officials to do what the residents wanted.

5. Answer: (D) Some employees who are otherwise scrupulously honest manage to justify stealing office supplies from their employers.
Here is another run-on, two independent clauses joined only by a comma. Choice (B) redundantly uses two conjunctions with similar meanings: *although* and *however*. Choice (C) incorrectly uses the pronoun *which* to refer to people and expresses a slightly different meaning than the original. Choice (E) illogically connects two contrasting ideas with the conjunction *and*. Only choice (D) keeps the original meaning of the sentence and expresses it in a grammatically correct way, by turning one of the main clauses into a descriptive subordinate clause

6. Answer: (A) controls the shared signals of different neurons and coordinates
Here's another question that tests your understanding of parallelism: using the same kind of grammatical structure for words linked by the conjunction *and*. The original sentence correctly joins two singular present-tense verbs: *controls* and *coordinates*. Choice (B) uses similar verb

forms but turns the sentence into a fragment, because the -ing forms used here cannot be the main verbs in the sentence. The verbs in choices (C) and (E) are not parallel. Choice (D) turns the sentence into a fragment by using the word *that* before the parallel verbs.

7. Answer: (B) photos; another craft that many Americans enjoy

Here is yet another run-on, two main clauses joined only by a comma. Changing the comma to a semicolon fixes the problem. Choice (C) leaves the comma problem. Choice (D) fixes that problem, but introduces an awkward passive-voice verb instead of matching the active present tense verb in the first clause. Choice (E) compounds the problem by using a passive-voice verb and not inserting any punctuation at all between the two clauses.

8. Answer: (E) was provided by

This sentence is a fragment that needs the verb *was* to be a complete sentence. The sentence already has a subject, *equipment*, so there is no need to add another subject, as choice (B) and (C) do. The word *equipment* is singular, so the plural verb *were* in choice (D) is incorrect. You need to remember that the plural nouns in a prepositional phrase that follow the subject are not part of the subject.

9. Answer: (D) could find producers and actors who were as dedicated and adventurous as she was

The first clause in the sentence uses the past-tense verb phrase *could not make*. Since there is no shift in time between the first clause and the second, the second clause should also consistently use the past tense. Only choice (D) does so, with the verbs *could*, *were*, and *was*.

10. Answer: (A) almost as gifted a student as he is an athlete

This kind of sentence is hard for most people because it is not the kind of structure we would normally use in conversation. However, the original sentence correctly uses the parallel comparing phrases *is as gifted a…as he is an*. The most helpful way to prepare for a question like this one is to memorize this sentence, or one like it, so that you can use it as a model for finding the correct answer.

11. Answer: (C) our teacher advised us not to get discouraged too quickly

Here's another sentence with a long introductory phrase. What do you do first? Ask yourself who is doing the explaining. Then find the answer choice that begins with that noun. Only choice (C) begins with the noun *our teacher*, the person who is doing the explaining.

12. Answer: (D) a staff of five childcare workers for each age level supervise the children's activities at all times

The structure *it is…who* adds an unnecessary and wordy complication to this sentence. Choice (D) expresses the same idea more simply, without the awkward construction. Choice (B) creates a fragment because it lacks a main verb. Choice (C) removes the original wordy construction but replaces it with another: *are the ones*. Choice (E) begins well, but combines the modifying prepositional phrase *for each age level* and *at all times* in an awkward, illogical way.

13. Answer: (D) At the end of the movie,

This is a classic example of the kind of "fancy" sentence students tend to write in their own papers when they want to sound intelligent and sophisticated. Look at it carefully, though. As written, the sentence begins with a long phrase that should be followed by the noun it describes. Are the heroes studying carefully the end of the movie? No. Since you need to keep the heroes as the subject of the sentence, the only answer that makes sense here is (D) because it doesn't include a verb form that would have to describe the heroes. This is a perfect example of when simplest is best.

14. Answer: (E) The American Diabetes Association advises you that as a diabetic patient you

Here is one last sentence with an introductory phrase. Who is the diabetic patient in this sentence? *the American Diabetes Association*? No, *you* are *the diabetic patient*. The correct answer must place *you* directly before or after *the diabetic patient*. Choice (C) does this, but adds an unnecessary passive-tense verb. Choice (D) turns the sentence into a fragment by adding *who* before the verb *advise*. Only choice (E) simply states the subject and the verb and then places *you* directly before the descriptive phrase *as a diabetic patient*.

PRACTICE TEST 3

The SAT Advantage

SECTION 1
(WRITING)
Time: 25 minutes
ESSAY

Directions: Write an essay based on the prompts given.

The essay section gives you an opportunity to demonstrate your effectiveness at written communication. A well-written essay will express a clear point of view, present ideas in a logical manner, and use language precisely.

Your essay must be written in your <u>Answer Grid Booklet</u>. Do not write your essay in your test book. Keep your handwriting legible so that readers who are unfamiliar with your handwriting will be able to read it.

DO NOT WRITE ON ANOTHER TOPIC. AN ESSAY ON AN UNRELATED TOPIC WILL RECEIVE A SCORE OF ZERO.

Consider carefully the matter presented in the following paragraph and the assignment below.

Topic: Economist Milton Friedman said that a corporation's only social responsibility was to increase its profits for its stockholders. People who agree with this point of view say that capitalism has lifted millions of people out of poverty and improved their lives by giving them more money to spend. People who disagree think that corporations must take into account their impact on the communities in which they operate, including the environment.

Assignment: Do corporations have responsibilities to society other than to make money? Develop and write an essay expounding on your viewpoint on this matter. You may use reasoning and your general knowledge based on your own experiences, observation of society, general reading or specific studies.

Excellent Quality Sample Essay (Score: 6 out of 6)

It is true that corporations make money in a society, and prosperity helps many people; yet corporations have responsibilities to the public too. The public responsibilities are as important as the profit motive, but both are important.

A corporation exists to make money. The profits corporations make benefit society in some ways. Corporations pay taxes and people's salaries, and then the government and those people spend money, which stimulates the economy. If a corporation can't make profits, then it has to let employees go who are people in the community, and that will have a negative impact on that community. Unemployed people need government assistance; they cannot spend money in the stores. Sometimes they get depressed or discouraged, and their families fall apart.

On the other hand, there are things like environmental and safety issues. A corporation may make huge profits while polluting the air or a nearby river. What if people get sick or even die because of the pollution? Corporations have a responsibility to make their profits without taking away from the quality of life of everyone and even future generations, as chemicals don't always go away after a few years. That includes keeping their own workers safe. If a corporation engages in unsafe work practices to save money and make more profits, such as failing to provide hard hats or hard shoes to workers, someone may be badly injured and they may even die. A life is worth more than a corporation's profits.

If it can't make money because of too many laws and restrictions, then the business has to decide if it should go out of business. Hiding from the law won't help, because eventually, the corporation will probably get caught. Then there will be penalties and damage control. Should such a corporation pollute a river or ignore safety standards just to make enough profits to employ people? No, that is not a good solution.

Hopefully, a corporation can be responsible to the community and also make enough profits to continue to employ people in the community. This is the best case scenario.

Medium Quality Sample Essay (Score: 3 – 4 out of 6)

Corporations have more responsibilities to society than just to make profits. They are making a lot of money off the public, and they owe the public. If it weren't for the public, the corporation wouldn't make any money. Corporations should be good to the public.

People like to know that a corporation does good things. It makes people feel good to shop at stores or go to companies that tell them about how they help the community or how they clean up the environment. When people say, "This is a good place to work," customers feel good spending their money there. If you hear about a corporation doing something bad, you don't want to spend your money there.

I always read customer feedback on the Internet. I won't buy from a company that doesn't have lots of good reviews and plenty of five star ratings, or I won't buy that product. I want to buy from companies that other people like and say are good.

Corporations have a responsibility to the environment. They should be taking care of things. If a corporation makes a mess, they should clean it up. If they use too much energy, they should learn how not to. If they are too big a building, they should build a smaller building and not use up so much land.

Corporations are not just there to exploit people and land. They should take care of things too or they will not be welcomed in a community or by the public.

Low Quality Sample Essay (Score: 1 – 2 out of 6)

Corporations need people to make money. They need people to like them and use their products. If corporations are hurting people, sooner or later, it will come out. They will go out of business.

Look at all the fancy buildings they have. If those were built by workers who were not paid, where are they now?

Sometimes they make huge profits. Only a few at the top get all the money, though. That isn't fair. When we hear about things like that, people feel cheated. The CEO of a company should make more than the employees because he or she has more responsibility. But not that much more. They have to be fair.

Pollution is serious business. No one wants pollution in their water or their air.

Most people want to be rich. Corporations can make people rich. Many of us will work for corporations. That is not a bad thing. I would like to make a lot of money out there in the world. I will probably have to work for a corporation, and I would not like that corporation to be bad.

SECTION 2
(CRITICAL READING)
Time: 25 minutes
24 questions

SENTENCE COMPLETION

Directions: For each of the following questions, choose the best answer and fill in the corresponding oval on the answer sheet to indicate your selection.

Each sentence contains one or two blanks indicating that something has been omitted from the sentence. Choose the word or set of words, labeled A through E, that when inserted into the sentence, best fits the meaning of the sentence as a whole.

1. Christopher was shocked when he heard that Sharon was engaged to Phil; Christopher had always assumed Sharon knew how much he loved her and that they had a(n) -------- agreement to marry after college.

   (A) expressed
   (B) illicit
   (C) revised
   (D) tacit
   (E) outspoken

2. The chief executive office of the corporation frowned over the accounts receivables notations in the bookkeeper's Excel files; there were simply too many -------- between the numbers and their sums to be accurate.

   (A) similarities
   (B) descriptions
   (C) relevancies
   (D) discrepancies
   (E) formulas

3. "I am tired of your evasiveness," the lawyer scolded his client, "for how can I defend you if I have to guess the -------- meaning of all your utterances?"

   (A) complicit
   (B) explicit
   (C) deficit
   (D) implicit
   (E) specificity

4. Writer Albert Payson Terhune, his wife, and their many dogs enjoyed their -------- home, Sunnybank, on the isolated shores of a lake, but they all suffered when his fans -------- on their privacy.

   (A) urban ... invaded
   (B) secluded ... encroached
   (C) suburban ... practiced
   (D) excluded ... pillaged
   (E) private ... pirated

5. The banquet was so -------- the guests all ate until they were -------- and then complained that they could not possibly eat the dessert.

   (A) sumptuous ... surfeited
   (B) scanty ... satisfied
   (C) marvelous ... hungry
   (D) skimpy ... satiated
   (E) mediocre ... modified

6. Because she had been -------- in the agreement to exclude Beth from their plans, a repentant Marcia tried hard to be -------- when Beth angrily complained about not being invited.

   (A) arbitrary ... argumentative
   (B) vacillating ... defensive
   (C) complicit ... conciliatory
   (D) justified ... courteous
   (E) neutral ... infuriated

7. The powerful former Soviet Union was not -------- by invading enemies; rather, its economic and political systems -------- from forces within.

   (A) conquered ... cohered
   (B) pacified ... gelled
   (C) befriended ... benighted
   (D) soothed ... collapsed
   (E) vanquished ... imploded

8. The -------- of love and death makes for an interesting statement that love equals loss in the movie *The English Patient*, for every time someone loves another person, the beloved one meets his or her doom.

   (A) juxtaposition
   (B) contrast
   (C) dissimilarities
   (D) adjacent
   (E) verticality

The SAT Advantage

READING BASED QUESTIONS

Directions: For each of the following questions, choose the best answer and fill in the corresponding oval on the answer sheet to indicate your selection.

The reading passages below are followed by questions based on their content. Questions that follow a pair of related passages may be based on both the content of the passages and/or the relationship between the passages. Answer the questions based on what is stated or implied in the passages.

Questions 9 – 14 are based on the following passage:

Our cultural perceptions of lawyers are sometimes negative, as if the profession is inherently immoral. We think all lawyers are rich and that they are "money-grubbing" tricksters. Shakespeare said in one of his plays that society should "kill all the lawyers." In the movie *Hook* starring Robin Williams, the protagonist (who is a corrupt lawyer) jokes that
5 scientists are considering substituting lawyers for rats in laboratory experiments because there are some things even rats won't do.

Charles Dickens paints an interesting portrait of two hard-nosed lawyers in *Great Expectations*. Toward the end of the book, we learn that these money-chasing, heartless lawyers both have private lives of some warmth and charity that they hide even from one
10 another. This is probably the most accurate cultural representation of lawyers and may hold a key to longevity in the legal profession.

Surveys by the American Bar Association consistently find that lawyers' main dissatisfaction is a lack of a sense that they are contributing to the social good. Most lawyers joined the legal profession because they cared about justice and the public weal. That
15 means they were idealistic and wanted to help people. When their work precludes that because of a soulless pursuit of profit, they feel less job satisfaction. ABA surveys of lawyers also show that most lawyers enjoy their *pro bono* work most of all. Some say volunteering to help those who cannot afford legal counsel is the best part of their week or day. They feel that they have touched lives and have used their abilities to help others who could not afford
20 their help otherwise.

Perhaps lawyers must present a hard, impersonal, money-pursuing front to the world because of our adversarial justice system. Yet those who contribute privately to charity and who cultivate warm, loving, human relationships may be the ones who are able to last the longest at their profession, for their rewards are more than monetary.

9. **The word "protagonist" is used in line 4 to mean:**

   (A) the main character of a story

   (B) the hero of a story

   (C) the person who experiences agony in a story

   (D) the person the audience is "pro" in the story

   (E) a professional lawyer

10. **Lines 1 – 11 all present cultural perceptions of lawyers, but lines 1 – 6 imply that cultural perceptions show that the word "lawyer" is:**

    (A) a pejorative term

    (B) a cultural construction

    (C) inaccurate; it should be "attorney" or "counsel"

    (D) a flattering term

    (E) a term of derision

11. **The description of Charles Dickens's depiction of two lawyers in lines 7 – 11 has as its purpose to provide an example of:**

    (A) yet another negative cultural perception of lawyers

    (B) an ambivalent cultural portrait of lawyers

    (C) historical records about lawyers

    (D) Dickens mixing fiction with non-fiction

    (E) truth being stranger than fiction

12. **Within the context of lines 12 – 20, the terms "weal" and "pro bono" most likely mean:**

    (A) welt and professionally good, respectively

    (B) welfare and probationary, respectively

    (C) woe and probability, respectively

    (D) well-being and charitable, respectively

    (E) wealth and in favor of goodness, respectively

13. **Lines 12 – 20 may be said to be:**

    (A) supporting points about lawyer's motivations by citing surveys done by the American Bar Association

    (B) drawing erroneous conclusions based upon unscientific data

    (C) purporting to represent most lawyers when in fact only a few were surveyed

    (D) drawing conclusions about the motivations of all lawyers based upon surveys done by an outside agency

    (E) making the case that lawyers do a great deal of their work for free in order to increase job satisfaction

14. **How do lines 21 – 24 relate to lines 7 – 11?**

    (A) Both sets of lines discuss the physical longevity of lawyers who lead healthy lives

    (B) Both sets of lines refer to cultural representations of lawyers

    (C) Both sets of lines imply that Charles Dickens's fictional portrait of two lawyers was inaccurate

    (D) Both sets of lines refer to Charles Dickens

    (E) Both sets of lines discuss the professional longevity of lawyers who contribute to charity and have warm relationships in their private lives

Questions 15 – 24 are based on the following two passages:

Passage 1

Creativity is considered to be of paramount importance in the business world. Business leaders say we have entered the "imagination economy." Creativity, they say, is what will give the razor's edge advantage to businesses in the present global marketplace of frequent and dizzyingly rapid change. It is good to see the faculty of creativity being embraced.

5   The terms creativity and innovation are used synonymously in the business world, but it seems "innovation" is the preferred term. Many businesses' mission statements now contain language about "innovation" but they are really talking about creativity. Both long-time corporations and budding entrepreneurs are on the hunt for creative ideas to jumpstart their companies' profits. Creativity and innovation are synonymous.

10   We should find the Thomas Edisons of our age and allow their creativity free rein. If we can find the inventive Edisons among the throng, we should pay them millions and millions of dollars just to sit and think. By the age of eighty, Edison owned over a thousand patents for creative ideas, many of which were never put to practical use. Let modern geniuses spill out their ideas into a sympathetic and eager environment. Surely out of thousands of new
15 ideas, as with Edison's, some will be useful.

When Edison died, millions of grateful people all over the world dimmed their lights to salute the man who had "lighted up the world." Let us find the lights of modern geniuses. With their brilliant creativity, they too can "light up the world" and generate innovation.

Perhaps modern business leaders should look to the creative arts to find people who
20 can think in original and revolutionary ways. Perhaps we should look to the painters, the sculptors, the musicians and composers, the writers, the poets, the designers, and the dancers. Businesses should hire these creative people, pay them well, and give them total freedom to explore their ideas. Build them special office spaces full of color and comfort where they can just explore their creativity. If innovation is the spark of the new economy,
25 let's by all means corral some creative talent and let their fountains flow.

Passage 2

The leaders in today's business industries absolutely love the word "innovation." Innovation is thought to be the main driving force of today's "imagination economy". To get ahead or stay ahead, companies know they need innovation.

Although the words "innovation" and "creativity" are used interchangeably, they are
30 demonstrably different. Creativity is but the beginning of a process: it is the catalyst that suddenly reveals something new or unveils new relationships between what already exists, resulting in a startling new synthesis. Innovation is the process of bringing creative ideas down to earth and into marketable commodities.

We call creative geniuses like Thomas Edison "inventors" (the similarity between this
35 word and "innovation" is clear). We do that because their creativity resulted in real creations (inventions) that could be put to practical use. Edison, for example, invented the phonograph. He recorded sound for the first time in human history. He invented the movies,

the storage battery, and numerous office machines. Not only did Edison's inventions generate whole new industries (pumping billions of dollars into the economy) he made our
40 daily lives more enjoyable and safer. No wonder people were grateful to him when he died—his creative genius touched our lives in truly hands-on ways.

The interesting thing about Edison is that he was not just a creative thinker. His genius was channeled into inventing practical things. Edison actually invented a high speed vote counting machine when he was young, but no one wanted it. The old-time politicians wanted
45 the time it took to count votes to continue to lobby voters to see things their way! Edison, whose family had struggled for years with poverty, vowed at that point never to create or invent something that had no market value.

The creative genius of Steve Jobs is also interesting in that it was not creativity for creativity's sake. Jobs did not even create the computer, though some would credit him with
50 that. He did figure out how to take the massive computers of the time (floor-to-ceiling computers took up a whole room in a business and had spaceship-like flashing lights) and make them fit on the top of a desk. He also figured out how to make them affordable. In so doing, and in making computers user-friendly, the personal computer revolution was spawned. People's lives were revolutionized, as was the world of business. With the
55 invention of the Apple MacIntosh, the iPhone, the iPod, and the iPad, Steve Jobs gave gifts to the entire world. Because he touched our daily lives with the practical results of his creative genius, when Jobs died, many people felt a sense of personal loss as well as a sense of gratitude.

Creativity is the mental inception; innovation is the physical substance. Innovation
60 always has a practical, usable, even user-friendly side to it. That's why we feel personally grateful to inventors like Edison and Jobs. Their creativity was lashed to the tiller of making useful and marketable products we can touch and use. Had that not been the case, they'd be forgotten as just two tinkerers in garages.

15. The authors of Passage 1 and Passage 2 can be shown to agree upon the following point:

   (A) Thomas Edison and Steven Jobs were creative geniuses

   (B) today's business leaders see the global marketplace as an "imagination economy"

   (C) the terms creativity and innovation are synonymous

   (D) artists, dancers, and writers should be hired by businesses

   (E) creative genius is important for its own sake

16. The authors of Passage 1 and Passage 2 would most likely disagree that:

   (A) creative genius can be cultivated through education

   (B) Thomas Edison and Steven Jobs were both creative geniuses

   (C) creativity and innovation are synonymous

   (D) creativity and innovation are related to one another

   (E) creativity and innovation are necessary into today's global economy

17. **In lines 10 – 15, the author seems to be suggesting that:**

    (A) Edison's practical ideas were only a percentage of his creative ideas

    (B) it took Edison decades of his life before any of his ideas were practical

    (C) because of his thousands of patents, Edison was considered by many to be a "crank" inventor

    (D) genius is merely a matter of percentages

    (E) genius cannot be compensated by money

18. **In line 25, the author uses alliteration for what likely purpose?**

    (A) to exhort and excite

    (B) to mix metaphors

    (C) to demonstrate creative thinking

    (D) to show the importance of creative writing

    (E) to urge the point of view of the author of Passage 2

19. **The author of Passage 2 might take issue with the author of Passage 1 about lines 19 – 25 on the following basis:**

    (A) not all artists, musicians, poets, etcetera are truly creative or innovative

    (B) creativity is not the same thing as innovation; innovation is always channeled to practical inventions that can become market commodities

    (C) business creativity is not the same as artistic creativity, and artistic creativity will not yield market commodities

    (D) artists, musicians, poets, etcetera are innovators, not creators

    (E) the "imagination economy" calls for people of imagination, not talent

20. **In line 20 the phrase "revolutionary ways" most likely means:**

    (A) politically correct ways

    (B) politically radical ways

    (C) innovative ways

    (D) mundane ways

    (E) thinking "inside the box" ways

21. The author of Passage 2 would say that people feel grateful toward inventors like Edison and Jobs because:

    (A) the inventions of these men touched and improved people's daily lives

    (B) electricity has sped up communications

    (C) their inventions improved the economies of nations

    (D) their inventions spurred on the "imagination economy"

    (E) they introduced the world to a global economy

22. According to lines 48 – 58, the author thinks Steve Jobs:

    (A) was not creative but could work with inventions already created

    (B) worked with already existing inventions and created new things of his own

    (C) was not really an innovator but did have a creative mind

    (D) down-sized the computer and "put the world in our pockets"

    (E) was too wrapped up in the ivory tower of Apple thinking

23. What kind of creative people are mentioned in Passage 1 but not in Passage 2?

    (A) Inventors like Thomas Edison

    (B) business leaders who see the global marketplace as "an imagination economy"

    (C) creative artists such as painters, musicians, sculptors, writers, poets, etcetera

    (D) consumers who prefer innovative products

    (E) tinkerers

24. In line 63 the phrase "tinkerers in garages" most likely means:

    (A) people who toy around with inventions that never make it out into the real world

    (B) people who do their thinking and tinkering in humble beginnings but go on to be famous

    (C) people whose inventions have vast practical applications

    (D) people who spend most of their time studying the internal combustion engine

    (E) people who do most of their creative thinking on paper

SECTION 3
(MATHEMATICS)
Time: 25 minutes
20 questions

MULTIPLE CHOICE

Directions: For the questions in this section, solve each problem and decide which of the given answer choices is the best choice. Fill in the corresponding oval on the answer sheet to indicate your selection. You may use any available space for scratchwork.

Note:

1. Calculator use is permitted.
2. All numbers used are real numbers.
3. All figures provided are drawn to scale and lie in a plane unless otherwise indicated.
4. Unless otherwise specified, the domain of any function f is assumed to be the set of all real numbers x for which $f(x)$ is a real number.

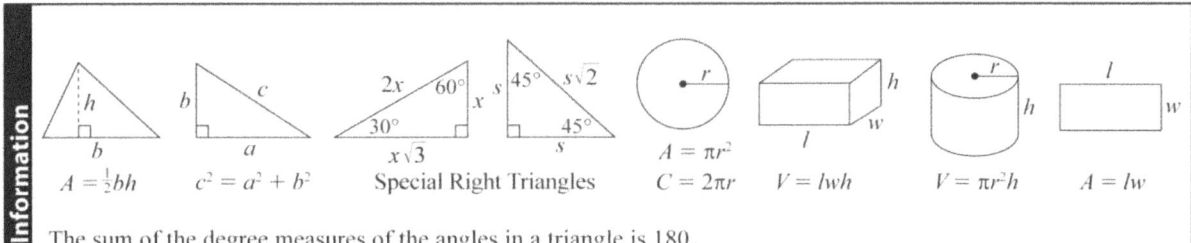

The sum of the degree measures of the angles in a triangle is 180.
The number of degrees of arc in a circle is 360.
A straight angle has a degree measure of 180.

1. Matt needs $\frac{3}{4}$ m long pieces of wood for a project. He cuts the pieces out of a 9 m long plank. How many $\frac{3}{4}$ m pieces of wood can he get out of the plank?

   (A) 3
   (B) 4
   (C) 7
   (D) 12
   (E) 15

2. In 2007 the number of students enrolled at Warren Middle School was 450. In 2008 the number increased by 8%. What was the enrollment in 2008?

   (A) 36
   (B) 414
   (C) 442
   (D) 458
   (E) 486

3. If a, b, and c are positive integers such that ab = 12 and bc = 48 and c = 16, what is the value of a?

(A) 4
(B) 6
(C) 12
(D) 16
(E) 24

4. What type of triangle is pictured below?

Note: Figure not drawn to scale.

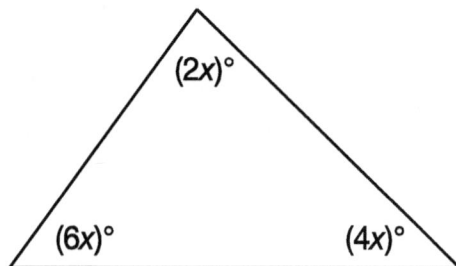

(A) Obtuse scalene
(B) Equilateral
(C) Acute isosceles
(D) 45-45-90
(E) 30-60-90

Questions 5 and 6 are based on the following table which shows sunrise and sunset times for a certain location for the first 10 days of May.

Date	Sunrise	Sunset
May 1	6:27 AM	8:32 PM
May 2	6:25 AM	8:33 PM
May 3	6:24 AM	8:35 PM
May 4	6:23 AM	8:36 PM
May 5	6:22 AM	8:37 PM
May 6	6:20 AM	8:38 PM
May 7	6:19 AM	8:39 PM
May 8	6:18 AM	8:40 PM
May 9	6:17 AM	8:41 PM
May 10	6:16 AM	8:42 PM

5. The length of the days from May 1st to May 10th

(A) doesn't change
(B) increases approximately linearly
(C) increases exponentially
(D) decreases approximately linearly
(E) decreases exponentially

6. The length of the day from May 1st to May 10th changes by about

(A) 0.01%
(B) 0.025%
(C) 0.05%
(D) 0.25%
(E) 2.5%

7. Jamie needs to earn an 80% average to receive a 'B' grade for a certain class. If all three of her tests are equally weighted and she scored 75% and 65% respectively on the first two tests, what must Jamie score on her final test to earn an 80% for the class?

   (A) 85
   (B) 90
   (C) 95
   (D) 100
   (E) 110

8. Which value for *s* makes the following expression a trinomial square?

   $x^2 + 7x + s$

   (A) $\dfrac{49}{2}$
   (B) 21
   (C) 14
   (D) $\dfrac{49}{4}$
   (E) 7

9. Which of the following must be added to $4x^2 + 2x - 7$ to get a sum of $2x^2 - 5x + 3$?

   (A) $2x^2 + 7x - 10$
   (B) $-2x^2 - 7x + 10$
   (C) $6x^4 + 3x^2 + 10$
   (D) $6x^2 + 3x + 10$
   (E) $8x^4 - 10x + 21$

10. In the figure below, line l is parallel to line m. If $m\angle 2 = (4x - 20)°$ and $m\angle 7 = (2x + 40)°$, what is the measure of $\angle 4$?

    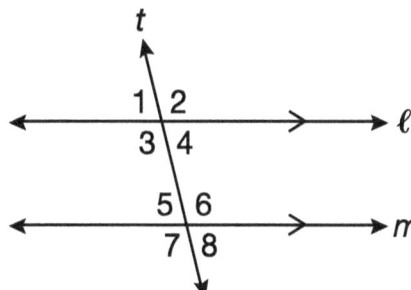

    (A) 15°
    (B) 25°
    (C) 30°
    (D) 60°
    (E) 80°

11. Which of the following is true for the given data set?

    3, 1, 1, 4, 7, 17, 5, 14, 36, 23, 2, 0, 1, 5, 1, 7, 5, 2

    I. There is more than one mode
    II. The median is greater than the mode
    III. The median and mean are equal

    (A) I only
    (B) II only
    (C) III only
    (D) I and II
    (E) I, II and III

12. Ethan's sister is twice as old as he is. Four years from now, Ethan will be five-eighth his sister's age. How old is Ethan's sister?

    (A) 4
    (B) 6
    (C) 10
    (D) 12
    (E) 14

13. If angle a = 65° and angle b = 140°, what is the value of angle c?

    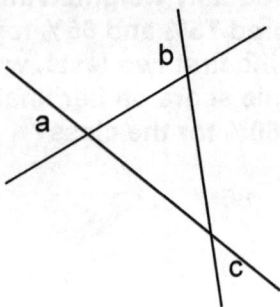

    (A) 45°
    (B) 50°
    (C) 65°
    (D) 75°
    (E) 140°

14. For all values of n greater than 4, which of the following is equivalent to the equation below?

    $$\sqrt{n+6} = n-4$$

    (A) $n = n^2 - 8n + 10$
    (B) $n = n^2 - 2$
    (C) $n = n^2 - 8n + 16$
    (D) $n = -n^2 - 8n + 10$
    (E) $n = n^2 - 8n - 2$

15. Two people run around a circular track at different speeds: 3 mph and 5 mph. If the circumference of the track is 1 mile and the two people start out at the same time, after how many minutes will they meet again at the starting point?

    (A) 12
    (B) 15
    (C) 20
    (D) 36
    (E) 60

16. $f(x) = -3x^2$. The number of points at which $f(x+3)$ touches the x-axis is

    (A) 0
    (B) 1
    (C) 2
    (D) 3
    (E) 4

17. The line 2ax + by = 3 forms an isosceles triangle with the x and y axes. What is $\dfrac{a}{b}$?

    (A) 6
    (B) 3
    (C) 2
    (D) $\dfrac{1}{2}$
    (E) $\dfrac{1}{3}$

18. For ease of stacking, a warehouse replaces cylindrical containers with cubic ones. If the volume and height of the new containers are the same as those for the old ones, what is the ratio of the side of a cubic container to the radius of a cylindrical one?

    (A) $\dfrac{\pi}{2}$
    (B) $\sqrt{\pi}$
    (C) π
    (D) $\sqrt{\dfrac{1}{\pi}}$
    (E) $\dfrac{\pi}{\sqrt{2}}$

19. If the first 10 powers of 2 are added up, what is the units digit?

   (A) 0
   (B) 2
   (C) 4
   (D) 6
   (E) 8

20. In a school, one-third of the students are girls. All students are allowed a choice of blue uniforms or red uniforms. On a particular day, one-fourth of the students wear blue uniforms. If a student is picked at random, what is the probability that the student is a girl wearing a blue uniform?

   (A) $\dfrac{3}{4}$
   (B) $\dfrac{7}{12}$
   (C) $\dfrac{1}{3}$
   (D) $\dfrac{1}{4}$
   (E) $\dfrac{1}{12}$

SECTION 4
(CRITICAL READING)
Time: 25 minutes
24 questions

SENTENCE COMPLETION

Directions: For each of the following questions, choose the best answer and fill in the corresponding oval on the answer sheet to indicate your selection.

Each sentence contains one or two blanks indicating that something has been omitted from the sentence. Choose the word or set of words, labeled A through E, that when inserted into the sentence, best fits the meaning of the sentence as a whole.

1. Although the political candidate was also considered competent, it was his -------- that won people over; he had made many friends and won many supporters with this warm and friendly quality.

    (A) ability
    (B) gullibility
    (C) flexibility
    (D) litheness
    (E) amiability

2. "I am -------- those orders," the rescuer Raoul Wallenberg dared to tell the Nazi SS guards who were herding Hungarian Jews onto trains to the death camps; "These people are under my authority and protection as a Swedish diplomat."

    (A) endorsing
    (B) contravening
    (C) carrying out
    (D) rescinding
    (E) supporting

3. The political science professor challenged his students, yet he -------- his astute and complex analyses of world events with fascinating stories and humor.

    (A) complicated
    (B) obfuscated
    (C) jeopardized
    (D) leavened
    (E) devastated

4. The -------- ideals of the Declaration of Independence declare that it is -------- that all are created equal.

    (A) egalitarian ... axiomatic
    (B) aristocratic ... obvious
    (C) monarchical ... elementary
    (D) plutocratic ... basic
    (E) oligarchic ... ludicrous

5. "What a -------- mass of unclear thinking," the professor said about the -------- philosopher's dense and nearly unreadable writings.

   (A) pristine ... famous

   (B) congealed ... obscure

   (C) crystalline ... venerable

   (D) massive ... prolific

   (E) porous ... witty

The SAT Advantage

> **READING BASED QUESTIONS**
>
> **Directions**: For each of the following questions, choose the best answer and fill in the corresponding oval on the answer sheet to indicate your selection.
>
> The reading passages below are followed by questions based on their content. Questions that follow a pair of related passages may be based on both the content of the passages and/or the relationship between the passages. Answer the questions based on what is <u>stated</u> or <u>implied</u> in the passages.

Questions 6 – 14 are based on the following passage:

Sociologists have a name for what happens when a person tries to become part of a gathered group of people: group entry skills. Who would have thought that entering and being welcomed and accepted by a group was a skill? It is a "soft" or "people" skill that has a great deal of significance when it comes to business networking, and business networking is the key
5 to attaining jobs, gaining contracts, finding affiliates, and overall success.

Some people have a natural knack for entering a group of people with grace and aplomb. Others do it more clumsily and risk rejection. What are some ways to enter a group of people seamlessly? There are some tricks to the trade.

First of all, make sure you are well-groomed and appropriately dressed. If everyone else
10 is wearing jeans, you're going to look funny in a tux and you're going to feel the brunt of people's curiosity and disapproval. Knowing how to dress appropriately for any kind of event is a skill in itself. Hint: it never hurts to ask. Women do this all the time; they call a friend and ask what she will be wearing to the event. For men, it is perfectly appropriate to ask the same thing of friends or colleagues or even to call the event-planners and ask if the
15 occasion calls for casual, business casual, business or formal attire. Some invitations or advertisement to events even include instructions like this: "Business casual dress advised." A quick trip to the Internet can help you define what terms like "business casual" really mean.

In addition to being appropriately dressed, you should make sure you are well-groomed
20 too. This means basic things like a good haircut, a clean shave, and a recent shower or bath. Fingernails should not have any dirt under the surfaces. Any makeup, jewelry, or accessories like scarves or ties should be understated. Scent should also be understated. Overpowering shaving lotion or clouds of heavy perfume are not pleasant, but a whiff of sweetness and cleanliness creates a fine impression. Shoes should be in good condition,
25 without any scuffs. Scratches should be polished out and repairs to the heels updated. Before going to any event, a good brushing, flossing, and mouthwash session will ensure your breath is clean. Carrying breath mints for post-snack close conversations is not a bad idea either.

Smile. Few people can resist a smile. If you approach a group of people with a warm
30 smile on your face, they will part to let you in like the proverbial Red Sea. The nice thing about a smile is that it doesn't matter if you are in Shanghai or Chicago—the whole human race recognizes a smile.

If you are by yourself and want people to find you approachable, turning the corners of your mouth slightly up helps. You don't have to go around with a big grin plastered on your face, but
35 the implications of a smile go a long way toward reassuring people that you are friendly and open to conversation.

If you are going to an event where you won't know anyone, it isn't the worst idea in the world to arrive early. As people trickle in, they will naturally notice you and move toward you to ask if they have the right room, what the time is, and other information-seeking questions. You
40 will be in the center of it all, acting almost like a host or hostess. You will soon have a friendly little group that you didn't even have to enter surrounding you.

Lost in the crowd? Finding it all too intimidating? Gravitate toward the refreshment table. It's easy to strike up a conversation with someone about the coffee, the snacks, where the cream is, etcetera. Hanging around for a few minutes, looking approachable, means that
45 everyone who comes to get refreshments is a candidate for being part of your group.

What if there is a group nearby engaged in conversation and laughter that you very much want to enter into? Stand nearby and incline an ear. Have a polite, inquiring, interested look on your face. Without horning in, add in a laugh, a short comment, or a question. Soon you will be moving into the space the group creates for you, accepting their
50 invitation to join them.

Be clean, well-groomed, friendly, and polite. Any mature group will then accept you. After the enjoyment of the conversation, a polite inquiry into whether the people near you would like your business card is appropriate. Then you are on your way to the next group to conquer!

6. **The author's attitude toward "soft skills" as expressed in lines 3 – 5 seems to be:**

   (A) contempt

   (B) that they are unnecessary and overrated

   (C) they are very important to business success

   (D) that they are a small part of business success

   (E) that "hard" skills like technological competence and training are far more important to business success

7. **In line 6, the word "aplomb" most likely means:**

   (A) confidence

   (B) a "plum," meaning a "plum job" to offer to others

   (C) an ability to deceive

   (D) an ability to appear more confident than they are

   (E) applied psychology

8. **Through lines 9 – 18 we can infer that the author's attitude toward conformity is:**

   (A) it is to be avoided in favor of just being yourself

   (B) conformity to socially acceptable norms of dress is appropriate

   (C) conformity is the only way you will get a job or a contract

   (D) conformity is a necessary evil of the business world

   (E) there is no point in questioning society's norms and ways

9. **The theme of lines 29 – 32 might be summed up as being:**

   (A) an inscrutable facial expression makes you mysterious and interesting

   (B) a smile will carry you through even if you are poorly dressed and poorly groomed

   (C) the universal acceptance of a smile

   (D) the deception of smiles in the Orient

   (E) always appear to be happy at networking events, even if you aren't

10. **Why is the phrase "that you didn't even have to enter" included in line 41?**

    (A) because the essay is about entering a room with grace and aplomb

    (B) because the subject of the essay is group entry skills

    (C) because the paragraph is about entering a room early

    (D) because a smile provides a key to entering a group

    (E) because you don't have to enter an event early; it is just advisable

11. **Lines 42 – 45 give advice for a networking strategy that is based on:**

    (A) people's boredom at networking events that makes them resort to the food and beverage table

    (B) people's insecurity about serving themselves in public

    (C) people's reluctance to talk with their mouths full

    (D) people's natural tendency to gather and be sociable around food and drink

    (E) people's inability to stick to their diets

12. Many of the strategies given in the passage seem to derive from:

(A) an understanding of Pavlov's conditioning

(B) an understanding of behaviorism

(C) an understanding of body English

(D) an understanding of manipulation

(E) an understanding of human nature and human behavior in groups

13. In line 51, the word "mature" is most likely used because:

(A) older people are lonely and will welcome most anyone in

(B) immature people tend to form cliques and practice exclusion

(C) the mature people at a business networking event are the ones who have jobs or contracts to offer

(D) social ostracism is a mark of maturity

(E) an immature group of people has no power and is not worth entering

14. The author speaks figuratively in line(s):

(A) 6

(B) 15 – 16

(C) 22

(D) 37 – 38

(E) 53 – 54

Questions 15 – 24 are based on the following passage:

In May of 1861, black spokesman and abolitionist Frederick Douglass wrote an important essay about the Civil War entitled "How to End the War." At that time, the cause of the North was "Union" against the secession of Southern states; yet secession was sparked by continuing disagreements between the region of the North and the region of the South
5 about slavery and its expansion. Douglass asserted that the banner of the North should be the emancipation of slaves.

    He wrote: "To our mind, there is but one easy, short and effectual way to suppress and put down the desolating war...Fire must be met with water, darkness with light, and war for the destruction of liberty must be met with war for the destruction of slavery..."
10 The "primal" cause of the war, Douglass went on to say, was slavery, and he believed that it should become the war cry of the North: "Freedom to the slave should now be

proclaimed from the Capitol, and should be seen above the smoke and fire of every battle field, waving from every loyal flag!"

Douglass was one of the first and most vociferous to call for the formation of black regiments: "Let the slaves and free colored people be called into service, and formed into a liberating army, to march into the South and raise the banner of Emancipation among the slaves," he wrote.

In the September 1861 issue of his abolitionist newspaper, *Douglass' Monthly*, Douglass bemoaned, "We are often asked by persons in the street as well as by letter, what our people will do in the present solemn crisis in the affairs of the country. Our answer is, would to God you would let us do something! We lack nothing but your consent. We are ready and would go, counting ourselves happy in being permitted to serve and suffer for the cause of freedom and free institutions. But you won't let us go."

The South, he said, was using black men in her army; why not the North? "The slaveholders have not hesitated to employ the sable arms of the Negroes at the South in erecting the fortifications which silenced the guns of Fort Sumter, and brought the star-spangled banner to the dust...They have no scruples against employing the Negroes to exterminate freedom."

Douglass predicted that black troops would be more than willing to be mustered to march into the South to end the slavery of their fellows: "We have no hesitation in saying that ten thousand black soldiers might be raised in the next thirty days to march upon the South...The very fact of color in this case would be more terrible than powder and balls."

Abraham Lincoln did elect to raise black troops. Black men responded to the call to arms to fight for a free country, and they formed regiments excelling in bravery, obedience, and discipline. The 1989 film *Glory* accurately depicts the recruiting, training, and battle exploits of the 54th Regiment of Massachusetts, one of the first black regiments. The film was studded with great actors like Morgan Freeman and Denzel Washington. Washington played a soldier with an "attitude" who eventually felt so much love for and identification with his fellow soldiers and the cause that he died a brave death upholding the flag of the Union as his regiment stormed Fort Wagner in South Carolina. The actual soldier who did that at the real Fort Wagner won the Medal of Honor. Denzel Washington won an Oscar for his show-stopping performance in the film, and the actor dedicated the golden statue to the fighting 54th black regiment of Massachusetts.

In welcoming black troops into the army of the United States, Frederick Douglass made speeches such as the one he made on March 21, 1863, calling upon black men to join up and fight for their freedom. On that occasion he said, "The day dawns; the morning star is bright upon the horizon! The iron gate of our prison stands half open. One gallant rush from the North will fling it wide open, while four millions of our brothers and sisters shall march out into liberty. The chance is now given you to end in a day the bondage of centuries, and to rise in one bound from social degradation to the place of common equality with all other varieties of men."

The brave men of the fighting 54th provided that "one gallant rush" when they stormed Fort Wagner in South Carolina. They won more than a battle. Although they could not take over the heavily manned fort, the men of the fighting 54th won a place in history as they proved the bravery, sincerity, and discipline of black troops. They won the undying respect and gratitude of their nation and were credited by Abraham Lincoln as having helped to turn the tide of war toward victory for the Union and for human freedom.

15. **In lines 1 – 6 Douglass is calling for:**

    (A) the end of the Civil War

    (B) a new flag or banner

    (C) the change of the national war aim from a war against secession to a war against slavery

    (D) the emancipation of the seceded states

    (E) the abolition of war

16. **In line 10, the word "primal" most likely means:**

    (A) primitive

    (B) ancient

    (C) underhanded

    (D) original

    (E) logistical

17. **The tone of lines 10 – 13 may be said to be:**

    (A) blissful

    (B) well-reasoned

    (C) impassioned

    (D) indifferent

    (E) loquacious

18. **In line 14 the word "vociferous" more likely means:**

    (A) veracious

    (B) voracious

    (C) vehement

    (D) vespertine

    (E) vocational

19. **What kind of people does Douglass believe should constitute a "liberating army" (line 16)?**

    (A) the Southern slave-owners themselves

    (B) the slaves and freemen

    (C) the sons of slaves

    (D) blacks and whites together

    (E) the Northern people

20. **What does Douglass see as the primary reason there are no blacks in the Northern army?**

    (A) white resistance

    (B) lack of uniforms

    (C) apathy

    (D) apartheid

    (E) inequality

21. **What line of reasoning does Douglass use in lines 24 – 28 to convince his audience that black men should be allowed into the Northern army?**

    (A) if A equals B, then C equals B

    (B) turn about is fair play

    (C) like should fight like

    (D) two wrongs don't make a right

    (E) there is no black or white when it comes to freedom

22. **In lines 30 – 32 the modern term we might apply to what Douglass is referring to is:**

    (A) racism

    (B) altruism

    (C) iconoclasm

    (D) psychological aggrandizement

    (E) psychological weapons

23. **Who are the "four millions of our brothers and sisters" Douglass is referring to in lines 47 – 49?**

    (A) relatives of soldiers who will be inspired to join the U. S. army

    (B) people around the world

    (C) the slaves in the South

    (D) prisoners behind an iron gate

    (E) freemen and free women in the North

24. **According to the passage, Abraham Lincoln's attitude toward black troops was:**

    (A) accepting of the idea and giving them full credit for their brave deeds

    (B) hesitant to integrate the army

    (C) worried they would be ill-supplied

    (D) worried they would be killed

    (E) worried they would be captured and put into slavery again

SECTION 5
(MATHEMATICS)
Time: 25 minutes
18 questions

MULTIPLE CHOICE

Directions: For the questions in this section, solve each problem and decide which of the given answer choices is the best choice. Fill in the corresponding oval on the answer sheet to indicate your selection. You may use any available space for scratchwork.

Note:

1. Calculator use is permitted.
2. All numbers used are real numbers.
3. All figures provided are drawn to scale and lie in a plane unless otherwise indicated.
4. Unless otherwise specified, the domain of any function f is assumed to be the set of all real numbers x for which $f(x)$ is a real number.

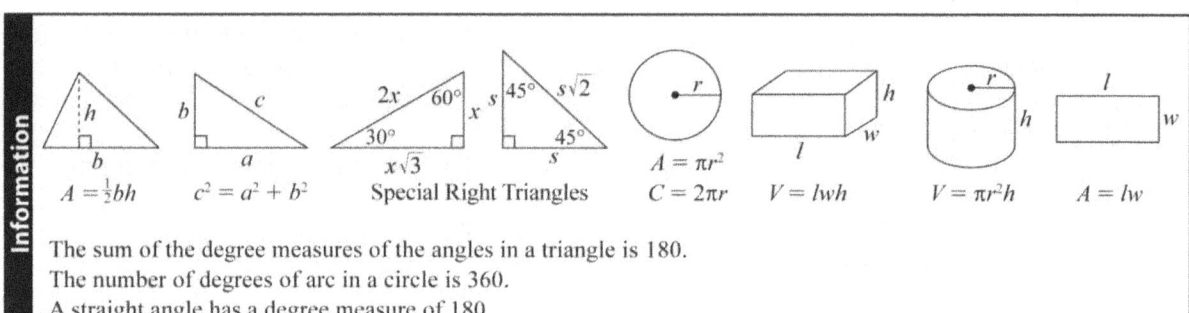

The sum of the degree measures of the angles in a triangle is 180.
The number of degrees of arc in a circle is 360.
A straight angle has a degree measure of 180.

1. Three friends went on vacation together. Lori drove three times as many miles as Lorna. Lauren drove 300 miles more than Lorna. Together, they drove 1100 miles. How many miles did Lori drive?

   (A) 200

   (B) 300

   (C) 420

   (D) 480

   (E) 600

The SAT Advantage

2. Scott and Mike share a pizza. Scott eats $\frac{3}{8}$ of the pizza while Mike eats $\frac{1}{2}$ of it. How much of the pizza is left?

(A) $\frac{1}{8}$

(B) $\frac{2}{5}$

(C) $\frac{1}{2}$

(D) $\frac{5}{8}$

(E) $\frac{7}{8}$

3. If a and b are positive integers such that $a^3 b^2 = 576$, what is the value of $2a - 3b$?

(A) 2
(B) 1
(C) 0
(D) -1
(E) -2

4. If $\angle A$ measures 87°, what is the total measure of the other four angles?

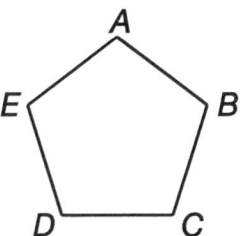

(A) 93
(B) 108
(C) 377
(D) 428
(E) 453

5. PRTS is a square and is adjacent to △. RV = 12 and $m\angle VRT = 45°$. In square units, what is the area of square PRTS?

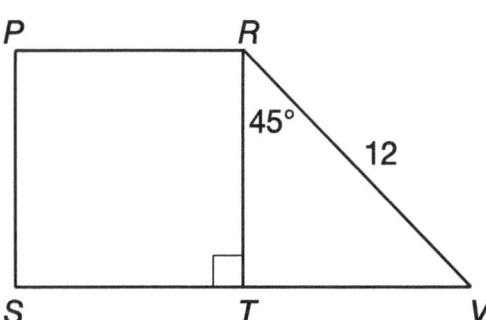

(A) $6\sqrt{2}$
(B) $24\sqrt{2}$
(C) 72
(D) $48\sqrt{3}$
(E) 96

6. The chart below shows the sales contributions of six different departments in a company. Which of the following departments together contribute more than half of the company's earnings?

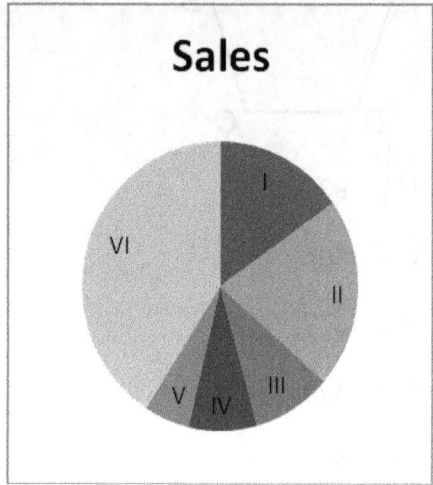

(A) I, III and V

(B) IV, V and VI

(C) I, II and III

(D) I, IV and V

(E) I, III and IV

7. The vertices of a triangle are at the points A (4, 0), B (0, 3) and C ($\frac{36}{5}$, $\frac{63}{5}$). Which of the following are true?

I. ABC is a right triangle.
II. ABC is an isosceles triangle.
III. The area of triangle ABC is 30 square units.

(A) I only

(B) II only

(C) III only

(D) I and III

(E) I and II

8. Over what range of x does the function $2x - 3x^2$ have positive values?

(A) 0 to $\frac{1}{3}$

(B) 0 to $\frac{2}{3}$

(C) 0 to $\frac{3}{2}$

(D) $-\frac{1}{3}$ to $\frac{1}{3}$

(E) $-\frac{2}{3}$ to $\frac{2}{3}$

The SAT Advantage

STUDENT-PRODUCED RESPONSE

Directions: For the Student-Produced Response questions 9 – 18, use the grids at the bottom of the same answer sheet page on which you answered questions 1 – 8. You may use any available space for scratchwork.

The 10 Student-Produced Response questions require you to solve the problem and enter your answer into special grids by filling in the appropriate ovals, as shown below.

Example: 2.25 or $\frac{9}{4}$ or 9/4. Write the answer in the boxes and grid-in the answers by filling in the ovals.

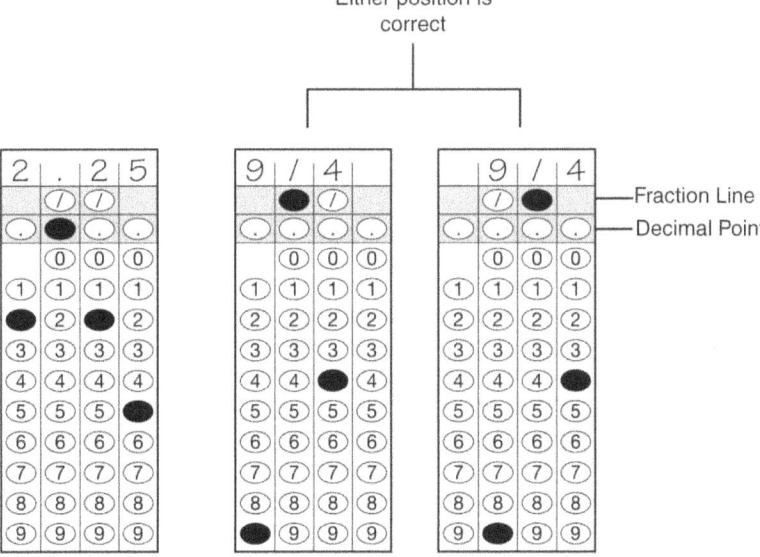

You may start your answers in any column, as shown above, as long as the answer fits. Columns not needed should be left blank. Only fill in one oval per column.

You are not required to write your answer in the boxes at the top of the columns, but it is recommended that you do so. Note, however, you will only receive credit for filling in the ovals correctly.

Only grid in one answer, even if a question has more than one correct answer.

No answers are negative.

Mixed numbers cannot be gridded. For example: the number $1\frac{1}{2}$ must be gridded as 1.5 or 3/2.

If it is gridded as 1 1 / 2, it will be interpreted as 11/2, not $1\frac{1}{2}$.

Enter decimal answers as accurately as possible. For example: the repeating decimal 0.1666... should be gridded as .166 or .167 (less accurate answers such as .16 or .17 are not acceptable). Examples of acceptable ways to grid 1/6 or .1666...

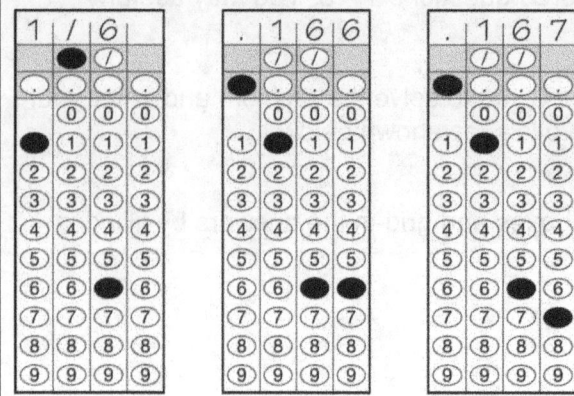

9. 2x + 3y = 3 and 3x + 2y = 7. What is the value of x + y?

10. A new container of detergent is advertised as containing 25% more detergent than the regular container. By what percentage is the price of the new detergent reduced compared to the regular detergent?

11. At how many separate points does the function $f(x) = x^2 - 3$ cross the x-axis?

12. Five times a number is equal to two more than twice the square of the number. What is the number?

13. What is the size of the area bounded by the x-axis and the following two lines in square units?

    2x − 3y = 6 and 2x + 3y = -6

14. $a = 3x + 2$; $b = \dfrac{6x^2 + 4x}{2x}$; x > 0. What is the value of $\dfrac{c}{d}$?

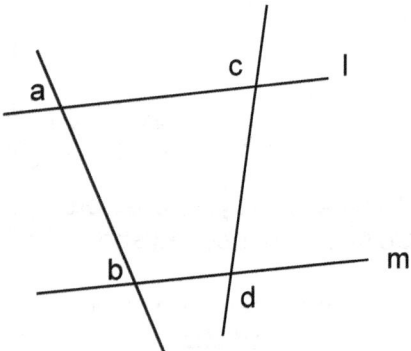

15. If 140% of a number is 70, what is 80% of the number?

16. There are 2 red (R) marbles and 2 white (W) marbles in a bag. Dan takes out one marble at a time without looking. What is the probability that he never pulls out marbles of the same color in two consecutive draws?

17. $n^2 + k^3 < 100$. If n and k are both integers and n > 5 and k > 0, what is the maximum possible value of k?

18. Max wants to arrange 9 books on a shelf. 5 of them are non-fiction and 4 are fiction. In how many ways can he arrange the books so that the fiction books stay together and the non-fiction books stay together?

SECTION 6
(WRITING)
Time: 25 minutes
35 questions

IMPROVING SENTENCES

Directions: For each of the following questions, choose the best answer and fill in the corresponding oval on the answer sheet to indicate your selection.

Part of each sentence (or the entire sentence) is underlined. The five answer choices present five ways of phrasing the underlined portion. Choice A repeats the original phrasing and the other four choices offer alternative phrasings. If you think the original phrasing is best, select choice A; if not, select one of the other options.

In choosing your answer, follow the requirements of standard written English. Pay attention to grammar, choice of words, sentence construction, and punctuation; your selection should result in the most effective, clear, and precise sentence—free of awkwardness or ambiguity.

1. **Once the home of "oldies" music from previous decades, the owners of our local radio station have** decided to switch to a talk-radio format.

    (A) Once the home of "oldies" music from previous decades, the owners of our local radio station have

    (B) The owners of the home of "oldies" music from previous decades, our local radio station, has

    (C) The owners of our local radio station, which was once the home of "oldies" music from previous decades, have

    (D) Though once the home of "oldies" music from previous decades, the owners of our local radio station

    (E) Once the home of "oldies" music from previous decades, the owners of the local radio station having

2. The literary character Sherlock Holmes, **based on one of Arthur Conan Doyle's medical school professors, a man who** possessed the amazing ability to deduce details about the lives of his patients.

    (A) based on one of Arthur Conan Doyle's medical school professors, a man who

    (B) is based on one of Arthur Conan Doyle's medical school professors, a man who

    (C) being based on one of Arthur Conan Doyle's medical school professors, an man that

    (D) basing himself on one of Arthur Conan Doyle's medical school professors, a man which

    (E) is based on one of Arthur Conan Doyle's medical school professors; this man being someone who

3. **Had Abraham Lincoln emancipated the slaves at the beginning of the Civil War,** he might have alienated the citizens of several slaveholding border states that had remained loyal to the Union.

   (A) Had Abraham Lincoln emancipated the slaves at the beginning of the Civil War,

   (B) If Abraham Lincoln emancipated the slaves at the beginning of the Civil War,

   (C) If Abraham Lincoln would have emancipated the slaves at the beginning of the Civil War,

   (D) Abraham Lincoln, by emancipating slaves at the beginning of the Civil War,

   (E) Abraham Lincoln having emancipated slaves at the beginning of the Civil War,

4. For years, many nutrition experts have blamed Americans' love of snacking for the nation's increasing obesity rates; **a recent study** found that eating two nutritious snacks a day, in addition to three meals, helped people lower their body mass index and maintain a healthy weight.

   (A) a recent study

   (B) but a recent study

   (C) therefore, a recent study

   (D) however, a recent study

   (E) furthermore, a recent study

5. In the decades after World War II, downtown Baltimore became a derelict port with decaying infrastructure and little appeal to vacationers; in recent decades, however, urban renewal successes such as the acclaimed Inner Harbor Project and the new Oriole Park at Camden Yards **have made it so it is significantly more appealing** to tourists.

   (A) have made it so it is significantly more appealing

   (B) have significantly made it more appealing

   (C) are causing it to be made significantly more appealing

   (D) significantly increasing its appeal

   (E) have significantly increased its appeal

6. **High school seniors face increasing pressure to choose and train for specific careers,** many employers prefer job candidates with curiosity, problem-solving skills, and the ability to communicate and work closely with others, rather than candidates with specific career-related training.

   (A) High school seniors face increasing pressure to choose and train for specific careers,

   (B) Because high school seniors face increasing pressure to choose and train for specific careers,

   (C) High school seniors are facing increased pressure to choose and train for specific careers,

   (D) Although high school seniors face increasing pressure to choose and train for specific careers,

   (E) With high school seniors facing increasing pressure to choose and train for specific careers,

7. Contrary to the popular view of the profession, the field of nursing has many different specialties, **each with its own distinct responsibilities and certification requirements**.

   (A) each with its own distinct responsibilities and certification requirements

   (B) when they each have their own distinct responsibilities and certification requirements

   (C) and each of them having its own distinct responsibilities and certification requirements

   (D) each with their own distinct responsibilities and certification responsibilities

   (E) each of them has its own distinct responsibilities and certification requirements

8. **The writer Joan Didion is known for her vivid details, controlled style, and in-depth characterizations, she has published several acclaimed novels and essay collections.**

   (A) The writer Joan Didion is known for her vivid details, controlled style, and in-depth characterizations, she

   (B) Known for her vivid details, controlled style, and in-depth characterizations, the writer Joan Didion

   (C) Joan Didion, the writer, known for her vivid details, controlled style, and in-depth characterizations, and she

   (D) The writer Joan Didion, known for her vivid details, controlled style, and in-depth characterizations; she

   (E) The writer Joan Didion is known for her vivid details, controlled style, and in-depth characterizations, however she

9. **Residents of New York City, as well as seasoned travelers to the Big Apple, say that tourists can expect to be dazzled by its exciting nightlife and experiencing bustling neighborhoods.**

   (A) and experiencing bustling neighborhoods

   (B) and to be dazzled by experiencing its bustling neighborhoods

   (C) and bustling neighborhoods

   (D) and they experience bustling neighborhoods as well

   (E) as well as by experiencing bustling neighborhoods

10. **Though older workers may not be as technologically savvy as their younger counterparts, many employers have found the work ethic and dependability of the older generation to be superior to younger workers.**

    (A) to younger workers

    (B) to that of younger workers

    (C) to those of younger workers

    (D) from those of a younger age

    (E) from the younger workers' work ethic and dependability

11. According to prevailing views in nineteenth-century society, women were supposed to be involved in domestic pursuits such as raising their children and beautifying their homes, <u>rather than in public concerns such as voting or entering professions</u>.

(A) rather than in public concerns such as voting or entering professions

(B) instead of the right to vote and to enter professions

(C) let alone becoming involved in the public concerns that voting and entering professions entailed

(D) rather than concerning themselves with the public voting or the entering of professions

(E) then with public concerns like voting and professions

IDENTIFYING SENTENCE ERRORS

Directions: For each of the following questions, choose the best answer and fill in the corresponding oval on the answer sheet to indicate your selection.

The following sentences test your ability to recognize grammar and usage errors. In making your selection, follow the requirements of standard written English.

Each sentence contains either a single error or no error at all; none of the sentences contain more than one error. If the sentence contains an error, select the underlined portion A through D that must be changed in order to fix the sentence. If the sentence is correct and contains no errors, select choice E.

12. In her deposition, the witness claimed <u>that</u> those <u>who</u> the company president
                A   B
    dismissed were <u>chosen not</u> because
                    C
    of their ineptitude on the job but <u>because of</u> their political opinions.
        D
    <u>No error</u>
       E

13. Prohibited <u>from</u> catching more than a
            A
    small number of profitable fish, local fishermen <u>have few</u> options if they
               B
    hope to succeed <u>in</u> the business <u>their</u>
             C   D
    ancestors have pursued for generations. <u>No error</u>
                 E

14. During their twenties, <u>a person</u> should
                  A
    have the <u>opportunity to</u> pursue
             B
    financial independence and <u>emotional</u>
                    C
    <u>maturity</u> without fear <u>of</u> permanent
                   D
    failure. <u>No error</u>
          E

15. <u>As</u> a young woman, Jessica refrained
     A
    <u>from making</u> <u>any</u> extravagant
        B   C
    purchases because she longed <u>for</u>
                      D
    <u>buying</u> her own home someday.
    <u>No error</u>
      E

16. A steep rise in energy prices, along with new rules <u>that have</u> tightened
                 A
    fuel-economy standards, <u>have led</u> to a
                  B
    sharp decrease <u>in</u> the <u>consumption of</u>
               C   D
    gasoline. <u>No error</u>
           E

17. So <u>sudden</u> was the arrival <u>of</u> the storm
       A   B
    that we <u>couldn't hardly</u> believe we
              C
    needed to seek shelter immediately or
    risk <u>being swept</u> away by the current.
          D
    <u>No error</u>
     E

18. The irony of our situation <u>lay</u> in the fact
                                A
    that we <u>had flew</u> halfway around the
              B
    world, <u>only to</u> eat <u>our</u> first meal in an
            C   D
    American fast-food restaurant.

    <u>No error</u>
     E

19. <u>Being prone to</u> stuttering can make
     A
    people self-conscious, <u>irregardless</u> of
                            B
    their intelligence and talent; <u>as a</u>
                                    C
    <u>result</u>, may stutterers <u>choose</u> the
                                D
    option of remaining quiet, rather than
    facing ridicule. <u>No error</u>
                       E

20. Among the factors <u>contributing to</u> the
                       A
    <u>rise of</u> the Industrial Revolution <u>was</u>
     B   C
    the invention of new machines and the
    <u>accumulation of</u> capital from trade.
     D
    <u>No error</u>
     E

21. A solar eclipse is a remarkable
    <u>phenomena</u> that <u>occurs when</u> the
     A   B
    moon passes <u>between</u> the earth and
                  C
    the sun, <u>obscuring</u> our view of the sun.
              D
    <u>No error</u>
     E

22. By a margin <u>that</u> impressed his
                 A
    supporters as much as <u>it</u> outraged his
                           B
    opponents, the candidate <u>easily won</u>
                              C
    the nomination and then named an
    obscure senator <u>as</u> his running mate.
                     D
    <u>No error</u>
     E

23. The condition called tendinitis increases blood flow to an injured area, raises the temperature of the surrounding tissue, and **releasing** (A) healing chemicals **that** (B) **repair** (C) any cells that **have been damaged** (D) by the injury. **No error** (E)

24. **Yearning for** (A) a project **in which to** (B) invest **his** (C) talent and energy, Damian **sought** (D) both self-fulfillment and a sense of purpose. **No error** (E)

25. Lily told Anna that **by applying** (A) diligence and perseverance **she** (B) could win the Alger Prize, **which was given** (C) **annually** (D) to the most versatile athlete. **No error** (E)

26. **Hopefully,** (A) you **have not forgotten** (B) to replace the windows on the second floor **that were broken** (C) during the howling winds and pounding hail **of** (D) last week's storm. **No error** (E)

27. **According to** (A) reports in the local media, the contestants from Salem **would have** (B) had a better chance **of** (C) **succeeding** in the competition if they had abided **with** (D) the rules. **No error** (E)

28. The scientist was considered **eccentric** (A) because she was much **more** (B) **interested** in quietly pursuing her research than in **widely publicizing** (C) her results, an activity she **deemed** (D) unprofessional. **No error** (E)

29. To increase productivity and encourage innovation, companies
                              A
    should provide employees of time to engage deeply in their projects,
                          B   C
    protecting workers from distracting interruptions. No error
                    D   E

IMPROVING PARAGRAPHS

Directions: The following passage is an early draft of an essay that may need parts rewritten.

Read the passage provided and select the best answer choice for each question. Some questions are about individual sentences or parts of individual sentences and ask you to improve the sentence structure or word choice. Some questions are about multiple sentences and ask you to consider the overall organization of the passage as a whole. In making your selection, follow the requirements of standard written English.

For each of the following questions, choose the best answer and fill in the corresponding oval on the answer sheet to indicate your selection.

(1) The feud between the Hatfields and McCoys began with a murder that took place when a McCoy, returning from the Union victory in the Civil War, was killed by Confederate Hatfields. (2) The Hatfields and McCoys lived in the border regions of Kentucky and West Virginia. (3) Both states had been in the Union. (4) But there were many Confederates there, including members of both families.
(5) Then the families argued about the ownership of some property. (6) A group of McCoy boys killed a Hatfield on an election day. (7) The Hatfields then captured three McCoy boys and executed them by gunshot after tying them to a clump of paw-paw bushes.
(8) One can only imagine what was in the hearts of these men roving the Kentucky and West Virginia woods, looking for their enemies. (9) Their enemies were either Hatfields or McCoys. (10) Sorrow, hatred, rage, fear, and guilt must have run high in those calm, unspoiled woods of yesteryear.
(11) Feuds of the blood are common in male pride codes of cultures. (12) Sicily, for example, has a strong code of male pride. (13) Entire villages have had their male populations wiped out because of revenge killings, and some families still live behind tall, concrete walls in Sicilian villages for self-protection.
(14) Revenge-retaliation-revenge is a cycle. (15) In societies with a strong code of pride, men must avenge an insult. (16) However, it is time to learn that it takes far more courage and honor to resist the vengeful urge. (17) It takes much more strength to forgive than it does to retaliate.

30. Of the following, which is the best way to revise the underlined portion of sentences 3 and 4 (reproduced below)?

    Both states had been in the <u>Union. But there</u> were many Confederates there, including members of both families.

    (A) No revision is necessary

    (B) Union, whereas there

    (C) Union, but there

    (D) Union; However, there

    (E) Union; but however there

31. In the interests of being clear and concise, what would be the best way to revise sentence 7 (reproduced below)?

    The Hatfields then captured three McCoy boys and executed them by gunshot after tying them to a clump of paw-paw bushes.

    (A) No revision is necessary

    (B) The Hatfields then captured and gunshot three McCoy boys.

    (C) The Hatfields then captured three McCoy boys in the paw-paw bushes and shot them.

    (D) The Hatfields tied up three McCoy boys they had captured and executed them at point blank range.

    (E) The Hatfields then captured three McCoy boys and executed them by gunshot.

32. What is the best way to revise and combine sentences 8 and 9 (reproduced below)?

    One can only imagine what was in the hearts of these men roving the Kentucky and West Virginia woods, looking for their enemies. Their enemies were either Hatfields or McCoys.

    (A) No revision is necessary

    (B) One can only imagine what was in the roving hearts of these Kentuckians and West Virginians as they went among the woods looking for enemy Hatfields or McCoys.

    (C) One can only imagine what was in the hearts of these men, Hatfields or McCoys, as they roved the woods of Kentucky and West Virginia, looking for their enemies.

    (D) One can only imagine what was in the enemy hearts of these Hatfields and McCoys as they roved Kentucky and West Virginia in the woods of their enemies.

    (E) One can only imagine what was in the hearts of these enemies, Hatfields and McCoys, as they roved the Kentucky and West Virginia woods, looking for the hearts of their enemies.

33. Of the following, which would be the best way to revise the underlined portion of sentence 10 (reproduced below)?

    Sorrow, hatred, rage, fear, and guilt must have run high in those calm, unspoiled woods of yesteryear.

    (A) No revision is necessary

    (B) Sorrow, hatred, rage, fear, and guilt must have run high in the hearts of the men who traversed those calm, unspoiled woods in yesteryear.

    (C) Sorrow, revenge, vengefulness, rage and anger, fear, guilt, and other emotions must have run high in those calm, unspoiled woods of yesteryear.

    (D) Sorrow, hatred, rage, fear and guilt must have run high in those calm, unspoiled hearts and woods of yesteryear.

    (E) Sorrow, hatred, rage, fear and guilt must have been elevated in those calm, unspoiled woods of yesteryear.

34. Which of the following is the best way to revise sentence 11 (reproduced below)?

    Feuds of the blood are common in male pride codes of cultures.

    (A) No revision is necessary

    (B) Blood feuds are common in male pride codes, culturally.

    (C) Feuds of the blood are common in cultures where there are male codes of pride.

    (D) Blood feuds are common culturally where there are prideful and honorable males.

    (E) Blood feuds are common in cultures where there is a strong code of male pride.

35. Which of the following is the best way to revise sentence 16 (reproduced below)?

However, it is time to learn that it takes far more courage and honor to resist the vengeful urge.

(A) No revision is necessary

(B) However and again, it is time to learn that it takes far more courage and honor to resist the vengeful urge.

(C) However, it is time to learn better that it takes far more courage and honor to resist the vengeful urge.

(D) However, it is time to learn that it takes fewer more courage and honor to resist the vengeful urge.

(E) However, time will tell that it takes far more courage and honor to resist the vengeful urge.

SECTION 7
(CRITICAL READING)
Time: 20 minutes
19 questions

> **SENTENCE COMPLETION**
>
> **Directions**: For each of the following questions, choose the best answer and fill in the corresponding oval on the answer sheet to indicate your selection.
>
> Each sentence contains one or two blanks indicating that something has been omitted from the sentence. Choose the word or set of words, labeled A through E, that when inserted into the sentence, best fits the meaning of the sentence as a whole.

1. The police officer asked the distraught grandmother to slow down, take a few deep breaths, and start over again calmly so that she could give a -------- account of the robbery she witnessed.

    (A) burdensome

    (B) blistering

    (C) truthful

    (D) coherent

    (E) disparaging

2. Few could believe that the seemingly kindly woman who claimed investors' money was coming from real estate was so -------- as to be perpetrating a Ponzi scheme.

    (A) ethical

    (B) principled

    (C) nefarious

    (D) astute

    (E) perspicacious

3. The editor -------- the proofreader for leaving many obvious errors on the website's home page: "You are not -------- enough," she told him.

    (A) praised ... dedicated

    (B) rebuked ... scrupulous

    (C) rebuffed ... careless

    (D) reviled ... meticulous

    (E) lauded ... sedulous

4. The set of mannerisms he adopted made his -------- appear quite -------- as a salesman of financial services, but in fact, he was himself in deep financial trouble.

    (A) expression ... guilty

    (B) visage ... troubled

    (C) aspect ... aggravated

    (D) demeanor ... questionable

    (E) persona ... plausible

5. The orchestra played with such technical precision, artistic transcendence, and celestial sweetness that the audience was moved to a sense of -------- joy.

   (A) ineffable
   (B) maddened
   (C) exhilarated
   (D) predatory
   (E) insatiable

6. The state official said, "I cannot -------- of the possibility that neighboring farmers thought that compound with the barbed wire, satellite dish, and armed guards was an -------- presence in that field."

   (A) deceive ... innocent
   (B) dispense ... alien
   (C) conceive ... innocuous
   (D) apprehend ... welcome
   (E) disavow ... altruistic

READING BASED QUESTIONS

Directions: For each of the following questions, choose the best answer and fill in the corresponding oval on the answer sheet to indicate your selection.

The reading passages below are followed by questions based on their content. Questions that follow a pair of related passages may be based on both the content of the passages and/or the relationship between the passages. Answer the questions based on what is <u>stated</u> or <u>implied</u> in the passages.

Questions 7 – 9 are based on the following passage:

A scientist, Dr. Harold J. Morowitz, was intrigued by the idea of human worth. Since he was a Yale University molecular biologist, he decided to approach the idea from a physiological rather than a metaphysical point of view.

The common wisdom at the time was that the human body, reduced down to its
5 chemical structure, was only worth about a dollar. Morowitz thought that was a little cheap.

He decided to do a detailed study of the monetary value of the human body. According to Dr. Morowitz's analysis, it turned out the chemicals needed to comprise a human body would cost a total of about six million dollars, or $6,000,015.44 to be precise. Dr. Morowitz arrived at this figure by adding up the costs of synthetic chemicals from the catalogue of a
10 biochemical company.

The synthesized chemicals offered in the catalogue came from animal sources. Dr. Morowitz calculated that if someone tried to synthesize the body's chemicals from natural, raw materials, the cost would be even more. What is more, organizing the chemicals into the body's tissues, organs, and systems would elevate the costs even more. Dr. Horowitz
15 estimated the cost would escalate to six billion dollars.

This is a good reason to esteem ourselves highly. If a person ever feels he or she is worthless, it is time to think again. Without adding in the incalculable value of a person's heart and mind, he or she is worth at least six billion dollars. Each person is invaluable.

7. The author of the passage talks about the physical, biochemical value of the human body yet also takes into account:

   (A) the metaphysical value of the human being
   (B) the astrophysical value of the human body
   (C) the neurological value of the human being
   (D) the physiological value of the human being
   (E) the physiognomic value of the human being

8. The tone of lines 4 – 6 may be said to be:

   (A) cynical
   (B) impersonal
   (C) humorous
   (D) straightforward
   (E) moronic

9. In line 18, the word "invaluable" most likely means:

   (A) of little worth
   (B) of immeasurable worth
   (C) invalid
   (D) unable to be validated by numbers
   (E) statistically insignificant

Questions 10 – 19 are based on the following passage:

Sometimes when people have an addiction problem, they don't know where to turn. After all, addictions—whether they are to alcohol, heroin, cocaine, food or other palliatives—are costly in multiple ways. Often, addicts and their family members have already suffered significant losses, including financial ones, due to the addiction. They cannot afford therapy.
5 They are at the end of their ropes. Where should they turn?
   There is one easily accessible, low-cost place where not only addicts but those who love and care about them can turn: the venerable institution of Alcoholics Anonymous and its companion program Al-Anon. Alcoholics Anonymous addresses the problems of addicts. Al-Anon addresses the problems of families and friends of addicts.
10 Alcoholics Anonymous began on June 10, 1935 when a man named Bill W. and his friend Dr. Bob addressed their chronic drinking problems. (The men's last names are usually not given, in keeping with AA being an anonymous organization.)
   Bill W. had ruined a successful business life and almost destroyed a happy marriage through his compulsive need to drink. His story and that of his wife, Lois, is told in the
15 poignant Hallmark Hall of Fame movie *When Love Is Not Enough*, starring Winona Ryder as Bill W.'s wife.
   Bill had been working with "The Oxford Group" to apply principles of living to learn to live alcohol-free. Bill worked toward sobriety with The Oxford Group, but he realized the

principles the program was based upon could use some expansion and broadening in order
20 to reach more diverse types of people. Together, Bill W. and Dr. Bob developed Twelve
Steps for fighting addiction to alcohol.

These Twelve Steps worked to establish order and harmony in alcoholics' chaotic lives. The support of other alcoholics in an "anonymous fellowship" from which Alcoholics Anonymous derived its name, helped men and women with alcohol addiction to overcome it
25 with privacy and dignity.

Over time, the pair also developed the Twelve Traditions, which are designed to keep AA non-hierarchical and non-judgmental. AA membership is open to anyone who has a problem with alcoholism or other addictions, regardless of his or her other affiliations or beliefs. However, the Twelve Traditions keep people from trying to impose their beliefs or
30 advertise their affiliations to other AA members. The Twelve Traditions limit AA's purpose to helping alcoholics get and become sober, period.

In 1951 Bill's wife Lois realized that her own behavior in relation to his addiction needed amending. This was the beginning of Al-Anon, the companion program to AA, where friends and family members of people with addictions work on their own lives and strive to achieve
35 serenity in order to ensure that they are not hindering the alcoholic's recovery. Friends and family members often find they have been "enabling" the addiction by paying fines, bailing the person out of jail, making excuses to employers for the alcoholic's missed work days, and in general covering up, protecting, and shielding the addict from the natural consequences of his or her addiction. This allows the addiction to go on longer. Through Al-
40 Anon, people who love addicts realize that a lot of their own behavior is neither helpful nor loving.

Many well-known experts and therapists recommend AA and Al-Anon to those affected by addictions. Although the Twelve Steps are not magic, they often bring about profound changes. They are simple, low-cost, readily available and effective programs. They have
45 helped countless people and those who love them cope with and overcome the agonies of addiction.

10. The word "palliatives" in line 2 most likely means:

(A) plentitudes

(B) parsimoniousness

(C) controlled substances

(D) things that comfort or relieve pain temporarily

(E) addictive substances

11. Line 5 contains a question the purpose of which is most likely:

(A) appositive effect

(B) literal effect

(C) rhetorical effect

(D) categorical effect

(E) cataclysmic effect

12. By the use of the word "venerable" in line 7, the author is expressing the following attitude toward Alcoholics Anonymous:

    (A) respect for a longstanding and successful institution

    (B) awe at the existence of such an institution

    (C) casual acceptance of the normalcy of such an institution

    (D) measured support of such an institution

    (E) skepticism toward such an old institution

13. The relationship between Alcoholics Anonymous and Al-Anon is described in the passage as being one of:

    (A) symbiosis

    (B) companion programs

    (C) complimentary programs

    (D) condiment programs

    (E) commiserating programs

14. The implications about Bill and Lois's marriage in lines 13 – 16 and lines 32 – 41 are most likely that:

    (A) Bill and Lois first met at AA meetings

    (B) Lois was not an active part of the founding and perpetuation of AA

    (C) the couple divorced and then remarried once Bill achieved sobriety

    (D) the couple sought many kinds of therapies before settling on AA and Al-anon

    (E) the couple kept their marriage together and Lois learned not to enable Bill's alcohol addiction

15. What significance does the passage ascribe to the Twelve Traditions of Alcoholics Anonymous?

    (A) they help keep alcoholics sober

    (B) they match the Twelve Steps in importance

    (C) they keep AA democratic, open to all comers, and focused in purpose

    (D) they keep AA functioning within a hierarchy of experts, elders, the newly sober, and those who are just beginning the path to sobriety

    (E) they serve as a companion program to Al-Anon

16. In using the word "period" in line 31, the author is most likely striving for the effect of:

    (A) a figure of speech

    (B) emphasis on AA's focused purpose

    (C) expressing the finality of AA's programs

    (D) making a clear delineation between AA and Al-Anon

    (E) transitioning to a discussion of Al-Anon

17. Line 42 mentions "Many well-known experts and therapists" for the likely purpose of:

    (A) trying to gain posthumous honorary degrees for Bill W.

    (B) trying to convince the reader to try AA and Al-anon

    (C) validating the ineffectiveness of this program because Dr. Bob was not a therapist but a medical doctor

    (D) validating the effectiveness of this program developed by someone who was not an expert or a therapist

    (E) repudiating the effectiveness of this program that was developed by an alcoholic

18. In general, the author's attitude toward alcoholics may be said to be:

    (A) judgmental

    (B) impartial

    (C) infuriated at the pain caused to family and friends of alcoholics

    (D) sympathetic

    (E) an attitude that supports the return of Prohibition

19. The author's perspective is that the "enabling" behavior of people who love alcoholics is "neither helpful nor loving" (lines 40 – 41) for the following reason:

    (A) a friend or family member can go broke paying fines and bail

    (B) a friend or family member might lose his or her own job making excuses to employers

    (C) a friend or family member might get in legal trouble for "covering up"

    (D) enabling the alcoholic may cause resentment in the friend or family member

    (E) shielding addicts from the natural consequences of their behavior may prolong their addictions

The SAT Advantage

SECTION 8
(MATHEMATICS)
Time: 20 minutes
16 questions

MULTIPLE CHOICE

Directions: For the questions in this section, solve each problem and decide which of the given answer choices is the best choice. Fill in the corresponding oval on the answer sheet to indicate your selection. You may use any available space for scratchwork.

Note:

1. Calculator use is permitted.
2. All numbers used are real numbers.
3. All figures provided are drawn to scale and lie in a plane unless otherwise indicated.
4. Unless otherwise specified, the domain of any function f is assumed to be the set of all real numbers x for which f(x) is a real number.

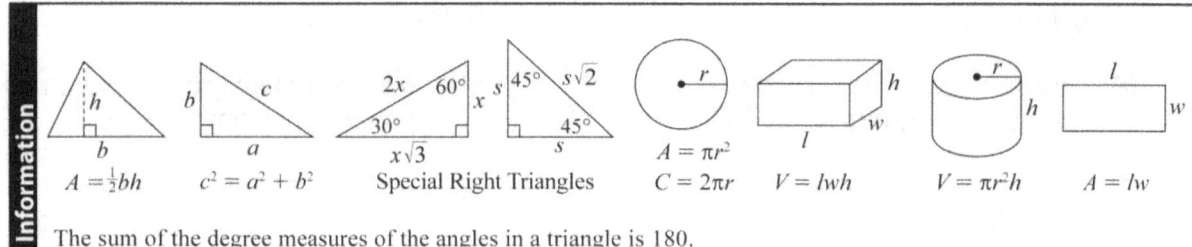

The sum of the degree measures of the angles in a triangle is 180.
The number of degrees of arc in a circle is 360.
A straight angle has a degree measure of 180.

1. If Sam can deliver 24 newspapers in 2 hours, how many newspapers can he deliver in 5 hours?

   (A) 65
   (B) 62
   (C) 60
   (D) 55
   (E) 52

2. A 50 ft by 30 ft rectangular garden has a circular fountain in the center. If the radius of the fountain is 6 ft, what is the area of the garden outside the fountain?

   (A) 113 sq. ft
   (B) 675 sq. ft
   (C) 1387 sq. ft
   (D) 1500 sq. ft
   (E) 1575 sq. ft

3. In the standard coordinate plane (x,y), the points (0,0), (2,4), (10,4), and (8,0) are the vertices of the parallelogram shown below. What is the area of the parallelogram?

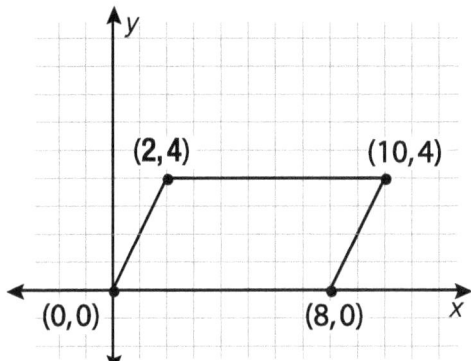

(A) 20

(B) 32

(C) $32\sqrt{2}$

(D) $32\sqrt{3}$

(E) $40\sqrt{3}$

4. The cost to join a movie rental club is $80.00 for annual dues and $12.00 per month for unlimited rentals. If Arnie has paid the club $164.00, how many monthly payments has he made?

(A) 7

(B) 6

(C) 5

(D) 4

(E) 3

5. In the figure below, D, A, and C are collinear and $\overline{BA} = \overline{BC}$. What is the value of x?

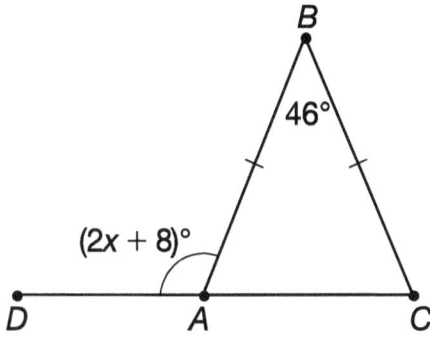

(A) 53

(B) 52.5

(C) 52

(D) 46

(E) 21.6

6. In the equation $\dfrac{12}{x} + x = 13$, x = ?

(A) x = 1

(B) x = 12

(C) x = 13

(D) x = 1 or x = 12

(E) x = 2 or x = 6

7. When water freezes, it expands by about 9%. When ice melts, by what percent does its volume decrease?

   (A) 7.8%
   (B) 8.3%
   (C) 9.0%
   (D) 9.8%
   (E) 18%

8. Square BCDE has a diagonal that measures 8 units. What is the perimeter of the square?

   (A) $4\sqrt{2}$
   (B) $8\sqrt{2}$
   (C) 16
   (D) $16\sqrt{2}$
   (E) 32

9. Angle BAD = 70° and angle ABC = 62°. If AD and BC are extended until they intersect, what angle will they form at the intersection?

   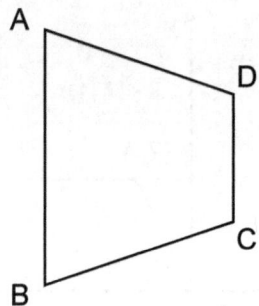

   (A) 48°
   (B) 60°
   (C) 76°
   (D) 132°
   (E) 228°

10. Matt buys 3 apples and 2 oranges for $2.40. Sally buys 6 apples and 5 oranges for $5.40. What is the cost of 1 apple and 1 orange?

    (A) $0.40
    (B) $0.60
    (C) $1.00
    (D) $2.00
    (E) $3.00

11. A school music program has 120 students. 45 students take violin and 30 students play the flute. At most, how many students play neither the violin nor the flute?

    (A) 105
    (B) 75
    (C) 45
    (D) 30
    (E) 0

12. A train 500 ft long enters a tunnel that is half a mile long at a speed of 100 mph. For how many seconds is the entire train in the tunnel? (1 mile = 5280 ft)

    (A) 14.6
    (B) 18
    (C) 21.4
    (D) 29.2
    (E) 36

13. $\dfrac{125a^3b^{12} - 27a^6}{64b^3}$ is equivalent to

    (A) $\left(\dfrac{5ab^4}{4b}\right)^3 - \left(\dfrac{3a^2}{4b}\right)^3$

    (B) $\left(\dfrac{5ab^4 - 3a^2}{4b}\right)^3$

    (C) $\dfrac{\left(5ab^4 - 3a^2\right)^3}{4b}$

    (D) $\dfrac{\left(5ab^4\right)^3}{4b} - \dfrac{\left(3a^2\right)^3}{4b}$

    (E) $\left(\dfrac{5ab^4}{4b}\right)^3 + \left(\dfrac{3a^2}{4b}\right)^3$

14. Alan buys pieces of wood of different lengths for a building project. There are 4 planks 5 m long, 6 planks 2 m long, 3 planks 10 m long, and 4 planks 12 m long. What is the median length of the planks?

    (A) 2m
    (B) 3m
    (C) 5m
    (D) 10m
    (E) 12m

15. A sculpture had a concrete sphere placed on a cylindrical pillar. If the sphere has a density of d pounds per cubic inch and the top of the pillar can withstand a pressure of p pounds per square inch, which of the following equations gives the relationship between the radius R of the largest sphere the pillar can support and the radius r of the base of the pillar?

(A) $\frac{4}{3}\pi R^2 d = p\pi r^3$

(B) $4\pi R^2 d = p\pi r^2$

(C) $Rd = pr$

(D) $\frac{4}{3}\pi R^3 p = d\pi r^2$

(E) $\frac{4}{3}\pi R^3 d = p\pi r^2$

16. A rectangular roof 20 ft by 50 ft will be covered with solar panels. If the entire surface of each panel must be placed on the roof and the panels cannot overlap, which of the following choices will cover the maximum area?

(A) circular panels of diameter 2 ft

(B) circular panels of diameter 4 ft

(C) circular panels of diameter 6 ft

(D) square panels of side 3 ft

(E) square panels of side 7 ft

SECTION 9
(WRITING)
Time: 10 minutes
14 questions

IMPROVING SENTENCES

Directions: For each of the following questions, choose the best answer and fill in the corresponding oval on the answer sheet to indicate your selection.

Part of each sentence (or the entire sentence) is underlined. The five answer choices present five ways of phrasing the underlined portion. Choice A repeats the original phrasing and the other four choices offer alternative phrasings. If you think the original phrasing is best, select choice A; if not, select one of the other options.

In choosing your answer, follow the requirements of standard written English. Pay attention to grammar, choice of words, sentence construction, and punctuation; your selection should result in the most effective, clear, and precise sentence—free of awkwardness or ambiguity.

1. **In order to feel energized and to function at their best, extroverts require regular periods of social interaction, introverts, on the other hand, need regular periods of time alone.**

    (A) In order to feel energized and to function at their best, extroverts require regular periods of social interaction, introverts, on the other hand, need regular periods of time alone.

    (B) Extroverts require regular periods of social interaction in order to feel energized and to function at their best, and introverts, on the other hand, they need regular periods of time alone.

    (C) Introverts need regular periods of time alone, with extroverts, on the other hand, requiring regular periods of social interaction, in order to feel energized and to function at their best.

    (D) In order to feel energized and to function at their best, extroverts require regular periods of social interaction; introverts, on the other hand, need regular periods of time alone.

    (E) While extroverts require regular periods of social interaction to feel energized and to function at their best; introverts, on the other hand, need regular periods of time alone.

2. **The auditorium at the high school does not have as many seats as the college does.**

    (A) as the college does

    (B) compared to what the college does

    (C) as the auditorium at the college does

    (D) like the ones at the college do

    (E) like the college auditorium does

3. The city council says that this year's budget, **which is 10 percent larger than projected and 20 percent larger than** last year's, is bound to create growing deficits.

   (A) which is 10 percent larger than projected and 20 percent larger than

   (B) which is 10 percent larger than projected and 20 percent as large when compared with

   (C) is 10 percent larger then projected but also 20 percent larger then

   (D) 10 percent larger than projected, and it creates a budget 20 percent larger than

   (E) with an amount 10 percent larger than the one that was projected, as well as being 20 percent larger than

4. **Recognized for its excellent food at reasonable prices, patrons will make reservations months in advance to entertain guests at the Riverside Inn, rather than settling for another local eatery.**

   (A) Recognized for its excellent food at reasonable prices, patrons will make reservations months in advance to entertain guests at the Riverside Inn, rather than settling for another local eatery.

   (B) Recognized for its excellence in food as well as for the reasonableness of its prices, patrons will make reservations months in advance to entertain guests at the Riverside Inn, rather than settling for another local eatery.

   (C) Recognized for its excellent food at reasonable prices, the Riverside Inn attracts patrons who will make reservations to entertain guests there months in advance, rather than settling for another local eatery.

   (D) The Riverside Inn, recognized for its excellent food at reasonable prices by patrons who will make reservations months in advance to entertain guests there but not to settle for another local eatery.

   (E) As recognized, the Riverside Inn, which is excellent in food and reasonable in price, has reservations made months in advance by patrons who want to entertain guests there, rather than settling for another local eatery.

5. **Establishing a regular exercise routine is both a challenge because of the demands of our busy daily schedules <u>but the rewards of strenuous physical activity make it a pleasure as well</u>.**

    (A) but the rewards of strenuous physical activity make it a pleasure as well

    (B) although it is a pleasure as well because of the rewards of strenuous physical activity

    (C) and its rewards make strenuous physical activity a pleasure as well

    (D) while having such rewards as to make strenuous physical activity also a reward

    (E) and a pleasure because of the rewards of strenuous physical activity

6. <u>**Reading the draft of his term paper in the morning, it needed much more revision than Sam had thought**</u> **when he looked at it the night before.**

    (A) Reading the draft of his term paper in the morning, it needed much more revision than Sam had thought

    (B) Reading the draft of his term paper in the morning, Sam realized that it needed much more revision than he had thought

    (C) Having read the draft of his term paper in the morning, it needed much more revision, Sam thought, than

    (D) Sam read the draft of his term paper in the morning, it needed much more revision than he had thought

    (E) Reading the draft of his term paper, it needed, the next morning, much more revision than Sam had thought

7. Unemployment rates in our state have increased dramatically during the recession—<u>in some cities by as much as 20 percent in the last two years</u>.

   (A) in some cities by as much as 20 percent in the last two years
   (B) which, in some cities, the increase amounts to 20 percent in the last two years
   (C) increasing the equivalent of 20 percent in the last two years, at least in some cities
   (D) in some cities having 20 percent more unemployment in the last two years
   (E) in some cities increasing about 20 percent in the last two years biennially

8. The students polled at our high school professed more interest in technical fields than <u>liberal arts</u>.

   (A) liberal arts
   (B) liberal arts fields
   (C) compared to liberal arts
   (D) in liberal arts
   (E) liberal arts ones

9. The main ideas in the newspaper article about dinosaurs <u>was that giant dinosaurs with feathers had once existed and their feathers may have served as insulation or as display plumage</u>.

   (A) was that giant dinosaurs with feathers had once existed and their feathers may have served as insulation or as display plumage
   (B) was the existence of giant dinosaurs with feathers and what they might have served as, namely insulation or display plumage
   (C) were giant dinosaurs with feathers having once existed and insulation or display plumage as their possible purpose
   (D) was that giant dinosaurs with feathers had once existed and their feathers possibly serving as insulation or display plumage
   (E) were that dinosaurs with feathers had once existed and that their feathers may have served as insulation or as display plumage

10. Singing together in perfect harmony with beautifully matched voices, Tim and Alanna were determined <u>to be the best duet teams</u> in the competition.

    (A) to be the best duet teams
    (B) to be the best duet team
    (C) to being the best duet team
    (D) at being the best of the duet teams
    (E) at having been the best duet teams

11. Sara, a brilliant engineer, has applied for a job with the company **Atlantic Systems, they produce** fiber-optic equipment.

    (A) Atlantic Systems, they produce

    (B) Atlantic Systems, it produces

    (C) Atlantic Systems, which produces

    (D) Atlantic Systems; for the producing of

    (E) Atlantic Systems is producing

12. Having trained and practiced for six months, **that the basketball coach decided not to choose him for the varsity team frustrated Darren greatly**.

    (A) that the basketball coach decided not to choose him for the varsity team frustrated Darren greatly

    (B) the basketball coach's deciding not to choose him for the varsity team was a great frustration for Darren

    (C) Darren was greatly frustrated by the basketball coach's decision not to choose him for the varsity team

    (D) Darren's great frustration resulted from the basketball coach deciding not to choose him for the varsity team

    (E) Darren's frustration at the basketball coach's deciding not to choose him for the varsity team was great

13. Recent information from hotels and travel agents **reveal that tourists want to travel to places** within a hundred-mile-radius of home these days.

    (A) reveal that tourists want to travel to places

    (B) reveal tourists that want to travel to places

    (C) reveals tourists wanting traveling to places

    (D) reveals that tourists want to travel to places

    (E) is revealing in that tourists are wanting to travel in places

The SAT Advantage

14. **Mayor Binns of Greenville has a tendency to accept speaking engagements only within the city limits, and** last week he spoke to a conference in Ashland.

　　(A) Mayor Binns of Greenville has a tendency to accept speaking engagements only within the city limits, and

　　(B) Although Mayor Binns of Greenville has a tendency to accept speaking engagements only within the city limits,

　　(C) Mayor Binns has a tendency to accept speaking engagements only within the city limits,

　　(D) As Mayor Binns of Greenvile has a tendency to accept speaking engagements only within the city limits,

　　(E) While Mayor Binns of Greenville has a tendency to accept speaking engagements only within the city limits, however,

PRACTICE TEST 3 ANSWER KEY

Section 1 (Writing)

Section 2 (Critical Reading)

1. D
2. D
3. D
4. B
5. A
6. C
7. E
8. A
9. A
10. A
11. B
12. D
13. A
14. E
15. B
16. C
17. A
18. A
19. B
20. C
21. A
22. B
23. C
24. A

Section 3 (Mathematics)

1. D
2. E
3. A
4. E
5. B
6. E
7. D
8. D
9. B
10. E
11. B
12. D
13. D
14. A
15. E
16. B
17. D
18. B
19. D
20. E

Section 4 (Critical Reading)

1. E
2. B
3. D
4. A
5. B
6. C
7. A
8. B
9. C
10. B
11. D
12. E
13. B
14. E
15. C
16. D
17. C
18. C
19. B
20. A
21. B
22. E
23. C
24. A

Section 5 (Mathematics)

1. D
2. A
3. D
4. E
5. C
6. B
7. D
8. B
9. 2
10. 20
11. 2
12. 2 or 1/2
13. 6
14. 1
15. 40
16. 1/3
17. 3
18. 5760

Section 6 (Writing)

1. C
2. B
3. A
4. D
5. E
6. D
7. A
8. B
9. C
10. C
11. A
12. B
13. E
14. A
15. D
16. B
17. C
18. B
19. B
20. C
21. A
22. E
23. A
24. E
25. B
26. A
27. D
28. E
29. B
30. C
31. E
32. C
33. B
34. E
35. A

Section 7 (Critical Reading)

1. D
2. C
3. B
4. E
5. A
6. C
7. A
8. C
9. B
10. D
11. C
12. A
13. B
14. E
15. C
16. B
17. D
18. D
19. E

Section 8 (Mathematics)

1. C
2. C
3. B
4. A
5. B
6. D
7. B
8. D
9. A
10. C
11. B
12. A
13. A
14. C
15. E
16. D

Section 9 (Writing)

1. D
2. C
3. A
4. C
5. E
6. B
7. A
8. D
9. E
10. B
11. C
12. C
13. D
14. B

PRACTICE TEST 3
ANSWER RATIONALES

The SAT Advantage

SECTION 1 (WRITING)

ESSAY

Excellent Quality Sample Essay (Score: 6 out of 6) Rationale

This essay is excellent because it shows mastery of the essay writing process. The writer has chosen the classic "five paragraph essay" format. The first sentence of each paragraph could be taken alone and formed into a cohesive paragraph that is a summary of the essay's points.

The writer reasons his or her way through the issue, presenting thoughts about both points of view. Although the essay maintains that profits are important and the reason for a corporation's existence, the writer also places great value on corporations' social responsibility and comes up with a "best case scenario" conclusion. The development of thought in this essay shows a progression from the position stated at the beginning to the conclusion.

The writer uses appropriate and specific vocabulary. "profit motive," "prosperity," "benefits," "stimulate the economy," "best case scenario," "unsafe work practices," and "failing to provide" are all examples of clear and concise vocabulary usage.

The writer brings in information that goes beyond the information provided in the excerpt. That is, the writer engages in some original thinking. He or she develops ideas regarding pollution and safety and the benefits corporations bring to communities through employing community members.

The writer varies sentence structure to keep the reading experience interesting. He or she uses simple sentences such as "This is the best case scenario"; compound sentences such as "It is true that corporations make money in a society, and prosperity helps many people; yet corporations have responsibilities to the public too"; and complex sentences "If a corporation engages in unsafe work practices to save money and make more profits, such as failing to provide hard hats or hard shoes to workers, someone may be badly injured and they may even die."

The writer also uses the device of a rhetorical question to make a point: "Should such a corporation pollute a river or ignore safety standards just to make enough profits to employ people?"

Due to its clarity, good structure, sound reasoning, and variety of word usage and sentence structure, this essay classifies as an excellent one.

Medium Quality Sample Essay (Score: 3 – 4 out of 6) Rationale

This essay takes a position and each point is made in support of the writer's point of view, which is stated in the first paragraph. This is a strength of the essay.

The essay shows some development of thought as the writer explores corporations doing good things such as helping the community, cleaning up the environment, etcetera. It takes into account a company's online reputation. The conclusion is firm and in harmony with the opening statements of the essay and with the essay's development.

The development of thought is limited, though. The essay writer says "Corporations should be good to the public" and "People like to know that a corporation does good things" but does not develop much what being good to the public and doing good things would look like. The writer does mention cleaning up the environment, but there is an overuse of over-simplified thinking, such as using the phrase "If you hear about a corporation doing something bad" without giving an example of what "doing bad" might be. The writer also talks about a situation in which a corporation "makes a mess," which is very non-specific and could mean a number of things. A clear example of "making a mess" would be very helpful and would strengthen the point.

The writer uses some appropriate vocabulary, such as "exploit," "five star ratings" and "customer feedback." However, the vocabulary is limited and there is much repetition. "The public" is overused, especially in the first paragraph. The terms "good" and "bad" are used too much. More specific and varied vocabulary, accompanied by examples, would improve the essay.

The essay does not progress as well as an excellent essay would. For example, the paragraph about customer feedback on the Internet is not clear. The writer seems to be talking about the products of a company rather than the company's behavior. That paragraph seems almost like a digression.

The essay does not consider another point of view. There is little critical thinking. Rather than proving points, the essay writer tends to rely strongly on opinion and assertion: "Corporations should" is a repeated thought, with little well-reasoned support for why they should do the things recommended.

For all these reasons, this is a medium quality essay.

Low Quality Sample Essay (Score: 1 – 2 out of 6) Rationale

This essay is poorly organized and shows little development of thought. The first, third, and fifth paragraphs do make statements that are followed by supporting and related thoughts, but some of the thoughts are only loosely related. The other paragraphs make random statements that are not clearly related to the previous paragraphs. There is little progression of thought throughout the essay.

Many of the sentences are simple sentences: "Sometimes they make huge profits," "That isn't fair," "They have to be fair," "Pollution is serious business," "Most people want to be rich," "Many of us will work for corporations," "That is not a bad thing." There are quite a few mistakes in sentence construction.

Some of the reasoning is not clear. For example, "Look at all the fancy buildings they have. If those were built by workers who were not paid, where are they now?" It is not clear who the "they" is in either sentence, although the reader assumes it is "corporations" in the first sentence. The thought is not complete; the reader does not understand the writer's point.

The simplistic, undeveloped quality of this essay makes it a low quality essay. The writer seems to be throwing out thoughts and opinions without properly supporting them with examples or further thought development or reasoning. The overall impression is a random set of thoughts written down on paper without much care.

The SAT Advantage

SECTION 2 (CRITICAL READING)

SENTENCE COMPLETION

1. Answer: (D) tacit
Since Christopher "had always assumed" that Sharon knew his feelings, the reader may surmise that he had not spoken to her explicitly about them or about any future plans. Therefore, an "expressed" (A) or "outspoken" (E) agreement is unlikely. "Revised" (C) means to alter or improve upon review. The couple clearly did not have an agreement to be reviewed or altered. An "illicit" (B) agreement would be an illegal or immoral one, so that answer does not fit. "Tacit" (D) means unspoken or not expressed in words and yet understood. "Tacit" fits in well with the meaning of the sentence that this young man thought they had an unspoken yet understood agreement.

2. Answer: (D) discrepancies
Because the chief executive officer "frowned" and questioned whether the figures were "accurate," there would not be "similarities" (A) or "relevancies" (C), as these would show accuracies. "Descriptions" (B) usually do not appear in an accounts ledger, and descriptions would have nothing to do with accuracy. Likewise, "formulas" (E) would not affect the accuracy of the accounts either. "Discrepancies" (D) mean that things are at variance; they do not fit together well or make sense together; they are inaccuracies. Answer (D) provides the most meaningful word.

3. Answer: (D) implicit
The key to the answer is the word "evasiveness": the client is not speaking clearly to his lawyer, so the lawyer has to "guess" what he means. This would eliminate answer (B) explicit, for "explicit" means something which is clear, with nothing left to be imagined. The adjective "specific" would fit the sentence in meaning and would describe the word "meaning" well, but "specificity" in answer (E) is a noun and cannot describe another noun; the sentence calls for an adjective. "Deficit," answer (C), refers to a shortage or shortfall of something, so does not fit the sentence, and "complicit" (A) is to take part in something unsavory. "Implicit" (D) means implied meaning. If the client is full of "evasiveness," the lawyer has to "guess" at his implied or "implicit" meaning.

4. Answer: (B) secluded ... encroached
The clue to the first missing word is in the phrase "on the isolated shores of a lake" later in the sentence. A home in such a setting would be "secluded," as in answer (B), not "urban" as in answer (A) or "suburban" as in answer (C). An "excluded" home (D) does not make sense, as excluded means "to be left out." The clue to the second missing word is the phrase that tells how the couple and their dogs "suffered" when his fans did something related to invading their privacy. The phrase "encroached on" means to intrude or to overstep into the rights or boundaries of another, so (B) is the correct answer. "Invaded" (A), "pillaged" (D), and "pirated" (E) are not used with the preposition "on," so they are incorrect. Although "practiced" (C) is used with the preposition "on", we have eliminated (C) because of the inappropriate first word answer "suburban." Only answer (B) provides two accurate answers that make sense in the context of the sentence.

5. Answer: (A) sumptuous ... surfeited
If the guests "could not possibly eat the dessert," they must have been filled up by a great feast. The first missing word should describe a great feast, so "sumptuous" (A) and "marvelous" (C)

are possibilities. All the other answers for the first missing word describe a feast that leaves something to be desired. The second missing word needs to describe how the guests were after they ate, so (C) "hungry" does not fit, since the guests were unable to go on to eat dessert. Answer (A) describes a sumptuous banquet that more than satisfied the guests. "Surfeit" is more than enough, so "surfeited" them, is the correct second word.

6. Answer: (C) complicit … conciliatory

Because Marcia is "repentant," she clearly regrets having been a party to the exclusion of Beth. Having been a party to or part of something wrong is the definition of the word "complicit" (C), so complicit is a good candidate for the first missing word. The fact that Marcia is "repentant" also means that she would likely want to soothe Beth's anger at not being invited. When we think of how a repentant Marcia might be in order to ascertain the second missing word, the word "conciliatory" (C) means to try to be friendly, agreeable, and to pacify or appease. It makes sense, along with its partner word "complicit" in the context and meaning of the sentence.

7. Answer: (E) vanquished … imploded

The sentence is contrasting "invading enemies" to "forces within." We can surmise that the Soviet Union was defeated somehow not by outside forces but from forces which caused a collapse within it. Synonyms for "defeated" are "conquered" (A), "pacified" (B), and "vanquished" (E). The second missing word, though, must imply a collapse of some sort. To say that the "economic and political systems" "cohered" (A) or "gelled" (B) means that they blended or came together well, so these answers can be eliminated. To "implode" means to "collapse inward," so answer (E) is the best combination of answers.

8. Answer: (A) juxtaposition

The word "equals" in the phrase "love equals loss" implies that "love" and "loss" are placed side by side in the movie. The statement that "every time someone loves another" that person "meets his or her doom" also implies that "love and death" are paired in the movie. This literary process is called "juxtaposition" (A) where two things or ideas are placed next to one another or side by side. "Adjacent" (D) means the same thing, but in the sentence, we need a noun in the missing space, for the preceding article "the" tells us we are going to be discussing a noun or pronoun. Since "love equals death" according to the sentence, we would not be talking about "dissimilarities" (C) or "contrast" (B) or "verticality" (E) since that implies something different from or higher than another.

READING BASED QUESTIONS

9. Answer: (A) the main character of a story

"Protagonist" is a term used in analyzing literature; it means the principal character of a story by whom or around whom most of the action of the story revolves. A protagonist may be a hero but not necessarily so; he or she may also be an anti-hero or even a villain, so answer (B) is incorrect. The audience may not be on the protagonist's side, so answer (D) is incorrect. In spite of starting with the same first three letters, "protagonist" and "professional" are not alike in meaning, nor does a protagonist necessarily have anything to do with law, so answer (E) is incorrect. Likewise, in spite of the similarity of the spelling of protagonist with "agony," the two terms are unrelated in modern meaning, so answer (C) is incorrect. A protagonist is simply the main character of a story, so answer (A) is correct.

The SAT Advantage

10. Answer: (A) a pejorative term
All languages are cultural constructions, so (B) is correct in a general sense, but the paragraph is too specific for (B) to be the correct answer. There is nothing in these lines that implies that the term lawyer is inaccurate, so (C) is incorrect. There is nothing that implies that lawyer is a "flattering term" either, so answer (D) is also incorrect. Although making fun of lawyers is demonstrated in the humorous quote from the movie Hook, the paragraph contains other serious perceptions of lawyers, so (E) is inaccurate. A "pejorative term" (A) means a term that has negative connotations, which is precisely the point of these lines. For example, the lines say their work is sometimes perceived as "inherently immoral" and that they are also sometimes perceived as "money-grubbing tricksters".

11. Answer: (B) an ambivalent cultural portrait of lawyers
These lines describe a cultural perception of lawyers arising from a famous piece of literature. It is not an entirely negative cultural perception, though, so answer (A) is inaccurate as evidenced by the words that "both have private lives of some warmth and charity." No points are made in the lines about fiction, so answers (D) and (E) are inaccurate; there is no mention of historical records either, so answer (C) is inaccurate. An "ambivalent cultural portrait of lawyers" (B) would be a cultural portrait that is contradictory. Since "hard-nosed lawyers" who are "money-chasing, heartless lawyers" is a strong contrast to lawyers who "both have private lives of some warmth and charity", this is indeed an "ambivalent cultural portrait of lawyers" (B).

12. Answer: (D) well-being and charitable, respectively
The author talks about lawyers being dissatisfied because of "a lack of a sense that they are contributing to the social good." Caring about justice and "the public weal" means "they were idealistic and wanted to help people." This must mean that they care about people's welfare or well-being, so answers (B) and (D) are both candidates. Pro bono is a Latin term meaning "for the good," which fits in with the idea of "charitable" work (D). These lines imply that pro bono work is the same as "volunteering to help those who cannot afford legal counsel," which would be charitable activity, so answer (D) is the best answer.

13. Answer: (A) supporting points about lawyer's motivations by citing surveys done by the American Bar Association
These lines specifically mention "Surveys by the American Bar Association" and "ABA surveys of lawyers" to discuss motivational issues in lawyers, so we know that these surveys are a reference for the material. This would point to answer (A). The ABA is not an "outside agency" as in answer (D). There is no reason to believe that the surveys done by such a prestigious organization would be "erroneous" or "unscientific" as in answer (B) or that the ABA would produce data "purporting to represent most lawyers" (C) rather than being really representative. While the passage certainly endorses pro bono work by lawyers, there is no mention that lawyers do "a great deal of their work for free" as in answer (E). For all these reasons, answer (A) is the correct one.

14. Answer: (E) Both sets of lines discuss the professional longevity of lawyers who contribute to charity and have warm relationships in their private lives
Much of the language in answer (E) is matched in the passage. The author refers to "longevity in the legal profession" and uses the words "last the longest at their profession." These lines are both referring to "professional longevity" as in answer (E). They are not discussing "physical longevity" so answer (A) can be eliminated. The author uses the words "warmth and charity" and also mentions "charity" and cultivating "warm, loving, human relationships." These references also match the language of answer (E) "contribute to charity" and "have warm

relationships in their private lives". That these factors "may hold a key to longevity in the legal profession" is a hint that this theme will be expanded on in the essay, as indeed it is throughout.

15. Answer: (B) today's business leaders see the global marketplace as an "imagination economy"
Both authors mention that business leaders see the global marketplace as an "imagination economy." Passage 1 says, "Creativity is considered to be of paramount importance in the business world. Business leaders say we have entered the 'imagination economy.'" Passage 2 says, "The leaders in today's business industries absolutely love the word 'innovation'" then goes on to say, "Innovation is thought to be the main driving force of today's 'imagination economy.'"

16. Answer: (C) creativity and innovation are synonymous
In Passage 1 the author says, "Creativity and innovation are synonymous," so we know the author's viewpoint on that. In Passage 2 the author says, "Although the words 'innovation' and 'creativity' are used interchangeably, they are demonstrably different." The author goes on to say, "Creativity is but the beginning of a process...Innovation is the process of bringing creative ideas down to earth and into marketable commodities." This distinction shows that the author of Passage 2 does not agree with the author of Passage 1 that creativity and innovation are the same thing.

17. Answer: (A) Edison's practical ideas were only a percentage of his creative ideas
The author of Passage 1 believes that if creative people were found and allowed to think, they would come up with enough ideas that some of them would be practical. This is evidenced by the lines, "If we can find the inventive Edisons among the throng, we should pay them millions and millions of dollars just to sit and think," coupled with the idea that, "Surely out of thousands of new ideas, as with Edison's, some will be useful." The sentence, "Out of thousands of new ideas...some will be useful," implies that the author thinks a certain percentage of ideas will be useful, and he compares this with Edison's thousands of ideas: "as with Edison's". The author also notes in that "Edison owned over a thousand patents for creative ideas, many of which were never put to practical use," showing that the author believes only a percentage of Edison's creative ideas were practical.

18. Answer: (A) to exhort and excite
The author of Passage 1 has come up with an idea as to how to introduce more creative thinking into business. The author is excited about this idea as shown when the author suggests "If we can find the inventive Edisons among the throng, we should pay them millions and millions of dollars just to sit and think." The author is becoming exhortatory, that is, trying to incite the reader to do something: "Let us find the lights of modern geniuses. With their brilliant creativity, they too can 'light up the world' and generate innovation." The author uses the repetition of initial consonants, known as alliteration, to continue to exhort and excite: "Let's by all means corral some creative talent and let their fountains flow."

19. Answer: (B) creativity is not the same thing as innovation; innovation is always channeled to practical inventions that can become market commodities
Passage 1 seems to suggest that creativity, if allowed to flow, will in and of itself bring about the kind of innovation businesses seek. The author says, "If innovation is the spark of the new economy, let's by all means corral some creative talent and let their fountains flow." The author of Passage 2, though, makes a distinction between creativity and innovation. In Passage 2, the author states, "Although the words 'innovation' and 'creativity' are used interchangeably, they

are demonstrably different," so the reader knows that part of the language of answer (B) matches that author's opinion.

Passage 2 says, "Innovation is the process of bringing creative ideas down to earth and into marketable commodities" which is language similar to that in answer (B). The author of Passage 2 also makes the point that, "The interesting thing about Edison is that he was not just a creative thinker. His genius was channeled into inventing practical things."

Creativity, in the author of Passage 2's mind, is the initial point on the continuum toward innovation, and innovation results in practical inventions. Passage 2 says, "Creativity is the mental inception; innovation is the physical substance. Innovation always has a practical, usable, even user-friendly side to it." All this language relates to the language in answer (B).

20. Answer: (C) innovative ways

The passage is not referring to "revolutionary ways" in the sense of politics, so answers (A) and (B) are incorrect. "Mundane" (D) means usual, every day, tied-to-the-earth, so it is not akin to "revolutionary" thinking. The business phrase "outside the box" means thinking that avoids insularity and "same old" thinking, so "inside the box" thinking (E) would be counterproductive. By process of elimination and the similarity of the word "innovative" to "innovation," we can see that (C) is the best answer.

21. Answer: (A) the inventions of these men touched and improved people's daily lives

In Passage 2, the author says in reference to Edison, "He made our daily lives more enjoyable and safer." This shows that the author believed Edison "improved people's daily lives" as in answer (A). The author goes on to say, "No wonder people were grateful to him when he died—his creative genius touched our lives in truly hands-on ways." In reference to Jobs, the author says, "Because he touched our daily lives with the practical results of his creative genius, when Jobs died, many people felt a sense of personal loss as well as a sense of gratitude." Again, this shows that answer (A), with its language about "the inventions of these men touched and improved people's daily lives" matches the author's ideas about why people feel grateful toward inventors like Edison and Jobs.

22. Answer: (B) worked with already existing inventions and created new things of his own

The author of Passage 2 makes the point that, "Jobs did not even create the computer," showing that Jobs worked with already existing inventions as in answers (A) and (B). However, since the author mentions "the creative genius of Steve Jobs," answer (A) is not correct, as it states that the author thought Jobs was not creative. Passage 2 mentions how downsizing the computer and making it affordable and user-friendly "spawned" the "personal computer revolution" and "revolutionized" the lives of people. This would seem to indicate answer (D), but the author of Passage 2 does not use the phrase "put the world in our pockets." We have eliminated answers (A) and (D). There is no mention of Apple being insular, so answer (E) is also incorrect. The author outlines Jobs's major innovations and inventions, so it is clear that the author of Passage 2 thinks Steve Jobs worked with already existing inventions and created new things of his own as well (B).

23. Answer: (C) creative artists such as painters, musicians, sculptors, writers, poets, etcetera

Thomas Edison figures importantly in both Passages 1 and 2, so answer (A) is incorrect. Likewise, business leaders who see the global marketplace as "an imagination economy" figure in both Passages, so answer (B) is also incorrect. "Consumers who prefer innovative products"

(D) are not "creative people," so answer (D) is incorrect. "Tinkerers" are only mentioned in Passage 2, so answer (E) is incorrect. Creative people such as (C) painters, musicians, sculptors, writers, poets, etcetera, are mentioned in Passage 1 but not at all in Passage 2, so answer (C) is correct.

24. Answer: (A) people who toy around with inventions that never make it out into the real world

Much of Passage 2 is devoted to the idea that innovation, as opposed to creativity, brings about real and marketable results. These lines show this: "Innovation is the process of bringing creative ideas down to earth and into marketable commodities." Later lines say, "The interesting thing about Edison is that he was not just a creative thinker. His genius was channeled into inventing practical things" and Edison "vowed at that point never to create or invent something that had no market value." About Steve Jobs, the author says, "Because he touched our daily lives with the practical results of his creative genius, when Jobs died, many people felt a sense of personal loss as well as a sense of gratitude." The author sees the practical worldly applications of Edison's and Jobs's work as an important part of their value. They were not just people who invented useless things for the fun of it, i.e., they were not people "who toy around with inventions that never make it out into the real world," answer (A).

SECTION 3 (MATHEMATICS)

MULTIPLE CHOICE

1. Answer: (D) 12

He's going to divide 9 m into $\frac{3}{4}$ m pieces, so you need to divide 9 by $\frac{3}{4}$. To divide by $\frac{3}{4}$, flip the fraction, and then multiply: $9 \times \frac{4}{3} = 12$.

2. Answer: (E) 486

To find 8% of 450, multiply 0.08 by 450. The result, 36, is the increase. To find the total enrollment in 2008, add 36 and 450: 450 + 36 = 486.

3. Answer: (A) 4

Substitute 16 for c:

$16b = 48$

$b = 3$

Substitute 3 for b:

$3a = 12$

$a = 4$

4. Answer: (E) 30-60-90

Since the sum of the angles in a triangle equals 180°, add the angles and set their sum equal to 180°.

$6x + 4x + 2x = 180$

$12x = 180$

$x = 15$

Substitute 15 for x in each angle:

$6 \times 15 = 90$

$4 \times 15 = 60$

$2 \times 15 = 30$

The triangle is a special right triangle called a 30-60-90 triangle.

5. Answer: (B) increases approximately linearly

Looking at the table carefully, you will notice that the sunrise time gets earlier and the sunset time gets later as the days go on. In the 9 days from May 1st to May 10th, the length of the day increases by 2 or 3 minutes every day. The change in day length on each successive day in minutes: 3, 3, 2, 2, 3, 2, 2, 2, 2. This indicates that the increase happens at a more or less constant rate, i.e., it is approximately linear. If the increase had been exponential, the day length would have grown faster and faster as the days went on.

6. Answer: (E) 2.5%

The change in the length of the day from May 1st to May 10th = 3 + 3 + 2 + 2 + 3 + 2 + 2 + 2 + 2 = 21 minutes.

The length of the day on May 1st from 6:27 AM to 8:32 PM = 14 hrs 5 min = 845 minutes.

Percentage change in day length = $\frac{21}{845}$ x 100 = 2.5%

7. Answer: (D) 100

To find the average of the three tests, let x equal the final test score:

$$\frac{75+65+x}{3} = 80$$

$$\frac{140+x}{3} = 80$$

$$140 + x = 240$$

$$x = 100$$

8. Answer: (D) $\frac{49}{4}$

A trinomial is an expression with three unlike terms. A trinomial is a square when it is in the form of $(a+b)^2 = a^2 + 2ab + b^2$. To make $x^2 + 7x + s$ a trinomial square, it is necessary to complete the square. Since in this case $a = 1$, to write the final term, multiply the middle coefficient, 7, by $\frac{1}{2}$ and square the product:

$$x^2 + 7x + (7 \times \frac{1}{2})^2$$

$$x^2 + 7x + \frac{49}{4}$$

9. Answer: (B) $-2x^2 - 7x + 10$

Subtract $4x^2 + 2x - 7$ from $2x^2 - 5x + 3$ to find the missing addend:

$(2x^2 - 5x + 3) - (4x^2 + 2x - 7) = -2x^2 - 7x + 10$

10. Answer: (E) 80°

When parallel lines are intersected by a transversal (line t in the diagram), groups of congruent and supplementary angles are formed. $\angle 2$ and $\angle 7$ are called alternate exterior angles and they have equal measures. Set their measures equal to each other and solve for x.

$4x - 20 = 2x + 40$

$2x = 60$

$x = 30$

Replace 30 for x in either equation to find the measure of $\angle 2$ or $\angle 7$.

$4(30) - 20 = 100$

$m\angle 2 = m\angle 7 = 100°$

$\angle 2$ and $\angle 4$ form a linear pair of angles. A linear pair of angles is a pair of adjacent, supplementary angles. Since the sum of supplementary angles is 180°, add 100° to the measure of $\angle 4$ and set the sum equal to 180.

$100 + m\angle 4 = 180$

$m\angle 4 = 80$.

11. Answer: (B) II only

Write the elements of the data set in order:

0, 1, 1, 1, 1, 2, 2, 3, 4, 5, 5, 5, 7, 7, 14, 17, 23, 36

The most frequently occurring value, 1, is the mode. Since every other element occurs fewer times than 1, there is no other mode. Hence option I is incorrect.

There are 18 elements in the data set. The median is the average of the two middle numbers 4 and 5. So the median is 4.5. This is clearly greater than the mode. Hence option II is correct.

The mean value of this data set = (1 + 1 + 1 + 1 + 2 + 2 + 3 + 4 + 5 + 5 + 5 + 7 + 7 + 14 + 17 + 23 + 36)/18 = $\frac{134}{18}$ = 7.44. So option III is incorrect.

12. Answer: (D) 12

If Ethan is x years old now, his sister is 2x years old. Four years from now, Ethan will be x + 4 years old and his sister will be 2x + 4 years old. From the information given,

$$x+4 = \frac{5}{8}(2x+4)$$
$$8(x+4) = 5(2x+4)$$
$$8x+32 = 10x+20$$
$$2x = 12$$
$$x = 6$$

So Ethan is 6 years old and his sister is 12.

13. Answer: (D) 75°

Two of the internal angles of the triangle shown can be found from the values of a and b.

The angle vertically opposite to a = 65°.

The angle supplementary to b = 180° – 140° = 40°.

Hence the third internal angle of the triangle = 180° – 65° – 40° = 75°.

This third angle is vertically opposite to angle c. Hence angle c is 75°.

14. Answer: (A) $n = n^2 - 8n + 10$

This problem does not require that the value of the variable be resolved. Rather, begin to solve the problem and check the answer choices each step of the way.

$$\sqrt{n+6} = n-4$$

Square both sides of the equation.
$$(\sqrt{n+6})^2 = (n-4)^2$$
$$n+6 = n^2 - 8n + 16$$
$$n-6+6 = n^2 - 8n + 16 - 6$$
$$n = n^2 - 8n + 10$$

15. Answer: (E) 60

The person running at 3 mph comes back to the starting point every $\frac{60}{3}$ = 20 minutes.

The person running at 5 mph comes back to the starting point every $\frac{60}{5}$ = 12 minutes.

They will meet at the starting point after a number of minutes that is a multiple of both 20 and 12. The multiples of 12 are 12, 24, 36, 48, 60, 72, and so on. The multiples of 20 are 20, 40, 60,

80, and so on. Hence the LCM (lowest common multiple) of 12 and 20 is 60. So the runners will meet again at the starting point after 60 minutes.

16. Answer: (B) 1

$f(x) = -3x^2$ is a downward-opening parabola with its vertex at (0,0). We know this because the coefficient of the x^2 term is negative. Also, the function is given in the vertex form $f(x) = K(x-a)^2 + b$ where (a, b) is the vertex. This function touches the x-axis only at the vertex point (0,0).

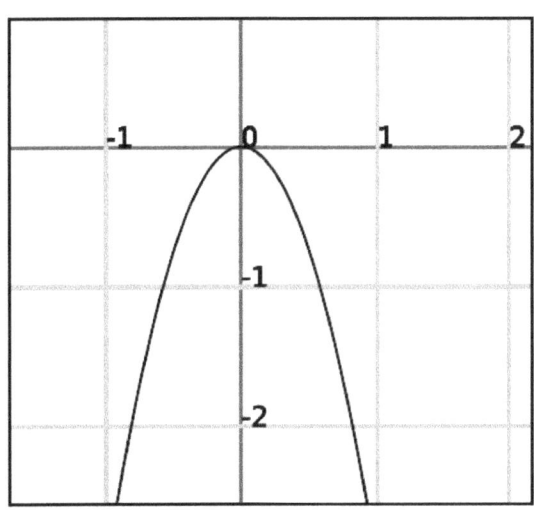

$f(x+3) = -3(x+3)^2$ is the above parabola moved 3 units to the left, i.e., the vertex of the parabola is at (-3,0). It still touches the x-axis at a single point since the transformation only moves the parabola in the x-direction and not in the y-direction.

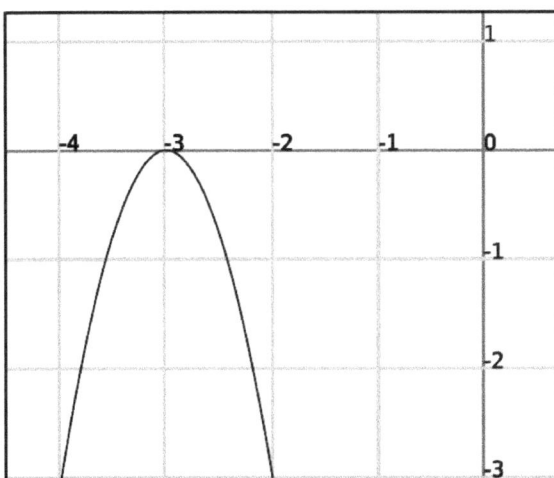

17. Answer: (D) $\frac{1}{2}$

The line 2ax + by = 3 forms a right triangle with the x and y axes. This triangle is isosceles if the two legs are equal, i.e., if the x and y intercepts of the line are equal.

The SAT Advantage

The x-intercept of the line when y = 0 is $x = \dfrac{3}{2a}$.

The y-intercept of the line when x = 0 is $y = \dfrac{3}{b}$.

Setting these equal to each other we get $\dfrac{3}{2a} = \dfrac{3}{b}$

Cross-multiplying, 3b = 6a; Dividing both sides by 3, 2a = b or $\dfrac{a}{b} = \dfrac{1}{2}$.

18. Answer: (B) $\sqrt{\pi}$

Let the cylindrical container have radius r and height h. Since the cubic container has the same height, the side of the cubic container is also h.

Both containers have the same volume. So $\pi r^2 h = h^3$.

Dividing both sides by h, $\pi r^2 = h^2$ or $\dfrac{h^2}{r^2} = \pi$ or $\dfrac{h}{r} = \sqrt{\pi}$.

19. Answer: (D) 6

To find the answer, we only need to know the units digit of each power of 2 since only the units digits will be added together to obtain the units digit of the sum.

The units digits of the first 10 powers of 2 are: 2, 4, 8, 6, 2, 4, 8, 6, 2, and 4. Adding these up we get 46 which has the units digit of 6.

20. Answer: (E) $\dfrac{1}{12}$

One-third of the students are girls. Since the choice of uniform color is not related to the gender of a student, we can assume that one-fourth of the girls and one-fourth of the boys are wearing blue uniforms. So the fraction of students who are girls wearing blue uniforms = $\dfrac{1}{4} \times \dfrac{1}{3} = \dfrac{1}{12}$. So the probability of a random student being a girl in a blue uniform = $\dfrac{1}{12}$.

The SAT Advantage

SECTION 4 (CRITICAL READING)

SENTENCE COMPLETION

1. Answer: (E) amiability
The key to the answer lies in the end of the sentence when the quality the politician has is described as "warm and friendly." "Amiability" (E) means friendliness and sociability in a person who is easy to get along with and easy to like. "Ability" (A) would be redundant with competent; "gullibility" (B) would mean easily fooled or taken in; "flexibility" (C) is not necessarily a "warm and friendly quality," nor is "litheness" (D) which means much the same thing as flexibility. By process of elimination and by word definition, (E) is the best answer.

2. Answer: (B) contravening
Since Raoul Wallenberg is described as a "rescuer" who is extending his "authority and protection as a Swedish diplomat," it is unlikely that he would be "endorsing" (A), "carrying out" (C), or "supporting" (E) orders to herd Hungarian Jews onto trains to the death camps. The word "rescinding" (D) means to take back or to breach a contract, but it implies that the person doing it was part of the original authority. Wallenberg, as a Swedish diplomat, would not be giving orders to Nazi SS guards, so he would not have been part of the original authority that gave the orders. Rather, Wallenberg was "contravening" (B) the orders, which means arguing against them or contradicting them.

3. Answer: (D) leavened
Because the sentence says the professor "challenged his students" and gave "astute and complex analyses," it seems the professor softens, eases, ameliorates, or mitigates this with "fascinating stories" and "humor." He would not make his analyses further "complicated" (A) or "obfuscated" (B), which means to make less clear. No professor would "jeopardize" or "devastate" his own analyses, as in answers (C) and (E). The word "leavened" (D) means to balance something or to ease or ameliorate the effects of something. If the professor "leavened" his astute and complex analyses with fascinating stories and humor, he balanced the complexity of his subject with things the students could relate to. Answer (D) makes sense in the context of the sentence.

4. Answer: (A) egalitarian … axiomatic
Since the phrase "all are created equal" describes the Declaration of Independence's declaration of ideals, by process of elimination, we can rule out that these ideals are "aristocratic" (B), "monarchical" (C), "plutocratic" (D), or "oligarchic" (E) as all of these adjectives refer to systems of inequality where birth, royal blood, wealth, or the power of a few refute the idea that all are created equal. What is more, the word "axiomatic" (A) is a synonym for "self-evident," which is the actual wording of the Declaration of Independence.

5. Answer: (B) congealed … obscure
The word "dense" describing the philosopher's writings gives the reader some clue as to what the first missing word is. Writings that are dense are not "pristine" (A) which means pure and untouched, nor are they "crystalline" (C) which means clear. They are not "porous" (E) because porosity allows liquid or other quantities in easily, and dense things are not porous. We are left with "congealed" (B) and "massive" (D) as candidates for the first missing word. "Congealed" matches "dense" as it means hardened into a rigid solid. What is more, the philosopher's meaning is hard to discern, full of "unclear thinking." Things that are unclear are "obscure" (B), and people who are not well-known are also considered obscure. An unclear thinking

philosopher would be obscure in both senses of the word. The combination of "congealed … obscure" (B) fits the sentence well.

READING BASED QUESTIONS

6. Answer: (C) they are very important to business success
The author says that the "soft" skill of group entry "has a great deal of significance when it comes to business networking." He or she also outlines how "business networking is the key to attaining jobs, gaining contracts, finding affiliates, and overall success." These lines show that the author's attitude toward these skills is (C) that they are very important to business success.

7. Answer: (A) confidence
"Aplomb" is synonymous with confidence; it also means with social dexterity, poise, and self-assurance; therefore, (A) is the correct answer.

8. Answer: (B) conformity to socially acceptable norms of dress is appropriate
The author uses the term "appropriately dressed." The language of answer (B) echoes this phrase. "Dress appropriately" is also used and the word "appropriate" appears again in a later line. Suggesting that people seek the opinions of others and information as to how to dress appropriately for an event shows that the author supports conformity to socially acceptable norms of dress and finds adherence to them "appropriate."

9. Answer: (C) the universal acceptance of a smile
Saying that people will "part…like the proverbial Red Sea" endorses the idea of a smile being universally acceptable as it alludes to ancient history. The phrases "it doesn't matter if you are in Shanghai or Chicago" and "the whole human race recognizes a smile" continue the theme of universality. A smile goes beyond time and location and affects "the whole human race." In other words, it is a universal key to social acceptance.

10. Answer: (B) because the subject of the essay is group entry skills
The opening lines state the subject of the essay, "Sociologists have a name for what happens when a person tries to become part of a gathered group of people: group entry skills." The lines are about attracting a group by arriving early and being available for questions. They describe a way to be a natural part of a group without having to exercise any group entry skills.

11. Answer: (D) people's natural tendency to gather and be sociable around food and drink
The author is giving advice to people who feel "lost" or intimidated at a networking event. The advice to "gravitate toward the refreshment table" is given because "it's easy to strike up a conversation with someone about the coffee, the snacks, where the cream is, etcetera." The word "easy" implies that people naturally are sociable and conversational around food and drink. The author also implies that many people will gather around the refreshment table: "everyone who comes to get refreshments is a candidate." All this adds up to the strategy being based on (D) people's natural tendency to gather and be sociable around food and drink.

12. Answer: (E) an understanding of human nature and human behavior in groups
The opening lines state the subject of the essay, "Sociologists have a name for what happens when a person tries to become part of a gathered group of people: group entry skills." Since sociology is the study of human behavior in groups, this is a key to the derivation of many of the strategies. Human nature, such as the tendency to be attracted to and sociable around food, is

also used to derive some of the strategies. Human nature is also recognized in the strategy of smiling: "the whole human race recognizes a smile."

13. Answer: (B) immature people tend to form cliques and practice exclusion
The author has given tips for basic human acceptance: "Be clean, well-groomed, friendly, and polite." The implication is that if a person is such, there is no reason for him or her to be rejected by a group. The word "mature" reassures the reader that well-behaved adults can be expected to accept him or her if he or she is "clean, well-groomed, friendly, and polite."

14. Answer: (E) 53 – 54
To speak figuratively means to speak symbolically, not literally. These lines do not literally mean that the person should "conquer" other groups: "Then you are on your way to the next group to conquer!" The essay is about gaining social skills so as to be accepted at networking events for business purposes. Any "conquering" means being socially winning and acceptable and being allowed to enter a group. Since the passage refers to business networking, "conquering" in the context of the passage might also mean "attaining jobs, gaining contracts, finding affiliates, and overall success."

15. Answer: (C) the change of the national war aim from a war against secession to a war against slavery
Although Douglass's article tells how to end the war, the article does not call for the end of the war. Rather, it tells *how* to end it by changing the war aim of the North. The passage states that the "cause of the North was 'Union' against the secession of Southern states." It is stated that Douglass "asserted" that the "banner," which would signify the North's cause, "should be the emancipation of slaves" instead.

16. Answer: (D) original
The word "primal" is related to the word "primary," which means first or original. Although "At that time, the cause of the North was 'Union' against the secession of Southern states," the passage goes on to state "secession was sparked by continuing disagreements between the region of the North and the region of the South about slavery and its expansion." Therefore, the original cause of the war was the nation's divisions over slavery, as Douglass points out with his use of the word "primal."

17. Answer: (C) impassioned
The use of an exclamation point at the end of this line, as well as the invocation of patriotism "waving from every loyal flag!" and the dramatic reference to "the smoke and fire of every battle field" indicate that Douglass has passionate feelings about what he is writing and wishes to appeal to the feelings of his readers.

18. Answer: (C) vehement
Douglass's language indicates that he feels very strongly about what he is advocating, making him "vehement" (C). By process of elimination, "veracious" (A) means "truthful," and while Douglass is truthful in content, the tone of the passage is different than content. "Voracious" (B) means of great appetite, and there is no evidence in the passage to show that. "Vespertine" (D) means of the evening, of which there is no mention in the passage, and "vocational" (E) means being called to a certain kind of work. The best word is "vehement" (C).

19. Answer: (B) the slaves and freemen
Douglass specifically calls for "slaves and free colored people" to be "called into service, and formed into a liberating army." These would be "slaves and freemen," as in answer (B).

20. Answer: (A) white resistance

Douglass says that most blacks' answer to the question of what they will do in the Civil War is "would to God you would let us do something!" He goes on to say, "We lack nothing but your consent. We are ready and would go." He later says, "But you won't let us go." Douglass is addressing the audience of his abolitionist newspaper, many of whom are white. The "you" he is referring to are white people who "won't let us go," therefore (A), white resistance, is the primary reason Douglass sees as obstructing the formation of black regiments.

21. Answer: (B) turn about is fair play

Douglass makes the point that Southerners have "not hesitated to employ the sable arms" of black men. They have used black men in a martial capacity "in erecting the fortifications which silenced the guns at Fort Sumter." They have used them to bring "the star-spangled banner to the dust." "They have no scruples against employing the Negroes to exterminate freedom." The implied reasoning here is that the North should do as the South is doing: "turn about is fair play" (B).

22. Answer: (E) psychological weapons

Douglass makes the point that "the very fact of color would be more terrible than powder and balls." "Powder and balls" refers to guns, artillery, and cannon. He is juxtaposing "the very fact of color" with "powder and balls" implying that he is talking about "the very fact of color" as a weapon. Since the South would be confronted with former slaves and freemen well aware of the injustices of slavery, it could well be imagined that this would have a powerful mental and emotional effect as "psychological weapons" (E).

23. Answer: (C) the slaves in the South

Since Douglass called for a "liberating army, to march into the South and raise the banner of Emancipation among the slaves," he is calling for an army to enter the South and liberate the slaves. Since he has called for an army of black men, i.e., former slaves and free men, to raise their "sable arms" in the cause of freedom, the term "brothers and sisters" refers to other black people in the South. The black people in the South at that time were slaves.

24. Answer: (A) accepting of the idea and giving them full credit for their brave deeds

Key words here are "According to the passage." It is likely that Lincoln worried about the black troops for a number of reasons, not least of which was that they would be "captured and put into slavery again" (E). He also likely worried that "they would be killed" (D) which is the danger every soldier faces in war, and that they might be "ill-supplied" (C) as well as possibly "hesitant to integrate the army" (B) in an era when there was a great deal of racism. However, according to the passage, "Abraham Lincoln did elect to raise black troops" and black troops "were credited by Abraham Lincoln as having helped to turn the tide of war toward victory for the Union and for human freedom." This shows that Lincoln's attitude toward black troops was (A) accepting of the idea and giving them full credit for their brave deeds.

The SAT Advantage

SECTION 5 (MATHEMATICS)

MULTIPLE CHOICE

1. Answer: (D) 480
Let x = the number of miles Lorna drove. Then $3x$ = the number of miles Lori drove.
$x + 300$ = the number of miles Lauren drove. The sum of these is 1100.

$x + 3x + x + 300 = 1100$; $5x + 300 = 1100$; $5x = 800$; $x = 160$. So Lorna drove 160 miles. Since Lori drove 3 times as much, she drove 480 miles.

2. Answer: (A) $\frac{1}{8}$

The fraction of pizza eaten = $\frac{3}{8} + \frac{1}{2}$. Expressing the two fractions using the common denominator 8, we can write the sum as $\frac{3}{8} + \frac{4}{8} = \frac{7}{8}$. So the fraction of pizza left = $1 - \frac{7}{8} = \frac{1}{8}$.

3. Answer: (D) -1
Small numbers can grow large quickly when cubed and squared. Use trial and error to test a few numbers.

$a = 3$ $b = 4$	$(3)^3(4)^2 = 27 \times 16 = 432$	Too small
$a = 5$ $b = 3$	$(5)^3(3)^2 = 125 \times 9 = 1125$	Too big
$a = 4$ $b = 3$	$(4)^3(3)^2 = 64 \times 9 = 576$	Correct values for a and b

Replace a and b with 4 and 3 respectively in the expression $2a - 3b$.

$2(4) - 3(3) = 8 - 9 = -1$

Another way to approach this problem would be to reduce 576 to its prime factors: $576 = 2^6 3^2$.

It's clear from this that the only choices that would satisfy $a^3 b^2 = 576$ are a = 4 and b = 3.

4. Answer: (E) 453
The sum of the measures of the interior angles of any polygon is found by using the formula $(n - 2)(180)$ where n is the number of sides. Since ABCDE is a pentagon, substitute 5 for n in the formula.

$(5 - 2)(180) = 540$.

Subtract 87 from 540 to find the sum of the measures of the remaining interior angles.

540 − 87 = 453.

5. Answer: (C) 72

The area of a square is found by using the formula $Area = s^2$, where s is the length of a side of the square. In the figure, the triangle and the square share $\overline{RT}$. Find the length of $\overline{RT}$ in ☐ and then input that value into the area formula for a square.

$\angle RTS$ and $\angle RTV$ are supplementary angles. The sum of the measures of supplementary angles is 180°. Given that $\angle RTS$ is a right angle, then $\angle RTV$ is also a right angle because 180 − 90 = 90.

The sum of the measures of the angles in a triangle is 180°. Add the measures of $\angle RTV$ and $\angle TRV$ and subtract their sum from 180 to find the measure of $\angle V$.

180 − (90 + 45) = 45.

The $m\angle V = 45°$, making ☐ a 45-45-90 triangle. The ratio of the sides of a 45-45-90 triangle is shown below.

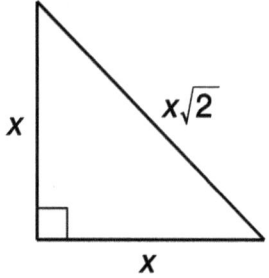

Find $\overline{RT}$ by setting 12, the hypotenuse in ☐, equal to $x\sqrt{2}$.

$x\sqrt{2} = 12$

$\dfrac{x\sqrt{2}}{\sqrt{2}} = \dfrac{12}{\sqrt{2}}$

$x = \dfrac{12}{\sqrt{2}} \times \dfrac{\sqrt{2}}{\sqrt{2}} = \dfrac{12\sqrt{2}}{2} = 6\sqrt{2}$

$x = RT = 6\sqrt{2}$

Input $6\sqrt{2}$ into the area formula for a square.

The SAT Advantage

$Area = s^2$

$Area = (6\sqrt{2})^2 = (36)(2) = 72$

6. Answer: (B) IV, V and VI
A contribution of more than half of the company's sales is shown by a total area that exceeds half the area of the circular pie chart. Of the options given, only the combination of departments IV, V, and VI adds up to more than half the area of the pie chart.

7. Answer: (D) I and III
Find the lengths of the 3 sides of the triangle using the distance formula
$d = \sqrt{(x_1-x_2)^2 + (y_1-y_2)^2}$.

Length of AB = $\sqrt{(4-0)^2 + (0-3)^2} = \sqrt{16+9} = \sqrt{25} = 5$.

Length of BC = $\sqrt{\left(\frac{36}{5}-0\right)^2 + \left(\frac{63}{5}-3\right)^2} = \sqrt{\frac{36^2}{5^2} + \frac{48^2}{5^2}} = \frac{12}{5}\sqrt{3^2+4^2} = \frac{12}{5} \times 5 = 12$.

Length of CA = $\sqrt{\left(\frac{36}{5}-4\right)^2 + \left(\frac{63}{5}-0\right)^2} = \sqrt{\frac{16^2}{5^2} + \frac{63^2}{5^2}} = \frac{1}{5}\sqrt{16^2+63^2} = \frac{1}{5} \times \sqrt{4225} = \frac{1}{5} \times 65 = 13$.

The triangle has sides 5, 12, and 13. So it is clearly not an isosceles triangle.

If it is a right triangle, the sides must satisfy the Pythagoras theorem, i.e., the square of the longest side must equal the sum of the squares of the other two sides. Check this:
$5^2 + 12^2 = 25 + 144 = 169 = 13^2$.

So ABC is a right triangle.

In this case, we can assume that one of the legs is the altitude of the triangle and the other leg is the base.

Therefore, the area of the triangle = $\frac{1}{2} \times 5 \times 12 = 30$ square units.

Hence options I and III are correct.

8. Answer: (B) 0 to $\frac{2}{3}$

Note that the function $2x-3x^2$ is a parabola that opens downwards since the x^2 term has a negative coefficient. If the vertex of the parabola lies above the x-axis, it will have positive values between the two points where the parabola intersects the x-axis.

The x coordinate of the vertex of parabola $ax^2 + bx + c$ is given by $x = -\dfrac{b}{2a}$.

For the parabola $-3x^2 + 2x$ the vertex is at $x = -\dfrac{2}{(-6)} = \dfrac{1}{3}$; $y = 2\left(\dfrac{1}{3}\right) - 3\left(\dfrac{1}{3}\right)^2 = \dfrac{2}{3} - \dfrac{1}{3} = \dfrac{1}{3}$.

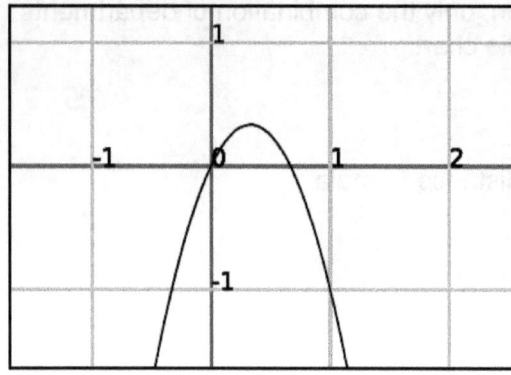

The range of positive values for the function is between the two points where the parabola crosses the x-axis. To find these values, we set the function equal to zero:

$2x - 3x^2 = 0$

$x(2 - 3x) = 0$

$x = 0$ or $2 - 3x = 0$

So the parabola crosses the x-axis at the points x = 0 and x = $\dfrac{2}{3}$ and the function has positive values within this range.

STUDENT-PRODUCED RESPONSE

9. Answer: 2

This problem can be solved using standard methods for systems of equations such as substitution or elimination. Notice, however, that the solution can be found very easily simply by adding the two equations together:

(2x + 3y) + (3x + 2y) = 3 + 7
5x + 5y = 10
5(x + y) = 10

Dividing both sides by 5 we get
x + y = 2

10. Answer: 20

Let the price of x oz. of the regular detergent be $1.

Since the new detergent contains 25% more for the same price, the quantity of new detergent available for $1 is 1.25x oz.

So the price of x oz. of the new detergent = $\$\dfrac{1}{1.25}$ = $0.80.

Hence the price of x oz. of the new detergent is $0.20 less than the $1 price of x oz. of the regular detergent.

Percentage reduction in price = $\dfrac{0.2}{1}$ x 100 = 20.

11. Answer: 2

$f(x) = x^2 - 3$ is the equation of a parabola. So it can cross the x-axis 0, 1, or 2 times depending on the position of its vertex on the y-axis.

Recall that $f(x) = x^2$ is a parabola with its vertex at the origin:

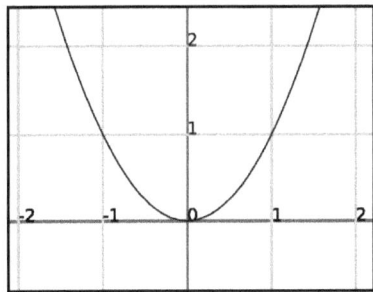

Adding -3 to the function transforms it by moving it 3 units downwards:

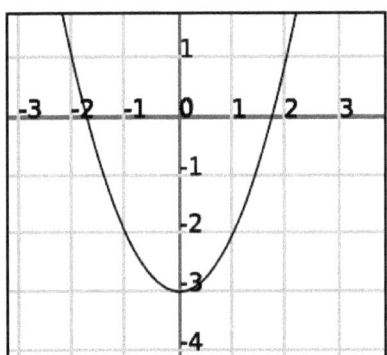

So the graph of the function crosses the x-axis at 2 separate points.

The SAT Advantage

12. Answer: 2 or $\frac{1}{2}$

Let the number be x. Based on the information given:
$5x = 2x^2 + 2$ or $2x^2 - 5x + 2 = 0$.

Factor the above equation to solve:

$2x^2 - 5x + 2 = (2x-1)(x-2) = 0$

$x = \frac{1}{2}$ or $x = 2$.

Some problems, like this one, may have more than one correct answer. Grid in any of the answers.

13. Answer: 6

First, visualize what the area looks like. To do that, reduce both equations to the slope-intercept form and find the x and y intercepts for the two lines.

$2x - 3y = 6 \Rightarrow 3y = 2x - 6 \Rightarrow y = \frac{2}{3}x - 2$

$2x + 3y = -6 \Rightarrow 3y = -2x - 6 \Rightarrow y = -\frac{2}{3}x - 2$

Notice that both lines have the same y-intercept y = -2.

The x-intercept for the first line is given by $\frac{2}{3}x - 2 = 0$; $\frac{2}{3}x = 2$; $2x = 6$; $x = 3$.

The x-intercept for the second line is given by $-\frac{2}{3}x - 2 = 0$; $\frac{2}{3}x = -2$; $2x = -6$; $x = -3$.

So this is what the area looks like:

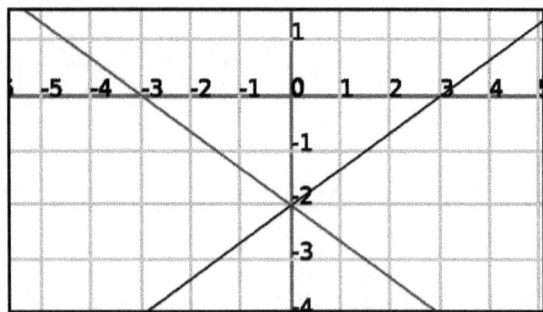

The area bounded by the x-axis and the two given lines is a triangle with height 2 and base length 6 (from -3 to 3). The size of the area = $\frac{1}{2} \times 6 \times 2 = 6$ square units.

The SAT Advantage

14. Answer: 1
Notice that the expression for b reduces to the one for a:

$$b = \frac{6x^2 + 4x}{2x} = \frac{6x^2}{2x} + \frac{4x}{2x} = 3x + 2 = a.$$

(It is fine to divide by 2x since x is not equal to zero.)

Since angles *a* and *b* are equal and they are corresponding angles, we can conclude that lines l and m are parallel.

This means that alternate exterior angles c and d are equal. Therefore $\frac{c}{d}$ = 1.

15. Answer: 40
Let x = the unknown number. Convert the percentages in the question into decimals to facilitate calculation.

140% of x = 1.4x

$1.4x = 70$

$\frac{1.4x}{1.4} = \frac{70}{1.4}$

$x = 50$

Find 80% of 50.

(0.8)(50) = 40

16. Answer: $\frac{1}{3}$

There are six ways in which Dan can pull out the marbles:
RRWW, RWRW, RWWR, WWRR, WRWR, WRRW

Of these six, only the following two do not include marbles of the same color in consecutive draws:

RWRW and WRWR

So the probability of not drawing out marbles of the same color consecutively = $\frac{2}{6}$, which reduces to $\frac{1}{3}$.

17. Answer: 3

The least possible value of n = 6 and the least possible value of n^2 = 36.

So k^3 must always be less than 100 − 36 = 64.

1^3 = 1, 2^3 = 8, 3^3 = 27, 4^3 = 64. So the maximum possible value of k = 3.

18. Answer: 5760

The 5 non-fiction books can be arranged in 5! = 1 x 2 x 3 x 4 x 5 = 120 ways.

The 4 fiction books can be arranged in 4! = 1 x 2 x 3 x 4 = 24 ways.

There are 2 ways the groups can be arranged: fiction first, then non-fiction or non-fiction first, then fiction.

So the total number of ways Max can arrange the books = 120 x 24 x 2 = 5760.

SECTION 6 (WRITING)

IMPROVING SENTENCES

1. Answer: (C) The owners of our local radio station, which was once the home of "oldies" music from previous decades, have
The sentence has a misplaced modifier: The opening phrase *Once the home of "oldies" music* describes *our local radio station*, not *the owners*. The first words after the opening phrase should be *our local radio station*. Choice (C) fixes the sentence correctly. Choice (B) fixes the modifier problem but is awkwardly worded, and the singular verb *has* does not agree with the subject *owners*. Choices (D) and (E) do not fix the misplaced modifier problem, and (E) is a fragment.

2. Answer: (B) is based on one of Arthur Conan Doyle's medical school professors, a man who
The sentence is a fragment because the past participle *based* cannot stand alone as the main verb in a sentence. Choice (B) corrects the problem by adding the helping verb *is* before the past participle *based*. Choices (C) and (D) do not make the fragment a complete sentence. Choice (E) correctly adds the helping verb *is*, but then introduces new errors by inserting a semicolon and the unnecessary awkward phrase *this man being someone*.

3. Answer: (A) Had Abraham Lincoln emancipated the slaves at the beginning of the Civil War,
The sentence is correct because it uses a logical sequence of tenses: *Had ... might have*. Although this is a sentence pattern we rarely hear in everyday speech, it is common in formal written English. The word *If* is understood: *If Abraham Lincoln had*. Choice (B) is incorrect because it does not convey that the choice Lincoln might have made had to occur *before* the possible result of that choice. The sequence of tenses in Choice (C) is not correct, although people commonly use this construction in everyday speech. *If he/she would have* is always incorrect. Choices (D) and (E) change the meaning of the sentence by suggesting that Lincoln did emancipate the slaves at the beginning of the Civil War, creating statements contrary to fact.

4. Answer: (D) however, a recent study
The use of a semicolon between the two independent clauses is correct, but this sentence also requires a conjunction to show that the information in the second clause is in contrast to the information in the first one. Choice (B) uses the conjunction *but* incorrectly after a semicolon. Choices (C) and (E) add conjunctions that do not prepare the reader for a contrast. Choice (D) correctly uses the conjunction *however*, followed by a comma, to introduce a contrast.

5. Answer: (E) have significantly increased its appeal
The underlined section is awkward and too wordy. Choice (E) expresses the same idea clearly and simply. Choices (B) and (C) are as awkward and wordy as the original. Choice (D) creates a fragment because it lacks a main verb that can stand on its own.

6. Answer: (D) Although high school seniors face increasing pressure to choose and train for specific careers,
The original sentence incorrectly joins two independent clauses with only a comma, and it does not convey the relationship between the ideas in the two clauses. This is another sentence in which the second clause presents information that is in contrast to the information in the first clause. Choice (D) begins with the conjunction *although*, which prepares the reader for a

contrast. Choices (B) and (E) do not convey the contrast between the ideas in the two clauses. Choice (C) merely changes the verb form in the first clause, which does not correct the original problems in the sentence.

7. Answer: (A) each with its own distinct responsibilities and certification requirements
The original sentence correctly places a modifying phrase after the word the phrase modifies: *specialties*. The pronoun *its* in the phrase agrees with its singular antecedent, *each*. Choices (B) and (D) incorrectly use the plural pronoun *their*. Choice (C) creates an awkward, muddled sentence. Choice (D) creates a run-on.

8. Answer: (B) Known for her vivid details, controlled style, and in-depth characterizations, the writer Joan Didion
The original sentence is a run-on, connecting two independent clauses with only a comma. Choice (B) corrects this error in a logical way: by changing one of the clauses to a descriptive participial phrase. Choice (C) combines the ideas in an awkward, illogical way. Choice (D) contains a fragment. Choice (E) is a run-on and uses *however* to suggest a contrast that doesn't exist.

9. Answer: (C) and bustling neighborhoods
Tourists can expect to be dazzled by two things: *exciting nightlife* and *bustling neighborhoods*. The phrases that follow the preposition *by* should be in the same grammatical form. Choice (C) is correct because *bustling neighborhoods* is in the same form as *exciting nightlife*: an adjective ending in *-ing* + a noun. Choice (B) is redundant, as it unnecessarily repeats the phrase *to be dazzled by*. Choices (A), (D), and (E) include grammatical structures that are not parallel.

10. Answer: (C) to those of younger workers
This sentence contains a very common error in making comparisons. Ask yourself: What is actually being compared here? You can't compare two traits of older workers—*work ethic and dependability*—to *younger workers*. You need to add a pronoun that refers to the two traits that are being compared. Choice (B) incorrectly uses the singular pronoun *that* to refer to the two traits. Choice (C) correctly uses the plural pronoun *those*. Choices (D) and (E) incorrectly use the preposition *from* after the adjective *superior*. In addition, choice (D) leaves out the needed word *workers*, and Choice (E) is redundant, needlessly repeating the phrase *work ethic and dependability*, rather than replacing the phrase with a pronoun.

11. Answer: (A) rather than in public concerns such as voting or entering professions
The original sentence correctly uses parallel grammatical structures to contrast two areas of life: *domestic pursuits such as raising their children and beautifying their homes* and *public concerns such as voting or entering professions*. The other choices are incorrect because they do not match the grammatical structure of *domestic pursuits such as raising their children and beautifying their homes*. In addition, Choice (E) includes the incorrect word *then*, instead of *than*.

IDENTIFYING SENTENCE ERRORS

12. Answer: (B) who
To decide between *who* and *whom*, look at the entire clause: *who the company president dismissed*. The subject of the clause is *president*, and the verb is *dismissed*. So you need the objective form *whom* as the direct object: *the company president dismissed whom*.

13. Answer: (E) No error
There are no errors: *Prohibited from* is correct idiomatic English, so choice (A) is correct. The verb *have* agrees with the plural subject *fishermen*, and *few* is the correct word to use for things that can be counted, so choice (B) is correct. *In* is the correct preposition to use after *to succeed*, so choice (C) is correct. The plural pronoun *their* agrees with the plural antecedent *fishermen*, so choice (D) is correct.

14. Answer: (A) a person
Since the phrase at the beginning of the sentence includes the plural pronoun *their*, which is not underlined, the noun that follows the phrase must also be plural. It should be *people* instead of *a person*.

15. Answer: (D) for buying
Correct idiomatic English requires an infinitive (*to* form), rather than the preposition *for* and a gerund (*-ing* form) after *longed*. The correct wording is *longed to buy*, rather than *longed for buying*.

16. Answer: (B) have led
Remember: Nouns in a phrase introduced by the words *along with* are never part of the subject. The subject of this sentence is the word *rise*, which requires the singular helping verb *has*.

17. Answer: (C) couldn't hardly
Remember: *Hardly* is considered a negative word. The phrase *couldn't hardly* is a double negative. The correct phrase is *could hardly*.

18. Answer: (B) had flew
The correct form of *fly* to use with *had* is *flown*. In choice (A), *lay* is correct here as the past tense of the verb *lie*.

19. Answer: (B) irregardless
Remember: *Irregardless* is not a word. The correct word is *regardless*. Whenever *irregardless* is offered as a choice, it is always incorrect.

20. Answer: (C) was
This is a really tricky subject-verb agreement item, not only because the subject comes after the verb, but also because the subject after the verb is compound: *invention* and *accumulation*. The sentence requires the plural verb *were*. In normal word order, the sentence would read as follows: *The invention of new machines and the accumulation of capital from trade were among the factors contributing to the rise of the Industrial Revolution.*

21. Answer: (A) phenomena
The word *phenomena* is actually the plural form of the noun *phenomenon*. The singular form is required here because of the singular verb *is*. To prepare for the SAT, you should review this and similar nouns derived from Greek, including *criterion* (singular) and *criteria* (plural).

22. Answer: (E) No error
The sentence is correct. *That* is the correct pronoun to introduce information that is essential to the meaning of the sentence and refers to the singular abstract noun *margin*, so (A) is correct. Choice (B) is correct because the singular pronoun *it* correctly refers to the antecedent *margin*. Choice (C) is correct because the adverb *easily* is needed to modify the verb *won*, which is the

correct past tense of the verb *win*. Choice (D) is correct because *as* is correct idiomatic usage after the verb *named*.

23. Answer: (A) releasing
This is an error in parallel structure. The verb *releases* is required to complete the series of words connected by *and*: *increases*, *raises*, and *releases*.

24. Answer: (E) No error
The sentence is correct: *For* is the correct preposition to follow *yearning*. *In which* correctly refers to *a project*. *His* correctly refers to *Damian*, and *sought* is the correct past-tense form of *seek*.

25. Answer: (B) she
Who could win the Alger Prize, Lily or Anna? The antecedent of the pronoun *she* is unclear. To clarify who could win the prize, you would need to repeat the noun *Lily* or *Anna* here.

26. Answer: (A) Hopefully,
Here is another tricky question. Although most people commonly use the word *hopefully* in this way, it is not technically correct standard usage. In standard English, *hopefully* should be used only as it is in the following sentence: *We waited hopefully for good news.* Correct usage in this sentence would require a construction such as *I hope that you have not forgotten…*

27. Answer: (D) with
Correct idiomatic usage requires the preposition *by* in this sentence: *abided by the rules*.

28. Answer: (E) No error
The sentence is correct. *Eccentric* is correct because an adjective is needed after *considered*. (The words *to be* are implied here: *considered to be eccentric*.) *More interested* is the correct comparative form of *interested*. *Widely publicizing* is a correct parallel construction to use in making a comparison because it matches *quietly pursuing*. The verb *deemed* is correctly followed by an adjective. (The words *to be* are implied here: *deemed to be unprofessional*.)

29. Answer: (B) of
This is another problem with correct idiomatic preposition usage. We *provide* people *with* something, not *of* something.

IMPROVING PARAGRAPHS

30. Answer: (C) Union, but there
Starting a sentence with "But" is usually considered improper, so some revision is called for. The two sentences can easily be combined, because they are closely related in thought. "But" is a transitional word that connects and compares information. In this example "But" leads to information that is true in sentence (4) in spite of the information in sentence (3), so the two sentences should be connected. The use of a simple comma and putting "But" into the lower case makes for a complete sentence that connects the information in the sentences in a meaningful way.

The SAT Advantage

31. Answer: (E) The Hatfields then captured three McCoy boys and executed them by gunshot.
The words "after tying them to a clump of paw-paw bushes" are not a necessary detail, so those words should be edited out. Keeping the word "executed" is important because then it is clear that the killings of the three McCoy boys were revenge killings for the murder of a Hatfield. That would make answer (B) incorrect, because it eliminates the word "executed." Answer (B) also uses the word "gunshot" as a verb; "shot" would be the usual verb used. Answer (C) keeps the unnecessary detail of the paw-paw bushes, so it is not correct. Answer (D) puts in words that are not in the original sentence and may make it incorrect: we do not know if the McCoy boys were executed "at point blank range." Answer (E) provides the most clear and concise revision.

32. Answer: (C) One can only imagine what was in the hearts of these men, Hatfields or McCoys, as they roved the woods of Kentucky and West Virginia, looking for their enemies.
Since sentence 9 is awkward, some revision is necessary, so answer (A) can be eliminated. Answer (B) introduces something inaccurate: "roving hearts". That expression usually refers to unfaithful hearts, and we do not know that the men had "roving hearts." Answer (D) twists information, because we do not know that the men went into the "woods of their enemies." Answer (E) is also inaccurate, as they were not "looking for the hearts of their enemies"; they were looking for their enemies. Answer (C) successfully combines sentences 8 and 9 by bringing in the thought that both sets of men—Hatfields and McCoys—must have felt similar emotions.

33. Answer: (B) Sorrow, hatred, rage, fear, and guilt must have run high in the hearts of the men who traversed those calm, unspoiled woods in yesteryear.
To revise this sentence well, attention must be paid to the prepositional phrases. The way the sentence is phrased, it appears that the woods felt the emotions, as the named emotions "must have run high in" the woods. We cannot leave the sentence as it is, since we know that emotions must be felt by people. That eliminates answer (A). Answer (C) adds unnecessary and repetitive words, so it is a poor revision: vengefulness is close in meaning to revenge; rage and anger are similarly close in meaning. In answer (D), the revision has changed the thought into something we have no information about: we do not know that the hearts of those times were calm and unspoiled. Answer (E) changes "run high" to "been elevated," which is a less effective expression of emotion in this case. It also does not correct the fact that the woods still seem to be the ones feeling the emotions. Answer (B) introduces the human element by the use of the words "hearts of the men." Changing the preposition "of" in "woods of yesteryear" to "in," as in "woods in yesteryear" also places the whole sentence in the past rather than just the woods, once again taking emphasis off the woods and putting it onto the men of the past.

34. Answer: (E) Blood feuds are common in cultures where there is a strong code of male pride.
Revisions should clarify sentences by expressing things in a better way and in fewer words, if possible. "Feuds of the blood" can be revised to read "blood feuds," so that eliminates answers (A) and (C). Answer (B) does not make it clear what "male pride codes" are, nor does the use of "culturally" as an adjective help in understanding what the sentence is trying to say, so answer (B) is a poor revision. Answer (D) revises the sentence so that it appears to be praising blood feuds by making the statement that they exist where there are prideful and honorable males. Answer (E) is both succinct and clear in meaning. With this revision, the reader understands that there are places where blood feuds are more common than in others, and these are in cultures where there is a strong code of male pride.

35. Answer: (A) No revision is necessary
Answer (B) adds in the unnecessary words "and again," so it is not a good revision. Answer (C) adds in the unnecessary word "better," so it is not a good revision. Answer (D) changes the word "far" to "fewer," which cancels out the word "more" and makes the sentence meaningless. Answer (E) introduces a new thought which changes the meaning of the sentence: "time will tell." The original sentence said, "it is time" now, rather than waiting for some time in the future. Revisions should not change the meaning of a sentence. The sentence is correct as it is, so no revision is necessary, answer (A).

SECTION 7 (CRITICAL READING)

SENTENCE COMPLETION

1. Answer: (D) coherent
A police officer would not be interested in a "burdensome" (A), "blistering" (B), or "disparaging" (E) eyewitness account of a robbery. He or she would want a "truthful" account (C); however, the beginning of the sentence shows that the grandmother's problem in giving a good account of what she saw was because she was "distraught." The officer needed to tell her to "slow down" and "take a few deep breaths" and "start over again calmly." All this indicates that her eyewitness account was full of emotion and probably did not hang together and make a lot of sense: it was incoherent. Therefore, the officer wanted her to calm herself down in order to give an account that did make sense and did hang together: a "coherent" account (D).

2. Answer: (C) nefarious
The words "seemingly kindly," "claimed," and "scheme" should alert readers that the woman in the sentence is up to no good. This would eliminate answers (A) and (B) "ethical" and "principled," respectively. "Astute" (D) and "perspicacious" (E) are synonyms meaning mentally sharp, able to discern things clearly, or shrewd. While a "seemingly kindly" person could be astute or perspicacious, a better choice would be "nefarious" (C), which means evil or wicked. "Nefarious" is a better contrast to "seemingly kindly" than any of the other answers and it goes along with someone perpetrating a phony financial scheme on investors, such as a Ponzi scheme.

3. Answer: (B) rebuked … scrupulous
Since the proofreader left "many obvious errors" we may be sure the editor did not praise him as in answer (A) or laud him (E), which also means to praise. Answer (C) can also be eliminated, because if the editor "rebuffed" the proofreader in a rejecting way, the editor would not then urge him to be more "careless." In answers (B) and (D) "scrupulous" and "meticulous" are synonymous, meaning taking great pains and care, so they fit well with the editor's complaint against the careless proofreader. However, "reviled" (D) is a very strong word, usually including verbal abuse. The best answer is "rebuked" (B), meaning to reprimand.

4. Answer: (E) persona … plausible
One key to the answers in this sentence is that the second half of the sentence changes direction with the word "but." Since "he was himself in deep financial trouble" the missing words will belie that, making him "appear" to be good at financial services. All of the first words of the answers would fit, as they have to do with the person's appearance or presentation of himself. However, if he appeared "guilty" (A), "troubled" (B), "aggravated" (C), or "questionable" (D) his appearance would not belie his real situation. Only "plausible" (E) fits in with the change of the direction of the sentence. The sales man had a good persona, or good image, that he presented to the public that made him believable (plausible) when he really wasn't.

5. Answer: (A) ineffable
The words "transcendence" and "celestial" suggest that the experience of the audience was out of the ordinary and elevating. It is unlikely that it would have given them "maddened" (B) or "predatory" (D) or "insatiable" (E) joy as the experience appears to have been one of great satisfaction for the audience. The word "exhilarated" (C) is almost synonymous with "joy" and also implies excitement, whereas the fact that the music was full of "sweetness" would imply that it was soothing and calming. Answer (A) "ineffable" means indescribable and unable to be

put into words. That the experience was transcendent and celestial suggests that it was an experience that would be hard to put into words, so (A) is the best answer.

6. Answer: (C) conceive ... innocuous

The state official in this sentence seems to be saying she cannot believe something about what the neighboring farmers thought. Since a "compound" with barbed wire, a satellite dish, and armed guards would be threatening, and the state official cannot believe the farmers thought it was not, the second missing word should be a positive word denoting harmlessness. "Innocent" (A), "innocuous" (C), "welcome" (D), and "altruistic" (E) all fit well. However, the preposition "of" right after the first missing word eliminates "deceive" (A), "apprehend" (D), and "disavow" (E) because these verbs are not used with the preposition "of". The verb "conceive" (C) is used with the preposition "of" as it means to have an idea of. Both words in answer (C) fit the sentence well.

READING BASED QUESTIONS

7. Answer: (A) the metaphysical value of the human body

The passage mentions that, "Since he was a Yale University molecular biologist," Dr. Morowitz's approach was "physiological" rather than "metaphysical." The mention of the word "metaphysical" shows that the author of the passage takes into account the value of a human being that goes beyond the physical. This is confirmed when the author says, "Without adding in the incalculable value of a person's heart and mind," the human person is extremely valuable, showing that the author acknowledges the "incalculable value" of the human being beyond just the physical.

8. Answer: (C) humorous

The first paragraph reads, "The common wisdom at the time was that the human body, reduced down to its chemical structure, was only worth about a dollar. Morowitz thought that was a little cheap." Although "ironic" would be an appropriate answer, "moronic" (E), is not. The tone is not "cynical" (A) because the lines affirm that Morowitz thought human beings were valuable. It is not "impersonal" (B) because it takes a tone of familiarity. Although it is "straightforward" (D), the clipped and colloquial language is clearly meant to be "humorous" (C) and is especially so because the passage talks about a Yale molecular biologist's thinking in contrast to the simple wording "a little cheap."

9. Answer: (B) of immeasurable worth

Far from meaning that something is of little value, "invaluable" means that the value of something cannot be estimated, it is so great. It is "priceless." The word "incalculable" and the quoting of the figure "at least six billion dollars" shows that the point of the passage, as summed up in this last paragraph, is that the human being is of incomparable, inestimable worth; each person is "invaluable" and "of immeasurable worth" (B).

10. Answer: (D) things that comfort or relieve pain temporarily

Answer (A) "plenitudes" is easily eliminated because things that are in "plenitudes" (there are plenty of them) are rarely "costly." "Parsimoniousness" (B) means being very close or frugal with money or the distribution of other resources and has little to do with the sentence. Answer (C) "controlled substances" does not fit as "other palliatives" because alcohol and food are not controlled substances. Likewise, "addictive substances" (E) does not strictly apply to food. The word has to mean something that will bring people comfort or ease their pain temporarily, answer (D).

11. Answer: (C) rhetorical effect

Although the question posed "Where should they turn?" is not strictly a rhetorical question because the answer is given in the next paragraph of the passage, switching from declarative sentences to an interrogative sentence creates a certain dramatic or rhetorical effect (C). The opening lines describe some people's difficult circumstances in dealing with addiction and the question at the end of the lines helps personalize these people and provides a lead-in to the answer.

12. Answer: (A) respect for a longstanding and successful institution

The definition of "venerable" is as a description of something that is both aged and benevolent. The implication is that distressed people can turn to this organization, which would show that it is benevolent and helpful. The reader soon finds that AA has been in existence since 1935, making it an aged institution. "Awe" (B) is too strong a word for what one would feel toward an institution like AA, while "casual" (C) is too weak a word. The passage is endorsing AA and Al-Anon, so it is unlikely that support would be "measured" (D) and there would be no reason for "skepticism" (E). Since AA is shown to be longstanding and successful, answer (A) is most appropriate.

13. Answer: (B) companion programs

The author describes "the venerable institution of Alcoholics Anonymous and its companion program Al-Anon." The passage states, "In 1951 Bill's wife Lois realized that her own behavior in relation to his addiction needed amending. This was the beginning of Al-Anon, the companion program to AA," so (B) is accurate. "Symbiosis" (A) is a relationship between dissimilar things, whereas AA and Al-Anon are closely related. "Complimentary programs" (C) would be correct if it were spelled "complementary," as the programs do "complement" one another but "complimentary" means "free." "Condiments" (D) are spices or flavorful additives to foods, and "commiserating" (E) means programs that would share their misery together.

14. Answer: (E) the couple kept their marriage together and Lois learned not to enable Bill's alcohol addiction

The author says that Bill W. "almost destroyed" his marriage. The word "almost" would imply that the marriage remained intact in spite of Bill's addiction. The fact that a Hallmark Hall of Fame movie was made about the couple and their story would imply that ultimately the couple triumphed. However, it is in later lines, where it says that "Lois realized that her own behavior...needed amending" and began Al-Anon where "friends and family members...work on their lives and strive to achieve serenity" that we know Lois remained a family member of Bill's and also took some responsibility for her own role in his addiction. The lines which say that through Al-Anon "Friends and family members often find they have been 'enabling' the addiction" also support answer (E).

15. Answer: (C) they keep AA democratic, open to all comers, and focused in purpose

The passage says that "the Twelve Traditions...are designed to keep AA non-hierarchical," which means it is democratic as in answer (C). AA is also stated as being open to "anyone who has a problem with alcoholism or other addictions, regardless of his or her other affiliations or beliefs," which shows AA is "open to all comers" as in answer (C). The passage makes clear that The Twelve Traditions limit AA's purpose to helping alcoholics get and become sober," which is similar to the wording in answer (C) "focused in purpose."

16. Answer: (B) emphasis on AA's focused purpose

Since the previous lines state, "However, the Twelve Traditions keep people from trying to impose their beliefs or advertise their affiliations to other AA members" and the passage says the "Twelve Traditions limit AA's purpose to helping alcoholics get and become sober," the word "period" puts emphasis on AA's focused purpose and the Twelve Tradition's role in making sure no distractions sway AA away from its focus.

17. Answer: (D) validating the effectiveness of this program developed by someone who was not an expert or a therapist

Throughout the passage, it is clear that Bill W. and his wife Lois were serious about combating alcoholism in their own and in others' lives. The author says that "Bill had been working with 'The Oxford Group' to apply principles of living to learn to live alcohol-free. Bill developed the Twelve Steps and Twelve Traditions with "Dr. Bob" who apparently had some medical credentials; the author states, "Together, Bill W. and Dr. Bob developed Twelve Steps for fighting addiction to alcohol," and "Over time, the pair also developed the Twelve Traditions." Although AA was founded in 1935, Lois founded Al-Anon in 1951, showing that the couple's commitment to Bill's sobriety spanned more than a decade. Effective support groups are often formed by people who share a difficulty rather than by experts, but the fact that "Many well-known experts and therapists recommend AA and Al-Anon to those affected by addictions" validates the effectiveness of this program developed by someone who was not an expert or therapist.

18. Answer: (D) sympathetic

The author includes "addicts" along with their family members when he or she says these people "Often...have already suffered significant losses...to the addiction." This language would seem to imply that the addiction rather than the people involved in it has caused the suffering and losses. The "addicts" or alcoholics are also included in the pronoun "They" in: "They cannot afford therapy. They are at the end of their ropes. Where should they turn?" implying that both addicts and those who love them are in the quandary of needing help and not knowing where to go to get it. Likewise, the author speaks of "the agonies of addiction" and the phrase "they have helped countless people and those who love them" includes not only the friends and family members of addicts or alcoholics, but also the alcoholic/addicts themselves. Similar to the language in the first paragraph, this language implies that addicts and alcoholics are as much victims suffering the agonies of addiction as are those who love them and implies an attitude of sympathy.

19. Answer: (E) shielding addicts from the consequences of their behavior may prolong their addictions

Since the question deals specifically with the reason an overly helpful or enabling relative or friend's actions might be "neither helpful nor loving," the answer should come from the perspective of what truly helpful and loving behavior toward an alcoholic is. Answers (A) – (D) deal with consequences that might come to the family or friend, so they have nothing to do with loving or helping the alcoholic. Only answer (E) deals with the effects the family member or friend's actions might have on the alcoholic, so only answer (E) deals with what would be "helpful" or "loving" to the alcoholic. Indeed, the most helpful and loving thing to do would be to help the person get over his or her addiction, which means not "enabling the addiction" and not "protecting" or "shielding" the alcoholic "from the natural consequences of his or her addiction."

SECTION 8 (MATHEMATICS)

MULTIPLE CHOICE

1. Answer: (C) 60
Set up the proportion $\frac{24}{2} = \frac{x}{5}$. To solve for x, multiply both sides of the equation by 10 to get $120 = 2x$. So $x = 60$.

2. Answer: (C) 1387 sq. ft
The area of the rectangular garden including the fountain = length × width = 50 ft × 30 ft = 1500 sq. ft.

The area of the fountain = $\pi r^2 = \pi(6^2) = 36\pi = 113$ sq. ft.
So the area of the garden outside the fountain = 1500 − 113 = 1387 sq. ft.

3. Answer: (B) 32
The area of a parallelogram is found by using the formula Area = (base)(height).

The length of the base is clearly 8 units from (0,0) to (8,0).

The height of the parallelogram can be found by drawing a line or segment from one base such that it is perpendicular to the other base. The vertex at (2,4) can be used to discern the height.

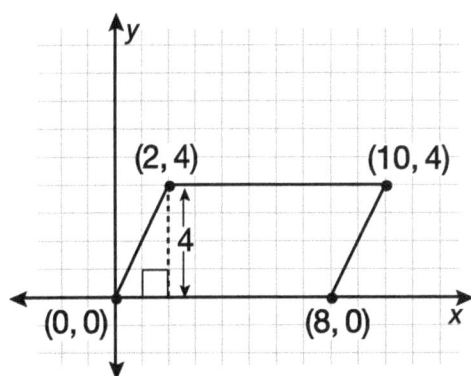

The y-coordinate, 4, is also the height of the parallelogram. Input 8 and 4 for the base and the height to find the area of the parallelogram.

Area = (base)(height) = $8 \times 4 = 32$

4. Answer: (A) 7
The movie rental membership can be modeled using a linear function in the form of y = mx + b where:

y = all payments made

m = the monthly fee
x = the number of months paid
b = the annual dues

Use the model to find the number of months for which Arnie has paid the fee.

164 = 12x + 80
84 = 12x
x = 7

5. Answer: (B) 52.5

☐ is an isosceles triangle because it has two congruent sides. When two sides of a triangle are congruent, the angles opposite those sides are also congruent.

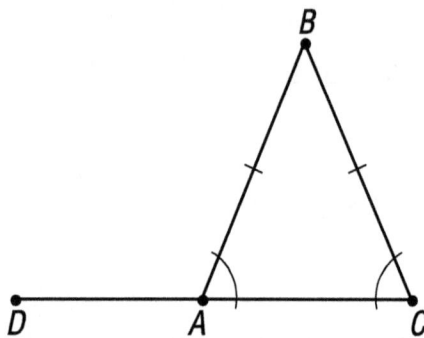

In the diagram, $m\angle BAC = m\angle BCA$. Begin solving this problem by finding the measures of $\angle BAC$ and $\angle BCA$. Since the sum of the measures of the angles in a triangle is 180°, create an equation by letting n equal the measures of $\angle BAC$ and $\angle BCA$.

$46 + n + n = 180$

$46 + 2n = 180$

$2n = 134$

$n = 67$

$\angle DAB$ and $\angle BAC$ form a linear pair. A linear pair is a pair of adjacent, supplementary angles. Since the sum of supplementary angles is 180°, set the sum of the measures of $\angle DAB$ and $\angle BAC$ to 180°.

$67 + 2x + 8 = 180$

$2x + 75 = 180$

$2x = 105$

$x = 52.5$

The SAT Advantage

6. Answer: (D) x = 1 or x = 12

Eliminate the denominator in the term $\frac{12}{x}$ by multiplying the entire equation by x.

$$\frac{12}{x} + x = 13$$

$$x(\frac{12}{x} + x = 13)x$$

$$12 + x^2 = 13x$$

$$x^2 - 13x + 12 = 0$$

Factor $x^2 - 13x + 12$. Since the coefficient of x^2 is 1, we find factors of 12 that add to -13.

(-1)(-12) = 12   -1 + -12 = -13

$$x^2 - 13x + 12 = (x-1)(x-12)$$

Since $x^2 - 13x + 12 = 0$, then $(x-1)(x-12) = 0$. Solve for x by setting x – 12 and x – 1 equal to 0.

x – 12 = 0
x = 12

x – 1 = 0
x = 1

In the equation $\frac{12}{x} + x = 13$, x = 1 or x = 12

7. Answer: (B) 8.3%
Water of volume x cubic units expands to 1.09x cubic units when it freezes.

This means that ice of volume 1.09x cubic units decreases in volume to x cubic units when it melts.

The decrease in volume = 1.09x – x = 0.09x cubic units.

The percentage decrease in volume = $\frac{0.09x}{1.09x}$ 100 = 8.3%

8. Answer: (D) $16\sqrt{2}$
The diagonal of a square is also a hypotenuse of an isosceles right triangle, which is also a 45-45-90 triangle. The ratio of the sides in a 45-45-90 triangle is x: x: x$\sqrt{2}$, where x is the length of a side. Use the Pythagorean theorem to find the length of one side of the square.

$x^2 + x^2 = 8^2$
$2x^2 = 64$
$x^2 = 32$
$x = 4\sqrt{2}$

Since each side of the square measures $4\sqrt{2}$, multiply $4\sqrt{2}$ by 4 to find the perimeter of the square.

$4\sqrt{2} \times 4 = 16\sqrt{2}$

9. Answer: (A) 48°

Let lines AD and BC intersect at E when extended and form angle x.

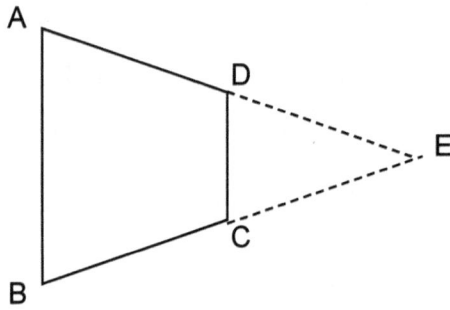

The sum of the angles of triangle ABE is equal to 180°:
70 + 62 + x = 180
132 + x = 180
x = 180 − 132 = 48

10. Answer: (C) $1.00

Let the cost of an apple be $x and the cost of an orange be $y. Then
3x + 2y = 2.4
6x + 5y = 5.4

These equations can be solved using standard methods such as substitution and elimination. There is, however, an easier way to find the answer to the question asked.

Notice that Sally buys 3 more apples and 3 more oranges than Matt. So the difference between the amounts they pay is the price of 3 apples and 3 oranges. Dividing this amount by 3 will give the price of 1 apple and 1 orange.

Subtracting the first equation from the second one:
(6x + 5y) − (3x + 2y) = 5.4 − 2.4

The SAT Advantage

3x + 3y = 3
3(x + y) = 3

Dividing both sides by 3, x + y = 1

11. Answer: (B) 75
The problem does not state how many students play both the violin and the flute. It is possible that all, some, or none of the flute students also play the violin.

If all 30 flute players also play the violin, then the number of students who don't play the violin or flute (the maximum possible number) = 120 − 45 = 75.

If none of the flute players play the violin, the number of students who don't play the violin or flute (the minimum possible number) = 120 − 45 − 30 = 45.

Therefore, at most 75 students play neither the violin nor the flute.

12. Answer: (A) 14.6

The length of the tunnel = $\frac{5280}{2}$ = 2640 ft

The entire train is in the tunnel from the time when the front of the train is 500 ft into the tunnel until the time when the front of the train is at the end of the tunnel.

The front of the train moves 2640 − 500 = 2140 ft in this time.

The speed of the train = 100 mph = 100 × $\frac{5280}{3600}$ ft/s = 146.67 ft/s

The time taken by the train to travel 2140 ft = $\frac{2140}{146.67}$ = 14.6 s.

Hence, the entire length of the train is in the tunnel for 14.6 s.

13. Answer: (A) $\left(\frac{5ab^4}{4b}\right)^3 - \left(\frac{3a^2}{4b}\right)^3$

Choices B and C are obviously wrong, since two separate cubic terms cannot just be combined within one set of parentheses. Choice D has the wrong denominator. Choice E has a plus sign instead of a minus sign between the terms. Check the accuracy of choice A by simplifying:

$$\left(\frac{5ab^4}{4b}\right)^3 - \left(\frac{3a^2}{4b}\right)^3 = \frac{125a^3b^{12}}{64b^3} - \frac{27a^6}{64b^3} = \frac{125a^3b^{12} - 27a^6}{64b^3}$$

The SAT Advantage

14. Answer: (C) 5m
Listing all the planks in order of length:
2, 2, 2, 2, 2, 2, 5, 5, 5, 5, 10, 10, 10, 12, 12, 12, 12
There are 17 planks in all. The length of the middle one (the 9th one) when they are arranged in order, is 5m.

15. Answer: (E) $\frac{4}{3}\pi R^3 d = p\pi r^2$

Since the weight of the sphere depends on its volume and the pressure the pillar can withstand depends on the area of its top surface, the relationship should involve R^3 and r^2. Choices A, B, and C can be eliminated since they don't meet this condition.

The volume of the sphere = $\frac{4}{3}\pi R^3$.

Since it has a density of d pounds per square inch, the total weight of the sphere = $\frac{4}{3}\pi R^3 d$.

The surface area of the top of the pillar = πr^2.

If the pillar can withstand a pressure of p pounds per square inch, the total weight the pillar can hold = $\pi r^2 p$.

The largest sphere the pillar can support will have a weight equal to the highest weight the pillar can hold. Hence

$$\frac{4}{3}\pi R^3 d = p\pi r^2$$

The SAT Advantage

16. Answer: (D) square panels of side 3 ft
Calculate how much area will be covered by each kind of panel.

Circular panels 2 ft in diameter can be arranged 25 along the length and 10 along the width. Total area covered by 250 panels = $250 \times \pi(1)^2 = 785$ sq. ft

Circular panels 4 ft in diameter can be arranged 12 along the length (up to 48 ft) and 5 along the width. Total area covered by 60 panels = $60 \times \pi(2)^2 = 240\pi = 754$ sq. ft

Circular panels 6 ft in diameter can be arranged 8 along the length (up to 48 ft) and 3 along the width (up to 18 ft). Total area covered by 24 panels = $24 \times \pi(3)^2 = 216\pi = 679$ sq. ft

Square panels of side 3 ft can be arranged 16 along the length (up to 48 ft) and 6 along the width (up to 18 ft). Total area covered by 96 panels = $96 \times 9 = 864$ sq. ft

Square panels of side 7 ft can be arranged 7 along the length (up to 49 ft) and 2 along the width (up to 14 ft). Total area covered by 14 panels = $14 \times 49 = 686$ sq. ft

So the maximum area will be covered if square panels of side 3 ft are used.

The SAT Advantage

SECTION 9 (WRITING)

IMPROVING SENTENCES

1. Answer: (D) In order to feel energized and to function at their best, extroverts require regular periods of social interaction; introverts, on the other hand, need regular periods of time alone.
The sentence is a run-on, incorrectly joining two independent clauses with just a comma. Choice (D) fixes the problem correctly by changing the comma to a semicolon. Choice (B) illogically uses the conjunction *and* to introduce a contrast and also uses the pronoun *they* redundantly, when the clause already has the subject *introverts*. Choice (C) is wordy and muddles the meaning of the sentence by moving critical information to the end of the sentence. Choice (E) is redundant because it uses two contrast clues—both *while* and *on the other hand*—when only one is needed.

2. Answer: (C) as the auditorium at the college does
The original sentence incorrectly compares *the auditorium at the high school* to *the college*. Choice (C) clarifies that the comparison is between one auditorium and another. Choice (B) does not fix the original problem. Choices (D) and (E) incorrectly use the preposition *like* to introduce the clause in the comparison. In addition, choice (D) incorrectly uses a plural pronoun and plural verb to refer to the singular antecedent, *auditorium*.

3. Answer: (A) which is 10 percent larger than projected and 20 percent larger than
The original sentence is correct. It uses the pronoun *which* to introduce parenthetical information that is not needed to understand the main idea of the sentence: *The city council says that this year's budget is bound to create growing deficits.* Choice (B) introduces the error *as large* and adds the redundant phrase *when compared with*. Choice (C) introduces the incorrect word *then* and the illogical conjunction *but*. Choice (D) adds another main clause in a part of the sentence that is supposed to be parenthetical. Choice (E) takes many more words to say something that was more simply expressed in the original sentence.

4. Answer: (C) Recognized for its excellent food at reasonable prices, the Riverside Inn attracts patrons who will make reservations to entertain guests there months in advance, rather than settling for another local eatery.
The sentence contains a misplaced modifier. The descriptive phrase that opens the sentence should be followed immediately by the noun that the phrase describes: *the Riverside Inn*. Choice (B) does not correct this problem. Choice (D) places the noun and the phrase next to each other, but it creates a fragment that is missing a main verb. Choice (E) completely muddles the meaning in a long, awkward sentence. Only choice (C) places the noun and the phrase together and expresses its ideas in a clear, logical way.

5. Answer: (E) and a pleasure because of the rewards of strenuous physical activity
The word *both* is always used with the conjunction *and*. The phrase *both a challenge because of ...* should be followed by the conjunction *and*, plus a noun in the same form as *challenge*. Choice (E) does this with the phrase *and a pleasure because of*. This correction clarifies that establishing a regular exercise routine is *both a challenge and a pleasure*. Choice (B) includes the parallel phrase *a pleasure ... because of*, but adds the word *although* instead of *and*. Choices (C) and (D) do not correct the original problem of ending the sentence with a construction that matches the one at the beginning of the sentence: *both a challenge because of*

6. Answer: (B) Reading the draft of his term paper in the morning, Sam realized that it needed much more revision than he had thought

Here's another misplaced modifier. Who was reading the draft of his term paper in the morning? Sam. The noun *Sam* should directly follow the opening phrase, as in Choice (B). Choices (C) and (E) do not fix the misplaced modifier problem. Choice (D) creates a run-on.

7. Answer: (A) in some cities by as much as 20 percent in the last two years

The sentence is correct because it uses a dash correctly to introduce extra information. You could read the information that follows the dash after the verb *increased* to form a sentence that makes sense. Choice (B) does not create a logical, idiomatic English sentence. Choice (C) is redundant, needlessly repeating the verb *increasing* and adding the phrase *the equivalent of*. Choice (D) creates a sentence that is not correct idiomatic English. Choice (E) needlessly repeats the verb *increasing* and adds the word *biennially*, changing the meaning of the sentence.

8. Answer: (D) in liberal arts

In a comparison like this, the items that come before and after the word *than* need to be in the same grammatical form: *more interest in* one thing … *than in* another thing. Choice (D) is the only one that corrects the comparison by adding the word *in*. Choice (B) does not correct the problem and adds the redundant word *fields*. Choice (C) does not correct the problem and adds the redundant phrase *compared to*. Choice (E) does not correct the problem and adds the redundant word *ones*.

9. Answer: (E) were that dinosaurs with feathers had once existed and that their feathers may have served as insulation or as display plumage

The newspaper article introduced two main ideas. The subject of the sentence is the plural noun *ideas*, which requires the plural verb *were*. That means you can automatically eliminate choices (A), (B), and (D), leaving only choices (C) and (E) as possible options. Choice (C) expresses the two main ideas in an awkward way, and the two ideas are not expressed in matching grammatical forms. Choice (E) uses the correct verb and adds the word *that* to the second main idea, creating two ideas expressed in the same form and with a logical sequence of tenses: *that giant dinosaurs with feathers had once existed and that their feathers may have served as insulation or as display plumage*.

10. Answer: (B) to be the best duet team

Tim and Alanna form one duet team, not more than one, so choice (A) is incorrect. Choice (B) correctly solves the problem by simply using the singular noun *team*, rather than the plural noun *teams*. The phrase *were determined to be* is correct idiomatic English, so the words *to be* should not be changed. Choices (C), (D), and (E) add errors by changing *to be* to the incorrect forms *to being*, *at being*, and *at having been*.

11. Answer: (C) Atlantic Systems, which produces

There are two problems with the original sentence: It is a run-on, joining two independent clauses with just a comma. It also uses the plural pronoun *they* to refer to *Atlantic Systems*, which is just one company, even though it has a plural word in its name. The correct answer must fix both of these problems. Choice (B) correctly uses the singular pronoun *it*, but does not correct the run-on problem. Choice (C) is the correct answer: It fixes the run-on problem by putting some of the information into a subordinate clause beginning with *which*. It also uses the singular verb *produces*, which agrees with the singular noun *Atlantic Systems*, the name of one company. Choice (D) does not make grammatical sense and incorrectly uses a semicolon when the words after the semicolon cannot stand alone as a complete sentence. Choice (E) does not fix the run-on problem.

12. Answer: (C) Darren was greatly frustrated by the basketball coach's decision not to choose him for the varsity team

Who trained and practiced for six months? The name *Darren* should immediately follow the introductory phrase that describes him. Since choice (C) is the only one that begins with the word *Darren*, you should be able to eliminate all of the other choices quickly.

13. Answer: (D) reveals that tourists want to travel to places

The subject of the sentence is the singular noun *information*, which requires the singular verb *reveals*. Therefore, you can automatically eliminate choices (A) and (B). Except for the wrong verb choice, however, choice (A) is correct grammatical English: *that tourists want to travel to*. Choice (D) is correct because it fixes the subject-verb agreement problem without adding any other errors. Choice (B) slightly changes the meaning of the sentence. The information doesn't reveal tourists; it reveals facts about tourists. Choice (E) also changes the meaning of the sentence, because *revealing* becomes an adjective, rather than a verb.

14. Answer: (B) Although Mayor Binns of Greenville has a tendency to accept speaking engagements only within the city limits,

This sentence expresses a contrast between what Mayor Binns usually does and what he did last week. The only problem with choice (A) is its use of the conjunction *and*, which is illogical in a sentence that shows a contrast. Choice (B) fixes this problem by using the word *although* to show contrast. Choice (C) creates a run-on and doesn't show a contrast. Choice (D) is completely illogical, suggesting a cause/effect relationship, rather than a contrast. Choice (E) is redundant, using two words to show a contrast—*while* and *however*—instead of just the one that is needed.

The SAT Advantage

SAT Practice Test Answer Sheet

Remove (or photocopy) the answer sheet and use it to complete the Practice Test. See the answer key following the test when finished.

Start with number 1 for each section. If a section has fewer questions than answer spaces, leave the extra spaces blank.

SECTION 1

Section 1 is the Writing section's essay component.

SECTION 2

1. Ⓐ Ⓑ Ⓒ Ⓓ Ⓔ   11. Ⓐ Ⓑ Ⓒ Ⓓ Ⓔ   21. Ⓐ Ⓑ Ⓒ Ⓓ Ⓔ   31. Ⓐ Ⓑ Ⓒ Ⓓ Ⓔ
2. Ⓐ Ⓑ Ⓒ Ⓓ Ⓔ   12. Ⓐ Ⓑ Ⓒ Ⓓ Ⓔ   22. Ⓐ Ⓑ Ⓒ Ⓓ Ⓔ   32. Ⓐ Ⓑ Ⓒ Ⓓ Ⓔ
3. Ⓐ Ⓑ Ⓒ Ⓓ Ⓔ   13. Ⓐ Ⓑ Ⓒ Ⓓ Ⓔ   23. Ⓐ Ⓑ Ⓒ Ⓓ Ⓔ   33. Ⓐ Ⓑ Ⓒ Ⓓ Ⓔ
4. Ⓐ Ⓑ Ⓒ Ⓓ Ⓔ   14. Ⓐ Ⓑ Ⓒ Ⓓ Ⓔ   24. Ⓐ Ⓑ Ⓒ Ⓓ Ⓔ   34. Ⓐ Ⓑ Ⓒ Ⓓ Ⓔ
5. Ⓐ Ⓑ Ⓒ Ⓓ Ⓔ   15. Ⓐ Ⓑ Ⓒ Ⓓ Ⓔ   25. Ⓐ Ⓑ Ⓒ Ⓓ Ⓔ   35. Ⓐ Ⓑ Ⓒ Ⓓ Ⓔ
6. Ⓐ Ⓑ Ⓒ Ⓓ Ⓔ   16. Ⓐ Ⓑ Ⓒ Ⓓ Ⓔ   26. Ⓐ Ⓑ Ⓒ Ⓓ Ⓔ   36. Ⓐ Ⓑ Ⓒ Ⓓ Ⓔ
7. Ⓐ Ⓑ Ⓒ Ⓓ Ⓔ   17. Ⓐ Ⓑ Ⓒ Ⓓ Ⓔ   27. Ⓐ Ⓑ Ⓒ Ⓓ Ⓔ   37. Ⓐ Ⓑ Ⓒ Ⓓ Ⓔ
8. Ⓐ Ⓑ Ⓒ Ⓓ Ⓔ   18. Ⓐ Ⓑ Ⓒ Ⓓ Ⓔ   28. Ⓐ Ⓑ Ⓒ Ⓓ Ⓔ   38. Ⓐ Ⓑ Ⓒ Ⓓ Ⓔ
9. Ⓐ Ⓑ Ⓒ Ⓓ Ⓔ   19. Ⓐ Ⓑ Ⓒ Ⓓ Ⓔ   29. Ⓐ Ⓑ Ⓒ Ⓓ Ⓔ   39. Ⓐ Ⓑ Ⓒ Ⓓ Ⓔ
10. Ⓐ Ⓑ Ⓒ Ⓓ Ⓔ   20. Ⓐ Ⓑ Ⓒ Ⓓ Ⓔ   30. Ⓐ Ⓑ Ⓒ Ⓓ Ⓔ   40. Ⓐ Ⓑ Ⓒ Ⓓ Ⓔ

SECTION 3

1. Ⓐ Ⓑ Ⓒ Ⓓ Ⓔ   11. Ⓐ Ⓑ Ⓒ Ⓓ Ⓔ   21. Ⓐ Ⓑ Ⓒ Ⓓ Ⓔ   31. Ⓐ Ⓑ Ⓒ Ⓓ Ⓔ
2. Ⓐ Ⓑ Ⓒ Ⓓ Ⓔ   12. Ⓐ Ⓑ Ⓒ Ⓓ Ⓔ   22. Ⓐ Ⓑ Ⓒ Ⓓ Ⓔ   32. Ⓐ Ⓑ Ⓒ Ⓓ Ⓔ
3. Ⓐ Ⓑ Ⓒ Ⓓ Ⓔ   13. Ⓐ Ⓑ Ⓒ Ⓓ Ⓔ   23. Ⓐ Ⓑ Ⓒ Ⓓ Ⓔ   33. Ⓐ Ⓑ Ⓒ Ⓓ Ⓔ
4. Ⓐ Ⓑ Ⓒ Ⓓ Ⓔ   14. Ⓐ Ⓑ Ⓒ Ⓓ Ⓔ   24. Ⓐ Ⓑ Ⓒ Ⓓ Ⓔ   34. Ⓐ Ⓑ Ⓒ Ⓓ Ⓔ
5. Ⓐ Ⓑ Ⓒ Ⓓ Ⓔ   15. Ⓐ Ⓑ Ⓒ Ⓓ Ⓔ   25. Ⓐ Ⓑ Ⓒ Ⓓ Ⓔ   35. Ⓐ Ⓑ Ⓒ Ⓓ Ⓔ
6. Ⓐ Ⓑ Ⓒ Ⓓ Ⓔ   16. Ⓐ Ⓑ Ⓒ Ⓓ Ⓔ   26. Ⓐ Ⓑ Ⓒ Ⓓ Ⓔ   36. Ⓐ Ⓑ Ⓒ Ⓓ Ⓔ
7. Ⓐ Ⓑ Ⓒ Ⓓ Ⓔ   17. Ⓐ Ⓑ Ⓒ Ⓓ Ⓔ   27. Ⓐ Ⓑ Ⓒ Ⓓ Ⓔ   37. Ⓐ Ⓑ Ⓒ Ⓓ Ⓔ
8. Ⓐ Ⓑ Ⓒ Ⓓ Ⓔ   18. Ⓐ Ⓑ Ⓒ Ⓓ Ⓔ   28. Ⓐ Ⓑ Ⓒ Ⓓ Ⓔ   38. Ⓐ Ⓑ Ⓒ Ⓓ Ⓔ
9. Ⓐ Ⓑ Ⓒ Ⓓ Ⓔ   19. Ⓐ Ⓑ Ⓒ Ⓓ Ⓔ   29. Ⓐ Ⓑ Ⓒ Ⓓ Ⓔ   39. Ⓐ Ⓑ Ⓒ Ⓓ Ⓔ
10. Ⓐ Ⓑ Ⓒ Ⓓ Ⓔ   20. Ⓐ Ⓑ Ⓒ Ⓓ Ⓔ   30. Ⓐ Ⓑ Ⓒ Ⓓ Ⓔ   40. Ⓐ Ⓑ Ⓒ Ⓓ Ⓔ

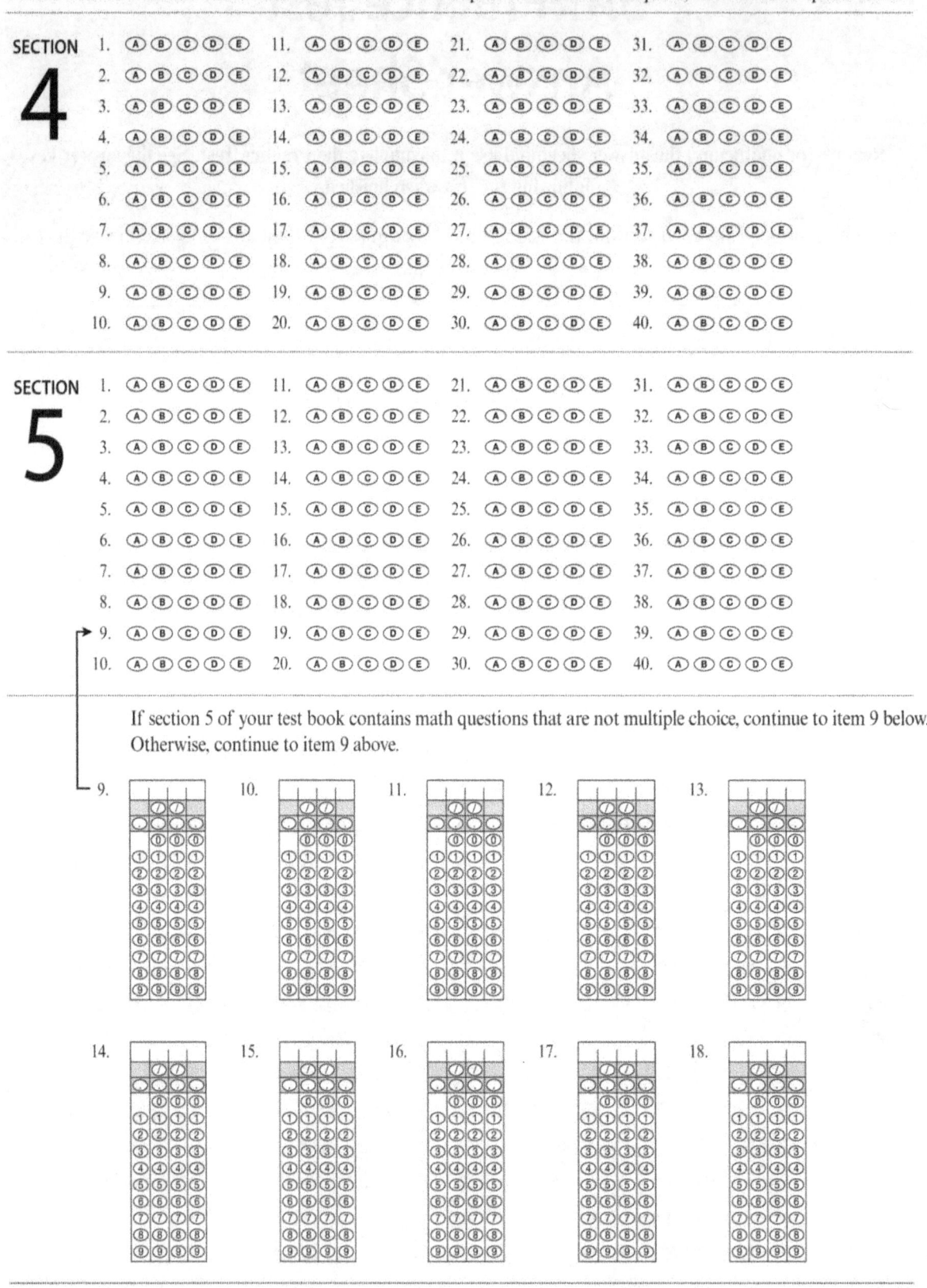

The SAT Advantage

Remove (or photocopy) this answer sheet and use it to complete the Practice Test.

Start with number 1 for each section. If a section has fewer questions than answer spaces, leave the extra spaces blank.

SECTION 6

1. Ⓐ Ⓑ Ⓒ Ⓓ Ⓔ   11. Ⓐ Ⓑ Ⓒ Ⓓ Ⓔ   21. Ⓐ Ⓑ Ⓒ Ⓓ Ⓔ   31. Ⓐ Ⓑ Ⓒ Ⓓ Ⓔ
2. Ⓐ Ⓑ Ⓒ Ⓓ Ⓔ   12. Ⓐ Ⓑ Ⓒ Ⓓ Ⓔ   22. Ⓐ Ⓑ Ⓒ Ⓓ Ⓔ   32. Ⓐ Ⓑ Ⓒ Ⓓ Ⓔ
3. Ⓐ Ⓑ Ⓒ Ⓓ Ⓔ   13. Ⓐ Ⓑ Ⓒ Ⓓ Ⓔ   23. Ⓐ Ⓑ Ⓒ Ⓓ Ⓔ   33. Ⓐ Ⓑ Ⓒ Ⓓ Ⓔ
4. Ⓐ Ⓑ Ⓒ Ⓓ Ⓔ   14. Ⓐ Ⓑ Ⓒ Ⓓ Ⓔ   24. Ⓐ Ⓑ Ⓒ Ⓓ Ⓔ   34. Ⓐ Ⓑ Ⓒ Ⓓ Ⓔ
5. Ⓐ Ⓑ Ⓒ Ⓓ Ⓔ   15. Ⓐ Ⓑ Ⓒ Ⓓ Ⓔ   25. Ⓐ Ⓑ Ⓒ Ⓓ Ⓔ   35. Ⓐ Ⓑ Ⓒ Ⓓ Ⓔ
6. Ⓐ Ⓑ Ⓒ Ⓓ Ⓔ   16. Ⓐ Ⓑ Ⓒ Ⓓ Ⓔ   26. Ⓐ Ⓑ Ⓒ Ⓓ Ⓔ   36. Ⓐ Ⓑ Ⓒ Ⓓ Ⓔ
7. Ⓐ Ⓑ Ⓒ Ⓓ Ⓔ   17. Ⓐ Ⓑ Ⓒ Ⓓ Ⓔ   27. Ⓐ Ⓑ Ⓒ Ⓓ Ⓔ   37. Ⓐ Ⓑ Ⓒ Ⓓ Ⓔ
8. Ⓐ Ⓑ Ⓒ Ⓓ Ⓔ   18. Ⓐ Ⓑ Ⓒ Ⓓ Ⓔ   28. Ⓐ Ⓑ Ⓒ Ⓓ Ⓔ   38. Ⓐ Ⓑ Ⓒ Ⓓ Ⓔ
9. Ⓐ Ⓑ Ⓒ Ⓓ Ⓔ   19. Ⓐ Ⓑ Ⓒ Ⓓ Ⓔ   29. Ⓐ Ⓑ Ⓒ Ⓓ Ⓔ   39. Ⓐ Ⓑ Ⓒ Ⓓ Ⓔ
10. Ⓐ Ⓑ Ⓒ Ⓓ Ⓔ 20. Ⓐ Ⓑ Ⓒ Ⓓ Ⓔ   30. Ⓐ Ⓑ Ⓒ Ⓓ Ⓔ   40. Ⓐ Ⓑ Ⓒ Ⓓ Ⓔ

SECTION 7

1. Ⓐ Ⓑ Ⓒ Ⓓ Ⓔ   11. Ⓐ Ⓑ Ⓒ Ⓓ Ⓔ   21. Ⓐ Ⓑ Ⓒ Ⓓ Ⓔ   31. Ⓐ Ⓑ Ⓒ Ⓓ Ⓔ
2. Ⓐ Ⓑ Ⓒ Ⓓ Ⓔ   12. Ⓐ Ⓑ Ⓒ Ⓓ Ⓔ   22. Ⓐ Ⓑ Ⓒ Ⓓ Ⓔ   32. Ⓐ Ⓑ Ⓒ Ⓓ Ⓔ
3. Ⓐ Ⓑ Ⓒ Ⓓ Ⓔ   13. Ⓐ Ⓑ Ⓒ Ⓓ Ⓔ   23. Ⓐ Ⓑ Ⓒ Ⓓ Ⓔ   33. Ⓐ Ⓑ Ⓒ Ⓓ Ⓔ
4. Ⓐ Ⓑ Ⓒ Ⓓ Ⓔ   14. Ⓐ Ⓑ Ⓒ Ⓓ Ⓔ   24. Ⓐ Ⓑ Ⓒ Ⓓ Ⓔ   34. Ⓐ Ⓑ Ⓒ Ⓓ Ⓔ
5. Ⓐ Ⓑ Ⓒ Ⓓ Ⓔ   15. Ⓐ Ⓑ Ⓒ Ⓓ Ⓔ   25. Ⓐ Ⓑ Ⓒ Ⓓ Ⓔ   35. Ⓐ Ⓑ Ⓒ Ⓓ Ⓔ
6. Ⓐ Ⓑ Ⓒ Ⓓ Ⓔ   16. Ⓐ Ⓑ Ⓒ Ⓓ Ⓔ   26. Ⓐ Ⓑ Ⓒ Ⓓ Ⓔ   36. Ⓐ Ⓑ Ⓒ Ⓓ Ⓔ
7. Ⓐ Ⓑ Ⓒ Ⓓ Ⓔ   17. Ⓐ Ⓑ Ⓒ Ⓓ Ⓔ   27. Ⓐ Ⓑ Ⓒ Ⓓ Ⓔ   37. Ⓐ Ⓑ Ⓒ Ⓓ Ⓔ
8. Ⓐ Ⓑ Ⓒ Ⓓ Ⓔ   18. Ⓐ Ⓑ Ⓒ Ⓓ Ⓔ   28. Ⓐ Ⓑ Ⓒ Ⓓ Ⓔ   38. Ⓐ Ⓑ Ⓒ Ⓓ Ⓔ
9. Ⓐ Ⓑ Ⓒ Ⓓ Ⓔ   19. Ⓐ Ⓑ Ⓒ Ⓓ Ⓔ   29. Ⓐ Ⓑ Ⓒ Ⓓ Ⓔ   39. Ⓐ Ⓑ Ⓒ Ⓓ Ⓔ
10. Ⓐ Ⓑ Ⓒ Ⓓ Ⓔ 20. Ⓐ Ⓑ Ⓒ Ⓓ Ⓔ   30. Ⓐ Ⓑ Ⓒ Ⓓ Ⓔ   40. Ⓐ Ⓑ Ⓒ Ⓓ Ⓔ

SECTION 8

1. Ⓐ Ⓑ Ⓒ Ⓓ Ⓔ   11. Ⓐ Ⓑ Ⓒ Ⓓ Ⓔ   21. Ⓐ Ⓑ Ⓒ Ⓓ Ⓔ   31. Ⓐ Ⓑ Ⓒ Ⓓ Ⓔ
2. Ⓐ Ⓑ Ⓒ Ⓓ Ⓔ   12. Ⓐ Ⓑ Ⓒ Ⓓ Ⓔ   22. Ⓐ Ⓑ Ⓒ Ⓓ Ⓔ   32. Ⓐ Ⓑ Ⓒ Ⓓ Ⓔ
3. Ⓐ Ⓑ Ⓒ Ⓓ Ⓔ   13. Ⓐ Ⓑ Ⓒ Ⓓ Ⓔ   23. Ⓐ Ⓑ Ⓒ Ⓓ Ⓔ   33. Ⓐ Ⓑ Ⓒ Ⓓ Ⓔ
4. Ⓐ Ⓑ Ⓒ Ⓓ Ⓔ   14. Ⓐ Ⓑ Ⓒ Ⓓ Ⓔ   24. Ⓐ Ⓑ Ⓒ Ⓓ Ⓔ   34. Ⓐ Ⓑ Ⓒ Ⓓ Ⓔ
5. Ⓐ Ⓑ Ⓒ Ⓓ Ⓔ   15. Ⓐ Ⓑ Ⓒ Ⓓ Ⓔ   25. Ⓐ Ⓑ Ⓒ Ⓓ Ⓔ   35. Ⓐ Ⓑ Ⓒ Ⓓ Ⓔ
6. Ⓐ Ⓑ Ⓒ Ⓓ Ⓔ   16. Ⓐ Ⓑ Ⓒ Ⓓ Ⓔ   26. Ⓐ Ⓑ Ⓒ Ⓓ Ⓔ   36. Ⓐ Ⓑ Ⓒ Ⓓ Ⓔ
7. Ⓐ Ⓑ Ⓒ Ⓓ Ⓔ   17. Ⓐ Ⓑ Ⓒ Ⓓ Ⓔ   27. Ⓐ Ⓑ Ⓒ Ⓓ Ⓔ   37. Ⓐ Ⓑ Ⓒ Ⓓ Ⓔ
8. Ⓐ Ⓑ Ⓒ Ⓓ Ⓔ   18. Ⓐ Ⓑ Ⓒ Ⓓ Ⓔ   28. Ⓐ Ⓑ Ⓒ Ⓓ Ⓔ   38. Ⓐ Ⓑ Ⓒ Ⓓ Ⓔ
9. Ⓐ Ⓑ Ⓒ Ⓓ Ⓔ   19. Ⓐ Ⓑ Ⓒ Ⓓ Ⓔ   29. Ⓐ Ⓑ Ⓒ Ⓓ Ⓔ   39. Ⓐ Ⓑ Ⓒ Ⓓ Ⓔ
10. Ⓐ Ⓑ Ⓒ Ⓓ Ⓔ 20. Ⓐ Ⓑ Ⓒ Ⓓ Ⓔ   30. Ⓐ Ⓑ Ⓒ Ⓓ Ⓔ   40. Ⓐ Ⓑ Ⓒ Ⓓ Ⓔ

The SAT Advantage

Remove (or photocopy) this answer sheet and use it to complete the Practice Test.

Start with number 1 for each section. If a section has fewer questions than answer spaces, leave the extra spaces blank.

SECTION 9

1. Ⓐ Ⓑ Ⓒ Ⓓ Ⓔ   11. Ⓐ Ⓑ Ⓒ Ⓓ Ⓔ   21. Ⓐ Ⓑ Ⓒ Ⓓ Ⓔ   31. Ⓐ Ⓑ Ⓒ Ⓓ Ⓔ
2. Ⓐ Ⓑ Ⓒ Ⓓ Ⓔ   12. Ⓐ Ⓑ Ⓒ Ⓓ Ⓔ   22. Ⓐ Ⓑ Ⓒ Ⓓ Ⓔ   32. Ⓐ Ⓑ Ⓒ Ⓓ Ⓔ
3. Ⓐ Ⓑ Ⓒ Ⓓ Ⓔ   13. Ⓐ Ⓑ Ⓒ Ⓓ Ⓔ   23. Ⓐ Ⓑ Ⓒ Ⓓ Ⓔ   33. Ⓐ Ⓑ Ⓒ Ⓓ Ⓔ
4. Ⓐ Ⓑ Ⓒ Ⓓ Ⓔ   14. Ⓐ Ⓑ Ⓒ Ⓓ Ⓔ   24. Ⓐ Ⓑ Ⓒ Ⓓ Ⓔ   34. Ⓐ Ⓑ Ⓒ Ⓓ Ⓔ
5. Ⓐ Ⓑ Ⓒ Ⓓ Ⓔ   15. Ⓐ Ⓑ Ⓒ Ⓓ Ⓔ   25. Ⓐ Ⓑ Ⓒ Ⓓ Ⓔ   35. Ⓐ Ⓑ Ⓒ Ⓓ Ⓔ
6. Ⓐ Ⓑ Ⓒ Ⓓ Ⓔ   16. Ⓐ Ⓑ Ⓒ Ⓓ Ⓔ   26. Ⓐ Ⓑ Ⓒ Ⓓ Ⓔ   36. Ⓐ Ⓑ Ⓒ Ⓓ Ⓔ
7. Ⓐ Ⓑ Ⓒ Ⓓ Ⓔ   17. Ⓐ Ⓑ Ⓒ Ⓓ Ⓔ   27. Ⓐ Ⓑ Ⓒ Ⓓ Ⓔ   37. Ⓐ Ⓑ Ⓒ Ⓓ Ⓔ
8. Ⓐ Ⓑ Ⓒ Ⓓ Ⓔ   18. Ⓐ Ⓑ Ⓒ Ⓓ Ⓔ   28. Ⓐ Ⓑ Ⓒ Ⓓ Ⓔ   38. Ⓐ Ⓑ Ⓒ Ⓓ Ⓔ
9. Ⓐ Ⓑ Ⓒ Ⓓ Ⓔ   19. Ⓐ Ⓑ Ⓒ Ⓓ Ⓔ   29. Ⓐ Ⓑ Ⓒ Ⓓ Ⓔ   39. Ⓐ Ⓑ Ⓒ Ⓓ Ⓔ
10. Ⓐ Ⓑ Ⓒ Ⓓ Ⓔ 20. Ⓐ Ⓑ Ⓒ Ⓓ Ⓔ   30. Ⓐ Ⓑ Ⓒ Ⓓ Ⓔ   40. Ⓐ Ⓑ Ⓒ Ⓓ Ⓔ

The SAT Advantage

The SAT Advantage

The SAT Advantage

The SAT Advantage